Criticism and
Aesthetics
1660-1800

Essays collected and edited by Oliver F. Sigworth

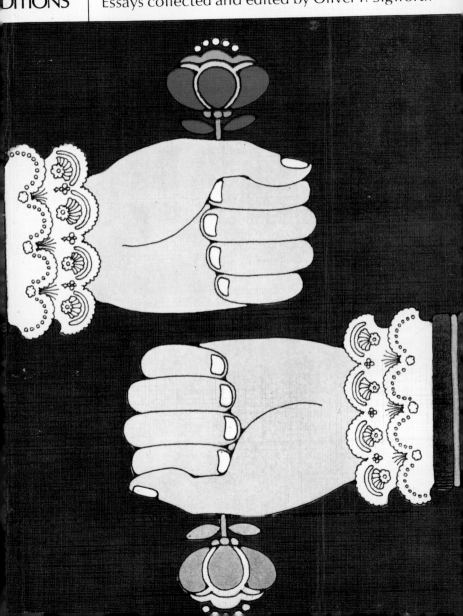

CRITICISM
AND
AESTHETICS

1660-1800

CRITICISM AND

AESTHETICS 1660-1800

ESSAYS COLLECTED AND EDITED BY
OLIVER F. SIGWORTH
THE UNIVERSITY OF ARIZONA

RINEHART PRESS SAN FRANCISCO

Criticism and Aesthetics 1660–1800
Essays Collected and Edited by
Oliver F. Sigworth

Copyright © 1971 by Rinehart Press,
A division of
Holt, Rinehart and Winston, Inc.
All rights reserved
Library of Congress Catalog Card Number: 76–122550
SBN: 03–079450–1
Printed in the United States of America
1 2 3 4   68   9 8 7 6 5 4 3 2 1

CONTENTS

Contents

PREFACE

This volume is intended to complement the other volumes of Rinehart Edition paperback books concerned with eighteenth-century literature, in which volumes are to be found the major critical statements of the chief poets and critics of the period. The obvious lacunae in this book are thereby accounted for—an accounting which is necessary, since the criticism of this period without the major statements of Dryden, Pope, Addison, and Johnson is like English medieval literature without Chaucer or Elizabethan drama without Shakespeare. Yet Chaucer is not all of the middle ages, nor Shakespeare all of Elizabethan drama; and just as what is left after the excision of these figures is worth examining, so much worthy of notice remains beyond the major statements of eighteenth-century critics. In fact, it must be fairly obvious that in thinking about an era so intellectually cosmopolitan and literary as that from 1660 to 1800 it is hardly possible to make sense of the major statements without viewing them against the intricate background which less famous pronouncements provide.

The essays collected here, then, are selected with a view to enabling the student to make connections between the major critical statements themselves, and between these statements and the literary accomplishments of the age. If I have presented more remarks on poetry than on other genres it is because the critics did not—for reasons which the Introduction will mention—display much interest in criticizing the novel, and because the criticism of the drama later in the century is generally not very interesting. And if I have presented some statements which seem, in the conventional sense, only tangentially literary, it is because these statements are the foundations upon which later literary theorizing is constructed; it is often to them rather than to specifically literary criticism that the poets of the early nineteenth century looked. Late renaissance (that is, neoclassic) literary theories were not so much developed or revised during the eighteenth century as they were replaced from different sources, and it is an examination of some of these sources, along with a view of their gradual application to literary questions, which enable us to see that the transition from neoclassic to romantic (that is, modern) poetic modes occurred at the same time earlier and more gradually than anthologies and handbooks of literature would generally have us believe.

The arrangement of the essays is roughly chronological. Where it seemed important and possible to do so I have presented entire essays or complete sections of larger works, but I have not hesitated to make relatively short excerpts where a significant remark is embedded in less relevant discourse. Some of the most revealing statements are in the form of *obiter dicta* dropped casually in the course of a discussion the whole of which would unconscionably swell the bulk of this anthology. The later writers, particularly the Scotsmen, were not given to writing briefly or incisively, yet their books, at the time read and discussed, were influential, and cannot be ignored in any overview of the criticism of the period.

The sources of the texts are given in the headnotes. The treatment of these texts is eclectic. Despite the loss of savor which such a procedure involves, I have modernized the older texts, since to students unaccustomed to the vagaries of typography in the late seventeenth and early eighteenth centuries the adventitious use of capitalization and italics and the mad abandon with which commas are distributed are merely confusing. Yet in cases where an oddity of capitalization or a striking use of italics seems to convey meaning otherwise lost I have retained the older usage, and in a few cases where there seemed no possibility of deciding whether, for example, a clause is restrictive or nonrestrictive, I have left the commas and allowed the attentive reader to puzzle matters out for himself. The later texts (after, say, 1760) usually present fewer difficulties, and are reprinted here essentially as they first appeared. Citations to classical sources, except where otherwise indicated in the notes, are from the volumes in the Loeb Library.

Anyone who deals at all with the criticism of this period must inevitably be deeply indebted to the collections by J. E. Spingarn (*Critical Essays of the Seventeenth Century*, 3 vols., 1907, reprinted 1957) and Scott Elledge (*Eighteenth Century Critical Essays*, 2 vols., 1961). I have frequently followed where they showed the way, but, as is obvious upon comparison, I have not hesitated to go on other bypaths. Their expensive collections, however, are for the scholar's library, not the student's. There are no other collections to put beside them.

I am happy to make other acknowledgments. To my wife, Heather, not alone for putting up with it all in the midst of other distractions, but also for concrete suggestions and help; to Marguerite Hunt, for onerous typing well done; to Michael Cohen, for his assiduity in tracking down more than one obscure reference; to Professor Richard Hosley, for valuable suggestions incorporated in the Introduction; most particularly to Professor A. L. Muir, Head of the Department of English at the University of Arizona, for plumbing the mysterious depths of the departmental sugar bowl and coming up with those few grains that made the difference. I am in eternal debt to my students in History of Criticism, Eighteenth-Century Prose, and Eighteenth-Century Poetry. They keep me alert, and by refusing to be taken in, keep me (I hope) sane.

O.F.S.

Tucson, Arizona
September, 1970

INTRODUCTION

Everyone now recognizes that we cannot look at literary criticism during the eighteenth century as a smoothly flowing neoclassic river rudely interrupted about midcourse by the tumultuous rapids of romanticism. Even in Dryden's criticism appear eddies which seem to forecast Wordsworth, and the "Preface" to the *Lyrical Ballads* reads at some points more like Samuel Johnson than Samuel Coleridge. The complications of the passage from late seventeenth- to early nineteenth-century criticism do not encourage brevity of exposition, nor do they facilitate lucidity. What is brief may be lucid yet misleading; what is both lucid and accurate can hardly be brief in telling the story. The reader must therefore be warned that the tale is not so simple as I make it seem, that every statement needs qualification, and that, on the whole, it is best to read the texts themselves.

Since any discussion of the criticism of the period 1660 to 1800 is inevitably saddled with the term "neoclassicism," it is as well to begin with an effort to determine what that term, as applied to criticism and nothing else, may mean. As used in the history of criticism in English the term is not a very happy one, for it implies that about 1600, when Charles II and his court came over from France, there was a sharp break with what all literary historians agree to call the English renaissance, and that thereafter criticism wandered, stultified, in dry and cold deserts until rescued by Wordsworth and Coleridge with the warm, life-giving waters of romanticism. Whether it was a rescue or not may be debated, but if it was a rescue it was not from any critical doctrines suddenly introduced or from a *critical* temper in any way new in 1660.

This is not the occasion to review the history of literary criticism in England from the beginnings to 1660, but we must recognize that such critical documents as exist before our period are generally what we can only call "neoclassic"—that is, they look back to the literary ideas of Plato, Aristotle, Cicero, Quintilian, and Horace, but they look back to these doctrines through the spyglass of Italian and French criticism of the sixteenth century. They are renaissance critical documents; but the renaissance itself was, after all, a revival of the classical ideal, at least as far as criticism is concerned, and no matter how exuberant English poetry of the sixteenth century was, when educated men talked about poetry they talked in "neoclassic" terms. Sidney's treatise is a case in point, a methodical and delightfully written exposition of the ideas received in the best literary society; even his famous remark about the old song of Percy and Douglas which so moved his heart concludes, in the best neoclassic tone, "what would it worke trymmed in the gorgeous eloquence of *Pindar?*"—a matter of regret, obviously, that "some blinde Crouder" had not sufficiently studied the classics. It is probably a pity that Ben Jonson never wrote a full-blown art of poetry, for there, judging from *Timber,* we would have seen neoclassicism as full-fledged as in Dryden, though probably somewhat less adaptable.

"Neoclassic" criticism, then, is renaissance criticism, and from the standpoint of the history of criticism, the early eighteenth century is the last phase of the renaissance. To the classic canon, however, one extremely important addition must be noted in the rediscovery of Longinus, whose *On the Sublime*, though available since 1554, was not much heeded on the Continent until Boileau's translation of 1674, after which it swept France and especially England like a winter tempest. One could argue that the Longinian storm heralded the spring of romanticism, and it may be necessary to do so, but the fact is also that his precepts (which, it must be emphasized, are rhetorical and have in themselves nothing to do with that "natural sublime" so beloved of the later eighteenth century) were quickly accommodated to the existing body of criticism, giving it added range but not yet disturbing the calm center.

The calm center of renaissance, or neoclassic, criticism looked at literature in a way quite foreign to the romantic, or modern, sensibility. At its basis was the conception of genre, of literary works existing as species in an absolute sense. The reality of a literary work and the means by which it imitated the "clear, unchanged, and universal light" of "nature" was a function of its partaking of the species which it singly represented. Just as we think of the "catness" of a cat as a function of the fact that it is representative of the feline species, so to renaissance critics the "tragicness" of a tragedy was a function of its relation to the Aristotelian norms as supplemented by Vida, Castelvetro, and others. There was considerable argument about the nature of the genres, and in favor of extending their scope or of establishing new ones, but the conception of genre as a basis for criticism was not seriously challenged.

For confirmation of this view one need again look no further than Sidney. After the few preliminary words by Sprat about language, the present collection begins with the Earl of Mulgrave's "Essay," modeled ultimately of course on Horace though directly on Boileau, a summary of conventional renaissance poetics with which Sidney would have been quite in

accord. Mulgrave is clearly familiar, whether at first or second
hand does not matter, with sixteenth- and seventeenth-century
Continental criticism and with critical traditions extending
back ultimately to the Ancients. He is telling us what every
cultivated man believed, though sometimes, as with Dryden,
diffidently. What the cultivated man believed was that when
a poet sat down to write he might indeed look in his heart and
might indeed be inspired by a divine afflatus, for the idea that
neoclassic precepts required only rigid adherence to "rules"
cannot be supported by any document known to me. Even
Aristotle had at one point equated the poet and the madman,
and Scaliger in the mid-sixteenth century had spoken of the
poet transforming himself "almost into a second Deity, fashioning images of things that are not, as well as images more
beautiful than life of those things which are." What we now
call "imagination" or "inspiration" was never discounted, but
such inspiration emerged *in form* as a tragedy, or comedy, or
ode, pastoral, elegy, satire, or epistle; if the inspiration were
really divine it might emerge as a *poem,* that is, an epic, which
Dryden, voicing the standard doctrine, called "undoubtedly
the greatest work which the soul of man is capable to perform." That Fielding had to write of the novel in terms of epic
and history is explained by this fact; there existed neither a
critical tradition into which the novel could fit, nor a vocabulary with which to describe it. The fact may also indicate at
least one reason why the novel as a form did not flower until
after neoclassic criticism as we are speaking of it had begun
to lose its power.

Each genre had its own rules, its own (to use the proper
term) *decorum,* which extended not only to matters of form
and structure—matters which we still vaguely understand—
but also to verse and diction. Nobody in the eighteenth century understood the precepts of decorum or observed them so
diligently as Pope, and in the works of no other poet in English is there to be found a wider variety or more precise use
of the various poetic dictions. In his use of couplet form and
diction in relation to the poetic species he was assaying, Pope
attempted and achieved the "correctness" which William
Walsh, the mentor of his youth, told him was the attribute of

no earlier poet in English. It is, aside from the very conception itself of genre, the eighteenth-century critics' conception of diction which most sets them apart from us. The fact that the greatest critic of the century, Samuel Johnson, still propounded the precepts relating to diction while no longer much interesting himself in questions of genre shows not only the pervasiveness of the idea, but shows also that the idea did, in fact, outlive its time, for during the latter part of Johnson's life criticism was becoming "modern."

It is, of course, a ridiculous oversimplification to speak of only two strains of criticism during any period as complex as the one we are considering. Something, however, did happen which leads us from the genre criticism of Mulgrave to the *aesthetics* of the later century (esthetics: a term which I shall use to mean the discussion of art in terms of feeling), and we can discuss the ideas to which this change may be attributed as a second strain of criticism during the eighteenth century. The term "esthetics," in fact, was invented during the 1750s, though it was invented by Baumgarten in Germany and did not appear in English (as "the science which treats of sensuous perception") until about 1800. The first use of the word in its modern philosophical sense—a sense to which I do not limit myself—is not recorded by the *Oxford English Dictionary* until 1832. The term was newly invented, but the possibility of discussing art in terms of its affective qualities was embryonic as early as Addison, and we would certainly need to look behind Addison to the third Earl of Shaftesbury's emphasis on sensibility and taste were we to attempt a history of the idea. We can, then, in fact we probably should, speak of Burke's *Philosophical Enquiry into the Origin of Our Ideas of the Sublime and the Beautiful* (1757) as a treatise on esthetics rather than as criticism. It is not even out of place to consider Addison's essays on the imagination in the same large context of esthetics.

In the *Spectator* papers on *Paradise Lost* (1712) Addison is practicing renaissance criticism. He discusses the poem from the standpoint of the rules for the epic (and finds it not wanting), and methodically pursues the prescribed course in examining the fable, characters, sentiments, and language, pointing out the faults under these headings, and then proceeding for twelve papers to discuss the "beauties." In his eleven essays of the same year on the "Pleasures of the Imagination," however, Addison is venturing into esthetics in the special sense in which I use the term. The emphasis is on the pleasure which natural objects as well as literary imitation of them may provide, rather than on generic form as a basis for judgment. The emphasis is not for that reason alone entirely remote from the best neoclassic doctrine, for the pseudo-Horatian dictum was, we must recall, "instruct *and delight*," and basic to Addison's criticism is the idea that it is the duty of the poet to generalize, that is, to imitate that unchanging nature which all men at all times know. We look back at least as far as Ronsard and Scaliger, just as we look ahead to Samuel Johnson, when we read:

> But because the mind of man requires something more perfect in matter, than what it finds there, and can never meet with any sight in nature which sufficiently answers its highest ideas of pleasantness; or, in other words, because the imagination can fancy to itself things more great, strange, or beautiful, than the eye ever saw, and is still sensible of some defect in what it has seen; on this account it is the part of a poet to humour the imagination in its own notions, by mending and perfecting nature where he describes a reality, and by adding greater beauties than are put together in nature, where he describes a fiction. (No. 418)

This is "imitation" in the truest sense of the complicated word so beloved of neoclassic critics; it is imitation in this sense that leads naturally to the investigation of the peculiar human qualities, possessed by some authors but not others, pursued in the numerous discussions of "genius." The genius is the man who has the ability to imitate truly and to transform himself "almost into a second deity" and mend and perfect nature, to see nature—the "nature of things"—as it really is behind the imperfect manifestations evident to our senses. The genius, then, is naturally one prone to the "great thoughts" which are the *sine qua non* of the noble rhetoric Longinus discussed in *On the Sublime*. The fact of his genius, of his capacity to see the eternal in nature, inspires the noble rhetoric; the great thoughts in noble rhetoric stir our feelings, and the imagination (still in the limited Addisonian sense of the image-making ability of the mind) is stimulated to see a higher reality.

It was not long before the rhetorical part of the progression of *great thoughts : rhetoric : feeling* took a secondary position or dropped out of sight. Nothing could stir great thoughts like great objects in nature (note the changing definition of that word!), therefore nothing could stir our feelings so profoundly as these great objects. Burke's *Philosophical Enquiry* is the crossroads. We have arrived at the "natural sublime," which the great genius was most able to imitate simply because he was most susceptible to great thoughts; but note that whereas in Longinus the author supplied the rhetoric which stimulated these profound feelings, in the new dispensation the feelings are stirred directly by the objects themselves, and the progression becomes *great objects : great thoughts : feeling : poetry*. From this position we do not have far to go to reach that "sense sublime / Of something far more deeply interfused" in nature which inspired Wordsworth, and before long we need only nature, not even great objects: "For me the meanest flower that blows can give / Thoughts that do often lie too deep for tears." We have, indeed, *esthetics*, for there becomes no way to discuss art (if one is discussing it from this standpoint) except in terms of feeling. The genres and the decorums associated with them become irrelevant.

Such seems to me the major movement of criticism during the eighteenth century, but there are so many byways, so many interruptions and deflections in the path which I have made seem all too plain, that to introduce any one of them without introducing them all would lead only to confusion and to the extending of this introduction to intolerable length. Neoclassicism, in the sense that men continued to resort to the Ancients for instruction and delight, persisted to the end of the century, as it persists today; in the truest sense of the word Burke was a neoclassicist, yet it was Burke who produced the most "romantic" esthetic document of the century. What we must keep in mind is that neoclassicism and romanticism are not polar. They are, rather, cultural constants. The change which I have described, great as it appears, was, finally, a change of emphasis.

This change is the one which the present anthology is designed to document, though the reader will find here a great many other ideas as well, and is invited to construct his own view of eighteenth-century criticism. As an aid in this enterprise the following volumes may be consulted:

Atkins, J. W. H.: *English Literary Criticism: 17th and 18th Centuries.* London, 1951; reprinted, University Paperbacks, 1966. [Standard views. See R. S. Crane's comments in "On Writing the History of Criticism in England, 1650–1800," *The Idea of the Humanities.* Chicago, 1967, vol. 2, pp. 157–75.]

Bate, Walter Jackson: *From Classic to Romantic.* Cambridge, Mass., 1946; reprinted, Harper Torchbooks, 1961. [A classic.]

Bosker, A.: *Literary Criticism in the Age of Johnson.* The Hague, 1930; revised edition, New York, 1953. [A view now somewhat outdated.]

Clark, A. F. B.: *Boileau and the French Classical Critics in England (1660–1700).* Paris, 1925.

Crane, R. S.: "English Neoclassical Criticism: An Outline Sketch," *Critics and Criticism.* Chicago, 1952.

Elioseff, Lee Andrew: *The Cultural Milieu of Addison's Literary Criticism.* Austin, Texas, 1963.

Monk, Samuel Holt: *The Sublime.* New York, 1935; reprinted, Ann Arbor Paperbacks, 1960. [Monk's views have been somewhat modified by subsequent discussions, but the book remains basic. R. S. Crane's brief review in *Philological Quarterly*, XV (April, 1936), pp. 165–67 should also be consulted.]

Marks, Emerson R.: *The Poetics of Reason: English Neoclassical Criticism.* New York, 1968. [The best study, and not only because it is recent and brief.]

Maurcordato, Alexandre: *La Critique classique en Angleterre de la Restauration à la mort de Joseph Addison.* Paris, 1964. [Perhaps not unnaturally over-emphasizes 17th century French influence, but otherwise a thorough and valuable study.]

Wellek, René: "Neoclassicism and the New Trends of the Time" and "Dr. Johnson," *A History of Modern Criticism, 1750–1950*, Vol. 1, *The Later Eighteenth Century*. New Haven, 1955.

————: *The Rise of English Literary History*. Chapel Hill, 1941; reprinted, McGraw-Hill Paperbacks, 1966.

Wimsatt, W. K., Jr., and Cleanth Brooks: *Literary Criticism: A Short History*. New York, 1957; reprinted, Vintage, 1967. Chapters 10–15.

CRITICISM
AND
AESTHETICS

1660-1800

THOMAS SPRAT
[1635–1713]

At Wadham College, Oxford, Sprat fell in with the group,
including Dr. John Wilkins, Seth Ward, Dr. Ralph
Bathurst, and Christopher Wren, who later formed a nucleus
for the foundation of the Royal Society, of which Sprat
was elected a Fellow in 1663. Sprat's involvement in the
actual foundation was probably not important, but in
his History of the Royal Society (1667) he justified at length
the existence of that body, and incidentally made remarks
on prose style which must be taken into account by any
student of Restoration literature. Before this he had been
known as a satirist and an imitator of Cowley, whose "Life"
(less a "Life" than a "character" according to Dr. Johnson) he
prefixed to an edition of Cowley's works in 1668. Sprat
had been ordained a priest in March 1660/61, and
after 1668 his interest with the Duke of Buckingham (in
whose spoof on Dryden's heroic plays, The Rehearsal, he
may have had a small share) led to advancement in the
Church. He was appointed Dean of Westminster in 1683,
and in 1684 he was elevated to the Bishopric of
Rochester, after which he was involved in various
ecclesiastical controversies of no interest to the student
of literature.

Sprat's attitude toward the new English prose speaks
for itself, and has obvious implications for literary criticism.
The easily perceptible change in English prose in the latter
half of the seventeenth century has been the subject of
complicated scholarly debate, which is best summed up
by Robert Adolph in The Rise of Modern Prose Style

(*Cambridge, Mass., M.I.T. Press, 1968*), *providing necessary
bibliography.* The History of the Royal Society *has been
reprinted in facsimile with an introduction by Jackson J. Cope
and H. W. Jones* (*Washington University, St. Louis,
1958*). *This facsimile is the basis for the present text.*

FROM THE HISTORY OF THE ROYAL SOCIETY

[1667]

THE FIRST PART,

SECTION XX

A Proposal for Erecting an English Academy

I hope now it will not be thought a vain digression if I step
a little aside to recommend the forming of such an Assembly[1]
to the gentlemen of our nation. I know indeed that the English
genius is not so airy and discursive as that of some of our
neighbors, but that we generally love to have reason set out
in plain, undeceiving expressions, as much as they to have
it delivered with color and beauty. And besides this, I understand well enough that they have one great assistance to the
growth of oratory which to us is wanting: that is, that their

---

[1] Sprat had previously spoken of such "Modern Academies for Language"
as the French Academy in Paris, founded in 1635 by Cardinal Richelieu
for the purpose of regulating the French language and literature.

nobility live commonly close together in their cities, and ours for the most part scattered in their country houses. For the same reason why our streets are not so well built as theirs will hold also for their exceeding us in the arts of speech: they prefer the pleasures of the town; we, those of the field: whereas it is from the frequent conversations in cities that the humor and wit and variety and elegance of language are chiefly to be fetched. But yet, notwithstanding these discouragements, I shall not stick to say that such a project is now seasonable to set on foot and may make a great reformation in the manner of our speaking and writing. First, the thing itself is no way contemptible. For the purity of speech and greatness of empire have in all countries still met together. The Greeks spoke best when they were in their glory of conquest. The Romans made those times the standard of their wit, when they subdued and gave laws to the world; and from thence by degrees they declined to corruption, as their valor, their prudence, and the honor of their arms did decay; and at last, did even meet the northern nations half way in barbarism, a little before they were over-run by their armies.

But besides, if we observe well the English language, we shall find that it seems at this time more than others to require some such aid to bring it to its last perfection. The truth is, it has been hitherto a little too carelessly handled; and, I think, has had less labor spent about its polishing than it deserves. Till the time of King Henry the Eighth there was scarce any man regarded it but Chaucer, and nothing was written in it which one would be willing to read twice but some of his poetry. But then it began to raise itself a little and to sound tolerably well. From that age down to the beginning of our late civil wars, it was still fashioning and beautifying itself. In the wars themselves (which is a time wherein all languages use, if ever, to increase by extraordinary degrees, for in such busy and active times there arise more new thoughts of men, which must be signified and varied by new expressions), then, I say, it received many fantastical terms which were introduced by our religious sects, and many outlandish phrases, which several writers and translators in that great hurry brought in and made free as they pleased; and with all it was enlarged by many sound and necessary forms and idioms which it before wanted. And now, when men's minds are somewhat settled, their passions allayed, and the peace of our country gives us the opportunity of such diversions, if some sober and judicious men would take the whole mass of our language into their hands as they find it, and would set a mark on the ill words, correct those which are to be retained, admit and establish the good, and make some emendations in the accent and grammar, I dare pronounce that our speech would quickly arrive at as much plenty as it is capable to receive, and at the greatest smoothness which its derivation from the rough German will allow it.

Nor would I have this new English Academy confined only to the weighing words and letters, but there may be also greater works found out for it. By many signs we may guess that the wits of our nation are not inferior to any other, and that they have an excellent mixture of the spirit of the French and the Spaniard; and I am confident that we only want a few more standing examples and a little familiarity with the ancients to excel all the moderns. Now the best means that can be devised to bring that about is to settle a fixed and impartial Court of Eloquence, according to whose censure all books or authors should either stand or fall. And above all, there might be recommended to them one principal work in which we are yet defective, and that is the compiling of a history of our late civil wars. Of all the labors of men's wit and industry I scarce know any that can be more useful to the world than civil history, if it were written with that sincerity and majesty as it ought to be, as a faithful idea of human actions. And it is observable that almost in all civilized countries it has been the last thing that has come to perfection. I may now say that the English can already show many industrious and worthy pieces in this kind; but yet I have some prophetical imagination in my thoughts that there is still behind, something greater than any we have yet seen, reserved for the glory of this age . . .

THE SECOND PART,

SECTION XX

Their Manner of Discourse

Thus they have directed, judged, conjectured upon, and improved experiments. But lastly, in these and all other businesses that have come under their care, there is one thing more about which the Society has been most solicitous, and that is the manner of their discourse: which unless they had been very watchful to keep in due temper, the whole spirit and vigor of their design had been soon eaten out by the luxury and redundance of speech. The ill effects of this superfluity of talking have already overwhelmed most other arts and professions; insomuch that when I consider the means of happy living and the causes of their corruption, I can hardly forbear recanting what I said before and concluding that eloquence ought to be banished out of all civil societies as a thing fatal to peace and good manners. To this opinion I should wholly incline if I did not find that it is a weapon which may be as easily procured by bad men as good, and that if these should only cast it away, and those retain it, the naked innocence of virtue would be upon all occasions exposed to the armed malice of the wicked. This is the chief reason that should now keep up the ornaments of speaking in any request, since they are so much degenerated from their original usefulness. They were at first, no doubt, an admirable instrument in the hands of wise men: when they were only employed to describe goodness, honesty, obedience in larger, fairer, and more moving images; to represent truth clothed with bodies; and to bring knowledge back again to our very senses from whence it was at first derived to our understandings. But now they are generally changed to worse uses: they make the fancy disgust the best things if they come sound and unadorned; they are in open defiance against reason, professing not to hold much correspondence with that but with its slaves, the passions; they give the mind a motion too changeable and bewitching to consist with right practice. Who can behold without indignation how many mists and uncertainties these specious tropes and figures have brought on our knowledge? How many rewards, which are due to more profitable and difficult arts, have been still snatched away by the easy vanity of fine speaking? For now I am warmed with this just anger, I cannot withhold myself from betraying the shallowness of all these seeming mysteries, upon which we writers and speakers look so big. And in few words I dare say that of all the studies of men, nothing can be sooner obtained than this vicious abundance of phrase, this trick of metaphors, this volubility of tongue, which makes so great a noise in the world. But I spend words in vain, for the evil is now so inveterate that it is hard to know whom to blame or where to begin to reform. We all value one another so much upon this beautiful deceit, and labor so long after it in the years of our education, that we cannot but ever after think kinder of it than it deserves. And, indeed, in most other parts of learning, I look on it to be a thing almost utterly desperate in its cure;[2] and I think it may be placed among those general mischiefs, such as the dissension of Christian princes, the want of practice in religion, and the like, which have been so long spoken against that men are become insensible about them, everyone shifting off the fault from himself to others; and so they are only made bare commonplaces of complaint. It will suffice my present purpose to point out what has been done by the Royal Society towards the correcting of its excesses in Natural Philosophy, to which it is, of all others, a most professed enemy.

They have therefore been most rigorous in putting in execution the only remedy that can be found for this extravagance, and that has been a constant resolution to reject all the amplifications, digressions, and swellings of style; to return back to the primitive purity and shortness, when men delivered so many things almost in an equal number of words. They have

[2] That is, "the need for a cure is desperate."

exacted from all their members a close, naked, natural way of speaking, positive expressions, clear senses, a native easiness, bringing all things as near the mathematical plainness as they can, and preferring the language of artisans, countrymen, and merchants before that of wits or scholars.

And here there is one thing not to be passed by, which will render this established custom of the Society well nigh everlasting, and that is the general constitution of the minds of the English. I have already often insisted on some of the prerogatives of England, whereby it may justly lay claim to be the head of a philosophical league above all other countries in Europe: I have urged its situation, its present genius, and the disposition of its merchants, and many more such arguments to encourage us still remain to be used; but of all others, this which I am now alleging is of the most weighty and important consideration. If there can be a true character given of the universal temper of any nation under heaven, then certainly this must be ascribed to our countrymen: that they have commonly an unaffected sincerity, that they love to deliver their minds with a sound simplicity, that they have the middle qualities between the reserved subtle southern and the rough unhewn northern people, that they are not extremely prone to speak, that they are more concerned what others will think of the strength than of the fineness of what they say, and that an universal modesty possesses them. These qualities are so conspicuous and proper to our soil that we often hear them objected to us by some of our neighbor satirists in more disgraceful expressions. For they are wont to revile the English with a want of familiarity; with a melancholy dumpishness; with slowness, silence, and with the unrefined sullenness of their behavior. But these are only the reproaches of partiality or ignorance: for they ought rather to be commended for an honorable integrity, for a neglect of circumstances and flourishes, for regarding things of greater moment more than less, for a scorn to deceive as well as to be deceived: which are the best endowments that can enter into a philosophical mind. So that even the position of our climate, the air, the influence of the heaven, the composition of the English blood, as well as the embraces of the ocean, seem to join with the labors of the

Royal Society to render our country a land of experimental knowledge. And it is a good sign that nature will reveal more of its secrets to the English than to others, because it has already furnished them with a genius so well proportioned for the receiving and retaining its mysteries.

JOHN SHEFFIELD,
EARL OF MULGRAVE,
DUKE OF BUCKINGHAM
[1648–1721]

_____

Sheffield was much involved in the complicated politics of
the late seventeenth and early eighteenth centuries, and
is to be considered no more than a very minor literary
figure. In 1666 he served as a volunteer in the fleet fighting
against the Dutch, and the next year, at the age of nineteen,
was appointed captain of a troop of horse. In the second
Dutch war in 1673 he received command of The Captain,
according to the DNB "the best second-rate ship in the navy."
His fortunes rose and fell with dynastic changes and the
winds of politics, but he was seldom out of favor for long.
Anne created him Duke of Buckingham shortly after her
accession, and he thereafter built the large house in London
still known by his name. An Essay on Poetry is his best
known poem, but he was also the author of An Essay upon
Satire (1680), of prose works of some historical value,
and of a curious rewriting of Shakespeare's Julius Caesar.

That An Essay on Poetry is of little intrinsic value as
criticism must be admitted without demur, but it is very
worth studying as showing what the cultivated public
considered the approved positions on literary and critical
matters. In its "genre criticism," treating the various kinds
of poems in ascending order from song to epic, the poem
echoes Renaissance criticism, as it does in its reference to
Horace and in its discussion of the mysteries of genius and
of the importance of reason. If neoclassical criticism exists,
it exists here as distillate, without the substance of major
statement.

Sheffield's poems were republished in the eighteenth

century in *Johnson's* collection (*with, of course, his "Life"
of Sheffield*), *and later by Chalmers*. A Miscellanea from the
Works *was published in* 1933 *by the Haworth Press, Halifax,
and* An Essay upon Satyr, *edited by* G. R. *Noyes and
Herman R. Mead, by the University of California Press,
Berkeley, in* 1948. *See also* V. *de Sola Pinto's* Restoration
Carnival, 1954. *The text printed here is based upon that in
Spingarn's* Critical Essays of the Sev.enteenth Century, 1907,
considerably modernized.

AN ESSAY UPON POETRY
[1682]

Of things in which mankind does most excell,
Nature's chief master-piece is writing well;
And of all sorts of writing none there are
That can the least with *Poetry* compare;
No kind of work requires so nice a touch,
And if well done, there's nothing shines so much;
But Heav'n forbid we should be so prophane,
To grace the vulgar with that sacred name;
'Tis not a flash of Fancy which sometimes
Dazzling our minds, sets off the slightest rimes,   10
Bright as a blaze, but in a moment done;
True wit is everlasting, like the sun,
Which though sometimes beneath a cloud retir'd,

Breaks out again, and is by all admir'd.
Number, and rime, and that harmonious sound,
Which never does the ear with harshness wound,
Are necessary, yet but vulgar arts,
For all in vain these superficial parts
Contribute to the structure of the whole
Without a Genius too, for that's the soul,—   20
A spirit which inspires the work throughout,
As that of Nature moves this world about:
A heat that glows in every word that's writ,
That's something of divine, and more than wit;
Itself unseen, yet all things by it shown
Describing all men, but describ'd by none:
Where dost thou dwell? what caverns of the brain
Can such a vast and mighty thing contain?
When I at idle hours in vain thy absence mourn,
O where dost thou retire? and why dost thou return,   30
Sometimes with powerful charms to hurry me away
From pleasures of the night and business of the day?
Ev'n now, too far transported, I am fain
To check thy course, and use the needfull rein:
As all is dullness, when the fancy's bad,
So without judgment, fancy is but mad;
And judgment has a boundless influence,
Not upon words alone, or only sense,
But on the world of manners, and of men:
Fancy is but the feather of the pen;   40
Reason is that substantial, useful part,
Which gains the head, while t' other wins the heart.

Here I should all the differing kinds rehearse
Of poetry with various sorts of verse;
But who that task can after *Horace* do,
That mighty master and example too?
Echoes at best, all we can say is vain,
Dull the design, and fruitless were the pain.
'Tis true, the Ancients we may rob with ease,
But who with that sad shift himself can please   50
Without an actor's pride? A players art

Is more than his who writes the borrow'd part.
Yet modern laws are made for later faults,
And new absurdities inspire new thoughts;
What need has Satire then to live on theft,
When so much fresh occasion still is left?
Folly abounds, nay, flourishes at court,
Where on its sphere it finds a kind support;
But hold, Whitehall [1] has nothing now to fear,
'Tis wit and sense that is the subject here.   60
Defects of witty men deserve a cure,
And those who are so will the worst endure.

   First then of *Songs*, that now so much abound:
Without his song no fop is to be found,
A most offensive weapon which he draws
On all he meets, against Apollo's laws:
Though nothing seems more easy, yet no part
Of poetry requires a nicer art;
For as in rows of richest Pearl there lies
Many a blemish that escapes our eyes,   70
The least of which defects is plainly shewn
In some small ring, and brings the value down;
So songs should be to just perfection wrought;
Yet where can we see one without a fault,
Exact propriety of words and thought?
Th' expression easy, and the fancy high,
Yet that not seem to creep, nor this to fly;
No words transpos'd, but in such just cadance,
As, though hard wrought, may seem the effect of chance;
Here, as in all things else, is most unfit   80
Bawdry barefac'd, that poor pretence to wit,—
Such nauseous songs as the late convert[2] made,
Which justly call this censure on his shade;
Not that warm thoughts of the transporting joy

---

[1] Then, as now, a reference to the government, though more specifically to the Royal Palace of Whitehall, burned in 1692, and hence to the court.
[2] The reference is to the Earl of Rochester, rake and poet, who was converted on his deathbed by Bishop Burnet in 1680.

Can shock the chastest or the nicest cloy,
But obscene words, too gross to move desire,
Like heaps of fuel do but choke the fire.
That author's name has undeserved praise,
Who pall'd the appetite he meant to raise.

   Next, *Elegie,* of sweet but solemn voice,   90
And of a subject grave, exacts the choice,
The praise of beauty, valour, wit contains,
And there too oft despairing love complains;
In vain, alas, for who by wit is moved?
That phoenix-she deserves to be beloved;
But noisy nonsense, and such fops as vex
Mankind, takes most with that fantastic sex:
This to the praise of those who better knew,
The many raise the value of the few.
But here, as I too oft, alas, have tried,   100
Women have drawn my wandering thoughts aside.
Their greatest fault, who in this kind have writ,
Is neither want of words, nor dearth of wit;
But though this Muse harmonious numbers yield,
And every couplet be with fancy fill'd,
If yet a just coherence be not made
Between each thought, and the whole model laid
So right that every step may higher rise,
As in a ladder, till it reach the skies;
Trifles like these perhaps of late have past,   110
And may be lik'd awhile, but never last;
'Tis epigram, 'tis point, 'tis what you will, ⎫
But not an elegie, nor writ with skill,   ⎬
No *Panegyrick,* nor a *Cooper's Hill.*[3]   ⎭

   A higher flight, and of a happier force,
Are *Odes,* the Muses' most unruly horse,
That bounds so fierce the rider has no rest,
But foams at mouth, and speaks like one possest.

---

[3] Johnson remarks, "Who would not suppose that Waller's *Panegyric* and
Denham's *Cooper's Hill* were elegies?"

The poet here must be indeed inspired,
And not with fancy, but with fury fired.   120
Cowley might boast to have perform'd this part,
Had he with Nature joyn'd the rules of Art;
But ill expression gives too great allay
To that rich fancy which can ne'er decay,
Though all appears in heat and fury done,
The language still must soft and easy run.
These laws may seem a little too severe,
But judgment yields, and fancy governs there,
Which, though extravagant, this Muse allows,
And makes the work much easier than it shews.   130

Of all the ways that wisest men could find
To mend the age, and mortify mankind,
Satyr[4] well writ has most successful prov'd,
And cures because the remedy is lov'd.
'Tis hard to write on such a subject more,
Without repeating things said oft before.
Some vulgar errors only let's remove,
That stain this beauty, which we chiefly love.
Of well-chose words some take not care enough,
And think they may be, as the subject, rough.   140
This great work must be more exactly made,
And sharpest thoughts in smoothest words convey'd:
Some think if sharp enough, they cannot fail,
As if their only business was to rail;
But 'tis men's foibles nicely to unfold,
Which makes a Satyr different from a scold.
Rage you must hide, and prejudice lay down:
A Satyr's smile is sharper than his frown.
So while you seem to scorn some rival youth,
Malice itself may pass sometimes for truth.   150
The Laureat[5] here may justly claim our praise,

[4] The spelling "satyr" is retained as appropriate to the belief then common that literary satire was originally associated with the mythological beings. The references in lines 146 and 148 must be read with this in mind.
[5] Dryden. Rochester believed Dryden the author of an attack on himself in Sheffield's *Essay on Satire* and hired ruffians to beat him.

Crown'd by *Mac-Fleckno* with immortal bays;
Though prais'd and punish'd for another's rimes,
His own deserve that glorious fate sometimes,
Were he not forc'd to carry now dead weight,
Rid by some lumpish Minister of State.

  Here rest, my Muse, suspend thy cares awhile,
A greater enterprise attends thy toil;
And as some eagle that intends to fly
A long and tedious journey through the sky,   160
Considers first the perils of her case,
Over what lands and seas she is to pass,
Doubts her own strength so far, and justly fears
That lofty road of airy travellers;
But yet incited by some great design,
That does her hopes beyond her fears incline,
Prunes every feather, views her self with care,
Then on a sudden flounces in the air;
Away she flies so strong, so high, so fast,
She lessens to us, and is lost at last: 170
So greater things my Muse prepares to sing,
Things that will malice, and may envy bring;
Yet why should truth offend, when only told
T' inform the ignorant, and warn the bold?
On then, my Muse, adventrously engage
To give instructions that concern the Stage.
The *unities* of action, time, and place,
Which, if observed, give plays so great a grace,
Are, though but little practis'd, too well known
To be taught here, where we pretend alone   180
From nicer faults to purge the present age,
Less obvious errors of the English stage.

  First then, *soliloquies* had need be few,
Extremely short, and spoke in passion too.
Our lovers talking to themselves, for want
Of others, make the pit their confidant;
Nor is the matter mended much, if thus
They trust a friend only to tell it us.

Th' occasion should as naturally fall,
As when *Bellario*[6] confesses all.   190

   Figures of speech, which poets think so fine,
Art's needless varnish to make Nature shine,
Are all but paint upon a beauteous face,
And in descriptions only claim a place.
But to make Rage declame, and Grief discourse,
From lovers in despair fine things to force,
Must needs succeed, for who can choose but pity
To see poor Hero's miserably witty?
But oh the dialogues, where jest and mock
Is held up like a rest at shuttlecock! [7]   200
Or else like bells eternally they chime,
Men die in simile, and live in rime.
What things are these who would be poets thought,
By Nature not inspir'd, nor Learning taught?
Some wit they have, and therefore may deserve
A better way than this by which they starve:
But to write plays? why, 'tis a bold pretence
To language, breeding, fancy, and good sense;
Nay, more, for they must look within to find
Those secret turns of Nature in the mind;   210
Without this part in vain would be the whole,
And but a body all without a soul.
All this together yet is but a part
Of dialogue, that great and powerful art,
Now almost lost, which the old Grecians knew, ⎤
From whence the Romans fainter copies drew, ⎬
Scarce comprehended since by but a few. ⎦
Plato and Lucian are the best remains
Of all the wonders which this art contains;
Yet to ourselves we justice must allow,   220
Shakespear and Fletcher are the wonders now:
Consider them, and read them o'er and o'er,

[6] In *Philaster,* by Beaumont and Fletcher.
[7] I.e., in the game of battledore and shuttlecock, the ancestor of what
became badminton.

Go see them play'd, then read them as before.
For though in many things they grosly fail,
Over our passions still they so prevail
That our own grief by theirs is rockt asleep,
The dull are forc'd to feel, the wise to weep.
Their beauties imitate, avoid their faults;
First on a plot employ thy carefull thoughts,
Turn it with time a thousand several ways,   230
This oft alone has given success to plays.
Reject that vulgar error which appears
So fair, of making perfect characters;
There's no such thing in Nature, and you'll draw
A faultless monster which the world ne'er saw;
Some faults must be, that his misfortunes drew,
But such as may deserve compassion too.
Besides the main design, composed with art,
Each moving scene must be a plot apart;
Contrive each little turn, mark every place,   240
As painters first chalk out the future face,
Yet be not fondly your own slave for this,
But change hereafter what appears amiss.
Think not so much where shining thoughts to place,
As what a man would say in such a case.
Neither in comedy will this suffice;
The actor too must be before your eyes;
And though 'tis drudgery to stoop so low,
To him you must your utmost meaning show.
Expose no single fop, but lay the load   250
More equally, and spread the folly broad;
The other way's too common: oft we see
A fool derided by as bad as he;
Hawks fly at nobler game, but in his way,
A very owl may prove a bird of prey;
Some poets so will one poor fop devour;
But to collect, like bees from every flower,
Ingredients to compose that precious juice,
Which serves the world for pleasure and for use,
In spite of faction this will favour get,   260
But *Falstaff* seems unimitable yet.

Another fault which often does befall,
Is when the wit of some great poet shall
So overflow, that is, be none at all,
That all his fools speak sense, as if possest,
And each by inspiration breaks his jest;
If once the justness of each part be lost,
Well may we laugh, but at the poet's cost.
That silly thing men call sheer wit avoid,
With which our age so nauseously is cloy'd;   270
Humour is all, and 'tis the top of wit
T' express agreeably a thing that's fit.
But since the poets we of late have known
Shine in no dress so well as in their own,
The better by example to convince,
Let's cast a view on this wrong side of sense.

First, a soliloquy is calmly made,
Where every reason is most nicely weigh'd;
At the end of which most opportunely comes
Some hero frighted at the noise of drums,   280
For her dear sake whom at first sight he loves,
And all in metaphor his passion proves;
But some sad accident, that's yet unknown,
Parting this pair, to leave the man alone,
He's jealous presently, we know not why,
Then, to oblige his rival needs must die,
But first he makes a speech, wherein he tells
The absent nymph how much his flame excells,
And yet bequeaths her generously now
To that dear rival whom he does not know,   290
Who, coming in, sent sure by Fate's command,
Too late, alas, withholds his hasty hand,
Which now has given that most lamented stroke,
At which this very stranger's heart is broke;
Who, more to his new friend than mistress kind,
Mourns the sad fate of being left behind,
Most naturally prefers those dying charms
To love and living in his lady's arms.
How shameful and what monstrous things are these!

And then they rail at th' age they cannot please,   300
Conclude us only partial for the dead,
And grudge the sin of old Ben Jonson's head;
When the intrinsic value of the stage
Can scarce be judg'd but by the following age;
For dances, flutes, Italian songs, and rime
May keep up sinking nonsense for a time,
But that will fail which now so much o'er rules,
And sense no longer will submit to fools.

   By painful steps we are at last got up
Parnassus' hill, upon whose airy top   310
The *Epic* poets so divinely show,
And with just pride behold the rest below.
Heroic poems have a just pretence
To be the chief effort of human sense,
A work of such inestimable worth,
There are but two the world has yet brought forth,
Homer and *Virgil:* with what awful sound
Each of those names the trembling air does wound!
Just as a changeling seems below the rest
Of men, or rather is a two legg'd beast,   320
So those gigantic souls, amaz'd, we find
As much above the rest of human kind.
Nature's whole strength united! endless fame,
And universal shouts attend their name!
Read Homer once, and you can read no more,
For all things else will seem so dull and poor,
You'll wish't unread; but oft upon him look,
And you will hardly need another book.
Had *Bossu*[8] never writ, the world had still
Like Indians view'd this wondrous piece of skill;   330
As something of divine the work admired,
Hoped not to be instructed, but inspired;
Till he, disclosing sacred mysteries,

[8] René Le Bossu, called by Dryden "the best of modern critics." His
Traité du Poëme Épique (1675) was generally regarded as the definitive
treatment of the epic.

Has shewn where all the mighty magic lies,
Describ'd the seeds, and in what order sown,
That have to such a vast proportion grown.
Sure from some angel he the secret knew,
Who through this labyrinth has given the clue!
But what, alas, avails it poor mankind
To see this promised land, yet stay behind?   340
The way is shewn, but who has strength to go?
Who can all sciences exactly know?
Whose fancy flies beyond weak reason's sight,
And yet has judgment to direct it right?
Whose nice distinction, Virgil-like, is such,
Never to say too little nor too much?
Let such a man begin without delay;
But he must do much more than I can say,
Must above *Cowley*, nay, and *Milton* too prevail,
Succeed where great *Torquato,* and our greater *Spenser*
     fail.[9]
                                                              350

---

[9] Johnson, in his "Life" of Sheffield remarks: "At the time when this work
first appeared, Milton's fame was not yet fully established, and therefore
Tasso and Spenser were set before him. . . . The last line in succeeding
editions was shortened, and the order of names continued; but now
Milton is at last advanced to the highest place, and the passage is thus
adjusted:

>   Must above Tasso's lofty flights prevail,
>   Succeed where Spenser, and ev'n Milton fail.

Amendments are seldom made without some token of a rent: *lofty* does
not suit Tasso so well as Milton."

THOMAS RYMER
[1641–1713]

Rymer's father, Ralph, was a roundhead Lord of the Manor who was hanged for joining the Presbyterian uprising of 1663. This event may not have contributed to his son's subsequent good nature. Thomas was educated at Cambridge and Gray's Inn, and called to the bar in 1673, but literature rather than law occupied his mind.

While no one, it is to be hoped, can read Rymer's critique of Othello today without flinching, we must admit while flinching that it is good fun to read. Rymer's criticism more than any other shows the perils of "common sense," particularly common sense infected with a mad reverence for those rules ultimately derived from the Ancients, but in their literal rigidity virtually invented by the critics of the Italian and French Renaissance, particularly Castelvetro (1505–1571) and Scaliger (1484–1558). It was from the seventeenth-century French formalists, whose literary classicism had passed through the crucible of Cartesian mathematicism, that Rymer received that tenet of rationalistic probability which tended to reduce poetry to an ingenious mechanism. Direct English influences can be traced to Hobbes, and almost certainly to the Royal Society in their desire to "bring all things to a mathematical plainness."

Rymer seems to have invented the term "poetic justice" to express the exact division of rewards and punishments— so exact that no character is to commit more crimes than he can at the end of the play be punished for! Abundant precedent for the doctrine exists in Classical prescriptions and in Scaliger, though nowhere previously is it applied

with quite such dogged literalness. Other of Rymer's doctrines
are, first, that of probability—ultimately derived from
Aristotle, but in Rymer interpreted in terms of the
commonplace; and, second, decorum—a character should
be representative of a type eternal in Nature, not of a
specific individual.

Pope calls Rymer as a critic "generally right, though
rather too severe in his opinion of the particular plays he
speaks of" (Spence), while Macaulay called him "simply, the
worst critic who ever lived." On the other hand, T. S.
Eliot has remarked of the critique on Othello that the
earlier critic "made out a very good case" and that "I have
never . . . seen a cogent refutation of Thomas Rymer's
objections to Othello." In his own day he was not publicly
refuted (though Dryden took issue with him in unpublished
"Heads of an Answer to Rymer"), and he exerted a
considerable influence upon Dennis, among others. Later,
both Voltaire and Byron commended him. It is much easier
to laugh at him than to argue with him. In any case, he
represents a high-water mark of what has since been almost
universally condemned as "rules criticism," a distinct phase
in the history of literary thought in Europe.

His chief critical works are the "Preface" to the
translation of Rapin's Reflections on Aristotle's treatise of
Poesie, containing the necessary, rational, and universal
rules for epick, dramatick, and the other sorts of Poetry.
With reflections on the works of the ancient and modern
poets, and their faults noted. (1674); The tragedies of the last
age consider'd and examin'd by the practice of ancients,
and by the common sense of all ages . . . (1678); and
A short view of tragedy; it's original, excellency, and
corruption. With some reflections on Shakespear, and other
practitioners for the stage. (1693), from which the
critique of Othello is taken. Curt A. Zimansky has edited
The Complete Critical Works of Thomas Rymer,
New Haven, 1956, with a perceptive introduction and notes,
to which I am happy to acknowledge my debt.

The text presented here is abbreviated from Spingarn's
text in Critical Essays of the Seventeenth Century (1907).
Spingarn presents the text with the original typographical
peculiarities, which I have modernized as far as possible
consistently with Rymer's apparent meaning, though I have

left the quotations from Othello *in their original form.*
Line numberings of quotations from the play follow the
numberings of the Globe edition as presented in the edition
of Shakespeare's works edited by W. A. Neilson and C. J.
Hill in the New Cambridge Edition, New York, 1942.

Rymer's importance in the history of criticism is
recognized by condescending nods, but not often discussed.
See, however, the following:

Alexander, Nigel: "Thomas Rymer and 'Othello,' "
    Shakespeare Survey XXI (1968), 67–77. [May be the
    cogent refutation which T. S. Eliot did not live to see.]
Shanahan, William: "The Critical System of Thomas Rymer,"
    Rendezvous (Idaho State University) I (Winter
    1966), 19–28.
Walcott, Fred G.: "John Dryden's answer to Thomas Rymer's
    The Tragedies of the Last Age, PQ XV (1936),
    194–214.
Watson, George: "Dryden's First Answer to Rymer," RES,
    n.s. XIV (1963), 17–23.

FROM SHORT VIEW OF TRAGEDY
[1693]

FROM CHAPTER VII

OTHELLO

From all the tragedies acted on our English stage, *Othello* is said to bear the bell away. The subject is more of a piece, and there is, as it were, some phantom of a fable. The fable is always accounted the soul of tragedy. And it is the fable which is properly the poet's part, because the other three parts of tragedy, to wit, the *characters* are taken from the moral philosopher; the *thoughts,* or sense, from them that teach rhetoric; and the last part, which is the *expression,* we learn from the grammarians.

This fable is drawn from a novel composed in Italian by Giraldi Cinthio, who also was a writer of tragedies, and to that use employed such of his tales as he judged proper for the stage. But with this of the Moor he meddled no farther.

Shakespear alters it from the original in several particulars, but always, unfortunately, for the worse. He bestows a name on his Moor, and styles him the Moor of Venice,—a note of pre-eminence which neither history nor heraldry can allow him. Cinthio, who knew him best, and whose creature he was, calls him simply a *Moor*. We say the Piper of Strasburgh, the Jew of Florence, and, if you please, the Pindar of Wakefield—all upon record, and memorable in their places. But we see no such cause for the Moor's preferment to that dignity. And it is an affront to all chroniclers and antiquaries to top upon 'um a Moor with that mark of renown, who yet had never fallen within the sphere of their cognisance.

Then is the Moor's wife, from a simple citizen in Cinthio, dress'd up with her top knots and rais'd to be *Desdemona*, a Senator's daughter. All this is very strange, and therefore pleases such as reflect not on the improbability. This match might well be without the parents' consent. Old Horace long ago forbad the banns:

> *Sed non ut placidis Coeant immitia, non ut*
> *Serpentes avibus geminentur, tigribus agni.*[1]

THE FABLE

Othello, a Blackmoor Captain, by talking of his prowess and feats of war, makes *Desdemona,* a Senator's daughter, to be in love with him, and to be married to him without her parent's knowledge; and having preferred *Cassio* to be his Lieutenant, a place which his Ensign, *Iago,* sued for, *Iago* in revenge works the Moor into a jealousy that *Cassio* cuckolds him—which he effects by stealing and conveying a certain handkerchief which had at the wedding been by the Moor presented to his bride. Hereupon *Othello* and *Iago* plot the deaths of *Desdemona* and *Cassio. Othello* murders her, and soon after is convinced of her innocence. And as he is about to be carried to prison in order to be punish'd for the murder, he kills himself.

---

[1] Horace, *Ars Poetica,* 12–13: "but not so far that savage should mate with tame, or serpents couple with birds, lambs with tigers."

Whatever rubs or difficulty may stick on the bark, the moral, sure, of this fable is very instructive.

First, this may be a caution to all maidens of quality how, without their parents' consent, they run away with Blackamoors.

> *Di non si accompagnare con huomo cui la natura & il cielo & il modo della vita disgiunge da noi.*——*Cinthio.*[2]

Secondly, this may be a warning to all good wives that they look well to their linen.

Thirdly, this may be a lesson to husbands that before their jealousy be tragical the proofs may be mathematical.

Cinthio affirms that *She was not overcome by a womanish appetite, but by the virtue of the Moor.* It must be a good-natur'd reader that takes Cinthio's word in this case, tho' in a novel. Shakespear, who is accountable both to the eyes and to the ears, and to convince the very heart of an audience, shews that *Desdemona* was won by hearing Othello talk.

> *Othello.*——I spake of most disastrous chances,
> Of Moving accidents by flood and field,
> Of hair-breadth scapes i' th' imminent deadly breach,
> Of being taken by the insolent foe,
> And sold to slavery, of my redemption thence,
> And portents in my Travels History;
> Wherein of Antars vast and Desarts idle,
> Rough Quarries, Rocks, and Hills whose heads touch Heaven,
> It was my hint to speak,—such was my process;
> And of the *Cannibals* that each others eat,
> The *Anthropophagi*, and men whose hands
> Do grow beneath their shoulders.——
>
> [I, iii, 134–45]

This was the charm, this was the philtre, the love-powder, that took the daughter of this noble Venetian. This was sufficient to make the Blackamoor white, and reconcile all, tho' there had been a cloven foot into the bargain.

---

[2] "Not to marry a man whom nature, heaven, and way of life disjoin from us."

A meaner woman might be as soon taken by *Aqua Tetra-chymagogon.*[3]

Nodes, cataracts, tumours, chilblains, carnosity, shankers, or any cant in the bill of an High German doctor is as good fustian circumstance, and as likely to charm a senator's daughter. But, it seems, the noble Venetians have an other sense of things. The Doge himself tells us:

Doge. I think this Tale wou'd win my Daughter too.

Horace tells us:

Intererit Multum——
Colchus an Assyrius, Thebis nutritus an Argis.[4]

Shakespear in this play calls 'em the *supersubtle Venetians.* Yet examine throughout the tragedy, there is nothing in the noble Desdemona that is not below any country chamber-maid with us.

And the account he gives us of their noblemen and senate can only be calculated for the latitude of Gotham.

The character of that state is to employ strangers in their wars: But shall a poet thence fancy that they will set a Negro to be their general, or trust a Moor to defend them against the Turk? With us a Blackamoor might rise to be a trumpeter; but Shakespear would not have him less than a Lieutenant-General. With us a Moor might marry some little drab or small-coal wench; Shakespear would provide him the daughter

---

[3] See *Tatler* 240: "About the same time [i.e., *c.* 1690] there was pasted a very hard word upon every corner of the streets. This, to the best of my remembrance, was

TETRACHYMAGOGON,

which drew great shoals of spectators about it, who read the bill that it introduced with unspeakable curiosity; and when they were sick, would have nobody but this learned man for their physician. [See Zimansky, p. 261.]

[4] *Ars Poetica,* 114–118: "Vast difference will it make, whether a god be speaking or a hero, a ripe old man or one still in the flower and fervour of youth, a dame of rank or a bustling nurse, a roaming trader or the tiller of a verdant field, a Colchian or an Assyrian, one bred at Thebes or at Argos."

and heir of some great lord or privy-councellor, and all the
town should reckon it a very suitable match. Yet the English
are not bred up with that hatred and aversion to the Moors
as are the Venetians, who suffer by a perpetual hostility from
them,—

Littora littoribus contraria.[5]

Nothing is more odious in Nature than an improbable lie;
and certainly never was any play fraught like this of *Othello*
with improbabilities.

The *characters* or manners, which are the second part in
a tragedy, are not less unnatural and improper than the fable
was improbable and absurd.

Othello is made a Venetian general. We see nothing done
by him nor related concerning him that comports with the
condition of a general, or indeed of a man, unless the killing
himself to avoid a death the law was about to inflict upon him.
When his jealousy had wrought him up to a resolution of's
taking revenge for the suppos'd injury, he sets Iago to the
fighting part to kill Cassio, and chuses himself to murder the
silly woman his wife, that was like to make no resistance.

His love and his jealousie are no part of a soldier's character, unless for comedy.

But what is most intolerable is Iago. He is no Blackamoor
soldier, so we may be sure he should be like other soldiers of
our acquaintance; yet never in tragedy, nor in comedy, nor in
Nature, was a soldier with his character; take it in the author's
own words:

> *Em.*—some Eternal Villain,
> Some busie and insinuating Rogue,
> Some cogging, couzening Slave, to get some Office.
>
> > [IV, ii, 130–32]

Horace describes a soldier otherwise:

> *Impiger, iracundus, inexorabilis, acer.*[6]

---

[5] *Æneid*, IV, 628: "May shore clash with shore."
[6] *Ars Poetica* 121: "impatient, passionate, ruthless, fierce."

Shakespear knew his character of Iago was inconsistent. In this very play he pronounces:

> If thou dost deliver more or less than Truth,
> Thou art no Souldier.
>
> [II, iii, 219–20]

This he knew; but to entertain the audience with something new and surprising, against common sense and Nature he would pass upon us a close, dissembling, false, insinuating rascal instead of an open-hearted, frank, plain-dealing soldier, a character constantly worn by them for some thousands of years in the world.

Tiberius Caesar had a poet arraigned for his life, because Agamemnon was brought on the stage by him with a character unbecoming a soldier.

Our ensigns and subalterns, when disgusted by the captain, throw up their commissions, bluster, and are bare-fac'd. Iago, I hope, is not brought on the stage in a red coat. I know not what livery the Venetians wear, but am sure they hold not these conditions to be *alla soldatesca*.

> *Non sia egli per far la vendetta con insidie, ma con la spada in mano.* Cinthio.[7]

Nor is our poet more discreet in his Desdemona. He had chosen a soldier for his knave, and a Venetian lady is to be the fool.

This senator's daughter runs away to a carrier's inn, the Sagittary, with a blackamoor, is no sooner wedded to him, but the very night she beds him is importuning and teasing him for a young smock-fac'd lieutenant, Cassio. And tho' she perceives the Moor jealous of Cassio, yet will she not forbear, but still rings *Cassio, Cassio*, in both his ears.

Roderigo is the cully of Iago, brought in to be murder'd by Iago, that Iago's hands might be the more in blood, and be yet the more abominable villain: who without that was too wicked on all conscience, and had more to answer for than any tragedy or Furies could inflict upon him. So there can be

---

[7] "He should not conduct a vendetta with plots, but with sword in hand." Zimansky points out that there is no such passage in the Cinthio story.

nothing in the characters, either for the profit or to delight an audience.

The third thing to be consider'd is the *thoughts*. But from such characters we need not expect many that are either true, or fine, or noble.

And without these, that is, without sense or meaning, the fourth part of tragedy, which is the *expression,* can hardly deserve to be treated on distinctly. The verse rumbling in our ears are of good use to help off the action.

In the neighing of an horse, or in the growling of a mastiff, there is a meaning, there is as lively expression, and, may I say, more humanity, than many times in the tragical flights of Shakespear.

Step then amongst the scenes to observe the conduct to this tragedy.

The first we see are Iago and Roderigo, by night in the streets of Venice. After growling a long time together, they resolve to tell Brabantio that his daughter is run away with the Blackamoor. Iago and Roderigo were not of quality to be familiar with Brabantio, nor had any provocation from him to deserve a rude thing at their hands. Brabantio was a noble Venetian, one of the sovereign lords and principal persons in the Government, peer to the most serene Doge, one attended with more state, ceremony, and punctillio than any English duke or nobleman in the government will pretend to. This misfortune in his daughter is so prodigious, so tender a point, as might puzzle the finest wit of the most supersubtle Venetian to touch upon it, or break the discovery to her father. See then how delicately Shakespear minces the matter:

> *Rod.* What ho, *Brabantio,* Signior *Brabantio,* ho!
> *Iago.* Awake! what ho, *Brabantio!* Thieves, thieves, thieves!
> Look to your House, your Daughter, and your Bags.
> Thieves, thieves!
> > Brabantio *at a window.*
> *Bra.* What is the reason of this terrible summons?
> What is the matter there?
> *Rod.* Signior, is all your Family within?
> *Iago.* Are your Doors lockt?

> *Bra.* Why, wherefore ask you this?
> *Iago.* Sir, you are robb'd; for shame, put on your
>   Gown;
> Your Heart is burst, you have lost half your Soul;
> Even now, very now, an old black Ram
> Is tupping your white Ewe: arise, arise,
> Awake the snorting Citizens with the Bell,
> Or else the Devil will make a Grandsire of you: arise,
>   I say.
>
> [I, i, 78–92]

.   .   .

In former days there wont to be kept at the courts of princes some body in a fool's coat, that in pure simplicity might let slip something which made way for the ill news, and blunted the shock, which otherwise might have come too violent upon the party.

Aristophanes put *Nicias* and *Demosthenes*[8] in the disguise of servants, that they might, without indecency, be drunk; and drunk he must make them that they might without reserve lay open the *arcana* of state, and the knavery of their ministers. . . .

This is address, this is truly satire, where the preparation is such that the thing principally design'd falls in as it only were of course.

But Shakespear shews us another sort of address; his manners of good breeding must not be like the rest of the civil world. Brabantio was not in masquerade, was not *incognito;* Iago well knew his rank and dignity.

> *Iago.* The *Magnifico* is much beloved,
> And hath in his effect a voice potential
> As double as the Duke.—
>
> [I, ii, 12–14]

But besides the manners to a *Magnifico*, humanity cannot bear that an old gentleman in his misfortune should be insulted over with such a rabble of scoundrel language, when no cause or provocation. Yet thus it is on our stage; this is our school of good manners, and the *speculum vitae.*

---

[8] *The Knights, passim.*

But our *Magnifico* is here in the dark, nor are yet his robes on: attend him to the senate house, and there see the difference, see the effects of Purple.

So, by and by, we find the Duke of Venice, with his senators in council, at midnight, upon advice that the Turks, or Ottamites, or both together, were ready in transport ships, put to sea, in order to make a descent upon Cyprus. This is the posture when we see Brabantio and Othello join them. By their conduct and manner of talk, a body must strain hard to fancy the scene at Venice, and not rather in some of our Cinq-ports, where the baily and his fishermen are knocking their heads together on account of some whale, or some terrible broil upon the coast. But to shew them true Venetians, the maritime affairs stick not long on their hand; the public may sink or swim. They will sit up all night to hear a Doctors' Commons, matrimonial cause, and have the merits of the cause at large laid open to 'em, that they may decide it before they stir. What can be pleaded to keep awake their attention so wonderfully?

Never, sure, was form of pleading so tedious and so heavy as this whole scene and midnight entertainment. Take his own words; says the respondent:

> *Oth.* Most potent, grave, and reverend Signiors,
> My very noble and approv'd good Masters:
> That I have tane away this old mans Daughter,
> It is most true; true, I have Married her;
> The very front and head of my offending
> Hath this extent, no more: rude I am in my speech,
> And little blest with the set phrase of peace;
> For since these Arms of mine had seven years pith,
> Till now some nine Moons wasted, they have us'd
> Their dearest action in the Tented Field;
> And little of this great World can I speak
> More than pertains to Broils and Battail;
> And therefore little shall I grace my Cause
> In speaking of my self; yet by your gracious patience,
> I would a round unravish'd Tale deliver,
> Of my whole course of love, what drags, what charms,
> What conjuration, and what mighty Magick,

> (for such proceedings am I charg'd withal)
> I won his Daughter.
>
>   [I, iii, 76–94]

All this is but preamble to tell the court that he wants words. This was the eloquence which kept them up all night, and drew their attention in the midst of their alarms.

One might rather think the novelty and strangeness of the case prevail'd upon them: no, the senators do not reckon it strange at all. Instead of starting at the prodigy, every one is familiar with Desdemona as he were her own natural father, rejoice in her good fortune, and wish their own several daughters as hopefully married. Should the poet have provided such a husband for an only daughter of any noble peer in England, the Blackamoor must have chang'd his skin to look our House of Lords in the face.

Aeschylus is noted in Aristophanes for letting Niobe be two or three acts on the stage before she speaks.[9] Our noble Venetian, sure, is in the other more unnatural extreme. His words flow in abundance; no butter-queen can be more lavish. Nay, he is for talking of state affairs, too, above anybody:

> *Bra.* Please it your Grace, on to the state Affairs.—
>
>   [I, iii, 190]

Yet is this Brabantio sensible of his affliction; before the end of the play his heart breaks, he dies.

> *Bra.* Poor *Desdemona,* I am glad thy Father's dead;
> Thy match was mortal to him, and pure grief
> Shore his old thread in twain.—
>
>   [V, ii, 204–206]

A third part in a tragedy is the *thoughts:* from Venetians, noblemen, and senators we may expect fine thoughts. Here is a trial of skill: for a parting blow, the Duke and Brabantio cap sentences. Where then shall we seek for the thoughts, if we let slip this occasion? Says the Duke:

> *Duk.* Let me speak like your self, and lay a *Sentence*

[9] *The Frogs.*

Which, like a greese or step, may help these lovers
Into your favour.
When remedies are past, the grief is ended
By seeing the worst, which late on hopes depended.
To mourn a mischief that is past and gone
Is the next way to draw more mischief on;
What cannot be preserv'd when Fortune takes,
Patience her injury a Mocker makes.
The rob'd that smiles steals something from a Thief;
He robs himself that spends an hopeless grief.
   Bra. So let the Turk of *Cyprus* us beguile;
We lose it not so long as we can smile.
He bears the sentence well, that nothing bears
But the free comfort which from thence he hears;
But he bears both the sentence and the sorrow,
That to pay grief must of poor patience borrow:
These *Sentences,* to Sugar or to Gall,
Begin strong on both sides, are equivocal.
But words are words; I never yet did hear
That the bruis'd Heart was pierced through the Ear.
Beseech you, now to the affairs of State.

[I, iii, 210–220]

How far wou'd the Queen of Sheba have travell'd to hear
the wisdom of our noble Venetians? . . .

What provocation or cause of malice our poet might have
to libel the most Serene Republic I cannot tell; but certainly
there can be no wit in this representation.

For the second act, our poet, having dispatched his affairs
at Venice, shews the action next (I know not how many leagues
off) in the island of Cyprus. The audience must be there too,
and yet our Bayes had it never in his head to make any provi-
sion of transport ships for them.

In the days that the Old Testament was acted in Clerken-
well by the parish clerks of London, the Israelites might pass
through the Red Sea; but alas, at this time, we have no Moses
to bid the waters make way and to usher us along. Well, the
absurdities of this kind break no bones. They may make fools
of us, but do not hurt our morals.

Come ashore then, and observe the countenance of the
people after the dreadful storm, and their apprehensions from

an invasion by the Ottomites, their succour and friends scatter'd and tost, nobody knew whither. The first that came to land was Cassio; his first salutation to the governor, Montanio, is:

> *Cas.* Thanks to the valiant of this Isle,
> That so approve the Moor, and let the Heavens
> Give him defence against their Elements,
> For I have lost him on the dangerous Sea.
>
> [II, i, 43–6]

To him the governor speaks, indeed, like a man in his wits.

> *Mont.* Is he well Shipt?

The lieutenant answers thus:

> *Cas.* His Bark is stoutly Tymber'd, and his Pilot
> Of very expert and approv'd allowance;
> Therefore my hopes (not surfeited to death)
> Stand in bold care.
>
> [II, i, 47–51]

The governor's first question was very proper; his next question, in this posture of affairs, is:

> *Mont.* But, good Lieutenant, is our general Wiv'd?
>
> [II, i, 60]

A question so remote, so impertinent and absurd, so odd and surprising never entered Bayes's *Pericranium*. Only the answer may tally with it:

> *Cas.* Most fortunately, he hath atcheiv'd a Maid,
> That Parragons description and wild fame:
> One that excels the quirks of blasoning Pens,
> And in the essential vesture of Creation,
> Does bear an excellency.—
>
> [II, i, 61–5]

They who like this author's writing will not be offended to find so much repeated from him. I pretend not here to tax either the sense or the language; those circumstances had their proper place in the Venetian senate. What I now cite is to shew how probable, how natural, how reasonable the conduct is all along.

I thought it enough that Cassio should be acquainted with a virgin of that rank and consideration in Venice as Desdemona. I wondered that in the senate-house everyone should know her so familiarly; yet here also at Cyprus everybody is in a rapture at the name of Desdemona, except only Montanio, who must be ignorant, that Cassio, who has an excellent cut in shaping an answer, may give him the satisfaction:

> *Mont.* What is she?
> *Cas.* She that I spoke of, our Captains Captain,
> Left in the Conduct of the bold Iago;
> Whose footing here anticipates our thoughts
> A Sennets speed: great Jove, *Othello* guard,
> And swell his Sail with thine own powerful breath,
> That he may bless this Bay with his Tall Ship,
> And swiftly come to *Desdemona's* Arms,
> Give renewed fire to our extincted Spirits,
> And bring all *Cyprus* comfort.
> > *Enter Desdemona, etc.*
> > O behold,
> The riches of the Ship is come on shoar!
> Ye men of *Cyprus,* let her have your Knees.
> Hail to the Lady! and the Grace of Heaven,
> Before, behind thee, and on every hand,
> Enwheel the round! [10]

[II, i, 73–87]

In the name of phrenzy, what means this soldier? Or would he talk thus if he meant anything at all? Who can say Shakespear is to blame in his character of a soldier? Has he not here done him reason? When could our *Tramontains* talk at this rate? but our *Jarsey* and *Garnsey* captains must not speak so fine things, nor compare with the Mediterranean, or garrisons in Rhodes and Cyprus.

The next thing our officer does is to salute Iago's wife, with this *conge* to the husband:

> *Cas.* Good Ancient, you are welcome; welcome, Mistriss:
> Let it not Gall your Patience, good Iago,

---

[10] The correct reading is "enwheel *thee* round." Zimansky points out that "*the* is probably a misprint, but Rymer, regarding the whole speech as frenzy, undoubtedly missed the image here." [Zimansky, p. 264.]

That I extend my Manners; 'tis my Breeding
That gives me this bold shew of Curtesy.
    Iago. Sir, would she give you so much of her lips,
As of her tongue she has bestow'd on me,
You'd have enough.
    Des. Alass! she has no speech.

                                [II, i, 97–103]

Now follows a long rabble of jack-pudden farce between
Iago and Desdemona, that runs on with all the little plays,
jingle, and trash below the patience of any country kitchen-
maid with her sweetheart. The Venetian *Donna* is hard put
to 't for pastime! And this is all when they are newly got on
shore from a dismal tempest, and when every moment she
might expect to hear her Lord (as she calls him), that she
runs so mad after, is arriv'd or lost: And moreover,

            —*In a Town of War,*
       —*The peoples Hearts brimful of fear.*
                       [II, iii, 213–14]

Never in the world had any Pagan poet his brains turn'd at
this monstrous rate. But the ground of all this Bedlam-buffoon-
ery we saw in the case of the French strollers;[11] the company
for acting *Christ's Passion* or the *Old Testament* were carpenters, cobblers, and illiterate fellows, who found that the drolls
and fooleries interlarded by them brought in the rabble and
lengthened their tune, so they got money by the bargain.

Our Shakespear, doubtless, was a great master in this
craft. These carpenters and cobblers were the guides he fol-

---

[11] Rymer had earlier referred to and translated an extract from the Regis-
ters of the French Parliament for 1541. The charge had been that, "It is
plain by Natural Reason, that without first knowing the Truth, one cannot
make a Fiction; for Fiction is to be something as near the Truth as may
be; whereas neither the Masters, nor the Actors know the A B C. They
understand neither the Bible, nor any prophane Learning, being Mecha-
nicks, as Cobblers, Botchers, Porters, that can neither read nor write, nor
have been train'd to the Stage, or that sort of exercise. . . . All of which,
the King's Attorney General being informed, hath put a stop to their
farther proceedings. They shew a Letter of Priviledge they had obtained
from the King." [Zimansky, pp. 114–115.] But Francis I permitted the
players to perform.

lowed. And it is then no wonder that we find so much farce
and Apocryphal matter in his tragedies, thereby un-hallowing
the theatre, profaning the name of tragedy; and instead of
representing men and manners, turning all morality, good
sense, and humanity into mockery and derision.

But pass we to something of a more serious air and complexion. Othello and his bride are the first night no sooner
warm in bed together, but a drunken quarrel happening in the
garrison, two soldiers fight, and the general rises to part the
fray. He swears:

> *Othel.* Now, by Heaven,
> My blood begins my safer guides to rule,
> And passion, having my best judgment cool'd,
> Assays to lead the way; if once I stir,
> Or do but lift this arm, the best of you
> Shall sink in my rebuke: give me to know
> How this foul rout began, who set it on,
> And he that is approv'd in this offence,
> Tho' he has twin'd with me, both at a birth,
> Should lose me: what, *in a Town of War*,
> *Yet wild, the peoples Hearts brimful of fear*,
> To manage private and domestick quarrels,
> In Night, and on the Court and guard of safety,
> 'Tis Monstrous; *Iago*, who began?

[II, iii, 204–17]

In the days of yore soldiers did not swear in this fashion.
What should a soldier say farther when he swears, unless he
blaspheme? Action shou'd speak the rest. What follows must
be *ex ore gladii*:[12] He is to rap out an oath, not wire-draw and
spin it out. By the style one might judge that Shakespear's soldiers were never bred in a camp, but rather had belong'd
to some affidavit-office. Consider also, throughout this whole
scene, how the Moorish general proceeds in examining into this
rout: no Justice Clod-pate could go on with more phlegm and
deliberation. The very first night that he lies with the *divine
Desdemona* to be thus interrupted might provoke a man's
Christian patience to swear in another style. But a Negro gen-

---

[12] "From the country of the gladiator."

eral is a man of strange mettle. Only his Venetian bride is a
match for him. She understands that the soldiers in the garrison are by th' ears together, and presently she, at midnight,
is in amongst them.

> *Desd.* What's the matter there?
> *Othel.* All's well now, Sweeting.
> Come away to Bed.
>
> [II, iii, 251–2]

In the beginning of this second act, before they had lain
together, Desdemona was said to be *our captain's captain*.
Now they are no sooner in bed together, but Iago is advising
Cassio in these words:

> *Iago.*—Our Generals Wife is now the General; I may say so
> in this respect, for that he hath devoted and given up himself
> to the contemplation, mark, and devotement of her parts and
> graces. Confess your self freely to her, importune her; she'll
> help to put you in your place again: she is so free, so kind, so
> apt, so blessed a disposition, that she holds it a vice in her
> goodness not to do more than she is requested. This broken
> joint between you and her Husband, intreat her to splinter.—
>
> [II, iii, 319–28]

And he says afterwards:

> *Iago.*—'Tis most easie
> The inclining *Desdemona* to subdue
> In any honest suit. She's fram'd as fruitful
> As the free Elements: And then for her
> To win the Moor, were 't to renounce his Baptism,
> All seals and symbols of redeemed sin,
> His soul is so enfetter'd to her love
> That she may make, unmake, do what she list;
> Even as her appetite shall play the God
> With his weak function.—
>
> [II, iii, 345–54]

This kind of discourse implies an experience and long
conversation, the honeymoon over, and a marriage of some
standing. Would any man in his wits talk thus of a bridegroom
and bride the first night of their coming together?

Yet this is necessary for our poet; it would not otherwise

serve his turn. This is the source, the foundation of his plot, hence is the spring and occasion for all the jealousy and bluster that ensues.

Nor are we in better circumstances for Roderigo. The last thing said by him in the former act was:

> *Rod.*—I'll go sell all my Land.
>
> [I, iii, 388]

A fair estate is sold to *put money in his purse* for this adventure. And lo, here, the next day:

> *Rod.* I do follow here in the Chace, not like a Hound that hunts, but one that fills up the cry. My Money is almost spent. I have been tonight exceedingly well cudgell'd. I think the issue will be, I shall have so much experience for my pains, and so no Money at all, and with a little more will return to Venice.
>
> [II, iii, 369-75]

The Venetian squire had a good riddance for his acres. The poet allows him just time to be once drunk, a very conscionable reckoning!

In this second act, the face of affairs could in truth be no other than

> —In a Town of War,
> Yet wild, the peoples Hearts brim-ful of fear.

But nothing, either in this act or in the rest that follow, shew any colour or complexion, any resemblance or proportion to that face and posture it ought to bear. Should a painter draw any one scene of this play, and write over it, *This is a Town of War*, would any body believe that the man were in his senses? Would not a *Goose* or *Dromedary* for it be a name as just and suitable? And what in painting would be absurd can never pass upon the world for poetry. . . .

Othello, the night of his arrival at Cyprus, is to consummate with Desdemona; they go to bed. Both are rais'd and run into the town amidst the soldiers that were a fighting, then go to bed again; that morning he sees Cassio with her: She importunes him to restore Cassio. Othello shews nothing of the soldier's mettle, but like a tedious, drawling, tame goose, is gaping after any paltry insinuation, labouring to be jealous, and catching at every blown surmize.

> *Iago.* My Lord, I see you are moved.
> *Oth.* No, not much moved.
> Do not think but *Desdemona* is honest.
> *Iago.* Long live she so, and long live you to think so!
> *Oth.* And yet how Nature erring from it self—
> *Iago.* I, There's the point: as, to be bold with you,
> Not to affect many proposed Matches
> Of her own clime, complexion, and degree,
> Wherein we see, in all things, Nature tends,
> Fye, we may smell in such a will most rank,
> Foul disproportion, thoughts unnatural.—
>
> [III, iii, 224–33]

The poet here is certainly in the right, and by consequence the foundation of the play must be concluded to be monstrous, and the constitution, all over, to be

> most rank,
> Foul disproportion, thoughts unnatural:

Which, instead of moving pity or any passion tragical and reasonable, can produce nothing but horror and aversion and what is odious and grievous to an audience. After this fair morning's work, the bride enters, drops a cur[t]sey:

> *Desd.* How now, my dear *Othello.*
> Your Dinner, and the generous Islanders
> By you invited, do attend your presence.
> *Oth.* I am to blame.
> *Desd.* Why is your speech so faint? Are you not well?
> *Oth.* I have a pain upon my Fore-head, dear.
>
> [III, iii, 279–84]

Michael Cassio came not from Venice in the ship with Desdemona, nor till this morning could be suspected of an opportunity with her. And 'tis now but dinner time; yet the Moor complains of his forehead. He might have set a guard on Cassio, or have lockt up Desdemona, or have observ'd their carriage a day or two longer. He is on other occasions phlegmatic enough; this is very hasty. But after dinner we have a wonderful flight:

   Othel. What sense had I of her stoln hours of lust?
I saw 't not, thought it not, it harm'd not me:
I slept the next night well, was free and merry;
I found not Cassio's kisses on her lips.—

[III, iii, 338–41]

A little after this, says he:

   Oth. Give me a living reason that she's disloyal.
   Iago.—I lay with *Cassio* lately,
And being troubled with a raging tooth, I could not sleep.
There are a kind of men so loose of Soul,
That in their sleeps will mutter their affairs:
One of this kind is *Cassio.*
In sleep I heard him say: sweet *Desdemona,*
Let us be wary, let us hide our loves:
And then, Sir, wou'd he gripe and wring my hand,
Cry out, sweet Creature! and then kiss me hard,
As if he pluckt up kisses by the roots,
That grew upon my Lips; then laid his leg
Over my Thigh, and sigh'd and kiss'd, and then
Cry'd: cursed fate that gave thee to the Moor!

[III, iii, 409–426]

By the rapture of Othello one might think that he raves,
is not of sound memory, forgets that he has not yet been two
nights in the matrimonial bed with his Desdemona. But we
find Iago, who should have a better memory, forging his lies
after the very same model. The very night of their marriage
at Venice, the Moor and also Cassio were sent away to Cyprus.
In the second act, Othello and his bride go the first time to bed:
The third act opens the next morning. The parties have been
in view to this moment. We saw the opportunity which was
given for Cassio to *speak his bosom* to her: *once,* indeed,
might go a great way with a Venetian. But *once* will not do
the poet's business. The audience must suppose a great many
bouts to make the plot operate. They must deny their senses
to reconcile it to common sense, or make it any way consistent
and hang together. . . .

ACT IV

>Enter *Iago* and *Othello.*
>*Iago.* Will you think so?
>*Othel.* Think so, *Iago!*
>*Iago.* What, to kiss in private?
>*Othel.* An unauthorized kiss.
>*Iago.* Or to be naked with her friend a-bed
>An hour or more, not meaning any harm?
>*Othel.* Naked a-bed, *Iago,* and not mean harm!—
>
>   [IV, i, 1–5]

At this gross rate of trifling, our General and his Ancient march on most heroically, till the jealous booby has his brains turn'd, and falls in a trance. Would any imagine this to be the language of Venetians, of soldiers and mighty captains? No Bartholomew droll could subsist upon such trash. But lo, a stratagem never presented in tragedy:

>*Iago.* Stand you a while a part—
>—Incave your self,
>And mark the Jeers, the Gibes, and notable scorns,
>That dwell in every region of his face;
>For I will make him tell the tale a new,
>Where, how, how oft, how long ago, and when
>He has and is again to Cope your Wife:
>I say, but mark his gesture.—
>
>   [IV, i, 75, 82–88]

With this device Othello withdraws. Says Iago aside:

>*Iago.* Now will I question Cassio of Bianca,
>A Huswife—
>That doats on *Cassio.*—
>He, when he hears of her, cannot refrain
>From the excess of Laughter.—
>As he shall smile, *Othello* shall go mad;
>And his unbookish jealousy must conster
>Poor *Cassio's* smiles, gesture, and light behaviour,
>Quite in the wrong.—
>
>   [IV, i, 94–104]

So to work they go: And Othello is as wise a commentator, and makes his applications pat, as heart could wish—but I would not expect to find this scene acted nearer than in Southwark Fair! But the handkerchief is brought in at last, to stop all holes and close the evidence. So now being satisfied with the proof, they come to a resolution that the offenders shall be murdered.

> *Othel.*—But yet the pity of it, *Iago!* ah, the pity!
> *Iago.* If you be so fond over her iniquity, give her
> Patent to offend. For if it touches not you, it comes near
> no Body.—
> Do it not with poison, strangle her in her Bed; Even the
> Bed she has contaminated.
> *Oth.* Good, good; the Justice of it pleases; very good.
> *Iago.* And for Cassio, let me be his undertaker.—
>
> [IV, i, 206–10, 220–24]

Iago had some pretence to be discontent with Othello and Cassio, and what passed hitherto was the operation of revenge. Desdemona had never done him harm, always kind to him and to his wife, was his country-woman, a dame of quality: for him to abet her murder shews nothing of a soldier, nothing of a man, nothing of Nature in it. The Ordinary of Newgate never had the like monster to pass under his examination. Can it be any diversion to see a rogue beyond what the devil ever finish'd? Or wou'd it be any instruction to an audience? Iago could desire no better than to set Cassio and Othello, his two enemies, by the ears together, so he might have been reveng'd on them both at once: And chusing for his own share the murder of Desdemona, he had the opportunity to play booty, and save the poor harmless wretch. But the poet must do everything by contraries, to surprize the audience still with something horrible and prodigious beyond any human imagination. At this rate he must out-do the devil to be a poet in the rank with Shakespear.

Soon after this, arrives from Venice Ludovico, a noble cousin of Desdemona; presently she is at him also on the behalf of Cassio.

    Desd. Cousin, there's fallen between him and my Lord
An unkind breach; but you shall make all well.
    Lud. Is there division 'twixt my Lord and *Cassio?*
    Desd. A most unhappy one; I wou'd do much
To attone them, for the love I bear to *Cassio.*

                [IV, i, 236–37, 242–44]

By this time we are to believe the couple have been a
week or two married, and Othello's jealousy, that had rag'd
so loudly and had been so uneasy to himself, must have reach'd
her knowledge. The audience have all heard him more plain
with her than was needful to Venetian capacity, and yet she
must still be impertinent in her suit for Cassio. Well, this
Magnifico comes from the Doge and Senators to displace
Othello.

    Lud.—Deputing *Cassio* in his Government.
    Desd. Trust me, I am glad on 't.
    Oth. Indeed!
    Desd. My Lord!
    Oth. I am glad to see you mad.
    Desd. How, *sweet Othello?*
    Oth. Devil!
    Desd. I have not deserved this.
    Oth. O Devil, Devil!—
Out of my sight.
    Desd. I will not stay to offend you.
    Lud. Truly, an obedient Lady.
I do beseech your Lordship call her back.
    Oth. Mistress!
    Desd. My Lord?
    Oth. What would you with her, Sir?
    Lud. Who, I, my Lord?
    Oth. I, you did wish that I wou'd make her turn:
Sir, she can turn, and turn, and yet go on,
And turn agen; and she can weep, Sir, weep;
And she is obedient, as you say, obedient,
Very obedient.—
    Lud. What, strike your Wife!

                [IV, i, 248–52, 255, 258–67]

Of what flesh and blood does our poet make these noble

Venetians,—the men without gall, the women without either
brains or sense? A senator's daughter runs away with this
Blackamoor; the government employs this Moor to defend
them against the Turks, so resent not the Moor's marriage at
present; but the danger over, her father gets the Moor cashier'd,
sends his kinsman, Seignior Ludovico, to Cyprus with the
commission for a new general; who, at his arrival, finds the
Moor calling the lady, his kinswoman, whore and strumpet,
and kicking her: what says the *Magnifico?*

> *Lud.* My Lord, this would not be believ'd in *Venice,*
> Tho' I shou'd swear I saw't; 'tis very much;
> Make her amends: she weeps.

> [IV, i, 253-55]

The Moor has no body to take his part, no body of his
colour; Ludovico has the new governor, Cassio, and all his
countrymen Venetians about him. What poet would give a
villainous blackamoor this ascendant? What Tramontain could
fancy the Venetians so low, so despicable, or so patient? This
outrage to an injur'd lady, the *Divine Desdemona,* might in a
colder climate have provoked some body to be her champion;
but the Italians may well conclude we have a strange genius
for poetry. In the next scene Othello is examining the supposed
bawd; then follows another storm of horror and outrage against
the poor chicken, his wife. Some drayman or drunken tinker
might possibly treat his drab at this sort of rate and mean no
harm by it; but for his excellency, a My Lord General, to
serenade a senator's daughter with such a volly of scoundrel
filthy language is sure the most absurd maggot that ever bred
from any poet's addle brain. . . .

The last act begins with Iago and Roderigo, who a little
before had been upon the huff:

> *Rod.* I say it is not very well. I will make my self known to
> *Desdemona:* if she will return me my Jewels, I will give over
> my suit and repent my unlawful sollicitation; if not, assure
> your self I'll seek satisfaction of you.

> [IV, ii, 199-203]

Roderigo, a noble Venetian, had sought Desdemona in
marriage, is troubled to find the Moor had got her from him,

advises with Iago, who wheadles him to sell his estate and go
over the sea to Cyprus in expectation to cuckold Othello; there
having cheated Roderigo of all his money and jewels on
pretence of presenting them to Desdemona, our gallant grows
angry, and would have satisfaction from Iago, who sets all
right by telling him Cassio is to be governor, Othello is going
with Desdemona into Mauritania. To prevent this, you are to
murder Cassio, and then all may be well.

> *Iago.* He goes into *Mauritania,* and takes with him the fair
> *Desdemona,* unless his abode be lingered here by some acci-
> dent, wherein none can be so determinate as the removing of
> *Cassio.*
>
> [IV, ii, 229–33]

Had Roderigo been one of the *Banditti,* he might not
much stick at the murder. But why Roderigo should take this
for payment, and risk his person where the prospect of advantage is so very uncertain and remote, nobody can imagine.
It had need be a *super-subtle* Venetian that this plot will pass
upon. Then, after a little spurt of villany and murder, we are
brought to the most lamentable that ever appear'd on any
stage. A noble Venetian lady is to be murdered by our poet,
—in sober sadness, purely for being a fool. No pagan poet but
would have found some machine for her deliverance. Pegasus
would have strain'd hard to have brought old Perseus on his
back, time enough to rescue this Andromeda from so foul
a monster. Has our Christian poetry no generosity, nor bowels?
Ha, Sir Lancelot! ha, St. George! will no ghost leave the shades
for us in extremity to save a distressed damosel?

But for our comfort, however felonious is the heart, hear
with what soft language he does approach her, with a candle
in his hand:

> *Oth.* Put out the light, and then put out the light:
> If I quench thee, thou flaming Minister,
> I can again thy former light restore.—
>
> [V, ii, 7–9]

Who would call him barbarian, monster, savage? . . .
One might think the general should not glory much in
this action, but make an hasty work on't, and have turn'd his

eyes away from so unsoldierly an execution; yet is he all pause
and deliberation, handles her as calmly and is as careful of her
soul's health as it had been her Father Confessor. *Have you
prayed tonight,* Desdemona? But the suspense is necessary that
he might have a convenient while so to roll his eyes, and so to
gnaw his nether lip to the spectators. Besides the greater
cruelty—*sub tam lentis maxillis.*[13]

But hard, a most tragical thing laid to her charge!

> *Oth.* That Handkerchief, that I so lov'd and gave thee,
> Thou gav'st to Cassio.
> *Desd.* No, by my Life and Soul!
> Send for the man, and ask him.
> *Oth.* By Heaven, I saw my Handkerchief in his hand.—
> —I saw the Handkerchief.

> [V, ii, 48–50, 62, 66]

So much ado, so much stress, so much passion and repetition about an handkerchief! Why was not this call'd the *Tragedy of the Handkerchief?* What can be more absurd than (as
Quintilian expresses it) *in parvis litibus has Tragoedias movere?*[14] We have heard of *Fortunatus his Purse* and of the
Invisible Cloak, long ago worn threadbare and stow'd up in the
wardrobe of obsolete romances: one might think that were a
fitter place for this handkerchief than that it, at this time of
day, be worn on the stage to raise every where all this clutter
and turmoil. Had it been Desdemona's garter, the sagacious
Moor might have smelt a rat; but the handkerchief is so remote
a trifle, no booby on this side Mauritania could make any
consequence from it.

We may learn here that a woman never loses her tongue,
even tho' after she is stiff'd:

---

[13] Suetonius, *Tiberius,* XXI (Loeb Library, *Suetonius,* v. 1, p. 325):
Miserum populum R., qui sub tam lentis maxillis ent. "Alas for the
Roman people, to be ground by jaws that crunch so slowly!"
[14] *Institutio* VI, i (tr. H. E. Butler, N.Y., 1921): *Nam in parvis quidem
litibus has tragoedias movere tale est, quasi si personam Herculis et
Cothurnos aptare infantibus velis.* "For to embark on such tragic methods
in trivial cases would be like putting the mask and buskins of Hercules
on a small child."

> *Desd.* O falsly, falsly murder'd!
> *Em.* Sweet *Desdemona,* O sweet Mistress, speak!
> *Desd.* A guiltless death I dye.
> *Em.* O who has done the deed?
> *Desd.* No body; I my self; farewel:
> Commend me to my kind Lord; O farewel!
>
> [V, ii, 117, 121–25]

This Desdemona is a black swan, or an old blackamoor
is a bewitching bedfellow. If this be Nature, it is a *lascheté* [15]
below what the English language can express.

For Lardella to *make love like an Humble Bee* was, in
The Rehearsal,[16] thought a fancy odd enough.

But hark what follows:

> *Oth.*—O heavy hour!
> Methinks it shou'd be now a huge Eclipse
> Of Sun and Moon, and that the affrighted globe
> Shou'd yawn at Alteration.
>
> [V, ii, 98–101]

This is wonderful! Here is poetry to elevate and amuse.
Here is sound all-sufficient. It would be uncivil to ask Flam-
stead [17] if the sun and moon can both together be so hugely
eclipsed in any *heavy hour* whatsoever. Nor must the spectators consult Gresham College whether a body is naturally
frighted till he *yawn* again. The fortune of Greece is not concern'd with these matters. These are physical circumstances
a poet may be ignorant in, without any harm to the public.
These slips have no influence on our manners and good life,
which are the poet's province.

Rather may we ask here what unnatural crime Desdemona
or her parents had committed to bring this judgment down
upon her: to wed a blackamoor, and innocent to be thus
cruelly murder'd by him. What instruction can we make out
of this catastrophe? Or whither must our reflection lead us?
Is not this to envenom and sour our spirits, to make us repine

---

[15] Law-French: negligence.
[16] *The Rehearsal,* IV, i.
[17] John Flamsteed (1646–1719), in 1675 appointed first astronomer royal.

and grumble at Providence and the government of the world? If this be our end, what boots it to be virtuous?

Desdemona dropped the handkerchief, and missed it that very day after her marriage; it might have been rumpled up with her wedding sheets, the fairy napkin (whilst Othello was stifling her) might have started up to disarm his fury and stop his ungracious mouth. Then might she (in a trance for fear) have lain as dead. Then might he, believing her dead, touched with remorse, have honestly cut his own throat, by the good leave and with the applause of all the spectators, who might thereupon have gone home with a quiet mind, admiring the beauty of Providence, fairly and truly represented on the theatre. . . .

But from this scene to the end of the play we meet with nothing but blood and butchery, described much-what to the style of *the last Speeches and Confessions of the persons executed at Tyburn,* with this difference, that there we have the *fact* and the due course of justice, whereas our poet, against all justice and reason, against all law, humanity, and Nature, in a barbarous, arbitrary way, executes and makes havock of his subjects, hab-nab, as they come to hand. Desdemona dropped her handkerchief; therefore she must be stifled. Othello, by law to be broken on the wheel, by the poet's cunning escapes with cutting his own throat. Cassio, for I know not what, comes off with a broken shin. Iago murders his benefactor Roderigo, as this were poetical gratitude. Iago is not yet killed, because there yet never was such a villain alive. The Devil, if once he brings a man to be dipped in a deadly sin, lets him alone to take his course; and now when the Foul Fiend has done with him, our wise authors take the sinner into their poetical service, there to accomplish him and do the Devil's drudgery.

Philosophy tells us it is a principle in the nature of man to be grateful.

History may tell us that John an Oaks, John a Stiles,[18] or Iago were ungrateful. *Poetry* is to follow Nature. Philosophy must be his guide: history and *fact* in particular cases of John

[18] Fictitious names used in law courts.

an Oaks or John of Styles are no warrant or direction for a poet. Therefore Aristotle is always telling us that poetry . . . is more general and abstracted, is led more by the philosophy, the reason and nature of things than history, which only records things higlety piglety, right or wrong, as they happen. History might without any preamble or difficulty say that Iago was ungrateful. Philosophy then calls him unnatural. But the poet is not without huge labour and preparation to expose the monster, and after shew the Divine Vengeance executed upon him. The poet is not to add wilful murder to his ingratitude: he has not antidote enough for the poison: his hell and furies are not punishment sufficient for one single crime of that bulk and aggravation.

> *Em.* O thou dull Moor, that Handkerchief thou
>   speakest on
> I found by Fortune and did give my Husband;
> For often with a solemn earnestness,
> More than indeed belong'd to such a trifle,
> He beg'd of me to steal it.
>
> [V, ii, 225–29]

Here we see the meanest woman in the play takes this handkerchief for a trifle below her husband to trouble his head about it. Yet we find it entered into our poet's head to make a tragedy of this trifle.

Then, *for the unraveling of the plot,* as they call it, never was old deputy recorder in a country town, with his spectacles, in summoning up the evidence, at such a puzzle, so blundered and be-doultefied, as is our poet to have a good riddance, and get the *catastrophe* off his hands.

What can remain with the audience to carry home with them from this sort of poetry for their use and edification? how can it work, unless (instead of settling the mind and purging our passions) to delude our senses, disorder our thoughts, addle our brain, pervert our affections, hair our imaginations, corrupt our appetite, and fill our head with vanity, confusion, *tintamarre,* and jingle-jangle, beyond what all the parish clerks of London with their Old Testament farces and interludes, in Richard the Second's time, could ever pretend to? Our only hopes for the good of their souls can be that these people go to the playhouse as they do to church, to sit still, look on one another, make no reflection, nor mind the play more than they would a sermon.

There is in this play some burlesk, some humor and ramble of comical wit, some shew and some mimickry to divert the spectators; but the tragical part is plainly none other than a bloody farce, without salt or savour.

JOHN DRYDEN
[1631–1700]

When one has said all the usual and necessary things about
Dryden's criticism—repeated Johnson's dictum that he is
the father of English criticism; pointed out that in his
criticism he not infrequently appears to contradict himself;
mentioned that the Essay of Dramatic Poesy is his only
formal critical work, the rest being prefatorial; quoted his
own remark on the skeptical turn of his mind; commented
on the easy grace of style and warm humanity of the later
prose—there remains yet much to say. He is the first of
the great critics in English, in the company of Johnson,
Coleridge, and Matthew Arnold, to speak only of those
before the twentieth century; yet of these he is the first,
and perhaps for that reason not always what we wish a
great critic to be. He did not create a critical system.
He did not reveal or make fashionable a new sensibility.
He did not memorably pontificate, except on one or two
occasions. What he did do that makes his criticism interesting
and important is to love literature, and to take us into his
workshop and reveal to us how a major poet (and playwright
too, we must not forget) accommodated himself to those a
priori standards of renaissance criticism which, although
he could look at them skeptically, he never disowned.
Some of his best criticism is an effort to justify himself
(perhaps sometimes also an effort to remind us, as Swift
in Tale of a Tub accuses him of doing, that he is a great
poet) by thinking through what he had done, and letting
us share in that process. The flattery he accords his patrons
is often embarrassing, but we should rather be dismayed

*that such flattery was still expected, that this particular
convention was still alive. To what extent either Dryden or
his patrons thought of it as more than merely a convention it
is now hard to say.*

*In two respects Dryden was an innovator. His "Examen
of the Silent Woman" in* Of Dramatic Poesy *is the first
extended critical discussion in English of a single literary
work. Dryden borrowed the term "Examen" and the concept
from Corneille, but to him belongs the honor of naturalizing
it in English. Dryden also displays a new consciousness of
English literary history. He does not write literary history,
but he takes the necessary first steps, and in the prefaces of
his last decade he points the direction we have all since
followed.*

*Although Dryden changed his mind on specific issues
(most notably on the question of rhymed verse in tragedy),
some principles he held to from first to last: the conviction
that poetry is valuable; the conviction that the most noble
kind of poetry, indeed the most noble human achievement,
is the epic, or heroic, poem; the conviction that great literature
can still be written despite the shadow of the Ancients.
These convictions everywhere illuminate his writing and are
everywhere brought to bear on the subjects he discusses.*

*An Essay of Dramatic Poesy and the "Preface to Fables
Ancient and Modern," the one almost his first critical work,
the other his last, are justly well known and easily accessible.
I have chosen to anthologize the "Preface" to Annus Mirabilis,
written just after the Essay though published first, and
selections from the immense "Discourse Concerning the
Original and Progress of Satire," 1693. The first is notable
for its attempt to define that key and elusive term "wit,"
and for its discussion of what we might now call "poetics."
From the second, neglected no doubt because of its length
—it runs to 35,000 words—and digressiveness, I have
selected several more or less independent essays, for the
"discourse" deals at one point or another with almost
every topic of concern to Dryden (even including satire!),
and also represents almost as well as the "Preface to Fables"
that last mellow vintage which readers of Dryden will always
gratefully return to quaff.*

*The texts printed here are adapted from the Scott-
Saintsbury edition of Dryden (1882–93). The standard*

*edition of Dryden's critical essays was long that by W. P. Ker
(1900), but this has been superseded by George Watson's
edition in Everyman's Library (2 vols., London and New
York, 1962). The Watson edition is textually superior to
Ker's, more inclusive, and has more helpful notes as well
as a sensitive introduction. The California edition of Dryden,
now in progress, will ultimately provide definitive texts, but
will not otherwise supersede Watson as a reading edition.
Dryden's criticism has excited discussion since the eighteenth
century. The following are only a few of the more helpful
twentieth-century comments:*

Aden, John H.: The Critical Opinions of John Dryden: A
    Dictionary, *Nashville, 1963.* [*Arranged alphabetically
    by topic, giving sources for Dryden's sometimes
    conflicting views on the same subject.*]
———: "Dryden and Boileau: The Question of Critical
    Influence," SP, L (1953), 491–509.
Eidson, John Oliver: "Dryden's Criticism of Shakespeare,"
    SP, XXXIII (1936), 273–80.
Eliot, T. S.: "The Critic," John Dryden: Three Essays, New
    York, 1932, 49–68.
Freedman, Morris: "Milton and Dryden on Rhyme,"
    Huntington Library Quarterly, XXIV (1961), 337–44.
Harth, Philip: Contexts of Dryden's Thought, Chicago, 1968.
Jensen, H. James: A Glossary of John Dryden's Critical Terms,
    Minneapolis, 1969. [*Aden, above, gives a classified
    arrangement of passages; Jensen explains, in context,
    the terminology.*]
Montgomery, Guy: "Dryden and the Battle of the Books,"
    Essays and Studies by Members of the Department
    of English (*University of California Publications in
    English, XIV*), 1943, pp. 57–72.
Smith, John H.: "Dryden's Critical Temper," Washington
    University Studies, Humanistic Series, XII (1925),
    201–20.
Trowbridge, Hoyt: "The Place of the Rules in Dryden's
    Criticism," MP, XLIV (1946), 84–96
Wolcott, Fred G.: "John Dryden's Answer to Thomas
    Rymer's The Tragedies of the Last Age," PQ, XV
    (1936), 194–214.

ANNUS MIRABILIS
[1667]

AN
Account of the Ensuing Poem,
IN A LETTER TO THE
Hon. Sir Robert Howard.

SIR,

I am so many ways obliged to you, and so little able to return your favours, that, like those who owe too much, I can only live by getting farther into your debt. You have not only been careful of my fortune, which was the effect of your nobleness, but you have been solicitous of my reputation, which is that of your kindness. It is not long since I gave you the trouble of perusing a play for me,[1] and now, instead of an acknowledgment, I have given you a greater, in the correction of a poem. But since you are to bear this persecution, I will at least give you the encouragement of a martyr, —you could never suffer in a nobler cause; for I have chosen the most heroic subject which any poet could desire. I have taken upon

[1] Perhaps *Secret Love* (1668), which had been performed early in 1667.

me to describe the motives, the beginning, progress, and successes, of a most just and necessary war; in it the care, management, and prudence of our king; the conduct and valour of a royal admiral, and of two incomparable generals; the invincible courage of our captains and seamen; and three glorious victories, the result of all. After this, I have in the Fire the most deplorable, but withal the greatest, argument that can be imagined; the destruction being so swift, so sudden, so vast and miserable, as nothing can parallel in story. The former part of this poem, relating to the war, is but a due expiation for my not serving my king and country in it. All gentlemen are almost obliged to it; and I know no reason we should give that advantage to the commonalty of England, to be foremost in brave actions, which the noblesse of France would never suffer in their peasants. I should not have written this but to a person who has been ever forward to appear in all employments, whither his honour and generosity have called him. The latter part of my poem, which describes the Fire, I owe, first, to the piety and fatherly affection of our monarch to his suffering subjects; and, in the second place, to the courage, loyalty, and magnanimity of the city; both which were so conspicuous that I have wanted words to celebrate them as they deserve. I have called my poem historical, not epic, though both the actions and actors are as much heroic as any poem can contain. But, since the action is not properly one, nor that accomplished in the last successes, I have judged it too bold a title for a few stanzas, which are little more in number than a single Iliad, or the longest of the Æneids. For this reason (I mean not of length, but broken action, tied too severely to the laws of history), I am apt to agree with those who rank Lucan rather among historians in verse, than Epic poets;[2] in whose room, if I am not deceived, Silius Italicus,[3] though a worse writer, may more justly be admitted. I have chosen to write my poem in quatrains, or stanzas of four in alternate rhyme, because I have ever judged them more noble, and of greater dignity, both for the sound and number, than any other verse in use amongst us; in which I am sure I have your approbation. The learned languages have certainly a great advantage of us, in not being tied to the slavery of any rhyme; and were less constrained in the quantity of every syllable, which they

[2] Lucan. Compelled to commit suicide by Nero at age 26 in A.D. 65, he left the *Pharsalia* in ten books, relating the struggle between Caesar and Pompey. Edited by A. E. Housman, 1926.
[3] *c.* A.D. 25–*c.* A.D. 100. His *Punica*, modeled after Virgil, glorifies the family of the Scipios, who were important in Roman history for 400 years.

might vary with spondees or dactyls, besides so many other helps
of grammatical figures, for the lengthening or abbreviation of them,
than the modern are in the close of that one syllable, which often
confines, and more often corrupts, the sense of all the rest. But in
this necessity of our rhymes, I have always found the couplet verse
most easy (though not so proper for this occasion), for there the
work is sooner at an end, every two lines concluding the labour of
the poet; but in quatrains he is to carry it farther on, and not only
so, but to bear along in his head the troublesome sense of four lines
together. For those who write correctly in this kind must needs
acknowledge that the last line of the stanza is to be considered in
the composition of the first. Neither can we give ourselves the
liberty of making any part of a verse for the sake of rhyme, or concluding with a word which is not current English, or using the
variety of female rhymes, all which our fathers practised; and for
the female rhymes, they are still in use amongst other nations—with
the Italian in every line, with the Spaniard promiscuously, with the
French alternately, as those who have read the Alaric, the Pucelle,[4]
or any of their later poems, will agree with me. And besides this,
they write in Alexandrines, or verses of six feet; such as, amongst
us, is the old translation of Homer by Chapman:[5] all which, by
lengthening of their chain, makes the sphere of their activity the
larger.

I have dwelt too long upon the choice of my stanza, which
you may remember is much better defended in the preface to
"Gondibert;"[6] and therefore I will hasten to acquaint you with my
endeavours in the writing. In general I will only say, I have never
yet seen the description of any naval fight in the proper terms
which are used at sea; and if there be any such, in another language, as that of Lucan in the third of his Pharsalia, yet I could not
prevail myself of it in the English; the terms of art in every tongue

---

[4] *Alaric* (1654) by Georges de Scudéry; *Pucelle* (1656) by Jean Chape-
lain.

[5] Neither of Chapman's translations is in Alexandrines, the *Iliad* being in
lines of seven feet, the *Odyssey* in lines of five.

[6] By Sir William Davenant, 1650. Davenant says: "I may declare that I
beleev'd it would be more pleasant to the Reader, in a Work of length,
to give this respite or pause between every *Stanza,* having endeavour'd
that each should contain a period, than to run him out of breath with
continu'd *Couplets.* Nor doth alternate Rime by any lowliness of Cadence
make the sound less Heroick, but rather adapt it to a plain and stately
composing of Musick . . ." (Spingarn, II, 19.)

bearing more of the idiom of it than any other words. We hear indeed among our poets of the thundering of guns, the smoke, the disorder, and the slaughter, but all these are common notions. And certainly, as those who, in a logical dispute, keep in general terms, would hide a fallacy; so those, who do it in any poetical description, would veil their ignorance:

> *Descriptas servare vices, operumque colores,*
> *Cur ego, si nequeo ignoroque, poeta salutor?* [7]

For my own part, if I had little knowledge of the sea, yet I have thought it no shame to learn; and if I have made some few mistakes, it is only, as you can bear me witness, because I have wanted opportunity to correct them; the whole poem being first written, and now sent you from a place, where I have not so much as the converse of any seaman. Yet though the trouble I had in writing it was great, it was more than recompensed by the pleasure. I found myself so warm in celebrating the praises of military men, two such especially as the prince and general,[8] that it is no wonder if they inspired me with thoughts above my ordinary level. And I am well satisfied, that, as they are incomparably the best subject I ever had, excepting only the royal family, so also, that this I have written of them is much better than what I have performed on any other. I have been forced to help out other arguments, but this has been bountiful to me; they have been low and barren of praise, and I have exalted them, and made them fruitful; but here— *Omnia sponte suà reddit justissima tellus.*[9] I have had a large, a fair, and a pleasant field; so fertile, that, without my cultivating, it has given me two harvests in a summer, and in both oppressed the reaper. All other greatness in subjects is only counterfeit; it will not endure the test of danger; the greatness of arms is only real. Other greatness burdens a nation with its weight; this supports it with its strength. And as it is the happiness of the age, so it is the peculiar goodness of the best of kings, that we may praise his subjects without offending him. Doubtless it proceeds from a just confidence of his own virtue, which the lustre of no other can be so great as to darken in

---

[7] Horace, *Ars Poetica*, 86–7: "If I fail to keep and do not understand these well-marked shifts and shades of poetic forms, why am I hailed as a poet?"

[8] Prince Rupert and General Monk, Duke of Albemarle.

[9] A line combining several classical sources: "The earth, with perfect justice, renders back everything freely." See Watson, I, 97.

him, for the good or the valiant are never safely praised under a bad or a degenerate prince.

But to return from this digression to a farther account of my poem, I must crave leave to tell you, that as I have endeavoured to adorn it with noble thoughts, so much more to express those thoughts with elocution. The composition of all poems is, or ought to be, of wit; and wit in the poet, or wit-writing (if you will give me leave to use a school-distinction), is no other than the faculty of imagination in the writer, which, like a nimble spaniel, beats over and ranges through the field of memory, till it spring the quarry it hunted after; or, without metaphor, which searches over all the memory for the species or ideas of those things, which it designs to represent. Wit written is that which is well defined, the happy result of thought, or product of imagination. But to proceed from wit, in the general notion of it, to the proper wit of an Heroic or Historical Poem, I judge it chiefly to consist in the delightful imagining of persons, actions, passions, or things. It is not the jerk or sting of an epigram, nor the seeming contradiction of a poor antithesis (the delight of an ill-judging audience in a play of rhyme), nor the jingle of a more poor paronomasia; neither is it so much the morality of a grave sentence, affected by Lucan, but more sparingly used by Virgil; but it is some lively and apt description, dressed in such colours of speech, that it sets before your eyes the absent object, as perfectly, and more delightfully than nature. So then the first happiness of the poet's imagination is properly invention, or finding of the thought; the second is fancy, or the variation, deriving, or moulding, of that thought, as the judgment represents it proper to the subject; the third is elocution, or the art of clothing and adorning that thought, so found and varied, in apt, significant, and sounding words. The quickness of the imagination is seen in the invention, the fertility in the fancy, and the accuracy in the expression. For the two first of these, Ovid is famous amongst the poets; for the latter, Virgil. Ovid images more often the movements and affections of the mind, either combating between two contrary passions, or extremely discomposed by one. His words therefore are the least part of his care; for he pictures nature in disorder, with which the study and choice of words is inconsistent. This is the proper wit of dialogue or discourse, and consequently of the drama, where all that is said is supposed to be the effect of sudden thought; which, though it excludes not the quickness of wit in repartees, yet admits not a too curious election of words, too frequent allusions, or use of tropes, or, in fine, anything that shows remoteness of thought or labour in the writer. On the other side, Virgil speaks not so often to us in the person of another, like Ovid, but in his own: he relates almost all things as from himself, and thereby gains more liberty than the other to express his thoughts with all the graces of elocution, to write more figuratively, and to confess as well the labour as the force of his imagination. Though he describes his Dido well and naturally, in the violence of her passions, yet he must yield in that to the Myrrha, the Byblis, the Althæa, of Ovid; for, as great an admirer of him as I am, I must acknowledge that if I see not more of their souls than I see of Dido's, at least I have a greater concernment for them: and that convinces me that Ovid has touched those tender strokes more delicately than Virgil could. But when action or persons are to be described, when any such image is to be set before us, how bold, how masterly, are the strokes of Virgil! We see the objects he presents us with in their native figures, in their proper motions; but so we see them, as our own eyes could never have beheld them, so beautiful in themselves. We see the soul of the poet, like that universal one of which he speaks, informing and moving through all his pictures—

> —— *Totamque infusa per artus*
> *Mens agitat molem, et magno se corpore miscet.*[10]

We behold him embellishing his images, as he makes Venus breathing beauty upon her son Æneas—

> ———— *lumenque juventæ*
> *Purpureum, & lœtos oculis afflârat honores:*
> *Quale manus addunt ebori decus, aut ubi flavo*
> *Argentum, Pariusve lapis, circumdatur auro.*[11]

See his Tempest, his Funeral Sports, his Combat of Turnus and Æneas: and in his "Georgics," which I esteem the divinest part of all his writings, the Plague, the Country, the Battle of Bulls, the labour of the Bees, and those many other excellent images of nature, most of which are neither great in themselves, nor have any natural ornament to bear them up; but the words wherewith he describes them are so excellent, that it might be well applied to him,

---

[10] *Æneid* VI, 726–7: ". . . and mind, pervading its members, sways the whole mass and mingles with its mighty frame."
[11] *Æneid* I, 590–93: ". . . and youth's ruddy bloom, and on his eyes a joyous lustre; even as the beauty which the hand gives to ivory, or when silver or Parian marble is set in yellow gold."

which was said by Ovid, *Materiam superabat opus:*[12] the very sound
of his words has often somewhat that is connatural to the subject;
and while we read him, we sit as in a play, beholding the scenes of
what he represents. To perform this, he made frequent use of
tropes, which you know change the nature of a known word by
applying it to some other signification; and this is it which Horace
means in his Epistle to the Pisos—

> *Dixeris egregiè, notum si callida verbum*
> *Reddiderit junctura novum.*————[13]

But I am sensible I have presumed too far to entertain you
with a rude discourse of that art, which you both know so well, and
put into practice with so much happiness. Yet before I leave Virgil,
I must own the vanity to tell you, and by you the world, that he
has been my master in this poem. I have followed him everywhere,
I know not with what success, but I am sure with diligence enough;
my images are many of them copied from him, and the rest are
imitations of him.[14] My expressions also are as near as the idioms of
the two languages would admit of in translation. And this, sir, I
have done with that boldness for which I will stand accountable to
any of our little critics, who, perhaps, are no better acquainted with
him than I am. Upon your first perusal of this poem, you have taken
notice of some words, which I have innovated (if it be too bold for
me to say refined) upon his Latin; which, as I offer not to introduce
into English prose, so I hope they are neither improper, nor altogether inelegant in verse; and, in this Horace will again defend
me—

> *Et nova, fictaque nuper, habebunt verba fidem, si*
> *Græco fonte cadunt, parcè detorta.*————[15]

The inference is exceeding plain; for, if a Roman poet might
have liberty to coin a word, supposing only that it was derived from
the Greek, was put into a Latin termination, and that he used this
liberty but seldom, and with modesty, how much more justly may I

---

[12] *Metamorphosis* II, 5: "The workmanship surpassed the material."
[13] *Ars Poetica,* 47–48: "You will express yourself most happily if a skilful
setting makes a familiar word new."
[14] It is to be noted that Dryden owns to this imitation not without some
pride. "Originality" had not yet become a fetish.
[15] *Ars Poetica,* 52–53: "While words, though new and of recent make, will
win acceptance, if they spring from a Greek fount and are drawn there-
from but sparingly."

challenge that privilege to do it with the same prerequisites, from the best and most judicious of Latin writers? In some places, where either the fancy or the words were his, or any other's, I have noted it in the margin, that I might not seem a plagiary; in others I have neglected it, to avoid as well tediousness, as the affectation of doing it too often. Such descriptions or images well wrought, which I promise not for mine, are, as I have said, the adequate delight of heroic poesy; for they beget admiration, which is its proper object; as the images of the burlesque, which is contrary to this, by the same reason beget laughter: for, the one shows nature beautified, as in the picture of a fair woman, which we all admire; the other shows her deformed, as in that of a lazar, or of a fool with distorted face and antic gestures, at which we cannot forbear to laugh, because it is a deviation from nature. But though the same images serve equally for the Epic poesy, and for the Historic and Panegyric, which are branches of it, yet a several sort of sculpture is to be used in them. If some of them are to be like those of Juvenal, *stantes in curribus Æmiliani,*[16] heroes drawn in their triumphal chariots, and in their full proportion; others are to be like that of Virgil, *spirantia mollius æra:*[17] there is somewhat more of softness and tenderness to be shown in them. You will soon find I write not this without concern. Some, who have seen a paper of verses, which I wrote last year to her Highness the Duchess, have accused them of that only thing I could defend in them. They said, I did *humi serpere,*[18]—that I wanted not only height of fancy, but dignity of words, to set it off. I might well answer with that of Horace, *Nunc non erat his locus;*[19] I knew I addressed them to a lady, and accordingly I affected the softness of expression, and the smoothness of measure, rather than the height of thought; and in what I did endeavour, it is no vanity to say I have succeeded. I detest arrogance; but there is some difference betwixt that and a just defence. But I will not farther bribe your candour, or the reader's. I leave them to speak for me; and, if they can, to make out that character, not pretending to a greater, which I have given them.[20]

[16] *Satires* VIII, 3: "The Aemiliani standing in chariots."
[17] *Æneid* VI, 847: *Excudent alii spirantia mollius aera,* "Others shall beat out the breathing bronze with softer lines."
[18] Horace, *Ars Poetica,* 28. *Serpit humi tutus nimium timidusque procellae,* "another, overcautious and fearful of the gale, creeps along the ground."
[19] *Ibid.,* 19: "For such things there was a place, but not just now."
[20] In the 1667 edition the "Verses to the Duchess" follow at this point.

And now, sir, it is time I should relieve you from the tedious
length of this account. You have better and more profitable employment for your hours, and I wrong the public to detain you longer.
In conclusion, I must leave my poem to you with all its faults, which
I hope to find fewer in the printing by your emendations. I know
you are not of the number of those, of whom the younger Pliny
speaks; *Nec sunt parum multi, qui carpere amicos suos judicium
vocant:* [21] I am rather too secure of you on that side. Your candour
in pardoning my errors may make you more remiss in correcting
them; if you will not withal consider that they come into the world
with your approbation, and through your hands. I beg from you
the greatest favour you can confer upon an absent person, since I
repose upon your management what is dearest to me, my fame and
reputation; and therefore I hope it will stir you up to make my
poem fairer by many of your blots; if not, you know the story of
the gamester who married the rich man's daughter, and when her
father denied the portion, christened all the children by his sur-
name, that if, in conclusion, they must beg, they should do so by
one name, as well as by the other. But, since the reproach of my
faults will light on you, it is but reason I should do you that justice
to the readers, to let them know, that, if there be anything tolerable
in this poem, they owe the argument to your choice, the writing to
your encouragement, the correction to your judgment, and the care
of it to your friendship, to which he must ever acknowledge himself
to owe all things, who is,

Sir,

The most obedient, and most

Faithful of your Servants,

John Dryden

From Charlton, in Wiltshire,
    Nov. 10, 1666.

[21] *Epistles* VII, 28: "There are many who think they show judgment by
criticizing their friends." (Watson).

FROM A DISCOURSE CONCERNING THE ORIGINAL AND PROGRESS OF SATIRE

[1693]

'Tis manifest that some particular ages have been more happy than others in the production of great men, in all sorts of arts and sciences: as that of Euripides, Sophocles, Aristophanes, and the rest for stage-poetry amongst the Greeks; that of Augustus, for heroic, lyric, dramatic, elegiac, and indeed all sorts of poetry, in the persons of Virgil, Horace, Varius, Ovid, and many others; especially if we take into that century the latter end of the Commonwealth, wherein we find Varro, Lucretius and Catullus; and at the same time lived Cicero, Sallust, and Cæsar. A famous age in modern times for learning in every kind was that of Lorenzo de Medici, and his son Leo the Tenth, wherein painting was revived, and poetry flourished and the Greek language was restored.

Examples in all these are obvious: but what I would infer is this; that in such an age, it is possible some great genius may arise, to equal any of the ancients, abating only for the language. For great contemporaries whet and cultivate each other, and mutual borrowing and commerce makes the common riches of learning, as it does of the civil government.

But suppose that Homer and Virgil were the only of their species, and that Nature was so much worn out in producing them that she is never able to bear the like again, yet the example only holds in heroic poetry: in tragedy and satire, I offer myself to maintain against some of our modern critics, that this age and the last, particularly in England, have excelled the ancients in both those kinds; and I would instance in Shakespeare of the former, of your Lordship in the latter sort.[22]

Thus I might safely confine myself to my native country; but if I would only cross the seas, I might find in France a living Horace and a Juvenal, in the person of the admirable Boileau; whose numbers are excellent, whose expressions are noble, whose thoughts are just, whose language is pure, whose satire is pointed, and whose sense is close; what he borrows from the ancients, he repays with usury of his own, in coin as good, and almost as universally valuable: for, setting prejudice and partiality apart, though he is our enemy, the stamp of a Louis, the patron of all arts, is not much inferior to the medal of an Augustus Cæsar. Let this be said without entering into the interests of factions and parties, and relating only to the bounty of that king to men of learning and merit; a praise so just, that even we, who are his enemies, cannot refuse it to him.

Now if it may be permitted me to go back again to the consideration of epic poetry, I have confessed, that no man hitherto has reached, or so much as approached, to the excel-

---

[22] The *Discourse* is in the form of a letter to the Earl of Dorset. Johnson remarks, in the concluding paragraphs of his "Life" of Dorset: "Would it be imagined that, of this rival to antiquity, all the satires were little personal invectives, and that his longest composition was a song of eleven stanzas?

"The blame, however, of this exaggerated praise falls on the encomiast, not upon the author; whose performances are, what they pretend to be, the effusions of a man of wit—gay, vigorous, and airy."

lences of Homer, or of Virgil; I must further add, that Statius,[23]
the best versificator next to Virgil, knew not how to design
after him, though he had the model in his eye; that Lucan is
wanting both in design and subject, and is besides too full of
heat and affectation; that amongst the moderns, Ariosto neither
designed justly, nor observed any unity of action, or compass
of time, or moderation in the vastness of his draught: his style
is luxurious, without majesty or decency, and his adventures
without the compass of nature and possibility. Tasso, whose
design was regular, and who observed the rules of unity in time
and place more closely than Virgil, yet was not so happy in his
action; he confesses himself to have been too lyrical, that is, to
have written beneath the dignity of heroic verse, in his Episodes of Sophronia, Erminia, and Armida. His story is not so
pleasing as Ariosto's; he is too flatulent sometimes, and sometimes too dry; many times unequal, and almost always forced;
and, besides, is full of conceits, points of epigram, and witti-
cisms; all which are not only below the dignity of heroic verse,
but contrary to its nature: Virgil and Homer have not one of
them. And those who are guilty of so boyish an ambition in so
grave a subject, are so far from being considered as heroic
poets, that they ought to be turned down from Homer to the
Anthologia, from Virgil to Martial and Owen's Epigrams,[24]
and from Spenser to Flecknoe; that is, from the top to the
bottom of all poetry. But to return to Tasso: he borrows from
the invention of Boiardo,[25] and in his alteration of his poem,
which is infinitely for the worse, imitates Homer so very ser-
vilely, that (for example) he gives the King of Jerusalem fifty
sons only because Homer had bestowed the like number on
King Priam; he kills the youngest in the same manner, and has
provided his hero with a Patroclus, under another name, only

---

[23] Statius, P. Papinius (*c.* A.D. 61–*c.* A.D. 96). His chief work is the
Thebaïs in twelve books on the war of the Seven against Thebes.

[24] John Owen (*c.* 1560–1622) published eleven books of Latin epigrams,
1606–1613.

[25] Matteo Maria Boiardo (1434–1494). The sixty-nine cantos of his uncompleted *Orlando Innamorato*, treating Carolingian epic matter in the
style of the Arthurian romances, was a point of departure for Ariosto's
Orlando Furioso.

to bring him back to the wars, when his friend was killed. The French have performed nothing in this kind which is not far below those two Italians, and subject to a thousand more reflections, without examining their *St. Lewis,* their *Pucelle,* or their *Alaric.*[26] The English have only to boast of Spenser and Milton, who neither of them wanted either genius or learning to have been perfect poets, and yet both of them are liable to many censures. For there is no uniformity in the design of Spenser: he aims at the accomplishment of no one action; he raises up a hero for every one of his adventures; and endows each of them with some particular moral virtue, which renders them all equal, without subordination, or preference. Every one is most valiant in his own legend: only we must do him that justice to observe, that magnanimity, which is the character of Prince Arthur, shines throughout the whole poem and succours the rest when they are in distress. The original of every knight was then living in the court of Queen Elizabeth, and he attributed to each of them that virtue which he thought was most conspicuous in them; an ingenious piece of flattery, though it turned not much to his account. Had he lived to finish his poem, in the six remaining legends, it had certainly been more of a piece; but could not have been perfect, because the model was not true. But Prince Arthur, or his chief patron Sir Philip Sidney, whom he intended to make happy by the marriage of his Gloriana, dying before him, deprived the poet both of means and spirit to accomplish his design. For the rest, his obsolete language, and the ill choice of his stanza, are faults but of the second magnitude; for, notwithstanding the first, he is still intelligible, at least after a little practice; and for the last, he is the more to be admired, that, labouring under such a difficulty, his verses are so numerous, so various, and so harmonious, that only Virgil, whom he professedly imitated, has surpassed him among the Romans, and only Mr. Waller among the English.

As for Mr. Milton, whom we all admire with so much justice, his subject is not that of an heroic poem, properly so called. His design is the losing of our happiness; his event is not

---

[26] *St. Lewis: Saint Louis* (1653) by Pierre Le Moyne. See note 4, above.

prosperous, like that of all other epic works; his heavenly machines are many, and his human persons are but two. But I will not take Mr. Rymer's work out of his hands: he has promised the world a critique on that author,[27] wherein, though he will not allow his poem for heroic, I hope he will grant us, that his thoughts are elevated, his words sounding, and that no man has so happily copied the manner of Homer, or so copiously translated his Grecisms, and the Latin elegances of Virgil. It is true, he runs into a flat of thought, sometimes for a hundred lines together, but it is when he is got into a track of Scripture. His antiquated words were his choice, not his necessity; for therein he imitated Spenser, as Spenser did Chaucer. And though, perhaps, the love of their masters may have transported both too far in the frequent use of them, yet, in my opinion, obsolete words may then be laudably revived, when either they are more sounding, or more significant, than those in practice; and when their obscurity is taken away by joining other words to them which clear the sense, according to the rule of Horace for the admission of new words.[28] But in both cases a moderation is to be observed in the use of them: for unnecessary coinage, as well as unnecessary revival, runs into affectation, a fault to be avoided on either hand. Neither will I justify Milton for his blank verse, though I may excuse him by the example of Hannibal Caro,[29] and other Italians who have used it; for whatever causes he alleges for the abolishing of rhyme (which I have not now the leisure to examine), his own particular reason is plainly this, that rhyme was not his talent; he had neither the ease of doing it, nor the graces of it; which is manifest in his *Juvenilia,* or verses written in his youth, where his rhyme is always constrained and forced, and comes hardly from him, at an age when the soul is most pliant

[27] Rymer makes such a promise at the end of *The Tragedies of the Last Age* (1678): "I shall also send you some reflections on that *Paradise Lost* of Milton's, which some are pleased to call a poem; and assert rhyme against the slender sophistry wherewith he attacks it." (*Critical Works,* ed. Zimansky, p. 76). Saintsbury remarks, "But this promise . . . he never filled up the measure of his presumption by attempting to fulfil."

[28] See note 15.

[29] Hannibal Caro (1507–1566) had published an Italian version of the *Æneid* in 1581.

and the passion of love makes almost every man a rhymer, though not a poet.

· · · ·

The most perfect work of poetry, says our master Aristotle, is tragedy.[30] His reason is, because it is the most united; being more severely confined within the rules of action, time, and place. The action is entire, of a piece, and one, without episodes; the time limited to a natural day; and the place circumscribed at least within the compass of one town, or city. Being exactly proportioned thus, and uniform in all its parts, the mind is more capable of comprehending the whole beauty of it without distraction.

But, after all these advantages, an heroic poem is certainly the greatest work of human nature.[31] The beauties and perfections of the other are but mechanical; those of the epic are more noble: though Homer has limited his place to Troy, and the fields about it; his actions to forty-eight natural days, whereof twelve are holidays, or cessation from business, during the funeral of Patroclus.—To proceed: the action of the epic is greater; the extension of time enlarges the pleasure of the reader, and the episodes give it more ornament and more variety. The instruction is equal; but the first is only instructive, the latter forms a hero, and a prince.

If it signifies anything which of them is of the more ancient family, the best and most absolute heroic poem was written by Homer long before tragedy was invented. But if we consider the natural endowments and acquired parts which are necessary to make an accomplished writer in either kind, tragedy requires a less and more confined knowledge; moderate learning and observation of the rules is sufficient, if a genius be not wanting. But in an epic poet, one who is worthy of that name, besides an universal genius is required universal learning, together with all those qualities and acquisitions which I

[30] *Poetics,* Ch. XXVI.
[31] Dryden is here anticipating what he will say again in the "Dedication" to his translation of the *Æneid,* 1697: "A Heroic Poem, truly such, is undoubtedly the greatest work which the soul of man is capable to perform." See also Pope's remarks in the same vein.

have named above, and as many more as I have, through haste
or negligence, omitted. And, after all, he must have exactly
studied Homer and Virgil as his patterns, Aristotle and Horace
as his guides, and Vida and Bossu as their commentators; with
many others, both Italian and French critics, which I want
leisure here to recommend.

In a word, what I have to say in relation to this subject,
which does not particularly concern satire, is that the greatness of an heroic poem, beyond that of a tragedy, may easily
be discovered by observing how few have attempted that work
in comparison to those who have written dramas; and, of those
few, how small a number have succeeded. But leaving the
critics on either side to contend about the preference due to
this or that sort of poetry, I will hasten to my present business,
which is the antiquity and origin of satire.

·   ·   ·

Thus I have treated, in a new method, the comparison
betwixt Horace, Juvenal, and Persius; somewhat of their particular manner belonging to all of them is yet remaining to be
considered. Persius was grave, and particularly opposed his
gravity to lewdness, which was the predominant vice in Nero's
court at the time when he published his Satires, which was
before that emperor fell into the excess of cruelty. Horace was
a mild admonisher, a court-satirist, fit for the gentle times of
Augustus, and more fit, for the reasons which I have already
given. Juvenal was as proper for his times as they for theirs;
his was an age that deserved a more severe chastisement; vices
were more gross and open, more flagitious, more encouraged
by the example of a tyrant, and more protected by his authority. Therefore, wheresoever Juvenal mentions Nero, he means
Domitian, whom he dares not attack in his own person, but
scourges him by proxy. Heinsius[32] urges in praise of Horace,
that, according to the ancient art and law of satire, it should be
nearer to comedy than tragedy; not declaiming against vice,
but only laughing at it. Neither Persius nor Juvenal were igno-

---

[32] Daniel Heinsius (1580–1655), Dutch classical philologist, published an
edition of Horace in 1612.

rant of this, for they had both studied Horace. And the thing itself is plainly true. But as they had read Horace, they had likewise read Lucilius, of whom Persius says,—*secuit urbem; . . . et genuinum fregit in illis;*[33] meaning Mutius and Lupus; and Juvenal also mentions him in these words—

> *Ense velut stricto, quoties Lucilius ardens*
> *Infremuit, rubet auditor, cui frigida mens est*
> *Criminibus, tacitâ sudant præcordia culpa.*[34]

So that they thought the imitation of Lucilius was more proper to their purpose than that of Horace. "They changed satire" (says Holyday), "but they changed it for the better; for the business being to reform great vices, chastisement goes further than admonition; whereas a perpetual grin, like that of Horace, does rather anger than amend a man."

Thus far that learned critic, Barten Holyday,[35] whose interpretation and illustrations of Juvenal are as excellent, as the verse of his translation and his English are lame and pitiful. For it is not enough to give us the meaning of a poet, which I acknowledge him to have performed most faithfully, but he must also imitate his genius and his numbers, as far as the English will come up to the elegance of the original. In few words, it is only for a poet to translate a poem. Holyday and Stapylton[36] had not enough considered this, when they attempted Juvenal: but I forbear reflections; only I beg leave to take notice of this sentence, where Holyday says, "a perpetual grin, like that of Horace, rather angers than amends a man." I cannot give him up the manner of Horace in low satire so

---

[33] Persius, *Satires* I, 114–15: "[Lucilius] lashed the town and chewed them up." Lucilius (148 B.C.–103 B.C.) was the first to mold Roman satire into the form later developed by Persius, Horace, and Juvenal.

[34] Juvenal, *Satire* I, 165–6. Dryden translates:

> But when Lucilius brandishes his pen,
> And flashes in the face of guilty men,
> A cold sweat stands in drops on ev'ry part;
> And rage succeeds to tears, revenge to smart.   [251–54].

[35] Barten Holyday (1593–1661). Translated Persius, 1616; his translation of Juvenal published after his death, 1673.

[36] Sir Robert Stapylton, d. 1669. Published a translation of Juvenal in 1647, 2nd ed., 1660.

easily. Let the chastisement of Juvenal be never so necessary for his new kind of satire; let him declaim as wittily and sharply as he pleases; yet still the nicest and most delicate touches of satire consist in fine raillery. This, my Lord, is your particular talent, to which even Juvenal could not arrive. It is not reading, it is not imitation of an author, which can produce this fineness; it must be inborn; it must proceed from a genius and particular way of thinking which is not to be taught; and therefore not to be imitated by him who has it not from nature. How easy is it to call rogue and villain, and that wittily! But how hard to make a man appear a fool, a blockhead, or a knave, without using any of those opprobrious terms! To spare the grossness of the names, and to do the thing yet more severely, is to draw a full face, and to make the nose and cheeks stand out, and yet not to employ any depth of shadowing. This is the mystery of that noble trade, which yet no master can teach to his apprentice; he may give the rules, but the scholar is never the nearer in his practice. Neither is it true, that this fineness of raillery is offensive. A witty man is tickled while he is hurt in this manner, and a fool feels it not. The occasion of an offence may possibly be given, but he cannot take it. If it be granted, that in effect this way does more mischief; that a man is secretly wounded, and though he be not sensible himself, yet the malicious world will find it out for him; yet there is still a vast difference betwixt the slovenly butchering of a man, and the fineness of a stroke that separates the head from the body and leaves it standing in its place. A man may be capable, as Jack Ketch's[37] wife said of his servant, of a plain piece of work, a bare hanging; but to make a malefactor die sweetly, was only belonging to her husband. I wish I could apply it to myself, if the reader would be kind enough to think it belongs to me. The character of Zimri in my "Absalom," is, in my opinion, worth the whole poem: it is not bloody, but it is ridiculous enough; and he, for whom it was intended, was too witty to resent it as an injury. If I had railed, I might have suffered for it justly; but I managed my own work

---

[37] John Ketch (d. 1686). The public executioner who executed Monmouth (1685) among very many others. He was notorious for his barbarity.

more happily, perhaps more dexterously. I avoided the mention of great crimes, and applied myself to the representing of blindsides, and little extravagances; to which, the wittier a man is, he is generally the more obnoxious. It succeeded as I wished; the jest went round, and he was laughed at in his turn who began the frolic.

.   .   .

Of the best and finest manner of satire, I have said enough in the comparison betwixt Juvenal and Horace: it is that sharp, well-mannered way of laughing a folly out of countenance, of which your Lordship is the best master in this age. I will proceed to the versification, which is most proper for it, and add somewhat to what I have said already on that subject. The sort of verse which is called burlesque, consisting of eight syllables, or four feet, is that which our excellent Hudibras has chosen. I ought to have mentioned him before when I spoke of Donne, but by a slip of an old man's memory he was forgotten. The worth of his poem is too well known to need my commendation, and he is above my censure. His satire is of the Varronian kind, though unmixed with prose. The choice of his numbers is suitable enough to his design, as he has managed it; but in any other hand the shortness of his verse and the quick returns of rhyme had debased the dignity of style. And besides, the double rhyme (a necessary companion of burlesque writings), is not so proper for manly satire, for it turns earnest too much to jest, and gives us a boyish kind of pleasure. It tickles awkwardly with a kind of pain to the best sort of readers: we are pleased ungratefully, and, if I may say so, against our liking. We thank him not for giving us that unseasonable delight, when we know he could have given us a better, and more solid. He might have left that task to others, who, not being able to put in thought, can only make us grin with the excrescence of a word of two or three syllables in the close. It is, indeed, below so great a master to make use of such a little instrument. But his good sense is perpetually shining through all he writes; it affords us not the time of finding faults. We pass through the levity of his rhyme, and are immediately carried into some admirable useful thought. After all, he has chosen this kind of verse, and has written the best in it: and had he taken another, he would always have excelled: as we say of a court favourite, that whatsoever his office be, he still makes it uppermost, and most beneficial to himself.

The quickness of your imagination, my Lord, has already prevented me; and you know beforehand, that I would prefer the verse of ten syllables, which we call the English heroic, to that of eight. This is truly my opinion; for this sort of number is more roomy; the thought can turn itself with greater ease in a larger compass. When the rhyme comes too thick upon us it straitens the expression; we are thinking of the close when we should be employed in adorning the thought. It makes a poet giddy with turning in a space too narrow for his imagination; he loses many beauties, without gaining one advantage. For a burlesque rhyme I have already concluded to be none; or, if it were, it is more easily purchased in ten syllables than in eight. In both occasions it is in a tennis-court, when the strokes of greater force are given, when we strike out and play at length.

. . . .

I have given your Lordship but this bare hint, in what verse and in what manner this sort of satire may be best managed. Had I time, I could enlarge on the beautiful turns of words and thoughts, which are as requisite in this, as in heroic poetry itself, of which the satire is undoubtedly a species. With these beautiful turns, I confess myself to have been unacquainted, till about twenty years ago, in a conversation which I had with that noble wit of Scotland, Sir George Mackenzie,[38] he asked me why I did not imitate in my verses the turns of Mr. Waller and Sir John Denham, of which he repeated many to me. I had often read with pleasure, and with some profit, those two fathers of our English poetry, but had not seriously enough considered those beauties which gave the last perfection to their works. Some sprinklings of this kind I had also formerly in my plays, but they were casual, and not designed.

[38] Mackenzie (1638–1691). Lord Advocate of Scotland; founded the Advocate's Library in Edinburgh.

But this hint, thus seasonably given me, first made me sensible
of my own wants, and brought me afterwards to seek for the
supply of them in other English authors. I looked over the
darling of my youth, the famous Cowley; there I found, instead
of them, the points of wit and quirks of epigram, even in the
Davideis, an heroic poem, which is of an opposite nature to
those puerilities; but no elegant turns either on the word or on
the thought. Then I consulted a greater genius (without offence to the manes of that noble author), I mean Milton; but
as he endeavours everywhere to express Homer, whose age had
not arrived to that fineness, I found in him a true sublimity,
lofty thoughts which were clothed with admirable Grecisms,
and ancient words, which he had been digging from the mines
of Chaucer and Spenser, and which, with all their rusticity,
had somewhat of venerable in them. But I found not there
neither that for which I looked. At last I had recourse to his
master, Spenser, the author of that immortal poem called the
Fairy Queen; and there I met with that which I had been looking for so long in vain. Spenser had studied Virgil to as much
advantage as Milton had done Homer; and amongst the rest of
his excellences had copied that. Looking further into the
Italian, I found Tasso had done the same; nay more, that all
the sonnets in that language are on the turn of the first thought,
which Mr. Walsh, in his late ingenious preface to his poems,
has observed. In short, Virgil and Ovid are the two principal
fountains of them in Latin poetry. And the French at this day
are so fond of them, that they judge them to be the first beauties: *délicat et bien tourné*, are the highest commendations
which they bestow on somewhat which they think a master-
piece.

·   ·   ·

GEORGE GRANVILLE,
BARON LANSDOWNE
[1667–1735]

George Granville entered Cambridge at the age of ten, and
two years later, it is said, recited verses before the Duchess
of York. At any rate, by the turn of the century he was
known as a poet and as the author of four plays, two of which,
Heroick Love, a Tragedy and The British Enchanters, were
very successful. He entered public life in 1702 at the
accession of Anne, becoming Secretary for War in 1710;
in 1711 he was raised to the peerage as one of the famous
twelve supporters of peace. His political star set under
George I, and in 1714 he was removed from his various
offices. He may have had something to do with a scheme
for a rising in Cornwall to help the Pretender; in any event,
he was in the Tower from September 1715 until February
1717, when he was restored to his seat in Parliament.
In 1722 he moved to Paris, where he lived for ten years.
    He was one who advised Pope to publish his Pastorals,
and he continued to encourage him:

> But why then publish? Granville the polite
> And knowing Walsh, would tell me I could write.
> "Epistle to Arbuthnot," 135–6

The Essay upon Unnatural Flights in Poetry, depending
very heavily upon the Horatian convention, is primarily
interesting for the "Explanatory Annotations," which have
been slightly abbreviated here by the elimination of some
self-exculpatory remarks added to the later editions.
The present text is adapted from The Genuine Works in
Verse and Prose, published by Tonson in 1736.

ESSAY UPON UNNATURAL FLIGHTS IN POETRY

[1701]

As when some image of a charming face
In living paint an artist tries to trace,
He carefully consults each beauteous line,
Adjusting to his object his design,
We praise the piece, and give the painter fame,
But as the just resemblance speaks the dame.
Poets are limners of another kind,
To copy out Ideas in the mind;
Words are the paint by which their thoughts are shown,
And Nature sits, the object to be drawn;
The written picture we applaud, or blame,
But as the due proportions are the same.
    Who driven with ungovernable fire,

Or void of Art, beyond these bounds aspire,
Gigantick forms, and monstrous births alone
Produce, which Nature, shockt, disdains to own.
By true reflexion I would see my face,
Why brings the fool a magnifying glass?
(1) "But Poetry in Fiction takes delight,
    And mounting in bold figures out of sight,
    Leaves Truth behind, in her audacious flight:
    Fables and metaphors that always lye,
    And rash hyperboles that soar so high,
    And every ornament of verse must die."
Mistake me not: No figures I exclude,
And but forbid intemperance, not food.
Who would with care some happy fiction frame,
So mimicks Truth, it looks the very same;
Not rais'd to force, or feign'd in Nature's scorn,
But meant to grace, illustrate, and adorn.
Important truths still let your fables hold,
And moral mysteries with art unfold.
Ladies and beaux to please is all the task,
But the sharp critick will instruction ask.
(2) As veils transparent cover, but not hide,
Such metaphors appear when right apply'd;
When thro' the phrase we plainly see the sense,
Truth, where the meaning's obvious, will dispense;
The reader what in reason's due believes,
Nor can we call that false, which not deceives.
(3) Hyperboles, so daring and so bold,
Disdaining bounds, are yet by rules control'd;
Above the clouds, but still within our sight,
They mount with truth, and make a tow'ring flight,
Presenting things impossible to view,
They wander thro' incredible to true:
Falsehoods thus mix'd, like metals are refin'd,
And truth, like silver, leaves the dross behind.
    Thus poetry has ample space to soar,
Nor needs forbidden regions to explore:
Such vaunts as his, who can with patience read,
Who thus describes his hero slain and dead:

(4) "Kill'd as he was, insensible of death,
         He still fights on, and scorns to yield his breath." *
The noisy culverin[1] o'ercharg'd, lets fly,
And burst unaiming in the rended sky:
Such frantick flights are like a mad-man's dream,
And Nature suffers in the wild extreme.
        The captive cannibal weigh'd down with chains,
Yet braves his foes, reviles, provokes, disdains,
Of nature fierce, untameable and proud,
He grins defiance at the gaping crowd,
And spent at last, and speechless as he lies,
With looks still threatning, mocks their rage, and dies.
This is the utmost stretch that Nature can,
And all beyond is fulsom, false, and vain.
        Beauty's the theme; some nymph divinely fair
Excites the Muse: Let Truth be even there:
As painters flatter, so may poets too,
But to resemblance must be ever true.
(5) "The day that she was born, the Cyprian Queen
         Had like t'have dy'd thro' envy and thro' spleen;
         The Graces in a hurry left the skies
         To have the honour to attend her eyes;
         And Love, despairing in her heart a place,
         Would needs take up his lodging in her face." †
Tho' wrote by great Corneille, such lines as these,
Such civil nonsense sure could never please.
Waller, the best of all th'inspir'd train,
To melt the fair, instructs the dying swain.
(6) The Roman Wit,‡ who impiously divides
His hero and his gods to diff'rent sides,
I would condemn, but that, in spight of sense,
Th'admiring world still stands in his defence.
How oft, alas! the best of men in vain
Contend for blessings which the worst obtain!
The Gods, permitting traitors to succeed,

* Ariosto.
† Corneille.
‡ Lucan.
[1] Culverin: cannon.

Become not parties in an impious deed:
And by the tyrant's murder we may find
That Cato and the Gods were of a mind.
　　　Thus forcing Truth with such prepost'rous praise,
Our characters we lessen when we'd raise:
Like castles built by magick art in air
That vanish at approach, such thoughts appear;
But rais'd on Truth, by some judicious hand,
As on a rock they shall for ages stand.
(7) Our King* return'd, and banish'd Peace restor'd,
The Muse ran mad to see her exil'd Lord;
On the crack'd stage the Bedlam heroes roar'd.
And scarce could speak one reasonable word;
Dryden himself, to please a frantick age,
Was forc'd to let his judgment stoop to rage,
To a wild audience he conform'd his voice,
Comply'd to custom, but not err'd by choice:
Deem then the peoples, not the writer's sin,
Almansor's rage, and rants of Maximin;
That fury spent in each elaborate piece,
He vies for fame with ancient *Rome and Greece.*
　　　First Mulgrave rose, Roscommon† next,
　　　　　like light
To clear our darkness, and to guide our flight;
With steady judgment, and in lofty sounds,
They gave us patterns, and they set us bounds;
The *Stagirite* and *Horace* laid aside,
Inform'd by them, we need no foreign guide:
Who seek from poetry a lasting name
May in their lessons learn the road to fame:
But let the bold adventurer be sure
That every line the test of Truth endure;
On this foundation may the fabrick rise,
Firm and unshaken, till it touch the skies.
　　　From pulpits banish'd, from the Court, from Love,
Forsaken Truth seeks shelter in the grove;

* King Charles II.
† Earl of Mulgrave's Essay upon Poetry; and Lord Roscommon's upon
Translated Verse.

Cherish, ye Muses! the neglected Fair,
And take into your train th'abandon'd wanderer.

EXPLANATORY ANNOTATIONS
ON THE FOREGOING POEM

(1) The poetick world is nothing but fiction; *Parnassus,
Pegasus,* and the *Muses,* pure imagination and chimæra: But
being however a system universally agreed on, all that has or
may be contrived or invented upon this foundation, according
to Nature, shall be reputed as Truth; but whatsoever shall
diminish from, or exceed the just proportions of Nature, shall
be rejected as false, and pass for extravagance; as dwarfs and
giants, for monsters.

(2) When *Homer,* mentioning *Achilles,* terms him a *Lion,*
this is a metaphor, and the meaning is obvious and true, tho'
the literal sense be false, the poet intending thereby to give
his reader some idea of the strength and fortitude of his hero.
Had he said *that* Wolf, or *that* Bear, this had been false, by
presenting an image not conformable to the nature and character of a Hero, etc.

(3) *Hyperboles* are of diverse sorts, and the manner of introducing them is different: Some are as it were naturalized and
established by a customary way of expression, as when we say,
such a one's "as swift as the wind; whiter than snow," or the
like. *Homer,* speaking of Nereus, calls him, *Beauty itself;* Martial of Zoilus, *Lewdness itself.* Such hyperboles lie indeed,
but deceive us not; and therefore Seneca terms them "Lies that
readily conduct our imagination to truths, and have an intelligible signification, tho' the expression be strain'd beyond cred-
ibility." Custom has likewise familiarized another way for
hyperboles, for example, by *irony;* as when we say of some
infamous woman, "She's a civil person," where the meaning's
to be taken quite opposite to the letter. These few figures are
mentioned only for example's sake; it will be understood that
all others are to be used with the like care and discretion.

(4) I needed not to have travelled so far for an extravagant
flight; I remember one of *British* growth of the like nature:

> See those dead bodies hence convey'd with care,
> Life may perhaps return—with change of air.

But I choose rather to correct gently, by foreign examples, hoping that such as are conscious of the like excesses will take the hint, and secretly reprove themselves. It may be possible for some tempers to maintain rage and indignation to the last gasp; but the soul and body once parted, there must necessarily be a determination of action.

> *Quodcunque ostendis mihi sic incredulus odi.*[2]

(5)   Le jour qu'elle nâquit, Venus bien qu'Immortelle,
        Pensa mourir de honte, en la voyant si belle,
        Les graces a l'envi descendirent des Cieux
        Pour avoir l'honeur d'accompagner ses yeux,
        Et l'Amour, qui ne pût entrer dans son courage,
        Voulut obstinément loger sur son Visage.[3]

This is a lover's description of his mistress, by the great *Corneille;* civil, to be sure, and polite as any thing can be. Let anybody turn over *Waller,* and he will see how much more naturally and delicately the *English* author treats the article of love than this celebrated Frenchman. I would not however be thought by any derogatory quotation to take from the merit of a writer whose reputation is so universally and so justly established in all nations; but as I said before, I rather choose, where any failings are to be found, to correct my own countrymen by foreign examples, than to provoke them by instances drawn from their own writings. *Humanum est errare.*

(6) *Victrix causa Deis placuit, sed victa Catoni.*[4]

The consent of so many ages having established the reputation of this line, it may perhaps be presumption to attack it; but it is not to be supposed that Cato, who is described to have been a man of rigid morals and strict devotion, more resembling the gods, than men, would have chosen any party in opposition to those gods, whom he profest to adore. The poet would give

---

[2] Horace, *Ars Poetica,* 188: "Whatever you thus show me, I discredit and abhor."

[3] Corneille, *Mélite,* I, i, 73–78.

[4] Lucan, *Pharsalia,* I, 118: "The conquering cause was pleasing to the gods, but the conquered to Cato."

us to understand that his hero was too righteous a person to accompany the divinities themselves in an unjust cause; but to represent a mortal man to be either wiser or juster than the Deity may shew the impiety of the writer, but add nothing to the merit of the hero; neither Reason nor Religion will allow it, and it is impossible for a corrupt being to be more excellent than a divine: Success implies permission, and not approbation; to place the gods always on the thriving side, is to make them partakers of all successful wickedness: To judge right, we must wait for the conclusion of the action; the catastrophe will best decide on which side is providence, and the violent death of Caesar acquits the gods from being companions of his usurpation.

Lucan was a determin'd Republican: no wonder he was a free-thinker.

(7) Mr. *Dryden* in one of his Prologues has these two lines:

> He's bound to please, not to write well, and knows
> There is a mode in plays, as well as cloaths.[5]

From whence it is plain where he has exposed himself to the criticks; he was forced to follow the fashion to humour an audience, and not to please himself—a hard sacrifice to make for present subsistence, especially for such as would have their writings live as well as themselves. Nor can the poet whose labours are his daily bread be deliver'd from this cruel necessity, unless some more certain encouragement can be provided than the bare uncertain profits of a third day, and the theatre be put under some more impartial management than the jurisdiction of players. Who write to live must unavoidably comply with their taste by whose approbation they subsist; some generous Prince, or Prime Minister like *Richelieu,* can only find a remedy. In his Epistle Dedicatory to the *Spanish Friar,* this incomparable poet thus censures himself:

> I remember some verses of my own, *Maximin* and *Almanzor,* which cry vengeance upon me for their extravagance, etc. All I can say for those passages, which are I hope not many, is, that I knew they were bad enough to please, even when I

---

[5] "Prologue" to *The Rival Ladies,* 21–22.

wrote them; but I repent of them among my sins: And if any of their fellows intrude by chance into my present writings, I draw a stroke over those Dalilah's of the theatre, and am resolved I will settle myself no reputation by the applause of fools: 'Tis not that I am mortified to all ambition, but I scorn as much to take it from half-witted judges, as I should to raise an estate by cheating of bubbles: Neither do I discommend the lofty style in tragedy, which is pompous and magnificent; but nothing is truly sublime that is not just and proper.[6]

This may stand as an unanswerable apology for Mr. *Dryden* against his criticks: And likewise for an unquestionable authority to confirm those principles which the foregoing poem pretends to lay down, for nothing can be just and proper but what is built upon Truth.

[6] See Watson's edition (Everyman), I, 276. *The Spanish Friar* was published in 1681. Maximin: from *Tyrannic Love;* Almanzor: from *Conquest of Granada.*

JOHN DENNIS
[1657–1734]

After taking his M.A. at Cambridge in 1683, Dennis
exhausted his small inheritance while mixing with literary
men in London, counting Mulgrave, Dryden, Congreve,
and Wycherley among his acquaintances. Later on he had
to live by his pen, which did not provide a good living.
Repeated failures as a dramatist no doubt soured his temper,
and led to his conviction that poetry in England was, as
he said, "on its last legs," a situation he designed his
criticism to correct.

Although he was ridiculed as a critic by Swift, Pope,
and Theobald, impartial commentators have generally
recognized his very considerable abilities, and in retrospect
we can see in his writings the seeds of many ideas which bore
splendid fruit in Addison, Burke, and Wordsworth. His
chief critical work is The Advancement and Reformation
of Modern Poetry (1701) and its sequel, The Grounds of
Criticism in Poetry (1704). In these, on grounds derived
from Longinus, he urged the scope which religion provides
for excellence in poetry, and exalted Milton above all
modern, and in certain respects above the ancient, poets.
Although his conception of "sublimity," one of his key terms,
is not quite that which became important later in the
century, the emphasis which Dennis places on this concept
is extremely important, if only for the vocabulary of criticism.

Edward N. Hooker has definitively edited The Critical
Works of John Dennis (2 vols., Baltimore, 1939–1943) with
an excellent introduction; no study of early eighteenth-
century criticism can proceed far without reference to this

edition. H. G. *Paul in* John Dennis, His Life and Criticism
(*New York,* 1911), *discusses Dennis' work in a historical
context, and Samuel H. Monk in* The Sublime (*New York,*
1935) *and Marjorie H. Nicolson in* Mountain Gloom and
Mountain Glory (*Ithaca,* 1959) *make significant comments.
Elledge anthologizes* The Grounds of Criticism in Poetry
with helpful notes and commentary. See also:

Heffernan, James A.: "*Words and Dennis: The
    Discrimination of Feelings,*" PMLA, LXXXII (1966),
    430–36.
Hooker, Edward N.: "*Pope and Dennis,*" ELH, VII (1940),
    188–98.
Wilkins, A. N.: "*John Dennis and Poetic Justice,*" N & Q,
    CCII (1957), 421–24.
———: "*John Dennis on Love as a 'Tragical Passion,'*"
    N & Q, CCIII (1958), 396–98, 417–19.
———: "*Tragedy and 'The True Politicks,'*" N & Q, CCIV
    (1959), 390–94.

FROM ADVANCEMENT AND REFORMATION OF POETRY
[1701]

CHAPTER II

That the Ancients Did Not Excel the Moderns by Any External Advantage

The external advantages which one writer has over another are chiefly two: the assistance which he receives from the age in which he writes, and the encouragement he meets with. Now we shall shew that the Ancients did not surpass the moderns on the account of either of these.

First, they had no advantage in the assistance which they received from the age in which they writ; on the contrary, the advantage here is clearly on the side of the moderns: for good thinking is the foundation of good writing, both in eloquence and in poetry. Now thoughts are but the images of things, and our knowledge of things is greater than that of the Ancients, for several which they knew are better known to us, and we know several which they never knew at all.

How many arts have the moderns improved? How many wonderful inventions are owing to them? And how many amazing discoveries? From which we have a supply of thoughts and images that is never to be exhausted. So that in the assistance which we receive from the age in which we live, we have the advantage of the Ancients.

Nor, secondly, is it from the encouragement which they received that the ancient poets excelled the moderns: though at the same time, I really believe that encouragement was one of the causes of the ancient excellence of the orators. For though good thinking is the foundation of good writing both in eloquence and in poetry, and the moderns are qualified to think as reasonably and as subtly as the Ancients thought, yet 'tis in these arts, as it is in architecture, there can be no beauty nor greatness without foundation; but 'tis not the foundation that makes the greatness or beauty. The chief design of eloquence is to persuade, and he persuading the most effectually who moves his hearers the most; that which makes the greatness and beauty of eloquence is not so much the thinking rightly, though without that there can be no excellence, as those violent passions, that reign and tyrannize over our souls, in the speeches of the ancient orators, which they chiefly derived from ambition. For the moving their popular assemblies among the ancient Grecians and Romans being almost the only way among them to arrive at the chief honours of the state, it can be no wonder to those who reflect upon the force of ambition and the stings it infixes into the minds of men, that the ancient Grecians and Romans, should be so great masters of eloquence. For, being instigated and stung by ambition, they not only were supported in the taking such pains as the moderns are utterly uncapable of taking, because they have not the same incentive to sustain them, but being moved and fired by ambition themselves, they the more easily roused and inflamed others; for if any one happens to urge that the love of glory being alike inseparable from moderns and ancients, they have equal incentives to eloquence, I desire him to take notice, that there is a very considerable difference between the love of glory, barely considered, and that which is joined to ambition, which is the desire of power and place. For I desire him to consider what nourishment and force the love of glory that was in the minds of the ancient orators must necessarily have received from the tumultuous applauses of the popular assemblies, and the glorious recompences that ensued upon them.

But now, if any one thinks that he has here found out the reason why the ancients surpassed us in the greater poetry, because passion making the greatness and beauty of poetry as well as it does of eloquence (which it certainly does, as shall be clearly shewn anon), and passion receiving access from encouragement, the ancient poets writ with a force superior to that of the moderns only because they were more encouraged: If any one, I say, thinks at this rate, he will find himself very much mistaken. For though I am convinced that encouragement does very much, yet I am satisfied that the difference is not chiefly owing to that; for, in the first place, though the encouragement which the ancients gave was more general than that which the moderns have met with, yet some of the moderns have been as much encouraged as most of the ancients were, and yet fall very much short of them in the greater poetry, of which Boileau and Racine are two illustrious examples. In the second place, Homer, the most admirable of all the ancients, was not at all encouraged. In the third place, one of the moderns received no encouragement, who has often transcendently soared above both ancients and moderns, and that is Milton, as shall be shewn in its proper place. And, lastly, comedy was as much encouraged by the Grecians and Romans as any other sort of poetry, witness what the Athenians did for Aristophanes, and Scipio and Lelius for Terence; and yet I am persuaded that the moderns have surpassed the ancients in comedy, and shall give my reasons below why I make no scruple of preferring Molière, and two or three of our own comic poets, to Terence and Aristophanes. So that we may seek for another cause of the excellence of the ancient poets than the encouragement they met with.

There are three other things which may be numbered among external advantages, and those are the climates in which the ancient poets lived, and the languages in which they writ, and the liberty which they enjoyed. But these are not the chief

things from which the ancients derived their pre-eminence.
For the greatest of the lyric poets writ in a country of downright blockheads, and one of the greatest of the epic poets in a
country that had lost its liberty; and besides, the Grecians
enjoyed all the advantages of their climate, and their language
and their liberty, long after the decay of poetry. 'Tis true,
indeed, the Grecians and Romans did derive one real excellence from the beauty of their language, and that was the
harmony of their versification, in which the moderns are not
likely to equal them. But harmony of versification is not the
chief thing in poetry, nor does the chief excellence of the
ancients consist in such a harmony. And thus we have shewn,
that they did not derive their pre-eminence from anything that
was external: Let us examine in the next chapter whether the
ancients derived their excellence from any internal advantage.

CHAPTER III

*That the Ancients Did Not Surpass the Moderns from Any Internal
Advantage*

There is nothing more certain than that he who handles
any subject excellently must do it by the power of his internal
faculties. And, consequently, he who treats any subject admirably has an inward advantage over him who treats it scurvily.
But either that advantage is naturally derived from the subject,
or it is not. If it is naturally derived from the subject, in that
case we can never pretend to deny that the ancients had an
inward advantage over the moderns. All that we shall endeavour to prove is that they had no internal advantage over them,
abstracted from the nature of the subjects of which they
treated.

Now all the internal advantages which the ancients may
be supposed to have had over the moderns may be reduced
to four: divine inspiration, inspiration by dæmons, a natural
superiority of the faculties of the soul, a greater degree of
virtue.

The first advantage that the ancient poets may be supposed to have had over the moderns is from divine inspiration. Now the ancient poets were the heathen theologues, and to affirm that the spirit of God should inspire those, to teach the adoration of idols, and inspire them more than he does the moderns, who are of the true religion, would be equally absurd and blasphemous.

Nor, secondly, can they have any advantage by inspiration of dæmons. For in the first place, 'tis absurd to give a supernatural cause of an effect of which we can give a very natural one. But we can give a very natural cause of the excellence of the ancient poets, as shall be shewn anon. In the second place, the ancients, before Socrates, owed all their moral philosophy to their poets. Now, though that philosophy was only dispersed up and down in sentences, yet had it a natural tendency to the forming that system, which afterwards the disciples of Socrates framed from the mouth of their master. And as that system was the utter overthrow of the heathen revelation, as we shall shew anon, anything that had a natural tendency to the forming that system could not be the work of dæmons. But, thirdly, supposing the ancient Grecian poets were really inspired by dæmons, it is hard to imagine that they should receive a greater advantage from such an inspiration as that than the moderns, who apply themselves to sacred poetry, should have from divine assistance.

Nor, thirdly, can the ancient poets be supposed to have had a greater share of virtue than the moderns. For all the Grecian poets who were famous for the greater poetry flourished before there was in that part of the world any system of morality. And, perhaps, most of the Roman poetry is only a copy of the Grecian. Now it is hard to imagine that they who had no system of morality, and no supernatural support, should transcend the moderns in virtue, who have a perfect system of morality, and divine assistance.

Nor, fourthly and principally, had the ancient any natural superiority of faculties over the modern poets. For if they surpass the moderns in the greater poetry out of any superiority of faculties which they had naturally as they were the ancients, it must be by a superiority of understanding or imagination, or both. But first, it was not from any superiority of understanding, because from hence it would follow that the minds of men grow weaker by succession of ages, and then the ancients would have surpassed one another as they preceded in time. Orpheus and Musæus would have excelled Homer; Alcæus and Stesichorus, Pindar; Thespis, Euripides and Æschylus, Sophocles; Tyrtæus. Virgil; and Alcmon, Horace, which is all absolutely false. But then again, if anyone urges that if the ancients did not surpass one another according to precedence of time, it was because art and experience were required to the perfection of poetry, and the younger in time had the advantage of the elder, both in art and experience; to that I answer, that some of the poets who are younger in time have, perhaps, the advantage of those who are older, more by nature than they have by art. For the tragic and lyric poets who preceded Sophocles and Pindar come more behind them in true genius, than they go before them in time. But now if the ancients did not surpass one another according to priority of time, why should they excel us? If it be objected that several very extraordinary men happened to be born at such and such particular times, to that I answer that this arrived by providence, or by chance. If you allege that it fell out by chance, to that I reply, that all the great poets among the Grecians flourished within four hundred years of one another, and all the great poets among the Romans within two hundred years; and then let me ask you whether this looked like chance? But if you pretend that these men, at these particular times, were designed such excellent poets by providence, and for that very end were formed with faculties so much superior to those who preceded them and who came after them, then let me ask you, for what design providence should so manifestly alter the course of nature? Or, why that which fell out by providence then, may not by providence arrive again?

Besides, if the ancient poets excelled the moderns by a superiority of understanding, it would necessarily follow that they understood their subjects better, which is false: For the subjects of the epic, tragic, and lyric poets are the virtues, vices, and passions of men, which the moderns ought to understand at least as well as the ancients, because they have all the knowledge of the ancients, and their own improvement besides.

Thus have I endeavoured to shew, that we have no reason to despair of equalling the ancients because of the transcendency of their understandings. And what has been said about their understandings may serve to shew that they as little excelled the moderns in their imaginations as they did in the other; though something more may be said for the last, for the violence of the passions, proceeding from the force of the imagination, and the corruption of mankind from the violence of the passions, and the corruption of mankind growing greater as the world grows older; it follows that the imaginations of men must grow stronger as the world grows older.

But, lastly, how vain is it to urge that the ancients excelled the moderns by a superiority of faculties, when it will appear a little lower, as clear as the sun, that one of the moderns very often excels them, both in his thoughts and spirit?

Thus we have endeavoured to shew that the ancients did not excel the moderns in the greater poetry from any external advantage—that is, from the assistance which they had from the ages in which they writ, or from the encouragement with which they met. We have shewn too that they did not surpass them from any internal advantage, whether it was from divine inspiration, or inspiration by dæmons, or transcendency of virtue, or superiority of faculties. The advantage, then, which the ancient poets had over the moderns, if they had any advantage, must be derived from the subjects of which they treated.

CHAPTER IV

That the Ancient Poets Derived Their Greatness from the Nature of Their Subjects

If the ancient poets excelled the moderns in the greatness of poetry, that is, in epic poetry, in tragedy, and in the greater ode, they must necessarily derive their pre-eminence from the subjects of which they treated, since it has been plainly made to appear that they could not derive it from any external or internal advantage. And it follows that the subjects which were handled by the ancients must be different from those which have been treated of by the moderns. And if the poems which have been writ by the ancients of the forementioned kinds were very much greater than those which have been produced by the moderns, why then it follows that the subjects were very different. But here the favourers of the moderns assert that the advantage which is to be drawn from the subject is purely on the side of the moderns. For who, for example, will compare the achievements of Achilles and Æneas, the event of which was only the reducing two pitiful paltry bourgs, with the glorious actions of some of our modern captains? But then the partisans of the ancients reply that there is a difference between one subject and another, which their adversaries seem not to have thought of. For, say they, human subjects can never differ so much among themselves, as sacred subjects differ from human; for the difference between the two last is as great as that between God and man, which we know is infinite. Now, say they, sacred subjects are infinitely more susceptible of the greatness of poetry than profane ones can be: and the subjects of the ancients in the forementioned poems were sacred. Now that we may engage the lovers of the ancients in their turns by supporting their just pretensions, let us endeavour to shew in the following chapters, that sacred poems must be greater than profane ones can be, supposing equality of genius and equal art in the writers, and that the poems of the ancients in the forementioned kinds were sacred. But in order to the doing that, we must declare what poetry is, and what is its chief excellence.

CHAPTER V

That Passion Is the Chief Thing in Poetry, and That All Passion Is Either Ordinary Passion, or Enthusiasm

But before we proceed, let us define poetry, which is the first time that a definition has been given of that noble art: For neither ancient nor modern critics have defined poetry in general.

Poetry then is an imitation of Nature, by a pathetic and numerous speech. Let us explain it.

As poetry is an art, it must be an imitation of Nature. That the instrument with which it makes its imitation is speech, need not be disputed. That that speech must be musical, no one can doubt: For numbers distinguish the parts of poetic diction from the periods of prose. Now numbers are nothing but articulate sounds, and their pauses measured by their proper proportions of time. And the periods of prosaic diction are articulate sounds, and their pauses unmeasured by such proportions. That the speech by which poetry makes its imitation must be pathetic, is evident, for passion is still more necessary to it than harmony. For harmony only distinguishes its instrument from that of prose, but passion distinguishes its very nature and character. For, therefore, poetry is poetry because it is more passionate and sensual than prose. A discourse that is writ in very good numbers, if it wants passion, can be but measured prose. But a discourse that is everywhere extremely pathetic, and, consequently, everywhere bold and figurative, is certainly poetry without numbers.

Passion, then, is the characteristical mark of poetry, and, consequently, must be everywhere: For wherever a discourse is not pathetic, there it is prosaic. As passion in a poem must be everywhere, so harmony is usually diffused throughout it. But passion answers the two ends of poetry better than harmony can do, and upon that account is preferable to it: For, first, it pleases more, which is evident: For passion can please without harmony, but harmony tires without passion. And in tragedy, and in epic poetry, a man may instruct without harmony, but never without passion, for the one instructs by admiration, and the other by compassion and terror. And as for the greater ode, if it wants passion it becomes hateful and intolerable, and its sentences grow contemptible.

Passion is the characteristical mark of poetry, and therefore it must be everywhere; for without passion there can be no poetry, no more than there can be painting. And though the poet and the painter describe action, they must describe it with passion. Let anyone who beholds a piece of painting, where the figures are shewn in action, conclude that if the figures are without passion, the painting is contemptible. There must be passion everywhere, in poetry and painting, and the more passion there is, the better the poetry and the painting, unless the passion is too much for the subject; and the painter and the poet arrive at the height of their art, when they describe a great deal of action with a great deal of passion. It is plain then, from what has been said, that passion in poetry must be everywhere, for where there is no passion, there can be no poetry; but that which we commonly call passion cannot be everywhere in any poem. There must be passion, then, that must be distinct from ordinary passion, and that must be enthusiasm. I call that ordinary passion whose cause is clearly comprehended by him who feels it, whether it be admiration, terror, or joy; and I call the very same passions enthusiasms, when their cause is not clearly comprehended by him who feels them. And those enthusiastic passions are sometimes simple, and sometimes complicated, of all which we shall shew examples lower. And thus I have shewn, that the chief thing in poetry is passion: But here the reader is desired to observe, that by poetry we mean poetry in general, and the body of poetry; for as for the form or soul of particular poems, that is allowed by all to be a fable. But passion is the chief thing in the body of poetry; as spirit is in the human body. For without spirit the body languishes, and the soul is impotent. Now everything that they call spirit, or genius in poetry, in short, everything that pleases, and consequently moves, in the poetic diction, is passion, whether it be ordinary or enthusiastic.

And thus we have shewn, what the chief excellence in the body of poetry is, which we have proved to be passion. Let us now proceed to the proofs of what we propounded, that sacred subjects are more susceptible of passion than profane ones; and that the subjects of the ancients were sacred in their greater poetry, I mean either sacred in their own natures, or by their manner of handling them.

FROM THE GROUNDS OF CRITICISM IN POETRY
[1704]

SPECIMEN

Being the Substance of What Will Be Said in the Beginning of the Criticism upon Milton

---

The next poet of whom we shall treat is Milton, one of the greatest and most daring geniuses that has appeared in the world, and who has made his country a glorious present of the most lofty, but most irregular, poem that has been produced by the mind of man. That great man had a desire to give the world something like an epic poem, but he resolved at the same time to break through the rules of Aristotle. Not that he was ignorant of them, or condemned them. On the contrary, no man knew them better or esteemed them more, because no man had an understanding that was more able to comprehend the necessity of them; and therefore when he mentioned them in the little treatise which he wrote to Mr. Hartlib, he calls the art which treats of them a "sublime" art. But at the same time he had discernment enough to see that if he wrote a poem which was within the compass of them, he should be subjected to the same fate which has attended all who have wrote epic poems ever since the time of Homer, and that is to be a copyist instead of an original. Tis true, the epic poets who have lived since Homer have most of them been originals in their fables, which are the very souls of their poems; but in their manner of treating those fables, they have too frequently been copyists. They have copied the spirit and the images of Homer; even the great Virgil himself is not to be excepted. Milton was the first who in the space of almost 4000 years resolved, for his country's honour and his own, to present the world with an original poem; that is to say, a poem that should have his own thoughts, his own images, and his own spirit. In order to this he was resolved to write a poem that, by virtue of its extraordinary subject, cannot so properly be said to be against the rules, as it may be affirmed to be above them all. He had observed that Aristotle had drawn his rules which he has given us for epic poetry from the reflections which he had made upon Homer. Now he knew very well that in Homer the action lay chiefly between man and man: for Achilles and Hector are properly the principals, and the gods are but seconds. He was resolved, therefore, that his principals should be the devil on one side and man on the other: and the devil is properly his hero, because he gets the better. All the persons in his poem, excepting two, are either divine or infernal, so that most of the persons and particularly one of the principals, being so very different from what Homer or Aristotle ever thought of, could not possibly be subjected to their rules, either for the characters or the incidents. We shall now shew for what reasons the choice of Milton's subject, as it set him free from the obligation which he lay under to the poetical laws, so it necessarily threw him upon new thoughts, new images, and an original spirit. In the next place we shall shew that his thoughts, his images, and by consequence too his spirit, are actually new, and different from those of Homer and Virgil. Thirdly, we shall shew that besides their newness, they have vastly the advantage of those of Homer and Virgil. And we shall make this appear from several things, but principally from the description of hell, which has been described by those three great poets with all their force and with all their art. After that, we shall proceed to say something of Milton's expression and his harmony; and then we shall come to mark his defects with so much the more exactness, because some of them ought to be avoided with the utmost caution, as being so great that they would be insupportable in any one who had not his extraordinary distinguishing qualities.

· · ·

CHAPTER II

That Poetry Is to be Establish'd, by Laying Down the Rules

That an art so divine in its instiution is sunk and profaned and miserably debased, is a thing that is confessed by all. But since poetry is fallen from the excellence which it once attained to, it must be fallen either by the want of parts, or want of industry, or by the errors of its professors. But that it cannot be for want of parts we have shewn clearly in the Advancement of Modern Poetry; nor can it be supposed to be for want of industry, since so many of its professors have no other dependence. It remains then that it must have fallen by their errors, and for want of being guided right. Since therefore 'tis for want of knowing by what rules they ought to proceed that poetry is fallen so low, it follows then that it is the laying down of those rules alone that can re-establish it. In short, poetry is either an art or whimsy and fanaticism. If it is an art, it follows that it must propose an end to itself, and afterwards lay down proper means for the attaining that end: For this is undeniable, that there are proper means for the attaining of every end, and those proper means in poetry we call the rules. Again, if the end of poetry be to instruct and reform the world, that is, to bring mankind from irregularity, extravagance, and confusion to rule and order, how this should be done by a thing that is in itself irregular and extravagant, is difficult to be conceived. Besides, the work of every reasonable creature must derive its beauty from regularity; for reason is rule and order, and nothing can be irregular either in our conceptions or our actions, any further than it swerves from rule, that is, from reason. As man is the more perfect the more he resembles his creator, the works of man must needs be more perfect the more they resemble his maker's. Now the works of God, though infinitely various, are extremely regular.

The universe is regular in all its parts, and it is to that exact regularity that it owes its admirable beauty. The microcosm owes the beauty and health both of its body and soul to order, and the deformity and distempers of both to nothing but the want of order. Man was created, like the rest of the creatures, regular, and as long as he remained so he continued happy; but as soon as he fell from his primitive state by transgressing order, weakness and misery was the immediate consequence of that universal disorder that immediately followed in his conceptions, in his passions and actions.

The great design of arts is to restore the decays that happened to human nature by the Fall, by restoring order: The design of logic is to bring back order, and rule, and method to our conceptions, the want of which causes most of our ignorance and all our errors. The design of moral philosophy is to cure the disorder that is found in our passions, from which proceeds all our unhappiness and all our vice, as from the due order that is seen in them comes all our virtue and all our pleasure. But how should these arts re-establish order, unless they themselves were regular? Those arts that make the senses instrumental to the pleasure of the mind, as painting and music, do it by a great deal of rule and order: Since, therefore, poetry comprehends the force of all these arts of logic, of ethics, of eloquence, of painting, of music, can anything be more ridiculous than to imagine that poetry itself should be without rule and order?

CHAPTER III

What Poetry Is, and That It Attains Its End by Exciting of Passion.

We have said above that as poetry is an art it must have a certain end, and that there must be means that are proper for the attaining that end, which means are otherwise called the rules: But that we may make this appear the more plainly, let us declare what poetry is. Poetry, then, is an art, by which a poet excites passion (and for that very cause entertains sense) in order to satisfy and improve, to delight and reform the mind, and so to make mankind happier and better: from which it appears that poetry has two ends, a subordinate, and a final one; the subordinate one is pleasure, and the final one is instruction.

First: The subordinate end of poetry is to please, for that pleasure is the business and design of poetry is evident; because poetry, unless it pleases, nay and pleases to a height, is the most contemptible thing in the world. Other things may be borne with if they are indifferent, but poetry, unless it is transporting, is abominable: nay, it has only the name of poetry, so inseparable is pleasure from the very nature of the things.

But, secondly, the final end of poetry is to reform the manners: As poetry is an art, instruction must be its final end; but either that instruction must consist in reforming the manners, or it cannot instruct at all, and consequently be an art; for poetry pretends to no other instruction as its final end. But since the final end of poetry is to reform the manners, nothing can be according to the true art of it, which is against religion, or which runs counter to moral virtue, or to the true politics, and to the liberty of mankind: and everything which is against the last, tends to the corruption and destruction of mankind; and consequently everything against the last, must be utterly inconsistent with the true art of poetry.

Now the proper means for poetry, to attain both its subordinate and final end, is by exciting passion.

First: The subordinate end of poetry, which is to please, is attained by exciting passion, because everyone who is pleased is moved, and either desires, or rejoices, or admires, or hopes, or the like. As we are moved by pleasure which is happiness, to do everything we do, we may find upon a little reflection that every man is incited by some passion or other, either to action, or to contemplation; and passion is the result either of action or of contemplation, as long as either of them please; and the more either of them pleases, the more they are attended with passion. The satisfaction that we receive from geometry itself comes from the joy of having found out truth, and the desire of finding more. And the satiety that seizes us upon too long a lecture proceeds from nothing but from the weariness of our spirits, and consequently from the cessation or the decay of those two pleasing passions. But,

Secondly, poetry attains its final end, which is the reforming the minds of men, by exciting of passion. And here I dare be bold to affirm, that all instruction whatever depends upon passion. The moral philosophers themselves, even the dryest of them, can never instruct and reform unless they move; for either they make vice odious and virtue lovely, or they deter you from one by the apprehension of misery, or they incite you to the other by the happiness they make you expect from it; or they work upon your shame, or upon your pride, or upon your indignation. And therefore poetry instructs and reforms more powerfully than philosophy can do, because it moves more powerfully; and therefore it instructs more easily too. For whereas all men have passions, and great passions of one sort or another; and whereas those passions will be employed, and whatever way they move they that way draw the man; it follows that philosophy can instruct but hardly, because it moves but gently: for the violent passions not finding their account in those faint emotions, begin to rebel and fly to their old objects; whereas poetry, at the same time that it instructs us powerfully, must reform us easily, because it makes the very violence of the passions contribute to our reformation.

For the generality of mankind are apparently swayed by their passions, nay, and perhaps the very best and wisest of them. The greatest philosophers and the greatest princes are influenced by their favourites, and so are the wisest magistrates. And 'tis for this reason that not only the devil, who must be supposed to understand human nature, corrupts mankind by their passions (for temptation is nothing but the inclining men to such and such actions, by the raising such and such passions in them), but God himself, who made the soul, and best understands its nature, converts it by its passions. For whereas philosophy pretends to correct human passions by human reason, that is, things that are strong and ungovernable, by something that is feeble and weak; poetry by the force of the passion, instructs and reforms the reason: which is the design of the true religion, as we have shewn in another place. So that we have here already laid down one great rule necessary for the succeeding in poetry: for since it can attain neither its subordinate nor its final end without exciting of passion, it follows that where there is nothing which directly tends to the moving of that, there can be no poetry; and that consequently a poet ought to contrive everything in order to the moving of passion, that not only the fable, the incidents and characters, but the very sentiments and the expressions, ought all to be designed for that. For since poetry pleases and instructs us more even than philosophy itself only because it moves us more, it follows that the more poetry moves, the more it pleases and instructs: and it is for this reason that tragedy, to those who have a taste of it, is both more pleasing and more instructing than comedy. And this naturally brings us to the dividing poetry into the greater and the less.

1. The greater poetry is an art by which a poet justly and reasonably excites great passion, that he may please and instruct; and comprehends Epic, Tragic, and the greater Lyric poetry.

2. The less poetry is an art by which a poet excites less passion for the forementioned ends, and includes in it comedy and satire, and the little ode, and elegiac and pastoral poems. But first we shall treat of the former.

CHAPTER IV

What the Greater Poetry Is, What Enthusiasm Is

The greater poetry then, is an art by which a poet justly and reasonably excites great passion, in order to please and instruct and make mankind better and happier; so that the first and grand rule in the greater poetry is, that a poet must everywhere excite great passion: but in some branches of the greater poetry it is impossible for a poet everywhere to excite in a very great degree that which we vulgarly call passion: as in the ode, for example, and in the narration of the epic poem. It follows then, that there must be two sorts of passion: First, that which we call vulgar passion; and secondly, enthusiasm.

First, vulgar passion, or that which we commonly call passion, is that which is moved by the objects themselves, or by the ideas in the ordinary course of life; I mean, that common society which we find in the world. As for example, anger is moved by an affront that is offered us in our presence, or by the relation of one; pity by the sight of a mournful object, or the relation of one; admiration or wonder (the common passion, I mean; for there is an enthusiastic admiration, as we shall find anon), by the sight of a strange object, or the relation of one. But,

Secondly, enthusiastic passion, or enthusiasm, is a passion which is moved by the ideas in contemplation, or the meditation of things that belong not to common life. Most of our thoughts in meditation are naturally attended with some sort and some degree of passion, and this passion, if it is strong, I call enthusiasm. Now the enthusiastic passions are chiefly six, Admiration, Terror, Horror, Joy, Sadness, Desire, caused by ideas occurring to us in meditation, and producing the same passions that the objects of those ideas would raise in us if they were set before us in the same light that those ideas give us of them. And here I desire the reader to observe, that ideas in meditation are often very different from what ideas of the same objects are in the course of common conversation. As for example, the sun mentioned in ordinary conversation gives the idea of a round, flat, shining body, of about two foot diameter. But the sun occurring to us in meditation gives the idea of a vast and glorious body, and the top of all the visible creation, and the brightest material image of the divinity. I leave the reader therefore to judge if this idea must not necessarily be attended with admiration; and that admiration I call enthusiasm. So thunder mentioned in common conversation gives an idea of a black cloud and a great noise, which makes no great impression upon us. But the idea of it occurring in meditation sets before us the most forcible, most resistless, and consequently the most dreadful phenomenon in nature: So that this idea must move a great deal of terror in us, and 'tis this sort of terror, or admiration, or horror, and so of the rest, which expessed in poetry make that spirit, that passion, and that fire, which so wonderfully please.

Thus there are two sorts of passions to be raised in poetry, the vulgar and the enthusiastic; to which last the vulgar is preferable, because all men are capable of being moved by the vulgar, and a poet writes to all: But the enthusiastic are more subtle, and thousands have no feeling and no notion of them. But where the vulgar cannot be moved in a great degree, there the enthusiastic are to be raised. Therefore in those parts of epic poetry where the poet speaks himself, or the eldest of the muses for him, the enthusiastic passions are to prevail, as likewise in the greater ode. And the vulgar passions are to prevail in those parts of an epic and dramatic poem where the poet introduces persons holding conversation together. And perhaps this might be one reason for which Aristotle might prefer tragedy to epic poetry, because the vulgar passions prevail more in it, and are more violently moved in it; and therefore tragedy must necessarily both please and instruct more generally than epic poetry. We shall then treat of the vulgar passions when we come to speak of tragedy, in which poem they ought most to prevail: we shall then more particularly shew the surest and most powerful ways of raising compassion and terror, which are the true tragical passions.

We shall at present treat of the enthusiastic passions, and how they are to be raised. We have taken notice above, that they are to be moved by ideas occurring in contemplation; that they are to be moved in a great degree, and yet justly and reasonably. We shall now shew that the strongest enthusiastic passions that are justly and reasonably raised, must be raised by religious ideas; that is, by ideas which either shew the attributes of the divinity, or relate to his worship. And this we shall endeavour to prove, first, by reason: secondly, by authority: thirdly, by examples.

.   .   .

I now come to the precepts of Longinus, and pretend to shew from them that the greatest sublimity is to be derived from religious ideas. But why then, says the reader, has not Longinus plainly told us so? He was not ignorant that he ought to make his subject as plain as he could, for he has told us in the beginning of his treatise that everyone who gives instruction concerning an art ought to endeavour two things: The first is to make his reader clearly understand what that is which he pretends to teach: The second is to shew him how it may be attained. And he blames Cecilius[1] very severely for neglecting the last; how then, says the objector, comes he himself to have taken no care of the first? Is it because Cecilius had done it before him? If so, it was a very great fault in Longinus to publish a book which could not be understood but by another man's writings, especially when he saw that those writings were so very defective that they would not probably last. But what, continues the objector, if Cecilius had not done it before him? For Longinus tells us that Cecilius makes use of a multitude of words to shew what it is; now he who knows anything clearly may, in a few words, explain it clearly to others; and he who does not, will make it obscure by many.

[1] *On the Sublime,* Chapters I, III.

To this I answer, that though Longinus did by long study and habitude know the sublime when he saw it as well as any man, yet he had not so clear a knowledge of the nature of it as to explain it clearly to others. For if he had done that, as the objector says, he would have defined it; but he has been so far from defining it that in one place he has given an account of it that is contrary to the true nature of it. For he tells us in that chapter which treats of the fountains of sublimity, that loftiness is often without any passion at all; which is contrary to the true nature of it. The sublime is indeed often without common passion, as ordinary passion is often without that. But then it is never without enthusiastic passion: For the sublime is nothing else but a great thought, or great thoughts moving the soul from its ordinary situation by the enthusiasm which naturally attends them. Now Longinus had a notion of enthusiastic passion, for he establishes it in that very chapter for the second source of sublimity. Now Longinus, by affirming that the sublime may be without not only that, but ordinary passion, says a thing that is not only contrary to the true nature of it, but contradictory to himself. For he tells us in the beginning of the treatise, that the sublime does not so properly persuade us, as it ravishes and transports us, and produces in us a certain admiration, mingled with astonishment and with surprize, which is quite another thing than the barely pleasing, or the barely persuading; that it gives a noble vigour to a discourse, an invincible force, which commits a pleasing rape upon the very soul of the reader; that whenever it breaks out where it ought to do, like the artillery of Jove, it thunders, blazes, and strikes at once, and shews all the united force of a writer. Now I leave the reader to judge, whether Longinus has not been saying here all along that sublimity is never without passion.

That the forementioned definition is just and good I have reason to believe, because it takes in all the sources of sublimity which Longinus has established. For, first, greatness of thought supposes elevation, they being synonymous terms: and, secondly, the enthusiasm or the pathetic, as Longinus calls it, follows of course; for if a man is not strongly moved by great thoughts, he does not sufficiently and effectually con-

ceive them. And, thirdly, the figurative language is but a consequence of the enthusiasm, that being the natural language
of the passions. And so is, fourthly, the nobleness of the
expression, supposing a man to be master of the language in
which he writes. For as the thoughts produce the spirit or the
passion, the spirit produces and makes the expression, which
is known by experience to all who are poets; for never anyone,
while he was wrapt with enthusiasm or ordinary passion,
wanted either words or harmony, as is self-evident to all who
consider that the expression conveys and shows the spirit, and
consequently must be produced by it.

Thus the definition which we have laid down being,
according to Longinus's own doctrine, the true definition of
the sublime, and shewing clearly the thing which he has not
done, nor given any definition at all of it; it seems plain to me
that he had no clear and distinct idea of it; and consequently
religion might be the thing from which 'tis chiefly to be derived, and he but obscurely know it: but that religion is that
thing from which the sublime is chiefly to be derived, let us
shew by the marks which he has given of the latter, which
will further strengthen our definition. 1. Says he, that which is
truly sublime has this peculiar to it, that it exalts the soul,
and makes it conceive a greater idea of itself, filling it with
joy and with a certain noble pride, as if itself had produced
what it but barely reads.

Now here it is plain, that the highest ideas must most
exalt the soul, but religious ideas are the highest.

The more the soul is moved by the greatest ideas, the more
it conceives them; but the more it conceives of the greatest
ideas, the greater opinion it must have of its own capacity.
By consequence the more it is moved by the wonders of religion, the more it values itself upon its own excellences. Again,
the more the soul sees its excellence, the more it rejoices. Besides, religious ideas are the most admirable; and what is
most admirable, according to the doctrine of Aristotle, is most
delightful. Besides, religious ideas create passion in such a
manner as to turn and incline the soul to its primitive object.
So that reason and passion are of the same side, and this peace

between the faculties causes the soul to rejoice; of which we shall have occasion to say more anon.

2. The second mark that Longinus gives of the sublime is, when a discourse leaves a great deal for us to think. But now this is certain, that the wonders of religion are never to be exhausted; for they are always new, and the more you enter into them, the more they are sure to surprize.

3. The third mark is, when it leaves in the reader an idea above its expression. Now no expressions can come up to the ideas which we draw from the attributes of God, or from his wondrous works, which only the author of them can comprehend.

4. The fourth mark is, when it makes an impression upon us which it is impossible to resist.

God, who made man for himself, and for his own glory, and who requires chiefly his heart, must by consequence have formed him of such a nature as to be most strongly moved with religious ideas, if once he enters into them. So that the impressions which they make are impossible to be resisted.

5. The fifth mark is, when the impression lasts, and is difficult to be defaced. Now that the impressions which religion makes upon us are difficult to be defaced is plain from this, that they who think it their interest to deface them, can never bring it about.

6. The sixth mark is, when it pleases universally people of different humours, inclinations, sexes, ages, times, climates. Now there is nothing so agreeable to the soul, or that makes so universal an impression, as the wonders of religion. Some persons are moved by love, and are not touched by ambition; others are animated by ambition, and only laugh at love. Some are pleased with a brave revenge, others with a generous contempt of injuries; but the eternal power, and the infinite knowledge of God, the wonders of the creation, and the beautiful brightness of virtue, make a powerful impression on all.

I must confess I have wondered very much, upon reflection, how it could happen that so great a man as Longinus, who whenever he met a passage in any discourse that was lofty enough to please him, had discernment enough to see that it had some of the preceding marks, should miss of finding so easy a thing as this, that never any passage had all these marks, or so much as the majority of them, unless it were religious.

But to return to Terror, we may plainly see by the foregoing precepts and examples of Longinus, that this enthusiastic terror contributes extremely to the sublime; and, secondly, that it is most produced by religious ideas.

First, ideas producing terror contribute extremely to the sublime. All the examples that Longinus brings of the loftiness of the thought consist of terrible ideas. And they are principally such ideas that work the effects, which he takes notice of in the beginning of his treaties, *viz.* that ravish and transport the reader, and produce a certain admiration, mingled with astonishment and with surprize. For the ideas which produce terror are necessarily accompanied with admiration, because everything that is terrible is great to him to whom it is terrible; and with surprize, without which terror cannot subsist; and with astonishment, because everything which is very terrible is wonderful and astonishing: and as terror is perhaps the violentest of all the passions, it consequently makes an impression which we cannot resist, and which is hardly to be defaced: and no passion is attended with greater joy than enthusiastic terror, which proceeds from our reflecting that we are out of danger at the very time that we see it before us. And as terror is one of the violentest of all passions, if it is very great, and the hardest to be resisted, nothing gives more force, nor more vehemence to a discourse.

But, secondly, it is plain from the same Longinus, that this enthusiastic terror is chiefly to be derived from religious ideas. For all the examples which he has brought of the sublime in his chapter of the Sublimity of the Thoughts, consists of most terrible and most religious ideas; and at the same time every man's reason will inform him, that everything that is terrible in religion is the most terrible thing in the world.

But that we may set this in a clearer light, let us lay before the reader the several ideas which are capable of producing this enthusiastic terror, which seem to me to be those which follow, *viz.* gods, dæmons, hell, spirits and souls of men, miracles, prodigies, enchantments, witchcrafts, thunder, tempests, raging seas, inundation, torrents, earthquakes, volcanos, monsters, serpents, lions, tygers, fire, war, pestilence, famine, *etc.*

Now of all these ideas none are so terrible as those which shew the wrath and vengeance of an angry God; for nothing is so wonderful in its effects: and consequently the images or ideas of those effects must carry a great deal of terror with them, which we may see was Longinus's opinion by the examples which he brings in his chapter of the Sublimity of the Thoughts.

.   .   .

JOSEPH ADDISON
[1672–1719]

Just as in his whiggism Addison reflected Locke's political
philosophy, so in the aesthetic theories expressed in his papers
on the imagination did he reflect Locke's psychology,
particularly the importance Locke placed on vision. That
Addison was a wide-ranging student of the most up-to-date
philosophical and scientific speculations of his day is
evident throughout his work, but he had also had a solid,
conventional education in the classics, a fact no less evident.
The result of the combination was a contribution to aesthetic
and critical writing basic to an understanding of the
development of criticism through the century.

The essay on Virgil's Georgics, anthologized here in its
entirety, is less well known than it ought to be. Probably
written as early as 1693, but not published until four years
later with Dryden's translation of the Georgics, it is not
markedly original, but it summarizes and rationalizes a
value judgment of which all students of eighteenth-century
literature must be aware, since the georgic mode is, in one
mutation or another, everywhere in the poetry of the century,
and it epitomizes that critical approach through the genres
which twentieth-century readers generally find alien and
puzzling. Addison's remarks on poetic diction are particularly
worth notice, as is the last paragraph of the essay.

"The Pleasures of the Imagination" was the third series
of Spectator papers dealing at some length with a critical
subject (see notes 12 and 13 below), and by all odds the
most valuable. Addison's comments on wit added little
to discussion of that vexed subject, and the papers on

Paradise Lost, *although again an excellent exemplification of a late renaissance method of criticism, are important principally in that they called to the attention of a wide public a poem already critically acclaimed. Of the papers on the imagination Elledge remarks:* "Though the essay has been overvalued . . . , students of the century must agree with George Saintsbury, Samuel Monk, and John Butt, who have said that it is the first real essay in aesthetics in English; and none would disagree that its great popularity had an important influence on both art and criticism." (Elledge, vol. 1, 498) *There are eleven papers in the series —a small book—introduced by No. 409 on* "Taste." *The four selected here by no means represent the whole argument, but will enable the student to gather some of Addison's major points.*

The Essay on Virgil's Georgics *is most recently edited in Elledge's collection, which also includes the entire series on the imagination. Donald F. Bond has definitively edited* The Spectator *in five volumes (Oxford, 1965). The present text is adapted from the edition by Richard Hurd, re-edited by Henry G. Bohn, London, 1893.*

Addison's critical writings have elicited considerable comment. Among the many scholarly contributions the following may be consulted:

Elioseff, Lee Andrew: The Cultural Milieu of Addison's Literary Criticism, *Austin, 1963.*

Hansen, David A.: "Addison on Ornament and Poetic Style," Studies in Criticism and Aesthetics, 1660–1800: Essays in Honor of Samuel Holt Monk *(ed. Howard Anderson and John S. Shea), Minneapolis, 1967, pp. 94–127.*

Kallich, Martin: "The Association of Ideas and Critical Theory: Hobbes, Locke, and Addison," *ELH, XII (1945), 290–315.*

Mahoney, John L.: "Addison and Akenside: The Impact of Psychological Criticism on Early English Romantic Poetry," *British Journal of Aesthetics, VI (1966), 365–74.*

Nicolson, Marjorie H.: Mountain Gloom and Mountain Glory, *Ithaca, 1959 [important passim, but particularly chapter VII, section iv.]*

Thorpe, Clarence D.: "Addison and Hutcheson on the
    Imagination," ELH, II (1935), 215–34.
————: "Addison's Contribution to Criticism," The
    Seventeenth Century: Studies in the History of English
    Thought and Literature from Bacon to Pope (*by
    Richard Foster Jones, and others writing in his honor*),
    Stanford, 1951, pp. 316–29.

AN ESSAY ON VIRGIL'S GEORGICS

[1697]

Virgil may be reckoned the first who introduced three new kinds of poetry among the Romans, which he copied after three the greatest masters of Greece. Theocritus and Homer have still disputed for the advantage over him in pastoral and heroics, but I think all are unanimous in giving him the precedence to Hesiod in his *Georgics*. The truth of it is, the sweetness and rusticity of a pastoral cannot be so well expressed in any other tongue as in the Greek, when rightly mixed and qualified with the Doric dialect; nor can the majesty of an heroic poem anywhere appear so well as in this language, which has a natural greatness in it, and can be often rendered more deep and sonorous by the pronunciation of the Ionians. But in the middle style, where the writers

in both tongues are on a level, we see how far Virgil has excelled all who have written in the same way with him.

There has been abundance of criticism spent on Virgil's
Pastorals and *Æneids,* but the *Georgics* are a subject which
none of the critics have sufficiently taken into their consideration, most of them passing over it in silence, or casting it
under the same head with pastoral—a division by no means
proper, unless we suppose the style of a husbandman ought
to be imitated in a georgic, as that of a shepherd is in
pastoral. But though the scene of both these poems lies in the
same place, the speakers in them are of a quite different character, since the precepts of husbandry are not to be delivered
with the simplicity of a ploughman, but with the simplicity of
a poet. No rules, therefore, that relate to pastoral can any
way affect the *Georgics,* since they fall under that class of
poetry which consists in giving plain and direct instructions
to the reader; whether they be moral duties, as those of
Theognis and Pythagoras; or philosophical speculations, as
those of Aratus and Lucretius; or rules of practice, as those of
Hesiod and Virgil. Among these different kinds of subjects,
that which the *Georgics* go upon is I think the meanest and
least improving, but the most pleasing and delightful. Precepts
of morality, besides the natural corruption of our tempers,
which makes us averse to them, are so abstracted from ideas
of sense, that they seldom give an opportunity for those beautiful descriptions and images which are the spirit and life of
poetry. Natural philosophy has indeed sensible objects to
work upon, but then it often puzzles the reader with the
intricacy of its notions, and perplexes him with the multitude
of its disputes. But this kind of poetry I am now speaking of,
addresses itself wholly to the imagination: it is altogether
conversant among the fields and woods, and has the most
delightful part of nature for its province. It raises in our
minds a pleasing variety of scenes and landscapes, whilst it
teaches us; and makes the dryest of its precepts look like a
description. A georgic, therefore, is some part of the science
of husbandry put into a pleasing dress, and set off with all the
beauties and embellishments of poetry. Now since this science

of husbandry is of a very large extent, the poet shows his
skill in singling out such precepts to proceed on as are useful,
and at the same time most capable of ornament. Virgil was so
well acquainted with this secret, that to set off his first georgic,
he has run into a set of precepts which are almost foreign
to his subject, in that beautiful account he gives us of the
signs in nature which precede the changes of the weather.

And if there be so much art in the choice of fit precepts,
there is much more required in the treating of them, that
they may fall in after each other by a natural, unforced
method, and show themselves in the best and most advanta-
geous light. They should all be so finely wrought together in
the same piece, that no course seam may discover where they
join, as in a curious brede of needle-work one colour falls
away by such just degrees, and another rises so insensibly,
that we see the variety, without being able to distinguish the
total vanishing of the one from the first appearance of the
other. Nor is it sufficient to range and dispose this body of
precepts into a clear and easy method, unless they are delivered to us in the most pleasing and agreeable manner: for
there are several ways of conveying the same truth to the
mind of man; and to choose the pleasantest of these ways
is that which chiefly distinguishes poetry from prose, and
makes Virgil's rules of husbandry pleasanter to read than
Varro's.[1] Where the prose writer tells us plainly what ought
to be done, the poet often conceals the precept in a description, and represents his countrymen performing the action
in which he would instruct his reader. Where the one sets
out as fully and distinctly as he can all the parts of the truth
which he would communicate to us; the other singles out
the most pleasing circumstance of this truth, and so conveys
the whole in a more diverting manner to the understanding.
I shall give one instance out of a multitude of this nature
that might be found in the *Georgics,* where the reader may
see the different ways Virgil has taken to express the same

---

[1] Varro (116 B.C.–28 B.C.). Called "the most learned of the Romans,"
only two of his 490 books have survived, one of which is *De Re Rustica.*

thing, and how much pleasanter every manner of expression is than the plain and direct mention of it would have been. It is in the second georgic, where he tells us what trees will bear grafting on each other.

> Et sæpe alterius ramos impune videmus
> Vertere in alterius, mutatamque insita mala
> Ferre pyrum, et prunis lapidosa rubescere corna.
> ————Steriles Platani malos gessire valentes
> Castaneæ fagos, ornusque incanuit albo
> Flore pyri: Glandemque sues fregere sub ulmis.
> ————Nec longum tempus: et ingens
> Exiit ad cœlum ramis felicibus arbos;
> Miraturque novas frondes et non sua poma.[2]

Here we see the poet considered all the effects of this union between trees of different kinds, and took notice of that effect which had the most surprise, and, by consequence, the most delight in it, to express the capacity that was in them of being thus united. This way of writing is everywhere much in use among the poets, and is particularly practised by Virgil, who loves to suggest a truth indirectly, and without giving us a full and open view of it, to let us see just so much as will naturally lead the imagination into all the parts that lie concealed. This is wonderfully diverting to the understanding thus to receive a precept that enters

---

[2] *Georgic* II, 32, 70, 80. Dryden translates:

> 'Tis usual now an inmate graff to see
> With insolence invade a foreign tree:
> Thus pears and quinces from the crab tree come,
> And thus the ruddy cornel bears the plum.

> And planes huge apples bear, that bore but leaves.
> Thus mastful beech the bristly chestnut bears,
> And the wild ash is white with blooming pears,
> And greedy swine from grafted elms are fed
> With falling acorns, that on oaks are bred.

> And in short space the laden boughs arise,
> With happy fruit advancing to the skies.
> The mother plant admires the leaves unknown
> Of alien trees, and apples not her own.

as it were through a by-way, and to apprehend an idea that draws a whole train after it. For here the mind, which is always delighted with its own discoveries, only takes the hint from the poet, and seems to work out the rest by the strength of her own faculties.

But since the inculcating precept upon precept will at length prove tiresome to the reader if he meets with no entertainment, the poet must take care not to encumber his poem with too much business, but sometimes to relieve the subject with a moral reflection, or let it rest a while for the sake of a pleasant and pertinent digression. Nor is it sufficient to run out into beautiful and diverting digressions (as it is generally thought) unless they are brought in aptly, and are something of a piece with the main design of the georgic: for they ought to have a remote alliance, at least, to the subject, that so the whole poem may be more uniform and agreeable in all its parts. We should never quite lose sight of the country, though we are sometimes entertained with a distant prospect of it. Of this nature are Virgil's descriptions of the original of agriculture, of the fruitfulness of Italy, of a country life, and the like, which are not brought in by force, but naturally rise out of the principal argument and design of the poem. I know no one digression in the *Georgics* that may seem to contradict this observation, besides that in the latter end of the first book, where the poet launches out into a discourse of the battle of Pharsalia and the actions of Augustus: but it is worth while to consider how admirably he has turned the course of his narration into its proper channel, and made his husbandman concerned even in what relates to the battle, in those inimitable lines,

> Scilicet et tempus veniet, cum finibus illis
> Agricola incurvo terram molitus aratro,
> Exesa inveniet scabra robigine pila:
> Aut gravibus rastris galeas pulsabit inanis,
> Grandiaque effossis mirabitur ossa sepulchris.

And afterwards speaking of Augustus's actions, he still remembers that agriculture ought to be some way hinted at through the whole poem.

Non ullus aratro
Dignus honos: squalent abductis arva colonis:
Et curvæ rigidum falces conflantur in ensem.[3]

We now come to the style which is proper to a georgic;
and indeed this is the part on which the poet must lay out
all his strength, that his words may be warm and glowing,
and that everything he describes may immediately present
itself, and rise up to the reader's view. He ought in particular to be careful of not letting his subject debase his
style and betray him into a meanness of expression, but
everywhere to keep up his verse in all the pomp of numbers
and dignity of words.

I think nothing which is a phrase or saying in common
talk should be admitted into a serious poem, because it
takes off from the solemnity of the expression, and gives it
too great a turn of familiarity: much less ought the low
phrases and terms of art that are adapted to husbandry have
any place in such a work as the georgic, which is not to
appear in the natural simplicity and nakedness of its subject,
but in the pleasantest dress that poetry can bestow on it.
Thus Virgil, to deviate from the common form of words,
would not make use of *tempore,* but *sydere,* in his first verse,
and everywhere else abounds with metaphors, Grecisms, and
circumlocutions, to give his verse the greater pomp and preserve it from sinking into a plebeian style. And herein consists Virgil's master-piece, who has not only excelled all other
poets but even himself in the language of his *Georgics,* where

[3] *Georgic* I, 493, 506. Dryden translates:

> Then, after length of time, the lab'ring swains
> Who turn the turfs of those unhappy plains
> Shall rusty piles from the plow'd furrows take,
> And over empty helmets pass the rake;
> Amaz'd at antic titles on the stones,
> And mighty relics of gigantic bones.
>
> The peaceful peasant to the wars is press'd;
> The fields lie fallow in inglorious rest;
> The plain no pasture to the flock affords;
> The crooked scythes are straighten'd into swords:

we receive more strong and lively ideas of things from his words than we could have done from the objects themselves, and find our imaginations more affected by his descriptions than they would have been by the very sight of what he describes.

I shall now, after this short scheme of rules, consider the different success that Hesiod [4] and Virgil have met with in this kind of poetry, which may give us some further notion of the excellence of the *Georgics*. To begin with Hesiod; if we may guess at his character from his writings, he had much more of the husbandman than the poet in his temper: he was wonderfully grave, discreet, and frugal. He lived altogether in the country, and was probably for his great prudence the oracle of the whole neighbourhood. These principles of good husbandry ran through his works, and directed him to the choice of tillage and merchandise, for the subject of that which is the most celebrated of them. He is everywhere bent on instruction, avoids all manner of digressions, and does not stir out of the field once in the whole georgic. His method in describing month after month, with its proper seasons and employments, is too grave and simple; it takes off from the surprise and variety of the poem, and makes the whole look but like a modern almanac in verse. The reader is carried through a course of weather, and may beforehand guess whether he is to meet with snow or rain, clouds or sun-shine, in the next description. His descriptions, indeed, have abundance of nature in them, but then it is nature in her simplicity and undress. Thus when he speaks of January: "The wild beasts," says he, "run shivering through the woods with their heads stooping to the ground, and their tails clapt between their legs; the goats and oxen are almost flayed with cold; but it is not so bad with the sheep, because they have a thick coat of wool about them. The old men too are bitterly pincht with the weather, but the young girls feel nothing of it, who sit at home with their mothers by a warm

---

[4] Hesiod, *fl. c.* 735 B.C. Greek poet whose *Works and Days* contains ethical, political, and economic precepts.

fire-side." Thus does the old gentleman give himself up to a loose kind of tattle, rather than endeavour after a just poetical description. Nor has he shown more of art or judgment in the precepts he has given us, which are sown so very thick that they clog the poem too much, and are often so minute and full of circumstances that they weaken and unnerve his verse. But after all, we are beholden to him for the first rough sketch of a georgic, where we may still discover something venerable in the antiqueness of the work; but if we would see the design enlarged, the figures reformed, the colouring laid on, and the whole piece finished, we must expect it from a greater master's hand.

Virgil has drawn out the rules of tillage and planting into two books which Hesiod has despatched in half a one, but has so raised the natural rudeness and simplicity of his subject with such a significancy of expression, such a pomp of verse, such a variety of transitions, and such a solemn air in his reflections, that if we look on both poets together we see in one the plainness of a downright countryman, and in the other something of a rustic majesty, like that of a Roman dictator at the plough-tail. He delivers the meanest of his precepts with a kind of grandeur, he breaks the clods and tosses the dung about with an air of gracefulness. His prognostications of the weather are taken out of Aratus,[5] where we may see how judiciously he has pickt out those that are most proper for his husbandman's observation, how he has enforced the expression and heightened the images which he found in the original.

The second book has more wit in it, and a greater boldness in its metaphors, than any of the rest. The poet, with a great beauty, applies oblivion, ignorance, wonder, desire, and the like, to his trees. The last georgic has, indeed, as many metaphors, but not so daring as this; for human thoughts and passions may be more naturally ascribed to a bee than to an inanimate plant. He who reads over the pleasures of a country life, as they are described by Virgil in the latter

---

[5] Aratus, *fl. c.* 270 B.C. at the court of Macedonia. He wrote an astronomical poem, *Phaenomena,* very popular in Rome and translated into Latin by Cicero.

end of this book, can scarce be of Virgil's mind in preferring even the life of a philosopher to it.

We may, I think, read the poet's clime in his description, for he seems to have been in a sweat at the writing of it:

> O quis me gelidis sub montibus Hæmi
> Sistat, et ingenti ramorum protegat umbrâ! [6]

And is everywhere mentioning among his chief pleasures the coolness of his shades and rivers, vales and grottos, which a more northern poet would have omitted for the description of a sunny hill and fire-side.

The third georgic seems to be the most laboured [7] of them all; there is a wonderful vigour and spirit in the description of the horse and chariot-race. The force of love is represented in noble instances and very sublime expressions. The Scythian winter-piece appears so very cold and bleak to the eye that a man can scarce look on it without shivering. The murrain at the end has all the expressiveness that words can give. It was here that the poet strained hard to outdo Lucretius in the description of his plague, and if the reader would see what success he had, he may find it at large in Scaliger.[8]

But Virgil seems nowhere so well pleased as when he is got among his bees in the fourth georgic, and ennobles the actions of so trivial a creature with metaphors drawn from the most important concerns of mankind. His verses are not in a greater noise and hurry in the battles of Æneas and Turnus than in the engagement of two swarms. And as in his *Æneis* he compares the labours of his Trojans to those of bees and pismires, here he compares the labours of the bees to those of the Cyclops. In short, the last georgic was

---

[6] *Georgic* II, 488: *O qui me gelidis convallibus Haemi* . . . Dryden translates:

> Or lift me high to Hæmus' hilly crown,
> Or in the plains of Tempe lay me down,
> Or lead me to some solitary place,
> And cover my retreat from human race!

[7] I.e., "carefully wrought."

[8] *Poetics*, V.

a good prelude to the *Æneis,* and very well showed what
the poet could do in the description of what was really great
by his describing the mock-grandeur of an insect with so
good a grace. There is more pleasantness in the little plat-
form of a garden, which he gives us about the middle of this
book, than in all the spacious walks and water-works of
Rapin.[9] The speech of Proteus at the end can never be
enough admired, and was, indeed, very fit to conclude so
divine a work.

After this particular account of the beauties in the *Georgics,* I should in the next place endeavour to point out its
imperfections, if it has any. But though I think there are some
few parts in it that are not so beautiful as the rest, I shall
not presume to name them, as rather suspecting my own
judgment than I can believe a fault to be in that poem
which lay so long under Virgil's correction, and had his last
hand put to it. The first georgic was probably burlesqued
in the author's life-time, for we still find in the scholiasts a
verse that ridicules part of a line translated from Hesiod,
Nudus ara, sere nudus—And we may easily guess at the
judgment of this extraordinary critic, whoever he was, from
his censuring this particular precept. We may be sure Virgil
would not have translated it from Hesiod had he not discovered some beauty in it; and indeed the beauty of it is
what I have before observed to be frequently met with in
Virgil, the delivering the precept so indirectly, and singling
out the particular circumstance of sowing and ploughing
naked, to suggest to us that these employments are proper
only in the hot season of the year.

I shall not here compare the style of the *Georgics* with
that of Lucretius, which the reader may see already done in
the Preface to the second volume of Miscellany Poems,[10] but
shall conclude this poem to be the most complete, elaborate,
and finished piece of all antiquity. The *Æneis,* indeed, is of
a nobler kind, but the *Georgics* is more perfect in its kind.

---

[9] "In his georgic *Hortorum,* René Rapin devoted one of the four books to
fountains, ponds and canals as parts of formal gardens." [Elledge]
[10] Dryden, "Preface to Sylvae," Watson, II, 23 ff.

The *Æneis* has a greater variety of beauties in it, but those of the *Georgics* are more exquisite. In short, the *Georgics* has all the perfection that can be expected in a poem written by the greatest poet in the flower of his age, when his invention was ready, his imagination warm, his judgment settled, and all his faculties in their full vigour and maturity.

SPECTATOR ESSAYS
[1712]

————————Musæo contingere cuncta lepore.
                                                    Lucr.
To grace each subject with enliv'ning wit.

Gratian[11] very often recommends the fine taste as the utmost perfection of an accomplished man. As this word arises very often in conversation, I shall endeavour to give some account of it, and to lay down rules how we may know whether we are possessed of it, and how we may acquire that fine taste of writing which is so much talked of among the polite world.

[11] Baltasar (pen-name Lorenzo) Gracián (1601–1658). Spanish Jesuit, euphuistic writer, author of (among many other works) *Arte de ingenio* (1642), praising the taste for conceits.

Most languages make use of this metaphor to express that faculty of the mind which distinguishes all the most concealed faults and nicest perfections in writing. We may be sure this metaphor would not have been so general in all tongues had there not been a very great conformity between that mental taste, which is the subject of this paper, and that sensitive taste which gives us a relish of every different flavour that affects the palate. Accordingly we find there are as many degrees of refinement in the intellectual faculty as in the sense which is marked out by this common denomination.

I knew a person who possessed the one in so great a perfection, that after having tasted ten different kinds of tea he would distinguish, without seeing the colour of it, the particular sort which was offered him; and not only so, but any two sorts of them that were mixt together in an equal proportion; nay, he has carried the experiment so far, as upon tasting the composition of three different sorts, to name the parcels from whence the three several ingredients were taken. A man of a fine taste in writing will discern, after the same manner, not only the general beauties and imperfections of an author, but discover the several ways of thinking and expressing himself which diversify him from all other authors, with the several foreign infusions of thought and language, and the particular authors from whom they were borrowed.

After having thus far explained what is generally meant by a fine taste in writing, and shewn the propriety of the metaphor which is used on this occasion, I think I may define it to be "that faculty of the soul which discerns the beauties of an author with pleasure and the imperfections with dislike." If a man would know whether he is possessed of this faculty, I would have him read over the celebrated works of antiquity which have stood the test of so many different ages and countries, or those works among the moderns which have the sanction of the politer part of our contemporaries. If upon the perusal of such writings he does not find himself delighted in an extraordinary manner, or if, upon reading the admired passages in such authors, he finds a coldness and indifference in his thoughts, he ought to conclude, not (as is too usual among tasteless readers) that the author wants those perfections which have been admired in him, but that he himself wants the faculty of discovering them.

He should, in the second place, be very careful to observe whether he tastes the distinguishing perfections, or, if I may be allowed to call them so, the specific qualities of the author whom he peruses; whether he is particularly pleased with Livy for his manner of telling a story, with Sallust for his entering into those internal principles of action which arise from the characters and manners of the persons he describes, or with Tacitus for his displaying those outward motives of safety and interest which give birth to the whole series of transactions which he relates.

He may likewise consider how differently he is affected by the same thought which presents itself in a great writer, from what he is when he finds it delivered by a person of an ordinary genius. For there is as much difference in apprehending a thought clothed in Cicero's language, and that of a common author, as in seeing an object by the light of a taper, or by the light of the sun.

It is very difficult to lay down rules for the acquirement of such a taste as that I am here speaking of. The faculty must in some degree be born with us, and it very often happens that those who have other qualities in perfection are wholly void of this. One of the most eminent mathematicians of the age has assured me that the greatest pleasure he took in reading Virgil was in examining Æneas his voyage by the map, as I question not but many a modern compiler of history would be delighted with little more in that divine author than in the bare matters of fact.

But notwithstanding this faculty must in some measure be born with us, there are several methods for cultivating and improving it, and without which it will be very uncertain and of little use to the person that possesses it. The most natural method for this purpose is to be conversant among the writings of the most polite authors. A man who has any relish for fine writing either discovers new beauties, or receives stronger impressions from the masterly strokes of a great author every time he peruses him: besides that he naturally wears himself into the same manner of speaking and thinking.

Conversation with men of a polite genius is another method of improving our natural taste. It is impossible for a man of the greatest parts to consider any thing in its whole extent and in all its variety of lights. Every man, besides those general observations which are to be made upon an author, forms several reflections that are peculiar to his own manner of thinking; so that conversation will naturally furnish us with hints which we did not attend to, and make us enjoy other men's parts and reflections as well as our own. This is the best reason I can give for the observation which several have made, that men of great genius in the same way of writing seldom rise up singly, but at certain periods of time appear together and in a body, as they did at Rome in the reign of Augustus, and in Greece about the age of Socrates. I cannot think that Corneille, Racine, Molière, Boileau, la Fontaine, Bruyère, Bossu, or the Daciers, would have written so well as they have done had they not been friends and contemporaries.

It is likewise necessary for a man who would form to himself a finished taste of good writing to be well versed in the works of the best critics both ancient and modern. I must confess that I could wish there were authors of this kind, who, beside the mechanical rules which a man of very little taste may discourse upon, would enter into the very spirit and soul of fine writing, and shew us the several sources of that pleasure which rises in the mind upon the perusal of a noble work. Thus although in poetry it be absolutely necessary that the unities of time, place, and action, with other points of the same nature, should be thoroughly explained and understood, there is still something more essential to the art, something that elevates and astonishes the fancy and gives a greatness of mind to the reader, which few of the critics besides Longinus have considered.

Our general taste in England is for epigram, turns of wit, and forced conceits, which have no manner of influence either for the bettering or enlarging the mind of him who reads them, and have been carefully avoided by the greatest writers, both among the ancients and moderns. I have endeavoured in several of my speculations to banish this Gothic taste which has taken possession among us. I entertained the town, for a week together, with an essay upon wit,[12] in which I endeavoured to detect several of those false kinds which have been admired in the different ages of the world, and at the same time to shew wherein the nature of true wit consists. I afterwards gave an instance of the great force which lies in a natural simplicity of thought to affect the mind of the reader, from such vulgar pieces as have little else besides this single qualification to recommend them. I have likewise examined the works of the greatest poet which our nation or perhaps any other has produced,[13] and particularized most of those rational and manly beauties which give a value to that divine work. I shall next Saturday enter upon an essay on "the pleasures of the imagination," which, though it shall consider that subject at large, will perhaps suggest to the reader what it is that gives a beauty to many passages of the finest writers both in prose and verse. As an undertaking of this nature is entirely new, I question not but it will be received with candour.

NO. 411. SATURDAY, JUNE 21.

Pleasures of the Imagination

> Avia Pieridum perago loca, nullius ante
> Trita solo; juvat integros accedere fonteis;
> Atque haurire:——
>
> > Lucr. i. 925.
>
> ——Inspir'd I trace the muses' seats,

---

[12] *Spectators* Nos. 58–63.
[13] *Spectator* papers on *Paradise Lost,* beginning with No. 267, and running for eighteen consecutive Saturdays from Jan. 5 to May 3, 1712.

      Untrodden yet; 'tis sweet to visit first
      Untouch'd and virgin streams, and quench my thirst.
                              CREECH.

Our sight is the most perfect and most delightful of all our senses. It fills the mind with the largest variety of ideas, converses with its objects at the greatest distance, and continues the longest in action without being tired or satiated with its proper enjoyments. The sense of feeling can indeed give us a notion of extension, shape, and all other ideas that enter at the eye, except colours; but at the same time it is very much straitened and confined in its operations, to the number, bulk, and distance of its particular objects. Our sight seems designed to supply all these defects, and may be considered as a more delicate and diffusive kind of touch, that spreads itself over an infinite multitude of bodies, comprehends the largest figures, and brings into our reach some of the most remote parts of the universe.

It is this sense which furnishes the imagination with its ideas, so that by the pleasures of the imagination or fancy (which I shall use promiscuously)[14] I here mean such as arise from visible objects, either when we have them actually in our view, or when we call up their ideas into our minds by paintings, statues, descriptions, or any the like occasion. We cannot, indeed, have a single image in the fancy that did not make its first entrance through the sight; but we have the power of retaining, altering, and compounding those images which we have once received into all the varieties of picture and vision that are most agreeable to the imagination; for by this faculty a man in a dungeon is capable of entertaining

---

[14] Readers of Coleridge take note! The two terms seem to have been used interchangeably through most of the century. As late as 1783 James Beattie wrote: "According to the common use of words, Imagination and Fancy are not perfectly synonymous. They are, indeed, names for the same faculty; but the former seems to be applied to the more solemn, and the latter to the more trivial, exertions of it. A witty author is a man of lively Fancy; but a sublime poet is said to possess a vast Imagination. However, as these words are often, and by the best writers, used indiscriminately, I shall not further distinguish them." *Dissertations Moral and Critical*, Dublin, 1783, I, 87 [Bond, III, 536].

himself with scenes and landscapes more beautiful than any that can be found in the whole compass of nature.

There are few words in the English language which are employed in a more loose and uncircumscribed sense than those of the fancy and the imagination. I therefore thought it necessary to fix and determine the notion of these two words, as I intend to make use of them in the thread of my following speculations, that the reader may conceive rightly what is the subject which I proceed upon. I must therefore desire him to remember that by the pleasures of the imagination I mean only such pleasures as arise originally from sight, and that I divide these pleasures into two kinds: my design being first of all to discourse of those primary pleasures of the imagination, which entirely proceed from such objects as are before our eyes; and in the next place to speak of those secondary pleasures of the imagination, which flow from the ideas of visible objects when the objects are not actually before the eye, but are called up into our memories, or formed into agreeable visions of things that are either absent or fictitious.

The pleasures of the imagination, taken in their full extent, are not so gross as those of sense, nor so refined as those of the understanding. The last are, indeed, more preferable, because they are founded on some new knowledge or improvement in the mind of man; yet it must be confest that those of the imagination are as great and as transporting as the other. A beautiful prospect delights the soul as much as a demonstration, and a description in Homer has charmed more readers than a chapter in Aristotle. Besides, the pleasures of the imagination have this advantage above those of the understanding, that they are more obvious, and more easy to be acquired. It is but opening the eye, and the scene enters. The colours paint themselves on the fancy with very little attention of thought or application of mind in the beholder. We are struck, we know not how, with the symmetry of any thing we see, and immediately assent to the beauty of an object without inquiring into the particular causes and occasions of it.

A man of polite imagination is let into a great many pleasures that the vulgar are not capable of receiving. He can converse with a picture, and find an agreeable companion in a statue. He meets with a secret refreshment in a description, and often feels a greater satisfaction in the prospect of fields and meadows than another does in the possession. It gives him, indeed, a kind of property in every thing he sees, and makes the most rude uncultivated parts of nature administer to his pleasures: so that he looks upon the world as it were in another light, and discovers in it a multitude of charms that conceal themselves from the generality of mankind.

There are, indeed, but very few who know how to be idle and innocent, or have a relish of any pleasures that are not criminal; every diversion they take is at the expence of some one virtue or another, and their very first step out of business is into vice or folly. A man should endeavour, therefore, to make the sphere of his innocent pleasures as wide as possible, that he may retire into them with safety, and find in them such a satisfaction as a wise man would not blush to take. Of this nature are those of the imagination, which do not require such a bent of thought as is necessary to our more serious employments, nor, at the same time, suffer the mind to sink into that negligence and remissness which are apt to accompany our more sensual delights, but, like a gentle exercise to the faculties, awaken them from sloth and idleness, without putting them upon any labour or difficulty.

We might here add that the pleasures of the fancy are more conducive to health than those of the understanding, which are worked out by dint of thinking, and attended with too violent a labour of the brain. Delightful scenes, whether in nature, painting, or poetry, have a kindly influence on the body as well as the mind, and not only serve to clear and brighten the imagination, but are able to disperse grief and melancholy, and to set the animal spirits in pleasing and agreeable motions. For this reason Sir Francis Bacon, in his Essay upon Health, has not thought it improper to prescribe to his reader a poem or a prospect, where he particularly dissuades him from knotty and subtile disquisitions, and advises him to pursue studies that fill the mind with splendid and illustrious objects, as histories, fables, and contemplations of nature.

I have in this paper, by way of introduction, settled the notion of those pleasures of the imagination which are the subject of my present undertaking, and endeavoured by several considerations, to recommend to my reader the pursuit of these pleasures. I shall, in my next paper, examine the several sources from whence these pleasures are derived.

NO. 412. MONDAY, JUNE 23.

Pleasures of the Imagination

———————Divisum sic breve fiet opus.

MART. Ep. iv. 83.

The work, divided aptly, shorter grows.

I shall first consider those pleasures of the imagination, which arise from the actual view and survey of outward objects: and these, I think, all proceed from the sight of what is great, uncommon, or beautiful. There may, indeed, be something so terrible or offensive that the horror or loathsomeness of an object may over-bear the pleasure which results from its greatness, novelty, or beauty; but still there will be such a mixture of delight in the very disgust it gives us, as any of these three qualifications are most conspicuous and prevailing.

By greatness I do not only mean the bulk of any single object, but the largeness of a whole view considered as one entire piece. Such are the prospects of an open champaign country, a vast uncultivated desert, of huge heaps of mountains, high rocks and precipices, or a wide expanse of waters, where we are not struck with the novelty or beauty of the sight, but with that rude kind of magnificence which appears in many of these stupendous works of nature. Our imagination loves to be filled with an object, or to grasp at any thing that is too big for its capacity. We are flung into a pleasing astonishment at such unbounded views, and feel a delightful stillness and amazement in the soul at the apprehension of them. The mind of man naturally hates everything that looks like a restraint upon it, and is apt to fancy itself under a sort of confinement when the sight is pent up in a narrow compass and shortened on every side by the neighbourhood of walls or mountains. On the contrary, a spacious horizon is an image of liberty, where the eye has room to range abroad, to expatiate at large on the immensity of its views, and to lose itself amidst the variety of objects that offer themselves to its observation. Such wide and undetermined prospects are as pleasing to the fancy as the speculations of eternity or infinitude are to the understanding. But if there be a beauty or uncommonness joined with this grandeur, as in a troubled ocean, a heaven adorned with stars and meteors, or a spacious landscape cut out into rivers, woods, rocks, and meadows, the pleasure still grows upon us, as it rises from more than a single principle.

Everything that is new or uncommon raises a pleasure in the imagination, because it fills the soul with an agreeable surprise, gratifies its curiosity, and gives it an idea of which it was not before possest. We are indeed so often conversant with one set of objects, and tired out with so many repeated shows of the same things, that whatever is new or uncommon contributes a little to vary human life, and to divert our minds, for a while, with the strangeness of its appearance: it serves us for a kind of refreshment, and takes off from that satiety we are apt to complain of in our usual and ordinary entertainments. It is this that bestows charms on a monster, and makes even the imperfections of nature please us. It is this that recommends variety, where the mind is every instant called off to something new, and the attention not suffered to dwell too long and waste itself on any particular object. It is this, likewise, that improves what is great or beautiful, and makes it afford the mind a double entertainment. Groves, fields, and meadows are at any season of the year pleasant to look upon, but never so much as in the opening of spring, when they are all new and fresh, with their first gloss upon them, and not yet too much accustomed and familiar to the eye. For this reason there is nothing that more enlivens a prospect than rivers, jetteaus, or falls of water, where the scene is perpetually shifting, and entertaining the sight every

moment with something that is new. We are quickly tired of
looking upon hills and vallies, where everything continues
fixed and settled in the same place and posture, but find our
thoughts a little agitated and relieved at the sight of such
objects as are ever in motion and sliding away from beneath
the eye of the beholder.

But there is nothing that makes its way more directly to
the soul than beauty, which immediately diffuses a secret
satisfaction and complacency through the imagination, and
gives a finishing to any thing that is great or uncommon. The
very first discovery of it strikes the mind with an inward
joy, and spreads a chearfulness and delight through all its
faculties. There is not perhaps any real beauty or deformity
more in one piece of matter than another, because we might
have been so made that whatsoever now appears loathsome
to us might have shewn itself agreeable; but we find by experience that there are several modifications of matter, which
the mind, without any previous consideration, pronounces at
first sight beautiful or deformed. Thus we see that every
different species of sensible creatures has its different notions
of beauty, and that each of them is most affected with the
beauties of its own kind. This is no where more remarkable
than in birds of the same shape and proportion, where we
often see the male determined in his courtship by the single
grain or tincture of a feather, and never discovering any
charms but in the colour of its species.

Scit thalamo servare fidem, sanctasque veretur
Connubii leges, non illum in pectore candor
Splendida lanugo, vel honesta in vertice crista,
Sollicitat niveus; neque pravum accendit amorem
Purpureusve nitor pennarum; ast agmina latè
Fœminea explorat cautus, maculasque requirit
Cognatas, paribusque interlita corpora guttis:
Ni faceret, pictis sylvam circum undique monstris
Confusam aspiceres vulgò, partusque biformes,
Et genus ambiguum, et Veneris monumenta nefandæ.
    Hinc merula in nigro se oblectat nigra marito,
Hinc socium lasciva petit Philomela canorum,
Agnoscitque pares sonitus, hinc noctua tetram

Canitiem alarum, et glaucos miratur ocellos.
Nempe sibi semper constat, crescitque quotannis
Lucida progenies, castos confessa parentes;
Dum virides inter saltus lucosque sonoros
Vere novo exultat, plumasque decora Juventus
Explicat ad solem, patriisque coloribus ardet.[15]

The feather'd husband, to his partner true,
Preserves connubial rites inviolate.
With cold indifference ev'ry charm he sees,
The milky whiteness of the stately neck,
The shining down, proud crest, and purple wings,
But cautious with a searching eye explores
The female tribes, his proper mate to find.
With kindred colours mark'd: did he not so,
The grove with painted monsters would abound,
Th' ambiguous product of unnatural love.
The black-bird hence selects her sooty spouse;
The nightingale her musical compeer,
Lur'd by the well-known voice; the bird of night,
Smit with his dusky wings, and greenish eyes,
Woos his dun paramour. The beauteous race
Speak the chaste loves of their progenitors;
When, by the spring invited, they exult
In woods and fields, and to the sun unfold
Their plumes, that with paternal colours glow.

There is a second kind of beauty that we find in the several products of art and nature which does not work in the imagination with that warmth and violence as the beauty that appears in our proper species, but is apt, however, to raise in us a secret delight, and a kind of fondness for the places or objects in which we discover it. This consists either in the gaiety or variety of colours, in the symmetry and proportion of parts, in the arrangement and disposition of bodies, or in a just mixture and concurrence of all together. Among these kinds of beauty the eye takes most delight in colours. We no where meet with a more glorious or pleasing show in nature than what appears in the heavens at the rising and

[15] The Latin verses are apparently by Addison. The translation first appeared anonymously in the 1744 edition of the *Spectator*.

setting of the sun, which is wholly made up of those different stains of light that shew themselves in clouds of a different
situation. For this reason we find the poets, who are always
addressing themselves to the imagination, borrowing more of
their epithets from colours than from any other topic.

As the fancy delights in every thing that is great, strange,
or beautiful, and is still more pleased the more it finds of
these perfections in the same object, so is it capable of receiving new satisfaction by the assistance of another sense.
Thus any continued sound, as the music of birds, or a fall
of water, awakens every moment the mind of the beholder,
and makes him more attentive to the several beauties of the
place that lie before him. Thus if there arises a fragrancy of
smells or perfumes, they heighten the pleasure of the imagination, and make even the colours and verdure of the landscape
appear more agreeable; for the ideas of both senses recommend each other, and are pleasanter together than when they
enter the mind separately, as the different colours of a
picture, when they are well disposed, set off one another and
receive an additional beauty from the advantage of their
situation.

NO. 417. SATURDAY, JUNE 28.

Pleasures of the Imagination.

Quem tu Melpomene semel
Nascentem placido lumine videris,
   Non illum labor Isthmius
Clarabit pugilem, non equus impiger, &c
Sed quæ Tibur aquæ fertile perfluunt,
   Et spissæ nemorum comæ
Fingent Æolio carmine nobilem.

                  Hor. 4. Od. iii. 1.

At whose blest birth propitious rays
The muses shed, on whom they smile,

           No dusty Isthmian game
    Shall stoutest of the ring proclaim,
        Or, to reward his toil,
    Wreath ivy crowns, and grace his head with bays.
        But fruitful Tibur's shady groves,
        Its pleasant springs and purling streams,
            Shall raise a lasting name,
        And set him high in sounding fame
            For Lyric verse.
                                                    CREECH.

We may observe that any single circumstance of what we
have formerly seen often raises up a whole scene of imagery,
and awakens numberless ideas that before slept in the imagination; such a particular smell or colour is able to fill the
mind, on a sudden, with the picture of the fields or gardens
where we first met with it, and to bring up into view all the
variety of images that once attended it. Our imagination takes
the hint, and leads us unexpectedly into cities or theatres,
plains or meadows. We may further observe, when the fancy
thus reflects on the scenes that have past in it formerly, those
which were at first pleasant to behold appear more so upon
reflection, and that the memory heightens the delightfulness
of the original. A Cartesian would account for both these instances in the following manner.

    The set of ideas, which we received from such a prospect
or garden, having entered the mind at the same time, have a
set of traces belonging to them in the brain, bordering very
near upon one another; when, therefore, any one of these
ideas arises in the imagination, and consequently dispatches a
flow of animal spirits to its proper trace, these spirits, in the
violence of their motion, run not only into the trace, to which
they were more particularly directed, but into several of those
that lie about it: by this means they awaken other ideas of
the same set, which immediately determine a new dispatch
of spirits, that in the same manner open other neighbouring
traces, till at last the whole set of them is blown up, and the
whole prospect or garden flourishes in the imagination. But
because the pleasure we received from these places far sur-
mounted and overcame the disagreeableness we found in

them, for this reason there was at first a wider passage worn in the pleasure traces, and on the contrary so narrow a one in those which belonged to the disagreeable ideas, that they were quickly stopt up, and rendered incapable of receiving any animal spirits, and consequently of exciting any unpleasant ideas in the memory.

It would be in vain to inquire, whether the power of imagining things strongly proceeds from any greater perfection in the soul, or from any nicer texture in the brain of one man than of another. But this is certain, that a noble writer should be born with this faculty in its full strength and vigour, so as to be able to receive lively ideas from outward objects, to retain them long, and to range them together, upon occasion, in such figures and representations as are most likely to hit the fancy of the reader. A poet should take as much pains in forming his imagination as a philosopher in cultivating his understanding. He must gain a due relish of the works of nature, and be thoroughly conversant in the various scenery of a country life.

When he is stored with country images, if he would go beyond pastoral and the lower kinds of poetry, he ought to acquaint himself with the pomp and magnificence of courts. He should be very well versed in every thing that is noble and stately in the productions of art, whether it appear in painting or statuary, in the great works of architecture which are in their present glory, or in the ruins of those which flourished in former ages.

Such advantages as these help to open a man's thoughts and to enlarge his imagination, and will therefore have their influence on all kinds of writing, if the author knows how to make a right use of them. And among those of the learned languages who excel in this talent, the most perfect in their several kinds are, perhaps, Homer, Virgil, and Ovid. The first strikes the imagination wonderfully with what is great, the second with what is beautiful, and the last with what is strange. Reading the *Iliad* is like travelling through a country uninhabited, where the fancy is entertained with a thousand savage prospects of vast deserts, wide uncultivated marshes, huge forests, misshapen rocks and precipices. On the contrary, the *Æneid* is like a well ordered garden, where it is impossible to find out any part unadorned, or to cast our eyes upon a single spot that does not produce some beautiful plant or flower. But when we are in the *Metamorphosis* we are walking on enchanted ground, and see nothing but scenes of magic lying round us.

Homer is in his province when he is describing a battle or a multitude, a hero or a god. Virgil is never better pleased than when he is in Elysium, or copying out an entertaining picture. Homer's epithets generally mark out what is great, Virgil's what is agreeable. Nothing can be more magnificent than the figure Jupiter makes in the first *Iliad*, nor more charming than that of Venus in the first *Æneid*.

῍Η, καὶ κυανέῃσιν ἐπ᾽ ὀφρύσι νεῦσε Κρονίων·
Ἀμβρόσιαι δ᾽ ἄρα χαῖται ἐπερρώσαντο ἄνακτος,
Κρατὸς ἀπ᾽ ἀθανάτοιο· μέγαν δ᾽ ἐλέλιξεν Ὄλυμπον.

Il. 1. v. 528

He spoke, and awful bends his sable brows,
Shakes his ambrosial curls, and gives the nod,
The stamp of fate, and sanction of the god:
High heav'n with trembling the dread signal took,
And all Olympus to the centre shook.

Pope

Dixit, et avertens roseâ cervice refulsit:
Ambrosiæque comæ divinum vertice odorem
Spiravere: pedes vestis defluxit ad imos:
Et vera incessu patuit Dea————

Æn, 1. v. 406

Thus having said, she turn'd, and made appear,
Her neck refulgent and dishevell'd hair;
Which flowing from her shoulders, reach'd the ground,
And widely spread ambrosial scents around:
In length of train descends her sweeping gown,
And by her graceful walk the queen of love is known.

Dryden

Homer's persons are most of them god-like and terrible;

Virgil has scarce admitted any into his poem who are not beautiful, and has taken particular care to make his hero so.

———————— lumenque juventæ
Purpureum, et lætos oculis afflavit honores.

Æn. 1. v. 594

And gave his rolling eyes a sparkling grace,
And breath'd a youthful vigor on his face.

DRYDEN

In a word, Homer fills his readers with sublime ideas and, I believe, has raised the imagination of all the good poets that have come after him. I shall only instance Horace, who immediately takes fire at the first hint of any passage in the *Iliad* or *Odyssey* and always rises above himself, when he has Homer in his view. Virgil has drawn together into his *Æneid* all the pleasing scenes his subject is capable of admitting, and in his *Georgics* has given us a collection of the most delightful landscapes that can be made out of fields and woods, herds of cattle, and swarms of bees.

Ovid, in his *Metamorphosis,* has shewn us how the imagination may be affected by what is strange. He describes a miracle in every story, and always gives us the sight of some new creature at the end of it. His art consists chiefly in well-timing his description before the first shape is quite worn off and the new one perfectly finished, so that he every where entertains us with something we never saw before, and shews monster after monster to the end of the *Metamorphosis.*

If I were to name a poet that is a perfect master in all these arts of working on the imagination, I think Milton may pass for one: and if his *Paradise Lost* falls short of the *Æneid* or *Iliad* in this respect, it proceeds rather from the fault of the language in which it is written than from any defect of genius in the author. So divine a poem in English is like a stately palace built of brick, where one may see architecture in as great a perfection as in one of marble, though the materials are of a coarser nature. But to consider it only as it regards our present subject: what can be conceived greater than the battle of angels, the majesty of Messiah, the stature and behaviour of Satan and his peers? What more beautiful than Pandæmonium, Paradise, Heaven, Angels, Adam and Eve? What more strange than the creation of the world, the several metamorphoses of the fallen angels, and the surprising adventures their leader meets with in his search after Paradise? No other subject could have furnished a poet with scenes so proper to strike the imagination, as no other poet could have painted those scenes in more strong and lively colours.

NO. 418. MONDAY, JUNE 30.

Pleasures of the Imagination.

——————————ferat et rubus asper amomum.
VIRG. Ecl. iii. 89.
The rugged thorn shall bear the fragrant rose.

The pleasures of these secondary views of the imagination are of a wider and more universal nature than those it has when joined with sight; for not only what is great, strange, or beautiful, but anything that is disagreeable when looked upon, pleases us in an apt description. Here, therefore, we must inquire after a new principle of pleasure, which is nothing else but the action of the mind, which compares the ideas that arise from words with the ideas that arise from the objects themselves; and why this operation of the mind is attended with so much pleasure, we have before considered. For this reason, therefore, the description of a dung-hill is pleasing to the imagination, if the image be presented to our minds by suitable expressions; though perhaps this may be more properly called the pleasure of the understanding than of the fancy, because we are not so much delighted with the image that is contained in the description, as with the aptness of the description to excite the image.

But if the description of what is little, common, or deformed, be acceptable to the imagination, the description of what is great, surprising, or beautiful, is much more so, because here we are not only delighted with comparing the representation with the original, but are highly pleased with the original itself. Most readers, I believe, are more charmed with Milton's description of Paradise than of Hell: they are both, perhaps, equally perfect in their kind, but in the one the brimstone and sulphur are not so refreshing to the imagination as the beds of flowers and the wilderness of sweets in the other.

There is yet another circumstance which recommends a description more than all the rest, and that is if it represents to us such objects as are apt to raise a secret ferment in the mind of the reader, and to work with violence upon his passions. For, in this case, we are at once warmed and enlightened, so that the pleasure becomes more universal, and is several ways qualified to entertain us. Thus, in painting, it is pleasant to look on the picture of any face where the resemblance is hit, but the pleasure increases if it be the picture of a face that is beautiful, and is still greater if the beauty be softened with an air of melancholy or sorrow. The two leading passions which the more serious parts of poetry endeavour to stir up in us are terror and pity. And, by the way, one would wonder how it comes to pass that such passions as are very unpleasant at all other times are very agreeable when excited by proper descriptions. It is not strange that we should take delight in such passages as are apt to produce hope, joy, admiration, love, or the like emotion in us, because they never rise in the mind without an inward pleasure which attends them. But how comes it to pass that we should take delight in being terrified or dejected by a description, when we find so much uneasiness in the fear or grief which we receive from any other occasion?

If we consider, therefore, the nature of this pleasure, we shall find that it does not arise so properly from the description of what is terrible, as from the reflection we make on ourselves at the time of reading it. When we look on such hideous objects, we are not a little pleased to think we

are in danger of them. We consider them at the same time
as dreadful and harmless, so that the more frightful appearance they make, the greater is the pleasure we receive from
the sense of our own safety. In short, we look upon the terrors
of a description with the same curiosity and satisfaction that
we survey a dead monster.

> ————Informe cadaver
> Protrahitur: nequeunt expleri corda tuendo
> Terribiles oculos, vultum, villosaque setis
> Pectora semiferi, atque extinctos faucibus ignes.
>
> VIRG. Æn. viii. v. 264

> ————They drag him from his den
> The wond'ring neighbourhood, with glad surprise,
> Beheld his shagged breast, his giant size,
> His mouth that flames no more, and his extinguished eyes.
>
> DRYDEN

It is for the same reason that we are delighted with the
reflecting upon dangers that are past, or in looking on a precipice at a distance which would fill us with a different kind
of horror if we saw it hanging over our heads.

In the like manner, when we read of torments, wounds,
deaths, and like dismal accidents, our pleasure does not flow
so properly from the grief which such melancholy descriptions give us, as from the secret comparison which we make
between ourselves and the person who suffers. Such representations teach us to set a just value upon our own condition, and make us prize our good fortune which exempts us
from the like calamities. This is, however, such a kind of
pleasure as we are not capable of receiving when we see
a person actually lying under the tortures that we meet with
in a description, because, in this case, the object presses too
close upon our senses, and bears so hard upon us that it
does not give us time or leisure to reflect on ourselves. Our
thoughts are so intent upon the miseries of the sufferer that
we cannot turn them upon our own happiness; whereas, on
the contrary, we consider the misfortunes we read in history
or poetry either as past or as fictitious, so that the reflection

upon ourselves rises in us insensibly, and over-bears the sorrow we conceive for the sufferings of the afflicted.

But because the mind of man requires something more perfect in matter than what it finds there, and can never meet with any sight in nature which sufficiently answers its highest ideas of pleasantness; or, in other words, because the imagination can fancy to itself things more great, strange, or beautiful than the eye ever saw, and is still sensible of some defect in what it has seen; on this account it is the part of a poet to humour the imagination in its own notions by mending and perfecting nature where he describes a reality, and by adding greater beauties than are put together in nature where he describes a fiction.[16]

He is not obliged to attend her in the slow advances which she makes from one season to another, or to observe her conduct in the successive production of plants and flowers. He may draw into his description all the beauties of the spring and autumn, and make the whole year contribute something to render it more agreeable. His rose-trees, woodbines, and jessamines may flower together, and his beds be covered at the same time with lilies, violets, and amaranths. His soil is not restrained to any particular set of plants, but is proper either for oaks or myrtles, and adapts itself to the products of every climate. Oranges may grow wild in it; myrrh may be met with in every hedge, and if he thinks it proper to have a grove of spices, he can quickly command sun enough to raise it. If all this will not furnish out an agreeable scene, he can make several new species of flowers, with richer scents and higher colours than any that grow in the gardens of nature. His concerts of birds may be as full and harmonious, and his woods as thick and gloomy as he pleases. He is at no more expence in a long vista than a short one, and can as easily throw his cascades from a precipice of half a mile high as from one of twenty yards. He has his choice of the winds, and can turn the course of his

[16] In this paragraph Addison is bringing to a focus a view of the poet as divine creator which derived from classical criticism and had been memorably expressed in the renaissance by Scaliger in the *Poetics* (see Smith and Parks, *The Great Critics*, 1951, p. 157).

rivers in all the variety of meanders that are most delightful to the reader's imagination. In a word, he has the modelling of nature in his own hands, and may give her what charms he pleases, provided he does not reform her too much, and run into absurdities by endeavouring to excel.

CHARLES GILDON
[1665–1725]

Charles Gildon ran through a modest estate, and then
attempted to maintain a livelihood as a hack author. His
first notable publication was a volume of critical remarks
on Shakespeare's plays published by Curll in 1709 and
intended to pass as a seventh volume of Rowe's edition
(and as such reprinted in 1968). A "Life of Betterton"
appeared with an edition of Betterton's The Amorous
Widow in 1710. He fell afoul of Pope in 1714 upon
publishing "The New Rehearsal, or Bays the Younger,
containing an examen of Mr. Rowe's Plays, and a word or
two on Mr. Pope's 'Rape of the Lock,' " and was thereafter
dependent upon the patronage of the Whigs.

The Complete Art of Poetry appeared in two volumes
in 1718. The critical work by which he is best known, the
book presents Gildon's defense of Homer against the
cavils of Scaliger, Perault, de la Motte, and Wotton,
among others. Gildon also conducted The Athenian Oracle,
published several miscellanies, and composed at least two
tragedies, neither of which were notably successful.

Gildon was described at his death as a "person of great
literature but mean genius." The present selection does
little to alter that opinion. The Laws of Poetry, as laid down
by the Duke of Buckinghamshire . . . explain'd and
Illustrated, however, shows that Gildon had learned well the
lessons which Dennis had been teaching, and his use of
the word "sublime" is worth considering, as are also his
remarks on blank verse and his vacillating efforts to define
"genius" and "wit." It is impossible to determine exactly the

*audience for which Gildon was writing, but from the general
tone of the writing and the unprepossessing physical
appearance of his book one can hardly suppose that it was
directed to the literary elite. His treatise, then, suggests a
public being prepared unknowingly for the subsequent
appearance of Thomson and of the new poetry of the 1740's.*

   *The present selection is adapted from the Library of
Congress copy of the first edition, 1721. See also:*

Litz, F. E.: "The Sources of Gildon's Complete Art of
    Poetry," ELH IX (1942), 118–35. [*Consult also the
    review of this article by Hoyt Trowbridge, PQ XXII
    (1943), 159.*]
Maxwell, J. C.: "Charles Gildon and the Quarrel of the
    Ancients and Moderns," RES, new ser. I (1950), 55–57.

Horace . . . , in his epistle to Lollius, assures us that Homer
has taught us morality much better than Chrysippus and
Crantor, two philosophers of a very considerable reputation
in those times; from all which it will appear, that as no particular prose author of Greece itself could pretend to all
those excellencies which are so eminent in Homer; so that
this maxim of the *Essay,* that *Soul-moving Poetry shines most
sublime,* is established beyond all manner of controversy.

Most sublime in its cause or rise, most sublime in its matter, most sublime in its manner, and most sublime in its aim
or end; most sublime in its cause or rise, if we respect either
its antiquity, or the occasion which produced it; for poetry
is as old as mankind, coeval with [the] human race, and was

invented as soon as man thought of addressing either his prayers or his praise to heaven, and that was as soon as man reflected on the supreme being that had given him life; for the first poetry is agreed to have been praise and thanksgiving to God; it was therefore truly sublime in its cause and rise; it was likewise sublime in its matter, or the subjects of which it treated; that is, not only the praise and thanksgiving of and to the Deity, which, as I have said, gave it birth, but it celebrated eminent virtue in great men or heroes; it taught all the useful and necessary arts that could contribute to the happiness of mankind, nor was there any thing instructive which was not originally delivered in verse; as religion, or the worship of God, the moral duties of men, and those political maxims which were necessary to the subsistence of human society.

It shines likewise *most sublime* in its manner, which consists of number and harmony, by which its instructions were conveyed with pleasure. It is likewise *most sublime* in its aim or end; for it is not only directed to praise and thanksgiving, to the celebration of great men, and great virtues, and those other things mentioned already, but to the polishing [of] mankind, refining and moderating their passions, and bringing them into perfect subjection to reason, without which we should seek for happiness in vain; but the wonders that this sublime art has done in the world, we find thus described in Horace's *Art of Poetry*, as translated by my lord Roscommon:

> *Orpheus,* inspired by more than human power,
> Did not (as Poets feign) tame savage beasts,
> But men as lawless and as wild as they,
> And first dissuaded from that rage and blood.
> Thus when *Amphion* built the *Theban* wall,
> They feigned the stones obeyed his magick lute.
> Poets, the first instructers of mankind,
> Brought all things to their proper native use:
> Some they appropriated to the gods,
> And some to publick, some to private ends:
> Promiscuous love by marriage was restrained,
> Cities were built, and useful laws were made.
> So ancient is the pedigree of verse,

And so divine a poet's function.
Then *Homer's* and *Tyrtæus'* martial muse
Wakened the world, and sounded loud alarms.
To verse we owe the sacred oracles,
And our best precepts of morality.
Some have by verse obtained the love of kings,
Who with the muses ease their wearied minds.
Then blush not, noble *Piso,* to protect
What gods inspire, and kings delight to hear.

[*Ars Poetica,* 390–407]

I think I may conclude from these considerations, and all that has been urged upon this head, that it is sufficiently evident, that

Among the famed remains of ancient time,
Soul-moving poetry shines most sublime.

From this eulogy of the ancients, the *Essay* brings us naturally and easily to the consideration of poetry in general.

No sort of work requires so nice a touch,
And, finished well, nothing delights so much.

The truth of these lines is founded not only upon the best authority, but reason; for though all sorts of polite writing require care and correctness, yet poetry challenges a nicer touch, something above all other arts, something more perfect and more accomplished, something that not only touches the soul, but penetrates into its inmost recesses, fully gratifies all its great faculties, and moves its passion; giving by that means a pleasure peculiar to itself, and much above all that we can derive from any other sort of writing. But to obtain this effect, it ought to be touched in the most nice and fine manner; for the pleasure it affords is greater or less, as the source of pleasure is managed with greater, or less address.

'Tis certain that though the author of the *Essay* has been pleased to take notice only of the pleasure of a well finished piece of poetry, yet there is nothing valuable in that art that does not convey instruction as well as delight. But the reason why my Lord has only taken notice of the latter I take to be because whatever instruction we receive from poetry must be delivered with pleasure, which, if wanting, we never can arrive at the profitable; and this is the reason why Horace will not admit of a mediocrity in poetry, because an indifferent poet can never give us that delight which is absolutely necessary to make his instructions of any force, since the very instructions themselves are the effect of the pleasure we receive from the performance; so that if that be languid and weak, the very end of this sort of writing is lost. Horace says,

> ————*Mediocribus esse poetis*
> *Non di, non homines, non concessere columnæ.*

which my lord Roscommon translates thus:

> Some things admit of mediocrity:
> A counsellor or pleader at the bar
> May want *Massala's* powerful eloquence,
> Or be less read then deep *Casselius;*
> Yet this indifferent lawyer is esteemed.
> But no authority of Gods nor men
> Allow of any mean in poesy.
>
> [*Ars Poetica* 370–373]

.   .   .

But though we have had no patrons of poetry, except Sir Philip Sidney, in this nation, yet we have not been without some very eminent poets, a fate peculiar to England; for poetry never appeared in any other nation in any manner of eminence without extraordinary encouragement, but here without the least.

Chaucer was the first that is of any consideration who enriched his mother-tongue with poetry; but Chaucer was a man of quality, a knight of the garter, and of so considerable a fortune as to marry into the family of John of Gaunt, the father of our Henry the Fourth, and grandfather to the second English monarch who conquered France; so that he had no need of encouragement to exert that excellent genius, of which he was master, in poetry. After him we had no man that made any figure in English verse, till the Earl of Surrey, in the time of Henry the Eighth, who very much improved our English numbers.

After the glorious Queen Elizabeth had thoroughly established the reformation, the spirit of poetry seemed to begin in a pleasing dawn to spread more wide, and that in several kinds. Though most of those first rude essays towards it are lost, yet we have still Sir Philip Sidney, whose *Arcadia* Sir William Temple prefers to all performances of that kind, and to which he allows the second rank after the ancients. Spencer, whose *Eclogues* are by some put on a foot with those of Theocritus and Virgil, and are praised by Sir Philip Sidney himself, in that happy age gave this nation a wonderful proof of his excellent genius in poetry, in his *Fairy Queen,* and makes us wish that he had rather chosen Homer and Virgil, with whom he was perfectly acquainted, for his pattern, than Ariosto, whom he very much excelled. But what was the fate of this great man? Why, after the death of his patron, Sir Philip Sidney, he starved.

In the same reign likewise appeared another great, but very irregular genius in Shakespear; but he being a player as well as a poet, the writer was handsomely supported and rewarded by the actor; for from the first appearance of the rude drama in the English tongue it was so popular that it enriched most of those who were concerned in the management of it, and Shakespear himself left above three hundred pounds a year acquired by that means.

Next in time we must place the immortal Ben Johnson, a man not only of complete learning, but of the most consummate comick genius that ever appeared in the world, ancient or modern; but I don't find that he met with encouragement which bore any manner of proportion to his merit: However, the propension of the people to theatrical entertainments produced so considerable an emolument to the poet, as well as the player, that we find the playwrights about this time grew very numerous; but there were none else of any great merit, not excepting Beaumont and Fletcher themselves, who at best have only written two or three tolerable comedies.

The next I shall mention is Mr. Waller; but he was a man of fortune, and stood not in need of any encouragement from others. To him I may add Sir John Suckling and Sir John Denham; the first being a very gallant writer, the second a

very good one in one or two pieces, but they were likewise
men of independent fortunes.

The last and greatest of all that I shall much insist upon,
is the immortal Milton, who, without the help of encouragement from the state, or any particular great and powerful
man, equalled the greatest poets of antiquity, who had the
happiness of enjoying all the encouragement of Greece and
Rome; but then Milton was likewise master of an independent
fortune, which, though not considerable in itself, was yet sufficient to answer all his demands and desires, and to give him
that happy tranquillity and ease which 'tis absolutely necessary a poet should enjoy to make him capable of producing
works truly perfect and admirable.

I might here mention several comick writers after the
restoration, and some few who have performed very well in
tragedy, especially Otway in his *Orphan* and *Venice Preserved*; but those gentlemen found no patrons, no encouragement worthy their labours and extraordinary merit that way.

I may, perhaps, seem to have done an injustice in allowing but one patron to poetry in this nation, since that great
and brave prince, Richard the First, was not only a poet himself, but a great favourer of the *Provencial* poets, who were
the only people of that age that made any figure in verse, and
from whom Petrarch and the first Italian versifiers borrowed
their manner and most of their beauties.

I mentioned not this king as an English patron because
all his favours were bestowed upon foreign poets; but this
might be because none of his country at that time appeared
worthy of his royal encouragement.

Thus it appears that we have had several considerable
poets in England, and some few of the first magnitude, without any encouragement from our great men; but their remissness in this particular cannot proceed from their being
naturally penurious in their pleasures, since, on the contrary,
we have instances too fresh in our memories of their extravagance and even profusion in that particular; witness
above a hundred and fifty thousand pounds subscribed by
them to Italian singers and operas, a sum, if rightly employed,
sufficient to have fixed the British muse in equal perfection

and glory with those of Greece and Rome. The reason therefore must be that we have never had so true a taste of the
sublime and divine art of Poetry as to find from it that transporting pleasure which has always ravished the finer spirits
of those few nations where it has ever eminently flourished,
for if they found this delight, or even a satisfaction equal to
that which they receive from the entertainment of mere sound,
they would be as forward in its encouragement.

.   .   .

[Gildon here introduces a long digression on the state of
literature in Europe, in the course of which he defends Homer
against Madame Dacier. He then turns to the corruption of
taste in England, ascribing it to the faulty system of education, which he describes in some detail.]

.   .   .

The only remedy that I know of (for to reform our education seems an impossible undertaking) is the publication
of books of criticism, which may, at least in time, touch the
minds of men of the finer sense and reason and bring them
over to the side of art and science, whose influence by degrees would bring in all the young *would-be-wits*, and so the
general readers and hearers of poetry.

It was very late before criticism came into England. After
that little Sir Philip Sidney has said of it in his apology for
poetry, Ben Johnson made the earliest steps toward it, not
only in his *Discoveries*, but in his translation of Horace's *Art
of Poetry*. After him I know not of anything until since the
restoration, and then the first attempts that way were very
faulty, that is, in some of the prefaces, and the *Essay on
Dramatic Poetry* of Mr. Dryden's, in which however there is
scarce one just criticism in ten. The first discourse that I remember of true value and excellence in this nature was the
present *Essay* under our consideration, which was followed
by my Lord Roscommon's *Essay on Translated Verse*. Mr.
Rymer, in his translation of Rapin's reflections upon Aristotle
and his criticisms upon the tragedies of the last age, Mr.
Dennis' several learned discourses upon this art, and some few

others, as the translation of Aristotle's *Poetics* with Dacier's notes, etc. have laid down principles enough to reform the taste of every considering man that will read them with any application.

But this must be said of my Lord Duke's *Essay on Poetry,* that as it was the first criticism that appeared in our tongue, at a time when the taste of the town was in a most abandoned condition, so it is alone sufficient to inspire a true knowledge and judgment of the art, and by consequence of giving us a good taste; and it is the more capable of doing this, because the instructions are conveyed in an easy manner, with abundance of good sense and reason, in harmonious verse, which methinks should have fixed it before this time in the minds even of the ladies, so far as to make them despise that wretched stuff which they have of late years so visibly encouraged. But the reason it has not had this effect upon them and some others I conclude is because they have not read it; which that they may is one of the chief reasons of my reviewing it now in this manner, and offering it to their hands, with my imperfect commentaries, to show, as well as I can, not only my value for it, but its real merit, and how worthy it is of their serious perusal, and how loudly it challenges all their attention and application to fix it in their understanding and memory.

I shall therefore now proceed to the Essay itself.

> Number, and rhime, and that harmonious sound,
> Which never does the ear with harshness wound,
> Are necessary, yet but vulgar arts;
> For all in vain these superficial parts
> Contribute to the structure of the whole,
> Without a genius too, for that's the soul.

Before I proceed to a consideration of the particular and judicious instruction of these lines, it seems incumbent upon me to remove an objection raised by the ignorant against the three first lines, as if the noble author were guilty of a sort of tautology, when he mentions,

> Number and ———— that harmonious sound,
> That never does the ear with harshness wound.

As two distinct qualities or perfections, of which the poet is obliged to be master; whereas, say they, Number includes

Harmonious sound,
That never does the ear with harshness wound.

But if the gentlemen who make this objection had been acquainted with the true force of the *rhythmus*, or fluency of numbers, in that necessary apposition of different numbers, and those which ought to proceed and follow each other in order to produce a perfect harmonious variety, they would have found that though a poet may be free from false quantities or numbers, he may yet fall short of that harmonious sound, which never wounds the ear with harshness of satiety; for example, a verse composed of five Iambics, or five long and five short syllables, has number, or true quantity, but yet may be often harsh, and must want, by the uniformity of cadence, that variety that produces the harmony which our author requires; and therefore Dryden and Milton, the greatest masters of English versification, have frequently given us two or three short quantities together, to attain this agreeable end. This I have shown of Mr. Dryden, in my *Complete Art of Poetry*, to which I refer the reader; the same may be found likewise in Milton by any nice and judicious reader.

It was a perfect skill in this particular, which gave Virgil that singular harmony of versification above all the other Latin poets, in so eminent a degree that it may be distinguished even by some that do not understand Latin; as we have an instance in France of a certain gentleman of figure, whose name I have forgot, who, at the hearing of certain verses of Virgil repeated in company with those of several other poets, would never fail to point out the verses of Virgil from all the rest.

·   ·   ·

A third thing in these verses of the *Essay*, and which it seems to make a necessary part of poetry, is the rhime. Though I cannot agree with the *Essay*, that rhime is a necessary part of poetry, yet this may be said in the author's excuse, that it was established as such at the time when this Essay was written, nothing having then appeared in blank verse (as they call it) but Milton's *Paradise Lost*, and that known then but to a few and esteemed by some of them defective in that particular, which made Dryden write his *State of Innocence* in rhime, thinking Milton's thoughts and images imperfect without that jingle; nay, Dryden was so fond of rhime that he brought it upon the stage, and established it so far by his success that he ventured in one of his prefaces to say that it had now so strong a possession of the stage that he durst prophesy no play would take without it; and yet he saw in less than a year's time that scarce any play would be received with it. This change was caused not only by the *Rehearsal,* but also by several admirable reflections in this *Essay,* which we shall hereafter take notice of

After Milton had prevailed in the world, the authors of jingle gave up the greater poetry, at least the epic and tragic poems, to blank verse, that is, to verse without rhime, to number and harmony of sound, in which rhime had really no share, and to which not the least just claim. But then they yet insist that it is necessary in all the shorter poems, but with no greater ground in truth than in the former; for wherever there is force and genius expressed in numbers and harmony, we shall find there is not the least occasion for rhime.

.   .   .

There is nothing more judicious than what is here delivered by the *Essay,* viz. that *number* and *rhime* are but vulgar arts, mean and low accomplishments, and mere superficial parts that have no share in the essence of poetry, since that consists in imitation, and imitation is not to be obtained in any sovereign degree without a great genius, but may subsist, and in great perfection too, without verse, and much more without rhime; the harmony of numbers are added to poetry, not as essential to that art, but as agreeable ornaments to recommend it. This is Aristotle's opinion, which he founds upon this reason, that if any one should turn Herodotus into verse, it would notwithstanding still be a history; and on the

other side, if any one should put the *Iliads* of Homer into
prose, it would however effectually remain a poem. But unknowing of this admirable precept of the *Essay*, most if not
all of our taking and popular versifiers have supposed that
the chief excellence of poetry lies in *number* and *rhime*, in
a flowing smoothness of verse, which is now very common,
and a sort of quaintness of expression; and this ignorance and
folly has spread so far, and is so grounded in the many, that
we have seen the whole art of poetry of English poetry (for
so they are pleased to distinguish it) is confined to these
alone in a book too scandalously mean to name, which, by
the arts of the booksellers concerned, has spread, by many
editions, through all England, and corrupted or at least continued the corruption of the young readers and lovers of
poetry.[1] But as that has no ground in reason and truth; so
this valuable Maxim of the *Essay* is founded on both, and
confirmed by the judgment of the learned and knowing of all
nations and ages.

> Without a genius too, for that's the soul.
> A spirit which inspires the work throughout,
> As that of nature moves the world about;
> A heat which glows in every word that's writ:
> 'Tis something of divine, and more than wit;
> It self unseen, yet all things by it shown,
> Describing all men, but described by none.

As it is sufficiently evident from what has been said, that
the *Essay* is perfectly in the right, and has judiciously determined that number and rhime are but superficial parts of
poetry and contribute very little to the structure of a poem
where there is not a genius to support them and render them
really valuable, so I believe that this assertion, which makes
the *genius* the soul of the work, is too self-evident to need any
confirmation: It is certainly granted on all sides. For whilst
there have been hot disputes whether *art* or *nature* contributed most to the forming of a poet, nobody ever yet con-

---

[1] Gildon is no doubt referring to *The Art of English Poetry* by Edward
Bysshe. First published in 1702, it ran through many editions, reaching
the tenth by 1739. The book is much as Gildon describes it.

tended that there could be a poet without a *genius;* Horace indeed having fixed this maxim, adds that he can't see what use or benefit a rude, uncultivated genius can be of, and by consequence that judgment, or art, is absolutely necessary for the rendering a genius truly valuable; but these conditions of art, or judgment, which Horace requires to be added to a genius, do by no means lessen the truth of what the *Essay* affirms, when he tells us that a *genius* is the *soul.*

> *A spirit which inspires the work throughout,*
> *As that of nature moves the world about.*

It may perhaps be thought proper in this place that I should define a term which is of that visible importance, since there is no greater obstruction to the clear and adequate knowledge of things than the leaving the terms we make use of to a vague and undetermined sense. It is no difficult matter to define a simple idea, or the term which expresses that simple idea; but when there is a term that stands for an idea that is extremely complex, or compounded of great variety of parts, it is not so easy a matter to give a perfect and adequate definition of it. Of this nature are these two terms, *wit* and *genius;* and this is the reason that the former has never yet been so compleatly defined, as to give full satisfaction that the definition was perfectly just; for the general term *wit* stands for so many things so very different in their nature, that they seem by no means capable of being reduced to one and the same individual definition: For example, what the Latins express by the word *ingenium,* we do by the term wit; what they mean by their metaphorical *sal,* by *acumen, lepos,* and some other words, we still express by that of *wit.* The beauties of Homer, Pindar, Sophocles, Euripides, Anacreon, Aristophanes, Menander, Virgil, Horace, Ovid, Terence, and even down to the points of Martial, the burlesk of Scarron and Butler, the biting of satire, and the mirth of our comic poets, and various other things, both serious and gay, we range under this general term *wit;* nay, even *genius* itself is often expressed by *wit;* it is therefore no wonder that we never have had a true and just definition of *wit,* that is, a definition that expresses all its parts and qualities; and I believe I may venture to prophesy that we never shall have any such definition.

What has been said of the term *wit*, will in great part hold good of that of *genius;* which consideration, joined with what is offered in the *Essay*, will, I dare persuade myself, sufficiently excuse me from pretending to define it; however, omitting the fine speculations that are to be found upon this head, as being above the capacity of the general readers, to whom I chuse to speak, I shall venture to say a word or two about a *genius*.

I think it is pretty plain that the Latins expressed what we call *genius* by the word *ingenium,* as it is evident Horace does in his *Art of Poetry;* and if I do not mistake the matter, that word is not embarrassed with so many doubts and so great an obscurity as our word *genius;* which, though I shall not here pretend to define, yet, as far as it relates to poetry, I shall venture to mention some particulars which compose it; as, a strong and clear imagination, or fancy, by which the poet is furnished with the lively images of all things, and enabled by them to form that imitation, which is the life and soul of poetry; for without imitation, there neither is, nor can be, any valuable poetry. There is, besides this, required to a *poetic genius* certain warmth and vigour, which by some is called enthusiasm, and which gives that force and transport to the images that are found in a great poet, and proves what the *Essay* says, that *a genius is the soul of poetry*.

.   .   .

The next sort of poem that the *Essay* takes notice of is the Ode. The words are these:

> A higher flight, and of a happier force
> Are *Odes*, the muses most unruly horse,
> That bounds so fierce, the rider has no rest,
> But foams at mouth, and moves like one possessed.
>
> The poet here must be indeed inspired,
> With fury too, as well as fancy fired.
> *Cowley* might boast to have performed this part,
> Had he with nature joined the rules of art;
> But ill expression gives sometimes allay

To nobler thoughts, whose fame will ne'er decay.
Though all appear in heat and fury done,
The language still must soft and easy run.
These laws may sound a little too severe,
But judgment yields, and fancy governs here;
Which, though extravagant, this muse allows,
And makes the work much easier than it shows.

It is plain that the *Essay* takes notice here only of those odes which we call pindaric; and this, without doubt, is the reason that there is no mention of the particular subjects which the ode admits, because the subjects this ode celebrates among us are sufficiently known to be all sublime, always great and magnificent, and which great subjects it always treats in the most sublime and lofty manner, with the highest warmth, and so great an extravagance of fancy, that it is apt to hurry the writer away beyond all the bounds of reason and judgment, and sometimes make him deviate into the borders of nonsense under the specious name of a heated imagination and poetic enthusiasm; but this warmth, this heat, this fire, their extent and liberties, and the caution which ought to be used in the managing of them, cannot be more fully and emphatically expressed than in the words of the *Essay* itself. [*See pp. 15–16 above.*]

ANTHONY ASHLEY COOPER, THIRD EARL OF SHAFTESBURY
[1671–1713]

Shaftesbury's father was the "shapeless lump" mentioned
in Dryden's famous character of the first earl as Achitophel;
the second earl is noted for nothing else. The education of the
third earl was supervised by John Locke and by a governess
named Elizabeth Birch, who had the accomplishment,
surprising at any time but particularly so in a
seventeenth-century woman, of being able to converse
fluently in Greek and Latin, an ability which she
communicated to her charge. After attending Winchester,
Shaftesbury made the Grand Tour, in the course of which
he learned French so expertly as to be mistaken for a native.
He played some small role in the complicated politics at
the turn of the century, but he had inherited his father's
feeble constitution, and failing health forced him to abandon
politics for literature.

Although educated in the principles of Locke,
Shaftesbury's immediate philosophical forebears were the
Cambridge Platonists and ultimately the Stoics. He believed
that Nature exhibited in itself an esthetic and moral order,
which man was able to discern through the development
of an innate taste, and ultimately through introspection.
In "The Moralists" he wishes to educate men to the
apprehension of the universal order; in "Advice to an
Author" he is concerned with the mode in which that
order can be achieved in poetry. The emphasis which we can
see in the present excerpt is on the conditions of liberty
furthering poetry (for Shaftesbury agreed with Locke in his
Whig principles, if scarcely in his philosophy), and on the

*"just standard of taste" which can only be attained when
Nature is properly perceived.*

*The standard is inward-looking, and to Shaftesbury
much of the subjectivity of later eighteenth-century poetry
and criticism can be traced. Leslie Stephen in 1881 could
speak of him as "one of the writers whose reputation is
scarcely commensurate with the influence which he once
exerted." Such a statement would hardly be made today,
when Shaftesbury is generally recognized as one of those
figures whose ideas are so prevalent and fruitful as themselves
almost to have been lost amongst the luxuriant growths they
stimulated.*

*Leslie Stephen's remains a good account of Shaftesbury
in the context of men in society; Cecil A. Moore's essays
are central to the more recent perception of his literary
importance.* The Characteristicks of Men, Manners, Opinions,
Times *is a collection of interrelated essays published in
1711. It went through many editions in the eighteenth
century, and was edited in 1900 by John M. Robertson.
The text of the selection below is based on the second
edition, 1714.* See also:

Aldridge, Alfred Owen: "Lord Shaftesbury's Literary
      Theories," PQ XXIV (1945), 46–64.
————: "Shaftesbury and the Test of Truth," PMLA LX
      (1945), 129–56.
Best, G. F. A.: Shaftesbury, New York, 1964.
Brett, R. L.: The Third Earl of Shaftesbury: a study in
      eighteenth-century literary theory, London, 1951.
Marsh, Robert: "Shaftesbury's Theory of Poetry: the
      Importance of 'Inward Colloquy,'" ELH XXVIII
      (1961), 54–69.
Moore, Cecil A.: Backgrounds of English Literature,
      1700–1760, Minneapolis, 1953 [including "Shaftesbury
      and the Ethical Poets in England, 1700–1760," PMLA
      XXXI (1916), 264–325; and "The Return to Nature
      in English Poetry of the Eighteenth Century," SP XIV
      (1917), 243–291.]
Morpurgo Tagliabue, Guido: "La nozione di 'gusto' nel
      secolo XVIII: Shaftesbury e Addision," Rivista di Estetica
      VII (1962), 198–228.
Tuveson, Ernest: "Shaftesbury and the Age of Sensibility,"

Studies in Criticism and Aesthetics, 1660–1800 [*ed.*
Howard Anderson and John S. Shea], *Minneapolis,*
1967.

Wolff, Erwin: Shaftesbury und seine Bedeutung für die
Englische Literatur des 18. Jahrhunderts; der Moralist
und die literarische Form, *Tübingen, 1960.*

FROM CHARACTERISTICKS: OR, ADVICE TO AN AUTHOR

[1711]

I must confess there is hardly anywhere to be found a more insipid race of mortals than those whom we moderns are contented to call *Poets* for having attained the chiming faculty of a language with an injudicious random use of wit and fancy. But for the man who truly and in a just sense deserves the name of *Poet*, and who as a real master or architect in the kind can describe both men and manners and give to an action its just body and proportions, he will be found, if I mistake not, a very different creature. Such a poet is indeed a second master, a just Prometheus under Jove. Like that sovereign artist or universal plastic Nature, he forms a *Whole*, coherent and proportioned in itself, with due subjection and subordinacy of constituent parts. He notes the boundaries of the passions, and knows their exact tones and measures, by which he justly represents them, marks the Sublime of sentiments and action, and distinguishes the Beautiful from the Deformed, the Amiable from the Odious. The moral artist, who can thus imitate the Creator, and is thus knowing in the inward form and structure of his fellow-creature, will hardly, I presume, be found unknowing in *himself*, or at a loss in those numbers which make the harmony of a mind. For knavery is mere dissonance and disproportion; and though villains may have strong tones and natural capacity of action, 'tis impossible that true judgment and ingenuity should reside* where harmony and honesty have no being.

But having entered thus seriously into the concerns of authors, and shewn their chief foundation and strength, their preparatory discipline, and qualifying method of self-examination, 'tis fit, ere we disclose this mystery any further, we should consider the advantages or disadvantages our authors may possibly meet with from abroad: and how far their genius may be depressed or raised by any external causes, arising from the humour or judgment of the World.

Whatever it be which influences in this respect must proceed either from the Grandees and men in power, the Criticks and men of art, or the People themselves, the common audience and mere vulgar. We shall begin therefore with the Grandees and pretended masters of the World, taking the liberty, in favour of Authors, to bestow some advice also on these high persons, if possibly they are disposed to receive it in such a familiar way as this.

.   .   .

'Tis scarce a quarter of an age since such a happy balance

---

* The maxim will hardly be disproved by fact or history, either in respect of philosophers themselves, or others who were the great geniuses or masters in the liberal arts. The characters of the ancient tragedians no less. And the great epic master, though of an obscurer and remoter age, was ever presumed to be far enough from a vile or knavish character. The Roman as well as the Grecian orator was true to his country, and died in like manner a martyr for its liberty. And those historians who are of highest value, were either in a private life approved good men, or noted such by their actions in the publick.

of power was settled between our Prince and People as has firmly secured our hitherto precarious liberties and removed from us the fear of civil commotions, wars and violence, either on account of religion and worship, the property of the subject, or the contending titles of the Crown. But, as the greatest advantages of this world are not to be bought at easy prices, we are still at this moment expending both our blood and treasure to secure to ourselves this inestimable purchase of our Free Government and National Constitution. And as happy as we are in this establishment at home, we are still held in a perpetual alarm by the aspect of affairs abroad, and by the terror of that power, which ere mankind had well recovered the misery of those barbarous ages consequent to the Roman yoke, has again threatened the world with a universal monarchy and a new abyss of ignorance and super-stition.[1]

The British Muses, in this din of arms, may well lie abject and obscure, especially being as yet in their mere infant state. They have hitherto scarce arrived to anything of shapeliness or person. They lisp as in their cradles, and their stammering tongues, which nothing beside their youth and rawness can excuse, have hitherto spoken in wretched pun and quibble. Our dramatic Shakespear, our Fletcher, Jonson, and our epic Milton preserve this style. And even a latter race, scarce free of this infirmity and aiming at a false sub-lime with crowded simile and mixed metaphor (the hobby-horse and rattle of the muses), entertain our raw fancy and unpractised ear, which has not as yet had leisure to form itself and become truly musical.

But those reverend bards, rude as they were, according to their time and age, have provided us, however, with the richest ore. To their eternal honour they have withal been the first of Europeans who, since the Gothick model of poetry, attempted to throw off the horrid discord of jingling rhyme. They have asserted ancient poetic Liberty, and have happily broken the ice for those who are to follow them, and who, treading in their footsteps, may at leisure polish our language,

[1] The Shaftesbury is referring to the conquests of Louis XIV.

lead our ear to finer pleasure, and find out the true *Rhythmus* and harmonious numbers which alone can satisfy a just judgment and Muse-like apprehension.

'Tis evident our natural genius shines above that airy neighboring nation, of whom, however, it must be confessed that with truer pains and industry they have sought politeness and studies to give the Muses their due body and proportion, as well as the natural ornaments of correctness, chastity, and grace of style. From the plain model of the Ancients, they have raised a noble satirist.* In the Epic kind their attempts have been less successful. In the Dramatic they have been so happy as to raise their stage to as great perfection as the genius of their nation will permit. But the high spirit of Tragedy can ill subsist where the spirit of liberty is wanting. The genius of this poetry consists in the lively representation of the disorders and misery of the great, to the end that the People and those of a lower condition may be taught the better to content themselves with privacy, enjoy their safer state, and prize the equality and justice of their guardian laws. If this be found agreeable to the just tragic model which the Ancients have delivered to us, it will easily be conceived how little such a model is proportioned to the capacity or taste of those who, in a long series of degrees, from the lowest peasant to the high slave of royal blood, are taught to idolize the next in power above them, and think nothing so adorable as that unlimited greatness and tyrannic power which is raised at their own expence and exercised over themselves.

'Tis easy, on the other hand, to apprehend the advantages of our BRITAIN in this particular, and what effect its established Liberty will produce in everything which relates to art when peace returns to us on these happy conditions. 'Twas the fate of Rome to have scarce an intermediate Age, or single period of time, between the rise of arts and fall of liberty. No sooner had that nation begun to lose the roughness and barbarity of their manners, and learn of

*Boileau

Greece to form their heroes, their orators and poets on a right model, than by their unjust attempt upon the liberty of the world they justly lost their own. With their liberty they lost not only their force of eloquence, but even their style and language itself. The poets who afterwards arose amongst them were mere unnatural and forced plants. Their two most accomplished, who came last, and closed the scene, were plainly such as had seen the days of liberty and felt the sad effects of its departure. Nor had these been ever brought in play otherwise than through the friendship of the famed Mæcenas, who turned a prince naturally cruel and barbarous to the love and courtship of the Muses. These tutoresses formed in their royal pupil a new nature. They taught him how to charm mankind. They were more to him than his arms or military virtue, and, more than Fortune herself, assisted him in his greatness and made his usurped dominion so enchanting to the world that it could see without regret its chains of bondage firmly riveted. The corrupting sweets of such a poisonous government were not indeed long-lived. The bitter soon succeeded. And, in the issue, the world was forced to bear with patience those natural and genuine tyrants who succeeded to this specious machine of arbitrary and universal power.

And now that I am fallen unawares into such profound reflections on the periods of government and the flourishing and decay of Liberty and Letters, I can't be contented to consider merely of the enchantment which wrought so powerfully upon mankind when first this universal monarchy was established. I must wonder still more when I consider how after the extinction of this Cæsarean and Claudian family, and a short interval of princes raised and destroyed with much disorder and public ruin, the Romans should regain their perishing dominion, and retrieve their sinking state by an after-race of wise and able princes successively adopted and taken from a private state to rule the empire of the world. They were men who not only possessed the military virtues and supported that sort of discipline in the highest degree, but as they sought the interest of the world they did what was in their power to restore Liberty, and raise again the perishing arts and decayed virtue of mankind. But the season was now past! The fatal form of government was become too natural: and the world, which had bent under it and was become slavish and dependent, had neither power nor will to help itself. The only deliverance it could expect was from the merciless hands of the Barbarians and a total dissolution of that enormous Empire and despotic power which the best hands could not preserve from being destructive to human nature. For even barbarity and Gothicism were already entered into arts, ere the savages had made any impression on the Empire. All the advantage which a fortuitous and almost miraculous succession of good princes could procure their highly favoured arts and sciences was no more than to preserve during their own time those perishing remains, which had for a while with difficulty subsisted after the decline of Liberty. Not a statue, not a medal, not a tolerable piece of architecture could shew itself afterwards. Philosophy, wit and learning, in which some of those good princes had themselves been so renowned, fell with them, and ignorance and darkness overspread the world and fitted it for the chaos and ruin which ensued.

We are now in an age when Liberty is once again in its ascendent, and we are ourselves the happy nation who not only enjoy it at home, but by our greatness and power give life and vigour to it abroad, and are the head and chief of the European League, founded on this common cause. Nor can it (I presume) be justly feared that we should lose this noble ardour or faint under the glorious toil, though, like ancient Greece, we should for succeeding Ages be contending with a foreign power and endeavoring to reduce the exorbitancy of a Grand Monarch. 'Tis with us at present, as with the Roman people in those early days when they wanted only repose from arms to apply themselves to the improvement of arts and studies. We should, in this case, need no ambitious monarch to be allured by hope of fame or secret views of power to give pensions abroad as well as at home, and purchase flattery from every profession and science. We should find a better fund within ourselves, and might, with-

out such assistance be able to excel by our own virtue and
emulation.

.   .   .

'Tis easy to imagine that amidst the several styles and
manners of discourse or writing the easiest attained, and
earliest practised, was the miraculous, the pompous, or what
we generally call the Sublime. Astonishment is of all other
passions the easiest raised in raw and unexperienced mankind.
Children in their earliest infancy are entertained in this
manner, and the known way of pleasing such as these is to
make them wonder, and lead the way for them in this passion
by a feigned surprize at the miraculous objects we set before
them. The best music of Barbarians is hideous and astonishing
sounds and the fine sights of Indians are enormous figures,
various odd and glaring colours, and whatever of that sort is
amazingly beheld with a kind of horror and consternation.
    In poetry, and studied prose, the astonishing part, or
what commonly passes for Sublime, is formed by the variety
of figures, the multiplicity of metaphors, and by quitting as
much as possible the natural and easy way of expression for
that which is most unlike to humanity or ordinary use. This
the Prince of Critics assures us to have been the manner of
the earliest poets, before the age of Homer, or till such time
as this Father-Poet came into repute, who deposed that
spurious race and gave rise to a legitimate and genuine Kind.
He retained only what was decent of the *figurative* or *meta-
phoric* style, introduced the *natural* and *simple,* and turned
his thoughts towards the real beauty of composition, the
unity of design, the truth of characters, and the just imitation
of Nature in each particular.
    The manner of this Father-Poet was afterwards variously
imitated and divided into several shares, especially when it
came to be copied in *Dramatic.* Tragedy came first, and
took what was most solemn and sublime. In this part the
poets succeeded sooner than in comedy or the facetious Kind,
as was natural indeed to suppose, since this was in reality the
easiest manner of the two and capable of being brought the
soonest to perfection (for so the same Prince of Critics

sufficiently informs us). And 'tis highly worth remarking what this mighty genius and judge of art declares concerning Tragedy, that whatever idea might be formed of the utmost perfection of this kind of poem, it could in practice rise no higher than it had been already carried in his time: "Having at length (says he) attained its ends, and being apparently consummate in itself." But for comedy, it seems, 'twas still in hand. It had been already in some manner reduced; but, as he plainly insinuates, it lay yet unfinished notwithstanding the witty labours of an Aristophanes and the other comick poets of the first manner, who had flourished a whole age before this critic. As perfect as were those Wits in style and language, and as fertile in all the varieties and turns of humour, yet the truth of characters, the beauty of order, and the simple imitation of Nature were in a manner wholly unknown to them, or through petulancy or debauch of humour were, it seems, neglected and set aside. A Menander had not as yet appeared, who arose soon after to accomplish the prophecy of our grand master of art and consummate philogist.

Comedy had at this time done little more than what the ancient *Parodies* had done before it. 'Twas of admirable use to explode the false sublime of early poets, and such as in its own age were on every occasion ready to relapse into that vicious manner. The good tragedians themselves could hardly escape its lashes. The pompous orators were its never-failing subjects. Every thing which might be imposing by a false gravity or solemnity was forced to endure the trial of this touchstone. Manners and characters, as well as speech and writings, were discussed with the greatest freedom. Nothing could be better fitted than this genius of Wit to unmask the face of things and remove those larvae naturally formed from the tragick manner and pompous style which had preceded:

> *Et docuit magnumque loqui, nitique*
> > *Cothurno.*
> SUCCESSIT *vetus his Comœdia.*[2]

'Twas not by chance that this succession happened in

[2] Horace, *Ars Poetica*, 280–81: "And taught a lofty speech and stately gait on the buskin. To these succeeded Old Comedy . . ."

Greece after the manner described, but rather through necessity and from the reason and nature of things. For in healthy
bodies Nature dictates remedies of her own, and provides
for the cure of what has happened amiss in the growth and
progress of a constitution. The affairs of this free people
being in the increase, and their ability and judgment every
day improving as letters and arts advanced, they would of
course find in themselves a strength of Nature, which by the
help of good ferments and a wholesome opposition of humours, would correct in one way whatever was excessive, or
peccant (as physicians say) in another. Thus the florid and
over-sanguine humor of the *high style* was allayed by something of a contrary nature. The comic genius was applied
as a kind of caustic to those exuberances and fungus's of the
swoln dialect and magnificent manner of speech. But after
a while even this remedy was found to turn into a disease as
medicines, we know, grow corrosive when the fouler matters
on which they wrought are sufficiently purged and the obstructions removed.

    *—In vitium Libertas excidit, et Vim
    Dignam Lege regi. ————[3]

'Tis a great error to suppose, as some have done, that
the restraining this licentious manner of wit by Law was a
violation of the liberty of the Athenian state, or an effect
merely of the power of foreigners, whom it little concerned
after what manner those citizens treated one another in their
comedies, or what sort of wit or humor they made choice of
for their ordinary diversions. If upon a change of government, as during the usurpation of the Thirty, or when that
nation was humbled at any time, either by a Philip, an Alexander, or an Antipater, they had been forced against their
wills to enact such laws as these, 'tis certain they would
have soon repealed them when those terrors were removed

---

* It follows————Lex est accepta, Chorusque Turpiter obticuit,
sublato jure nocendi.
[3] *Ibid.*, 282–84: "But its freedom sank into excess and a violence deserving
to be checked by law. The law was obeyed, and the chorus to its shame
became mute, its right to injure being withdrawn.

(as they soon were) and the people restored to their former liberties. For notwithstanding the dominion and power they lost *abroad*, they preserved the same government *at home*. And how passionately interested they were in what concerned their diversions and public spectacles, how jealous and full of emulation in what related to their *Poetry, Wit, Music*, and other arts, in which they excelled all other Nations, is well known to persons who have any comprehension of ancient manners, or been the least conversant in history.

.   .   .

However difficult or desperate it may appear in any artist to endeavor to bring perfection into his work, if he has not at least the idea of perfection to give him aim he will be found very defective and mean in his performance. Though his intention be to please the world, he must nevertheless be, in a manner, *above* it, and fix his eye upon that consummate Grace, that beauty of Nature, and that perfection of numbers, which the rest of mankind, feeling only by the effect whilst ignorant of the cause, term the *Je-ne-sçay-quoy*, the unintelligible, or the I know not what, and suppose to be a kind of charm or enchantment of which the artist himself can give no account.

But here, I find, I am tempted to do what I have myself condemned. Hardly can I forbear making some apology for my frequent recourse to the rules of common artists, to the matters of exercise, to the academies of painters, statuaries, and to the rest of the virtuoso-tribe. But in this I am so fully satisfied I have reason on my side, that let custom be ever so strong against me I had rather repair to these inferior schools to search for Truth and Nature than to some other places where higher arts and sciences are professed.

I am persuaded that to be a Virtuoso (so far as befits a Gentleman) is a higher step towards the becoming a man of vitrue and good sense, than the being what in this age we call a *Scholar**. For even rude Nature itself, in its primitive

* It seems indeed somewhat improbable, that according to modern erudition, and as science is now distributed, our ingenious and noble youths should obtain the full advantage of a just and liberal education by unit-

simplicity, is a better guide to judgment than improved sophistry and pedantic learning. The *faciunt, næ, intellegendo, ut nihil intellegant*[4] will be ever applied by men of discernment and free thought to such logic, such principles, such forms and rudiments of knowledge as are established in certain schools of literature and science. The case is sufficiently understood even by those who are unwilling to confess the truth of it. Effects betray their causes. And the known turn and figure of those understandings which sprout from Nurseries of this kind give a plain idea of what is judged on this occasion. 'Tis no wonder, if after so wrong a ground of education, there appears to be such need of redress and amendment from that excellent school which we call the World. The mere amusements of gentlemen are found more improving than the profound researches of pedants. And in the managment of our youth we are forced to have recourse to the former as an antidote against the genius peculiar to the latter. If the Formalists of this sort were erected into patentees with a

---

ing the Scholar-part with that of the real Gentlemen and Man of Breeding. Academies for exercises so useful to the public and essential in the formation of a genteel and liberal character are unfortunately neglected. Letters are indeed banished, I know not where, in distant cloisters and unpractised cells, as our Poet has it, confined to the commerce and mean fellowship of bearded boys. The sprightly arts and sciences are severed from *Philosophy*, which consequently must grow dronish, insipid, pedantic, useless, and directly opposite to the real knowledge and practice of the world and mankind. Our youth accordingly seem to have their only chance between two widely different roads, either that of pedantry and school-learning, which lies amidst the dregs and most corrupt part of ancient literature, or that of the fashionable illiterate world, which aims merely at the character of the fine gentleman, and takes up with the foppery of modern languages and foreign wit. The frightful aspect of the former of these roads makes the journey appear desperate and impracticable. Hence that aversion so generally conceived against a *learned character*, wrong turned and hideously set out under such difficulties and in such seeming labyrinths and mysterious forms. As if a Homer or a Xenophon, imperfectly learnt in raw years, might not afterwards, in a riper age, be studied as well in a capital city and admidst the world as at a college or country-town.

[4] Terence, *Andria*, "Prologue," line 17: *Faciuntne intellegendo ut nil intellegant?* "Do they not show [by too much] knowing that they know nothing?"

sole commission of authorship, we should undoubtedly see such writing in our days as would either wholly wean us from all books in general, or at least from all such as were the product of our own nation under such a subordinate and conforming government.

.   .   .

One who aspires to the character of a man of breeding and politeness is careful to form his judgment of arts and sciences upon right models of *Perfection*. If he travels to Rome he inquires which are the truest pieces of architecture, the best remains of statues, the best paintings of a Raphael or a Carache. However antiquated, rough, or dismal they may appear to him at first sight, he resolves to view them over and over till he has brought himself to relish them and finds their hidden graces and perfections. He takes particular care to turn his eye from everything which is gaudy, luscious, and of a false taste. Nor is he less careful to turn his ear from every sort of music besides that which is of the best manner, and truest harmony.

'Twere to be wished we had the same regard to a right taste in life and manners. What mortal being once convinced of a difference in *inward* character, and of a preference due to one Kind above another, would not be concerned to make *his own* the best? It Civility and Humanity be a taste; if Brutality, Insolence, Riot be in the same manner a taste; who, if he could reflect, would not chuse to form himself on the amiable and agreeable rather than the odious and perverse model? Who would not endeavor to force Nature as well in this respect as in what relates to a taste or judgment in other arts and sciences? For in each place the force on Nature is used only for its redress. If a natural good taste be not already formed in us, why should not we endeavor to form it and become *natural?*

"I like! I fancy! I admire! How? By accident: or as I please. No. But I learn to fancy, to admire, to please as the subjects themselves are deserving and can bear me out. Otherwise, I like at this hour but dislike the next. I shall be weary of my pursuit, and, upon experience, find little pleasure in the main if my choice and judgment in it be from no other rule than that single one, *because I please*. Grotesque and monstrous figures often please. Cruel spectacles and barbarities are also found to please, and, in some tempers, to please beyond all other subjects. But is this pleasure right? And shall I follow it if it presents? Not strive with it, or endeavor to prevent its growth or prevalency in my temper?—How stands the case in a more soft and flattering kind of pleasure?—Effeminancy pleases me. The Indian figures, the Japan-work, the enamel strike my eye. The luscious colours and glossy paint gain upon my fancy. A French or Flemish style is highly liked by me at first sight, and I pursue my liking. But what ensues?—Do I not forever forfeit my good relish? How is it possible I should thus come to taste the beauties of an Italian master, or of a hand happily formed on Nature and the Ancients? 'Tis not by wantonness and humour that I shall attain my end, and arrive at the enjoyment I propose. The Art itself is severe: the rules rigid. And if I expect the knowledge should come to me by accident or in play, I shall be grosly deluded and prove myself, at best, a mock-virtuoso, or mere pedant of the kind."

Here therefore we have once again exhibited our moral science, in the same method and manner of soliloquy as above. To this correction of humour and formation of a taste, our reading, if it be of the right sort, must principally contribute. Whatever company we keep, or however polite and agreeable their characters may be with whom we converse or correspond, if the authors we read are of another kind we shall find our palate strangely turned their way. We are the unhappier in this respect for being scholars if our studies be ill chosen. Nor can I, for this reason, think it proper to call a man well-read who reads many authors, since he must of necessity have more ill models, than good, and be more stuffed with bombast, ill fancy, and wry thought than filled with solid sense and just imagination.

But notwithstanding this hazard of our taste from a multiplicity of reading, we are not, it seems, the least scrupulous in our choice of subject. We read whatever comes next us. What was first put into our hand when we were young serves us afterwards for serious study and wise research when we are old. We are many of us, indeed, so grave as

to continue this exercise of youth through our remaining life.
. . . We care not how Gothic or barbarous our models are,
what ill-designed or monstrous figures we view, or what
false proportions we trace or see described in history, romance, or fiction. And thus our eye and ear is lost. Our
relish or taste must of necessity grow barbarous whilst barbarian customs, savage manners, Indian wars, and wonders
of the Terra Incognita employ our leisure hours, and are
the chief materials to furnish out a library. . . .

'Tis the same taste which makes us prefer a Turkish
history to a Grecian or a Roman, an Ariosto to a Virgil, and
a Romance, or novel, to an *Iliad.* We have no regard to the
character or genius of our author, nor are so far curious as
to observe how able he is in the judgment of facts, or how
ingenious in the texture of his lies. For facts unably related,
though with the greatest sincerity and good faith, may prove
the worst sort of deceit and mere lies, judiciously composed,
can teach us the Truth* of things beyond any other manner.
But to amuse ourselves with such authors as neither know
how to lie nor tell truth discovers a taste which methinks one
should not be apt to envy. Yet so enchanted we are with the
travelling Memoirs of any casual adventurer, that be his
character or genius what it will we have no sooner turned
over a page or two than we begin to interest ourselves highly
in his affairs. No sooner has he taken shipping at the mouth
of the Thames, or sent his baggage before him to Gravesend
or Buoy in the Nore, than strait our attention is earnestly
taken up. If in order to [? undertake] his more distant
travels, he takes some part of Europe in his way, we can with
patience hear of inns and ordinaries, passage-boats and ferries,
foul and fair weather, with all the particulars of the author's
diet, habit of body, his personal dangers and mischances on
land and sea. And thus, full of desire and hope, we accompany
him till he enters on his great scene of action, and begins by
the description of some enormous fish or beast. From mon-

* The greatest of critics says of the greatest poet, when he extols him
the highest, "That above all others he understood how TO LYE."
[Aristotle, *Poetics,* 1460ᵃ.]

strous brutes he proceeds to yet more monstrous men. For in this race of authors he is ever compleatest and of the first rank who is able to speak of things the most unnatural and monstrous.

This humour our old Tragick Poet* seems to have discovered. He hit our taste in giving us a Moorish hero full fraught with prodigy: a wondrous story-teller! But for the attentive part, the poet chose to give it to woman-kind. What passionate reader of travels, or student in the prodigious sciences, can refuse to pity that fair lady who fell in love with the miraculous Moor, especially considering with what suitable grace such a lover could relate the most monstrous adventures and satisfy the wondring appetite with the most wondrous tales: Wherein (says the Hero-Traveller)

> *Of Antars vast, and Desarts idle,*
> *It was my Hint to speak:*
> *And of the Cannibals that each other eat!*
> *The Anthropophagie! and Men whose Heads*
> *Do grow beneath their Shoulders. These to hear*
> *Wou'd DESDEMONA seriously incline.*[5]

Seriously, 'twas a woeful tale! unfit, one would think, to win a tender fair-one. It's true, the poet sufficiently condemns her fancy, and makes her (poor Lady!) pay dearly for it in the end. But why, amongst his Greek names, he should have chosen one which denoted the lady *superstitious* I can't imagine, unless as poets are sometimes prophets too, he should figuratively, under this dark type, have represented to us that about a hundred years after his time the Fair Sex of this Island should, by other monstrous tales, be so seduced as to turn their favour chiefly on the persons of the tale-tellers, and change their natural inclination for fair, candid, and courteous Knights into a passion for a mysterious race of black enchanters: such as of old were said to *creep into houses, and lead captive silly women.*

·   ·   ·

* Shakespear.
[5] Misquoted from *Othello* I, iii, 140–46.

But whatever monstrous zeal or superstitious passion the poet might foretell, either in the Gentlemen, Ladies, or common people of an after age, 'tis certain that as to books the same Moorish fancy, in its plain and literal sense, prevails strongly at this present time. Monsters and monster-lands were never more in request, and we may often see a philosopher or a wit run a tale-gathering in those idle deserts as familiarly as the silliest woman or merest boy.

One would imagine that our philosophical writers, who pretend to treat of morals, should far out-do mere poets in recommending virtue and representing what was fair and amiable in human actions. One would imagine that if they turned their eye towards remote countries (of which they affect so much to speak) they should search for that simplicity of manners and innocence of behaviour which has been often known among mere savages ere they were corrupted by our commerce and, by sad example, instructed in all kinds of treachery and inhumanity. 'Twould be of advantage to us to hear the causes of this strange corruption in ourselves, and be made to consider of our deviation from Nature and from that just purity of manners which might be expected, especially from a people so assisted and enlightened by Religion. For who would not naturally expect more justice, fidelity, temperance, and honesty from Christians than from Mahometans or mere pagans? But so far are our modern moralists from condemning any unnatural vices or corrupt manners, whether in our own or foreign climates, that they would have Vice itself appear as natural as Virtue, and from the worst examples, would represent to us, "That all actions are naturally indifferent; that they have no note or character of good or ill in themselves; but are distinguished by mere fashion, law, or arbitrary decree." Wonderful philosophy! raised from the dregs of an illiterate, mean kind which was ever despised among the great Ancients and rejected by all men of action or sound erudition; but, in these ages, imperfectly copied from the original, and, with much disadvantage, imitated and assumed in common both by devout and indevout attempters in the moral kind.

Should a writer upon music, addressing himself to the students and lovers of the art, declare to them, "That the measure or rule of harmony was caprice or will, humour or fashion," 'tis not very likely he should be heard with great attention or treated with real gravity. For harmony is harmony by Nature, let men judge ever so ridiculously of music. So is symmetry and proportion founded still in Nature, let men's fancy prove ever so barbarous, or their fashions ever so Gothic in their architecture, sculpture, or whatever other designing art. 'Tis the same case where Life and Manners are concerned. Virtue has the same fixed standard. The same numbers, harmony, and proportion will have place in morals, and are discoverable in the characters and affections of mankind, in which are laid the just foundations of an art and science superior to every other of human practice and comprehension.

This, I suppose therefore, is highly necessary that a writer should comprehend. For things are stubborn, and will not be as we fancy them or as the fashion varies, but as they stand in Nature. Now whether the writer be poet, philosopher, or of whatever kind, he is in truth no other than *a copyist after Nature*. His style may be differently suited to the different times he lives in, or to the different humour of his age or nation; his manner, his dress, his colouring may vary. But if his drawing be uncorrect, or his design contrary to Nature, his piece will be found ridiculous when it comes thoroughly to be examined. For Nature will not be mocked. The prepossession against her can never be very lasting. Her decrees and instincts are powerful and her sentiments in-bred. She has a strong party abroad, and as strong a one within ourselves: and when any slight is put upon her she can soon turn the reproach, and make large reprisals on the taste and judgment of her antagonists.

Whatever philosopher, critic, or author is convinced of this prerogative of Nature will easily be persuaded to apply himself to the great work of reforming his Taste, which he will have reason to suspect if he be not such a one as has deliberately endeavored to frame it by the just Standard of Nature. Whether this be his case he will easily discover by appealing to his memory. For custom and fashion are powerful seducers, and he must of necessity have fought hard against these to have attained that justness of taste which is required in one who pretends to follow Nature. But if no such conflict can be called to mind, 'tis a certain token that the party has his taste very little different from the vulgar. And on this account he should instantly betake himself to the wholesome practice recommended in this treatise. He should set afoot the powerfullest faculties of his mind, and assemble the best forces of his wit and judgment, in order to make a formal descent on the Territories of the Heart: resolving to decline no combat, nor hearken to any terms till he had pierced into its inmost provinces and reached the seat of Empire. No treaties should amuse him, no advantages lead him aside. All other speculations should be suspended, all other mysteries resigned till this necessary campaign was made and these inward conflicts learnt, by which he would be able to gain at least some tolerable insight into *himself*, and knowledge of *his own natural Principles*.

ALEXANDER POPE
[1688–1744]

Although Pope began his career writing literary criticism
(in the "Discourse on Pastoral Poetry," written, he said,
when he was sixteen), and although his concern with
formal and technical literary matters continued through
his life and appears constantly in his poetry as well as in
miscellaneous prose writings and in his letters, it is only
fairly recently that his eighteenth-century reputation as a
critic is being revived, and that he is coming to be recognized
as writing criticism of far wider range and broader sympathy
than a cursory reading of the Essay on Criticism would
indicate. The Essay on Criticism is the last major example
of the renaissance Ars Poetica modeled on Horace's not
only in its easy though epigrammatic tone but also in its
apparent prescriptiveness. Pope is there taking Boileau and
Vida, most notably, as his models and turning the
established pattern of Horace's Art of Poetry to a discussion
emphasizing criticism rather than poetry itself. The Essay
cannot be viewed apart from this renaissance genre, which
continued through the early eighteenth century in such
unlikely forms as "The Art of Cooking," "The Art of
Politics," and "The Art of Preserving Health." Pope was
the last author who was able to imbue this moribund
convention with poetic vitality (though to an age in which
the educated man still read Horace before he read English
poetry the fact that the convention was dying would not
necessarily have been obvious), and the fact that the Essay
on Criticism is, indeed, still vital as poetry is what may lead
to confusions as to the dicta it seems to be enforcing.

It is enough to say here about the Essay on Criticism
that even though it was written when Pope was young—at
an age when poets are most apt to be dogmatic—it is more
than merely a ragout of received ideas, though one must
recognize that received ideas are the meat of the dish. Even

> From vulgar bounds with brave disorder part
> And snatch a grace beyond the reach of Art,
> Which, without passing through the judgment, gains
> The heart, and all its end at once attains . . .

was not an idea strange to the renaissance critical convention.
It is, in fact, at the very root of that convention.

In the "Postscript to the Odyssey" Pope is discussing
what he perhaps knew best—poetic style. The discussion
proceeds, however, on grounds which many commentators
today would probably not find immediately relevant, since
the basis of his argument is still profoundly rooted in the
classical and renaissance conception of decorous poetic
diction. One could, as a matter of fact, virtually reconstruct
that conception inductively from Pope's discussion. As a
vital force for practicing poets these dicta also, along with
the very conception of the genres, were near the end of their
tether (even Johnson did not seem to have understood them
quite as Pope did), but we must recognize that to listen
to poets of the early eighteenth and the seventeenth centuries
(even Donne!) without an awareness of these prescriptions
is to hear their possible verbal music through velour curtains
of our own preconceptions—the melody may come through,
but the overtones are lost.

The "Postscript" was, of course, first published in 1726 in
the final volume of Pope's translation of Homer. Warburton
did not include it in his edition of Pope, hence it was not
included in most editions which derive from Warburton
(including Elwin and Courthope, the standard edition
until the publication of the Twickenham volumes over the
last thirty years). It was frequently reprinted with editions
of Pope's translation, but Joseph Warton for the first time
re-edited it among the prose selections in his edition of 1797.
The text below is adapted from Warton's edition.

The books by Austin Warren (Alexander Pope as Critic
and Humanist, Princeton, 1929) and George Sherburn
(The Early Career of Alexander Pope, Oxford, 1934) can

still not be ignored by students. Warren's insights,
particularly, remain basic. Among a mass of more recent
studies, the following having relevance to Pope's criticism
are worth consulting:

Aden, John M.: " 'First Follow Nature': Strategy and
    Stratification in An Essay on Criticism," JEGP, LV
    (1956), 604–17.
Adler, Jacob H.: "Pope and the Rules of Prosody," PMLA,
    LXXVI (1961), 218–26.
Goldgar, Bertrand A. [ed.]: Literary Criticism of Alexander
    Pope (Regent's Critics Series), Lincoln, Nebraska, 1965.
Hooker, Edward Niles: "Pope on Wit: the Essay on
    Criticism," The Seventeenth Century: Studies in the
    History of English Thought and Literature from Bacon
    to Pope (by Richard Foster Jones and others writing
    in his honor), Stanford, 1951, pp. 225–46.
Ramsey, Paul: "The Watch of Judgment: Relativism and
    An Essay on Criticism," Studies in Criticism and
    Aesthetics, 1660–1800: Essays in Honor of Samuel Holt
    Monk (ed. Howard Anderson and John S. Shea),
    Minneapolis, 1967, pp. 140–55.

POSTSCRIPT TO THE ODYSSEY
[1726]

I cannot dismiss this work without a few observations on the true character and style of it. Whoever reads the *Odyssey* with an eye to the *Iliad*, expecting to find it of the same character, or of the same sort of spirit, will be grievously deceived, and err against the first principle of criticism, which is to consider the nature of the piece, and the intent of its author. The *Odyssey* is a moral and political work, instructive to all degrees of men, and filled with images, examples and precepts of civil and domestic life. Homer is here a person

Qui didicit, patriae quid debeat, & quid amicis,
Quo sit amore parens, quo frater amandus, & hospes:

> Qui quid sit pulcrum, quid turpe, quid utile, quid non,
> Plenius & melius Chrysippo & Crantore dicit.[1]

The *Odyssey* is the reverse of the *Iliad* in moral, subject, manner, and style, to which it has no sort of relation but as the story happens to follow in order of time, and as some of the same persons are actors in it. Yet from this incidental connection many have been misled to regard it as a continuation or second part, and thence to expect a parity of character inconsistent with its nature.

It is no wonder that the common reader should fall into this mistake when so great a critic as Longinus seems not wholly free from it, although what he has said has been generally understood to import a severer censure of the *Odyssey* than it really does, if we consider the occasion on which it is introduced and the circumstances to which it is confined.

> The *Odyssey* (says he) is an instance, how natural it is to a great genius, when it begins to grow old and decline, to delight itself in narrations and fables. For that Homer composed the *Odyssey* after the *Iliad,* many proofs may be given, etc. From hence in my judgment it proceeds, that as the *Iliad* was written while his spirit was in its greatest vigour, the whole structure of that work is dramatic and full of action; whereas the greater part of the *Odyssey* is employed in narration, which is the taste of old age: so that in this latter piece we may compare him to the setting sun, which has still the same greatness but not the same ardor or force. He speaks not in the same strain; we see no more that sublime of the *Iliad* which marches on with a constant pace, without ever being stopped or retarded: there appears no more that hurry and that strong tide of motions and passions pouring one after another; there is no more the same fury, or the same volubility of diction so suitable to action, and all along drawing in such innumerable images of nature. But Homer, like the ocean, is

---

[1] Horace, *Ars Poetica* 312–13: "He who has learned what he owes his country and friends, what love is due a parent, a brother, and a guest"; and *Epistle* I. ii. 3–4: "Who tells us what is fair, what is foul, what is helpful, what is not, more plainly and better than Chrysippus or Crantor."

always great, even when he ebbs and retires, even when he is lowest and loses himself most in narrations and incredible fictions: as instances of this we cannot forget the descriptions of tempests, the adventures of Ulysses with the Cyclops, and many others. But though all this be age, it is the age of Homer —And it may be said for the credit of these fictions that they are beautiful dreams, or if you will, the dreams of Jupiter himself. I spoke of the *Odyssey* only to show that the greatest poets, when their genius wants strength and warmth for the pathetic, for the most part employ themselves in painting the manners. This Homer has done in characterising the suitors and describing their way of life, which is properly a branch of comedy, whose peculiar business is to represent the manners of men."

We must first observe, it is the Sublime of which Longinus is writing: that, and not the nature of Homer's poem, is his subject. After having highly extolled the sublimity and fire of the *Iliad,* he justly observes the *Odyssey* to have less of those qualities, and to turn more on the side of moral, and reflections on human life. Nor is it his business here to determine whether the *elevated spirit* of the one, or the *just moral* of the other, be the greater excellence in itself.

Secondly, that fire and fury of which he is speaking cannot well be meant of the general spirit and inspiration which is to run through a whole epic poem, but of that particular warmth and impetuosity necessary in some parts to image or represent actions or passions of haste, tumult, and violence. It is on occasion of citing some such particular passages in Homer that Longinus breaks into this reflection, which seems to determine his meaning chiefly to that sense.

Upon the whole, he affirms the *Odyssey* to have less sublimity and fire than the *Iliad,* but he does not say it wants the sublime or wants fire. He affirms it to be narrative, but not that the narration is defective. He affirms it to abound in fictions, not that those fictions are ill invented or ill executed. He affirms it to be nice and particular in painting the manners, but not that those manners are ill painted. If Homer has fully in these points accomplished his own design, and done all that the nature of his poem demanded or allowed, it still remains perfect in its kind, and as much a master-piece as the *Iliad.*

The amount of the passage is this, that in his own particular taste, and with respect to the Sublime, Longinus preferred the *Iliad*: and because the *Odyssey* was less active and lofty, he judged it the work of the old age of Homer.

If this opinion be true, it will only prove that Homer's age might determine him in the choice of his subject, not that it affected him in the execution of it: and that which would be a very wrong instance to prove the decay of his imagination, is a very good one to evince the strength of his judgment. For had he (as Madam Dacier[2] observes) composed the *Odyssey* in his youth and the *Iliad* in his age, both must in reason have been exactly the same as they now stand. To blame Homer for his choice of such a subject as did not admit the same incidents and the same pomp of style as his former is to take offence at too much variety, and to imagine that when a man has written one good thing he must ever after only copy himself.

The "Battle of Constantine" and the "School of Athens" are both pieces of Raphael: shall we censure the "School of Athens" as faulty because it has not the fury and fire of the other? Or shall we say that Raphael was grown grave and old because he chose to represent the manners of old men and philosophers? There is all the silence, tranquility, and composure in the one, and all the warmth, hurry, and tumult in the other which the subject of either required; both of them had been imperfect if they had not been as they are. And let the painter or poet be young or old who designs and performs in this manner, it proves him to have made the piece at a time of life when he was master not only of his art, but of his discretion.

Aristotle makes no such distinction between the two poems; he constantly cites them with equal praise, and draws the rules and examples of epic writing equally from both. But it is rather to the *Odyssey* that Horace gives the preference in the *Epistle to Lollius,* and in the *Art of Poetry.* It is remarkable how opposite his opinion is to that of Longinus, and that the particulars he chooses to extol are those very fictions and pic-

---

[2] Madame Dacier: Anne, *neé* Lefebvre (1654–1720), published a prose translation of the *Iliad* with a prefatory essay, 1711.

tures of the manners which the other seems least to approve. Those fables and manners are of the very essence of the work; but even without that regard, the fables themselves have both more invention and more instruction, and the manners more moral and example, than those of the *Iliad*.

In some points (and those the most essential to the epic poem) the *Odyssey* is confessed to excel the *Iliad*, and principally in the great end of it, the moral. The conduct, turn, and disposition of the fable is also what the critics allow to be the better model for epic writers to follow: accordingly we find much more of the cast of this poem than of the other in the *Aeneid*, and (what next to that is perhaps the greatest example) in the *Telemachus*. In the manners it is no way inferior: Longinus is so far from finding any defect in these that he rather taxes Homer with painting them too minutely. As to the narrations, although they are more numerous as the occasions are more frequent, yet they carry no more the marks of old age, and are neither more prolix nor more circumstantial, than the conversations and dialogues of the *Iliad*. Not to mention the length of those of Phoenix in the ninth book, and of Nestor in the eleventh (which may be thought in compliance to their characters), those of Glaucus in the sixth, of Aeneas in the twentieth, and some others, must be allowed to exceed any in the whole *Odyssey*. And that the propriety of style and the numbers in the narrations of each are equal, will appear to any who compare them.

To form a right judgment whether the genius of Homer had suffered any decay, we must consider, in both his poems, such parts as are of a similar nature and will bear comparison. And it is certain we shall find in each the same vivacity and fecundity of invention, the same life and strength of imaging and colouring, the particular descriptions as highly painted, the figures as bold, the metaphors as animated, and the numbers as harmonious and as various.

The *Odyssey* is a perpetual source of poetry: the stream is not the less full for being gentle, though it is true (when we speak only with regard to the sublime) that a river foaming and thundering in cataracts from rocks and precipices is what more strikes, amazes, and fills the mind, than the same body of water flowing afterwards through peaceful vales and agreeable scenes of pasturage.

The *Odyssey* (as I have before said) ought to be considered according to its own nature and design, not with an eye to the *Iliad*. To censure Homer because it is unlike what it was never meant to resemble, is as if a gardener who had purposely cultivated two beautiful trees of contrary natures, as a specimen of his skill in the several kinds, should be blamed for not bringing them into pairs, when in root, stem, leaf, and flower, each was so entirely different that one must have been spoiled in the endeavour to match the other.

Longinus, who saw this poem was "partly of the nature of comedy," ought not for that very reason to have considered it with a view to the *Iliad*. How little any such resemblance was the intention of Homer may appear from hence, that although the character of Ulysses there was already drawn, yet here he purposely turns to another side of it, and shows him not in that full light of glory but in the shade of common life, with a mixture of such qualities as are requisite to all the lowest accidents of it, struggling with misfortunes, and on a level with the meanest of mankind. As for the other persons, none of them are above what we call the higher comedy; Calypso, though a goddess, is a character of intrigue, the suitors yet more approaching to it; the Phæacians are of the same cast; the Cyclops, Malanthius, and Irus descend even to droll characters; and the scenes that appear throughout are generally of the comic kind—banquets, revels, sports, loves, and the pursuit of a woman.

From the nature of the poem we shall form an idea of the style. The diction is to follow the images, and to take its colour from the complexion of the thoughts. Accordingly the *Odyssey* is not always clothed in the majesty of verse proper to tragedy, but sometimes descends into the plainer narrative, and sometimes even to that familiar dialogue essential to comedy. However, where it cannot support a sublimity, it always preserves a dignity, or at least a propriety.

There is a real beauty in an easy, pure, perspicuous description even of a low action. There are numerous instances of this both in Homer and Virgil, and perhaps those natural passages are not the least pleasing of their works. It is often the same in history, where the representations of common, or even domestic things, in clear, plain, and natural words, are frequently found to make the liveliest impression on the reader.

The question is how far a poet, in pursuing the description or image of an action, can attach himself to *little circumstances* without vulgarity or trifling; what particulars are proper and enliven the image, or what are impertinent and clog it? In this matter painting is to be consulted, and the whole regard had to those circumstances which contribute to form a full, and yet not a confused, idea of a thing.

Epithets are of vast service to this effect, and the right use of these is often the only expedient to render the narration poetical.

The great point of judgment is to distinguish when to speak simply and when figuratively, but whenever the poet is obliged by the nature of his subject to descend to the lower manner of writing, an elevated style would be affected, and therefore ridiculous; and the more he was forced upon figures and metaphors to avoid that lowness, the more the image would be broken and consequently obscure.

One may add that the use of the grand style on little subjects is not only ludicrous, but a sort of transgression against the rules of proportion and mechanics: 'tis using a vast force to lift a feather.

I believe, now I am upon this head, it will be found a just observation that the *low actions* of life cannot be put into a figurative style without being ridiculous, but *things natural* can. Metaphors raise the latter into dignity, as we see in the Georgics, but throw the former into ridicule, as in the *Lutrin.*[3] I think this may very well be accounted for; laughter implies censure; inanimate and irrational beings are not objects of censure; therefore these may be elevated as much as you please, and no ridicule follows: but when rational beings are

---

[3] A mock epic poem relating an ecclesiastical quarrel over the placing of a lectern, by Nicolas Boileau-Despréaux (1636–1711). Published in 1674, it is one of the important forebears of *The Rape of the Lock.*

represented above their real character, it becomes ridiculous in art, because it is vicious in morality. The *bees* in Virgil,[4] were they rational beings, would be ridiculous by having their actions and manners represented on a level with creatures so superior as men, since it would imply folly or pride, which are the proper objects of ridicule.

The use of pompous expression for low actions or thoughts is the *true sublime* of *Don Quixote*. How far unfit it is for epic poetry appears in its being the perfection of the mock epic. It is so far from being the sublime of tragedy, that it is the cause of all bombast; when poets, instead of being (as they imagine) constantly lofty, only preserve throughout a painful equality of fustian, that continued swell of language (which runs indiscriminately even through their lowest characters, and rattles like some mightiness of meaning in the most indifferent subjects) is of a piece with that perpetual elevation of tone which the players have learned from it, and which is not *speaking*, but *vociferating*.

There is still more reason for a variation of style in epic poetry than in tragic, to distinguish between that language of the gods proper to the muse who sings and is inspired, and that of men who are introduced speaking only according to nature. Farther, there ought to be a difference of style observed in the speeches of human persons and those of deities; and again, in those which may be called set harangues or orations, and those which are only conversation or dialogue. Homer has more of the latter than any other poet; what Virgil does by two or three words of narration, Homer still performs by speeches; not only replies, but even rejoinders are frequent in him, a practice almost unknown to Virgil. This renders his poems more animated, but less grave and majestic, and consequently necessitates the frequent use of a lower style. The writers of tragedy lie under the same necessity if they would copy nature, whereas that painted and poetical diction which they perpetually use would be improper even in orations designed to move with all the arts of rhetoric: This is plain from the practice of Demosthenes and Cicero; and Virgil in those

---

[4] In the fourth *Georgic*. See Dryden's translation, 220 ff.

of Drances and Turnus[5] gives an eminent example how far
removed the style of them ought to be from such an excess of
figures and ornaments, which indeed fits only that *language
of the gods* we have been speaking of, or that of a *muse* under
inspiration.

To read through a whole work in this strain is like
travelling all along on the ridge of a hill, which is not half so
agreeable as sometimes gradually to rise and sometimes gently
to descend as the way leads, and as the end of the journey
directs.

Indeed, the true reason that so few poets have imitated
Homer in these lower parts, has been the extreme difficulty
of preserving that mixture of ease and dignity essential to
them. For it is as hard for an epic poem to stoop to the narrative with success as for a prince to descend to be familiar without diminution of his greatness.

The *sublime* style is more easily counterfeited than the
natural; something that passes for it, or sounds like it, is common in all false writers: but nature, purity, perspicuity, and
simplicity never walk in the clouds; they are obvious to all
capacities, and where they are not evident they do not exist.

The most plain narration not only admits of these, and of
harmony (which are all the qualities of style), but it requires
every one of them to render it pleasing. On the contrary, whatever pretends to a share of the sublime may pass notwithstanding any defects in the rest, nay sometimes without any of them,
and gain the admiration of all ordinary readers.

Homer in his lowest narrations or speeches is ever easy,
flowing, copious, clear, and harmonious. He shews not less
invention in assembling the humbler than the greater thoughts
and images, nor less judgment in proportioning the style and
the versification to these than to the other. Let it be remembered that the same genius that soared the highest, and from
whom the greatest models of the sublime are derived, was
also he who stooped the lowest, and gave to the simple narrative its utmost perfection. Which of these was the harder task
to Homer himself I cannot pretend to determine, but to his

---

[5] Æneid XI, 340–444. See Dryden's translation, 510–681.

translator I can affirm (however unequal all his imitations must be) that of the latter has been much the more difficult.

Whoever expects here the same pomp of verse and the same ornaments of diction as in the *Iliad*, he will and he ought to be disappointed. Were the original otherwise, it had been an offence against nature; and were the translation so, it were an offence against Homer, which is the same thing.

It must be allowed that there is a majesty and harmony in the Greek language which greatly contribute to elevate and support the narration. But I must also observe that this is an advantage grown upon the language since Homer's time, for things are removed from vulgarity by being out of use: and if the words we could find in any present language were equally sonorous or musical in themselves, they would still appear less poetical and uncommon than those of a dead one from this only circumstance, of being in every man's mouth. I may add to this another disadvantage to a translator from a different cause: Homer seems to have taken upon him the character of an historian, antiquary, divine, and professor of arts and sciences as well as a poet. In one or other of these characters he descends into many particularities, which as a poet only perhaps he would have avoided. All these ought to be preserved by a faithful translator, who in some measure takes the place of Homer; and all that can be expected from him is to make them as poetical as the subject will bear. Many arts, therefore, are requisite to supply these disadvantages in order to dignify and solemnize these plainer parts, which hardly admit of any poetical ornaments.

Some use has been made, to this end, of the style of Milton. A just and moderate mixture of old words may have an effect like the working old abbey stones into a building, which I have sometimes seen, to give a kind of venerable air, and yet not destroy the neatness, elegance, and equality requisite to a new work; I mean without rendering it too unfamiliar or remote from the present purity of writing, or from that ease and smoothness which ought always to accompany narration or dialogue. In reading a style judiciously antiquated, one finds a pleasure not unlike that of travelling on an old Roman way: but then the road must be as good as the way is ancient; the style must be such in which we may evenly proceed without being put to short stops by sudden abruptnesses, or puzzled by frequent turnings and transpositions. No man delights in furrows and stumbling blocks: and let our love to antiquity be ever so great, a fine ruin is one thing and a heap of rubbish another. The imitators of Milton, like most other imitators, are not *copies,* but *caricaturas* of their original; they are a hundred times more obsolete and cramp than he, and equally so in all places: whereas it should have been observed of Milton that he is not lavish of his exotic words and phrases everywhere alike, but employs them much more where the subject is marvellous, vast and strange, as in the scenes of heaven, hell, chaos, etc. than where it is turned to the natural and agreeable, as in the pictures of Paradise, the loves of our first parents, the entertainments of angels, and the like. In general, this unusual style better serves to awaken our ideas in the descriptions and in the imaging and picturesque parts, than it agrees with the lower sort of narrations, the character of which is simplicity and purity. Milton has several of the latter, where we find not an antiquated, affected, or uncouth word for some hundred lines together, as in his fifth book, the latter part of the eighth, the former of the tenth and eleventh books, and in the narration of Michael in the twelfth. I wonder indeed that he, who ventured (contrary to the practice of all other epic poets) to imitate Homer's lownesses in the narrative, should not also have copied his plainness and perspicuity in the dramatic parts, since in his speeches (where clearness above all is necessary) there is frequently such transposition and forced construction that the very sense is not to be discovered without a second or third reading: and in this certainly he ought to be no example.

To preserve the true character of Homer's style in the present translation, great pains has been taken to be easy and natural. The chief merit I can pretend to is not to have been carried into a more plausible and figurative manner of writing, which would better have pleased all readers, but the judicious ones. My errors had been fewer had each of those gentlemen who joined with me shown as much of the severity of a friend to me, as I did to them, in a strict animadversion and correction. What assistance I received from them was made known in general to the public in the original proposals for this work, and the particulars are specified at the conclusion of it; to which I must add (to be punctually just) some part of the tenth and the fifteenth books. The reader will now be too good a judge how much the greater part of it, and consequently of its faults, is chargeable upon me alone. But this I can with integrity affirm, that I have bestowed as much time and pains upon the whole as were consistent with the indispensable duties and cares of life, and with that wretched state of health which God has been pleased to make my portion. At the least, it is a pleasure to me to reflect that I have introduced into our language this other work of the greatest and most ancient of poets with some dignity, and I hope with as little disadvantage as the *Iliad*. And if, after the unmerited success of that translation, any one will wonder why I would enterprize the *Odyssey*, I think it sufficient to say that Homer himself did the same, or the world would never have seen it.

RICHARD STEELE
[1672–1729]

Steele cannot properly be considered a critic, yet his occasional
writings on literary subjects deserve some notice as another
indication of the increasing attention writers necessarily
paid to the interests of the new middle class during the early
decades of the eighteenth century. Addison, too, displays
this concern, but Addison is still writing with the air of the
renaissance gentleman patiently explaining what the proper
attitudes should be according to the rules. Steele by no
means neglects those rules, rather he is warning his public
—and most notably the ladies, who were always his special
concern—against being misled by shallow critics who misapply
the rules. Ultimately he is suggesting that readers must judge
for themselves, a suggestion the revolutionary effects of
which on literature could hardly have been foreseen.

  This stance is what one might expect to find in The
Guardian, the most successful of the immediate successors
of the Spectator, but openly oriented toward the Whigs
and hence toward the newly important, but still culturally
diffident, bourgeoisie. Steele appealed to this audience also
in his most successful play, The Conscious Lovers, commonly
said to be one of the earliest "sentimental" plays, and
certainly one of the most influential dramas of the century.

  Steele as a critic has not been discussed, nor has The
Guardian been adequately edited. The present text is adapted
from Chalmers' edition, 1808. Steele's early life, through
the period of The Guardian, is well treated in Calhoun
Winton's Captain Steele (Baltimore, 1964).

GUARDIAN NO. 12
ON POETRY AND CRITICS
[1713]

Vel quia nil rectum, nisi quod placuit sibi, ducunt:
Vel quia turpe putant parere minoribus—

Hor. 2. Ep. i. 84.

IMITATED.

You'd think no fools disgraced the former reign,
Did not some grave examples yet remain,
Who scorn a lad should match his father's skill,
And having once been wrong, will be so still.

Pope.

When a poem makes its first appearance in the world, I have always observed that it gives employment to a greater number of critics than any other kind of writing. Whether it be that most men, at some time of their lives, have tried their talent that way, and thereby think they have a right to judge; or whether they imagine that their making shrewd observations upon the polite arts gives them a pretty figure; or whether there may not be some jealousy and caution in bestowing applause upon those who write chiefly for fame. Whatever the reasons be, we find few discouraged by the delicacy and danger of such an undertaking.

I think it certain that most men are naturally not only capable of being pleased with that which raises agreeable pictures in the fancy, but willing also to own it. But then there are many who, by false applications of some rules ill understood, or out of deference to men whose opinions they value, have formed to themselves certain schemes and systems of satisfaction, and will not be pleased out of their own way. These are not critics themselves, but readers of critics, who, without the labour of perusing authors, are able to give their characters in general, and know just as much of the several species of poetry as those who read books of geography do of the genius of this or that people or nation. These gentlemen deliver their opinions sententiously, and in general terms: to which it being impossible readily to frame complete answers, they have often the satisfaction of leaving the board in triumph. As young persons, and particularly the ladies, are liable to be led aside by these tyrants in wit, I shall examine two or three of the many stratagems they use, and subjoin such precautions as may hinder candid readers from being deceived thereby.

The first I shall take notice of is an objection commonly offered, viz. 'that such a poem hath indeed some good lines in it, but it is not a regular piece.' This, for the most part, is urged by those whose knowledge is drawn from some famous French critics, who have written upon the epic poem, the drama, and the great kinds of poetry, which cannot subsist without great regularity; but ought by no means to be required in odes, epistles, panegyrics, and the like, which naturally admit of greater liberties. The enthusiasm in odes, and the freedom of epistles, is rarely disputed: but I have often heard the poems upon public occasions, written in heroic verse, which I choose to call panegyrics, severely censured upon this account; the reason whereof I cannot guess, unless it be that because they are written in the same kind of numbers and spirit as an epic poem, they ought therefore to have the same regularity. Now [in] an epic poem, consisting chiefly in narration, it is necessary that the incidents should be related in the same order that they are supposed to have been transacted. But in works of the above-mentioned kind there is no more reason that such order should be observed than that an oration should be as methodical as an history. I think it sufficient that the great hints, suggested from the subject, be so disposed that the first may naturally prepare the reader for what follows, and so on; and that their places cannot be changed without disadvantage to the whole. I will add further, that sometimes gentle deviations, sometimes bold and even abrupt digressions, where the dignity of the subject seems to give the impulse, are proofs of a noble genius; as winding about and returning artfully to the main design are marks of address and dexterity.

Another artifice made use of by pretenders to criticism, is an insinuation, 'that all that is good is borrowed from the ancients.' This is very common in the mouths of pedants, and perhaps in their hearts too; but is often urged by men of no great learning, for reasons very obvious. Now nature being still the same, it is impossible for any modern writer to paint her otherwise than the ancients have done. If, for example, I was to describe the general's horse at the battle of Blenheim, as my fancy represented such a noble beast, and that description should resemble what Virgil hath drawn for the horse of his hero, it would be almost as ill-natured to urge that I had stolen my description from Virgil, as to reproach the duke of Marlborough for fighting like Æneas. All that the most exquisite judgment can perform is, out of that great variety of circumstances wherein natural objects may be considered, to select the most beautiful; and to place images in such views and lights as will affect the fancy after the most delightful manner. But, over and above a just painting of nature, a learned reader will find a new beauty superadded in a happy imitation of some famous ancient, as it revives in his mind the pleasure he took in his first reading such an author. Such copyings as these give that kind of double delight which we perceive when we look upon the children of a beautiful couple, where the eye is not more charmed with the symmetry of the parts, than the mind, by observing the resemblance transmitted from parents to their offspring, and the mingled features of the father and mother. The phrases of holy writ, and allusions to several passages in the inspired writings (though not produced as proofs of doctrine) add majesty and authority to the noblest discourses of the pulpit; in like man-

ner, an imitation of the air of Homer and Virgil raises the
dignity of modern poetry, and makes it appear stately and
venerable.

The last observation I shall make at present is upon the
disgust taken by those critics who put on their clothes prettily,
and dislike every thing that is not written with ease. I hereby
therefore give the genteel part of the learned world to understand, that every thought which is agreeable to nature, and
expressed in language suitable to it, is written with ease.
There are some things which must be written with strength,
which nevertheless are easy. The statue of the gladiator,
though represented in such a posture as strains every muscle,
is as easy as that of Venus, because the one expresses strength
and fury as naturally as the other doth beauty and softness.
The passions are sometimes to be roused, as well as the fancy
to be entertained; and the soul to be exalted and enlarged,
as well as soothed. This often requires a raised figurative
style, which readers of low apprehensions, or soft and languid dispositions (having heard of the words, fustian and
bombast) are apt to reject as stiff and affected language. But
nature and reason appoint different garbs for different things;
and since I write this to the men of dress, I will ask them if a
soldier who is to mount a breach should be adorned like a
beau who is spruced up for a ball?

JOHN HUGHES
[1677–1720]

Hughes was a constant invalid, and through much of his
life in straighted circumstances. In 1717, however, an
appointment as a secretary in the Court of Chancery
provided him with independence for the few remaining years
of his life. He died of consumption on the night of the first
performance of his enormously successful, last, and best
work, The Siege of Damascus, which continued to hold the
stage until the end of the century.

Hughes was a literary man-of-all-work, producing poems,
libretti, essays, and translations. In 1713 he published a
translation of the spurious letters between Heloise and
Abelard which were the basis for Pope's poem, and in 1715
he edited Spenser, with a glossary. Hughes' edition remained
the standard Spenser for forty years.

The contribution to The Guardian reprinted here is
interesting as an obviously direct reply to Rymer, whose
chief objections to Othello Hughes answers not in terms
of the rules, but in terms of audience reaction. The emphasis
on the true-to-life quality of the emotions portrayed is
significant in that while the decorum required by the rules,
which Rymer applied so brutally to the play, has application
to an ideal reality, the reality to which Hughes is appealing
is that which any sensible man can himself feel and observe.
The anecdote at the end of the essay, for Hughes and his
audience the final argument, would have been for Rymer
preposterously irrelevant.

The text of this essay is adapted from Chalmers edition
of The Guardian, 1808.

GUARDIAN NO. 37
ON *OTHELLO*
[1713]

Me duce damnosas homines compescite curas.

OVID. Rem. Amor. v. 69.

Learn, mortals, from my precepts to controul
The furious passions that disturb the soul.

It is natural for an old man to be fond of such entertainments
as revive in his imagination the agreeable impressions made
upon it in his youth: the set of wits and beauties he was first
acquainted with, the balls and drawing-rooms in which he
made an agreeable figure, the music and actors he heard and
saw when his life was fresh and his spirits vigorous and quick,
have usually the preference in his esteem to any succeeding
pleasures that present themselves when his taste is grown
more languid. It is for this reason I never see a picture of
Sir Peter Lely, who drew so many of my first friends and
acquaintance, without a sensible delight; and I am in raptures
when I reflect on the compositions of the famous Mr. Henry
Laws, long before Italian music was introduced into our na-

tion. Above all, I am pleased in observing that the tragedies of Shakespeare, which in my youthful days have so frequently filled my eyes with tears, hold their rank still, and are the great support of our theatre.

It was with this agreeable prepossession of mind, I went some time ago, to see the old tragedy of Othello, and took my female wards with me, having promised them a little before to carry them to the first play of Shakespeare's which should be acted. Mrs. Cornelia, who is a great reader and never fails to peruse the play-bills, which are brought to her every day, gave me notice of it early in the morning. When I came to my lady Lizard's at dinner, I found the young folks all drest, and expecting the performance of my promise. I went with them at the proper time, placed them together in the boxes, and myself by them in a corner seat. As I have the chief scenes of the play by heart, I did not look much on the stage, but formed to myself a new satisfaction in keeping an eye on the faces of my little audience, and observing, as it were by reflection, the different passions of the play represented in their countenances. Mrs. Betty told us the names of several persons of distinction, as they took their places in their boxes, and entertained us with the history of a new marriage or two, till the curtain drew up. I soon perceived that Mrs. Jane was touched with the love of Desdemona, and in a concern to see how she would come off with her parents. Annabella had a rambling eye, and for some time was more taken up with observing what gentlemen looked at her, and with criticising the dress of the ladies, than with any thing that passed on the stage. Mrs. Cornelia, who I have often said is addicted to the study of Romances, commended that speech in the play, in which Othello mentions his 'hair-breadth scapes in th' imminent deadly breach,' and recites his travels and adventures with which he had captivated the heart of Desdemona. The Sparkler looked several times frighted; and as the distress of the play was heightened, their different attention was collected, and fixed wholly on the stage, 'till I saw them all, with a secret satisfaction, betrayed into tears.

I have often considered this play as a noble, but irregular, production of a genius, who had the power of animating the

theatre beyond any writer we have ever known. The touches
of nature in it are strong and masterly; but the œconomy of
the fable, and in some particulars the probability, are too
much neglected. If I would speak of it in the most severe
terms, I should say, as Waller does of the Maid's Tragedy,

> 'Great are its faults, but glorious is its flame.' [1]

But it would be a poor employment in a critic to observe
upon the faults, and shew no taste for the beauties, in a work
that has always struck the most sensible part of our audiences
in a very forcible manner.

The chief subject of this piece is the passion of jealousy,
which the poet hath represented at large, in its birth, its
various workings and agonies, and its horrid consequences.
From this passion, and the innocence and simplicity of the
person suspected, arises a very moving distress.

It is a remark, as I remember, of a modern writer, who is
thought to have penetrated deeply into the nature of the passions, 'that the most extravagant love is nearest to the strongest
hatred.' The Moor is furious in both these extremes. His love
is tempestuous, and mingled with a wildness peculiar to his
character, which seems very artfully to prepare for the change
which is to follow.

How savage, yet how ardent is that expression of the raptures of his heart, when, looking after Desdemona as she
withdraws, he breaks out,

> 'Excellent wench! Perdition catch my soul,
> But I do love thee; and when I love thee not,
> Chaos is come again.'   [III, iii, 90–92]

The deep and subtle villainy of Iago, in working this
change from love to jealousy in so tumultuous a mind as that
of Othello, prepossessed with a confidence in the disinterested
affection of the man who is leading him on insensibly to his
ruin, is likewise drawn with a masterly hand. Iago's broken

---

[1] "Prologue to The Maid's Tragedy Alter'd," lines 4–6:
                    Of all our elder Plays,
        This, and PHILASTER, have the loudest fame:
        Great are their faults, and glorious is their flame.

hints, questions, and seeming care to hide the reason of them;
his obscure suggestions to raise the curiosity of the Moor; his
personated confusion, and refusing to explain himself while
Othello is drawn on and held in suspense till he grows impatient and angry; then his throwing in the poison, and naming to him in a caution the passion he would raise,

'————O beware of jealousy!————'

are inimitable strokes of art, in that scene which has always
been justly esteemed one of the best which was ever represented on the theatre.

To return to the character of Othello; his strife of passions, his starts, his returns of love, and threatenings to Iago,
who puts his mind on the rack, his relapses afterwards to jealousy, his rage against his wife, and his asking pardon of
Iago, whom he thinks he had abused for his fidelity to him,
are touches which no one can overlook that has the sentiments
of human nature, or has considered the heart of man in its
frailties, its penances, and all the variety of its agitations. The
torments which the Moor suffers are so exquisitely drawn as
to render him as much an object of compassion, even in the
barbarous action of murdering Desdemona, as the innocent
person herself who falls under his hand.

But there is nothing in which the poet has more shewn
his judgment in this play than in the circumstance of the
handkerchief, which is employed as a confirmation to the jealousy of Othello already raised. What I would here observe is
that the very slightness of this circumstance is the beauty of
it. How finely has Shakespeare expressed the nature of jealousy in those lines, which, on this occasion, he puts into the
mouth of Iago,

'Trifles light as air
Are to the jealous, confirmation strong
As proofs of holy writ.'   [III, iii, 322–24]

It would be easy for a tasteless critic to turn any of the
beauties I have here mentioned into ridicule: but such an
one would only betray a mechanical judgment, formed out
of borrowed rules and common-place reading, and not aris-

ing from any true discernment in human nature and its passions.

As the moral of this tragedy is an admirable caution against hasty suspicions, and the giving way to the first transports of rage and jealousy, which may plunge a man in a few minutes into all the horrors of guilt, distraction and ruin, I shall further enforce it by relating a scene of misfortunes of the like kind, which really happened some years ago in Spain, and is an instance of the most tragical hurricane of passion I have ever met with in history. It may be easily conceived that a heart ever big with resentments of its own dignity, and never allayed by, reflections which make us honour ourselves for acting with reason and equality, will take fire precipitantly. It will on a sudden flame too high to be extinguished. The short story I am going to tell is a lively instance of the truth of this observation, and a just warning to those of jealous honour to look about them, and begin to possess their souls as they ought, for no man of spirit knows how terrible a creature he is, till he comes to be provoked.

Don Alonzo, a Spanish nobleman, had a beautiful and virtuous wife, with whom he had lived for some years in great tranquillity. The gentleman, however, was not free from the faults usually imputed to his nation; he was proud, suspicious, and impetuous. He kept a Moor in his house, whom, on a complaint from his lady, he had punished for a small offence with the utmost severity. The slave vowed revenge, and communicated his resolution to one of the lady's women with whom he lived in a criminal way. This creature also hated her mistress, for she feared she was observed by her; she therefore undertook to make Don Alonzo jealous, by insinuating that the gardener was often admitted to his lady in private, and promising to make him an eye-witness of it. At a proper time agreed on between her and the Morisco, she sent a message to the gardener, that his lady, having some hasty orders to give him, would have him come that moment to her in her chamber. In the mean time she had placed Alonzo privately in an outer room, that he might observe who passed that way. It was not long before he saw the gardener appear. Alonzo had not patience, but, following him into the apartment, struck him at one blow with a dagger to the heart; then dragging his lady by the hair, without inquiring farther, he instantly killed her.

Here he paused, looked on the dead bodies with all the agitations of a dæmon of revenge; when the wench who had occasioned these terrors, distracted with remorse, threw herself at his feet, and in a voice of lamentation, without sense of the consequence, repeated all her guilt. Alonzo was overwhelmed with all the violent passions at one instant, and uttered the broken voices and motions of each of them for a moment, till at last he recollected himself enough to end his agony of love, anger, disdain, revenge, and remorse, by murdering the maid, the Moor, and himself.

JAMES THOMSON
[1700–1748]

Thomson spent his boyhood in the countryside of southern Scotland and studied for the Presbyterian ministry at the University of Edinburgh, but when in 1725 he moved to London he decided to become a poet. "Winter," the first installment of The Seasons, was published next year to instant acclaim, going through four editions in 1726 alone. The Seasons as a whole was possibly the most popular poem of the century. The public required at least seventy-two editions in one form or another between 1730 and 1800, and another forty-four editions between 1800 and 1820. Not knowing the size of the various editions, we cannot know precisely what these statistics mean, and we must take into account the fact that elegantly bound and illustrated volumes of The Seasons came to be regarded, particularly in the early nineteenth century, as appropriate objects to remain visible on drawing-room tables. Yet even books on drawing-room tables may occasionally be read, and we must surely regard as an indicator of taste the fact that Thomson's rested there along with editions of Shakespeare, the Bible, and Young's Night Thoughts.

Thomson cannot be considered a critic, but any statement about his own poetic ideas from the author of so ubiquitous a poem must be read with some interest. The short Preface reproduced here appeared with the second edition of the poem in June 1726, and continued to be published with separate editions of "Winter" until 1730. Why Thomson dropped it then we do not know; it would *be extremely important if we could be sure that he believed it no longer necessary.*

The present text is that of J. Logie Robertson in the Oxford Standard Authors Edition (London, 1908). I can discover no discussion of the "Preface" as criticism. A. D. McKillop's The Background of Thomson's 'Seasons' *(Minneapolis, 1942) is essential for the study of Thomson's esthetic ideas. Ralph Cohen's* The Art of Discrimination: Thomson's The Seasons and the Language of Criticism *(Berkeley, 1964) should also be consulted. The most helpful general study is Douglas Grant's* James Thomson: Poet of "The Seasons" *(London, 1951).*

PREFACE
TO WINTER
[1726]

I am neither ignorant nor concerned how much one may suffer in the opinion of several persons of great gravity and character by the study and pursuit of poetry.

Although there may seem to be some appearance of reason for the present contempt of it as managed by the most part of our modern writers, yet that any man should seriously declare against that divine art is really amazing. It is declaring against the most charming power of imagination, the most exalting force of thought, the most affecting touch of sentiment—in a word, against the very soul of all learning and politeness. It is affronting the universal taste of mankind, and declaring against what has charmed the listening world from Moses down to Milton. In fine, it is even declaring against the sublimest passages of the inspired writings themselves, and what seems to be the peculiar language of heaven.

The truth of the case is this: These weak-sighted gentlemen cannot bear the strong light of poetry and the finer and more amusing scene of things it displays. But must those therefore whom heaven has blessed with the discerning eye shut it to keep them company?

It is pleasant enough, however, to observe frequently in these enemies of poetry an awkward imitation of it. They sometimes have their little brightnesses when the opening glooms will permit. Nay, I have seen their heaviness on some occasions deign to turn friskish, and witty, in which they make just such another figure as Æsop's Ass when he began to fawn. To complete the absurdity, they would even in their efforts against Poetry fain be poetical; like those gentlemen that reason with a great deal of zeal and severity against reason.

That there are frequent and notorious abuses of Poetry is as true as that the best things are most liable to that misfortune; but is there no end of that clamorous argument against the use of things from the abuse of them? and yet, I hope, that no man who has the least sense of shame in him will fall into it after the present sulphureous attacker of the stage.

To insist no further on this head, let poetry once more be restored to her ancient truth and purity; let her be inspired from heaven, and in return her incense ascend thither; let her exchange her low, venal, trifling, subjects for such as are fair, useful, and magnificent; and let her execute these so as at once to please, instruct, surprise, and astonish: and then of necessity the most inveterate ignorance, and prejudice, shall be struck dumb; and poets yet become the delight and wonder of mankind.

But this happy period is not to be expected, till some long-wished, illustrious man of equal power and beneficence rise on the wintry world of letters: one of a genuine and unbounded greatness and generosity of mind; who, far above all the pomp and pride of fortune, scorns the little addressful flatterer; pierces through the disguised designing villain; discountenances all the reigning fopperies of a tasteless age: and who, stretching his views into late futurity, has the true interest of virtue, learning, and mankind entirely at heart—a character so nobly desirable that to an honest heart it is almost incredible so few should have the ambition to deserve it.

Nothing can have a better influence towards the revival of poetry than the choosing of great and serious subjects, such as at once amuse the fancy, enlighten the head, and warm the heart. These give a weight and dignity to the poem; nor is the pleasure—I should say rapture—both the writer and the reader feels unwarranted by reason or followed by repentant disgust. To be able to write on a dry, barren theme is looked upon by some as the sign of a happy, fruitful genius:—fruitful indeed! like one of the pendant gardens in Cheapside, watered every morning by the hand of the Alderman himself. And what are we commonly entertained with on these occasions save forced unaffecting fancies, little glittering prettinesses, mixed turns of wit and expression, which are as widely different from native poetry as buffoonery is from the perfection of human thinking? A genius fired with the charms of truth and nature is tuned to a sublimer pitch, and scorns to associate with such subjects.

I cannot more emphatically recommend this poetical ambition than by the four following lines from Mr. Hill's poem, called *The Judgment Day*,[1] which is so singular an instance of it:—

> For me, suffice it to have taught my Muse,
> The tuneful Triflings of her tribe to shun;
> And rais'd her warmth such heavenly themes to chuse,
> As, in past ages, the best garlands won.

I know no subject more elevating, more amusing; more ready to awake the poetical enthusiasm, the philosophical reflection, and the moral sentiment, than the works of Nature. Where can we meet with such variety, such beauty, such

---

[1] Aaron Hill (1685–1750). Prolific dramatist; published *Judgment Day* in 1721.

magnificence? All that enlarges and transports the soul! What more inspiring than a calm, wide survey of them? In every dress nature is greatly charming—whether she puts on the crimson robes of the morning, the strong effulgence of noon, the sober suit of the evening, or the deep sables of blackness and tempest! How gay looks the Spring! how glorious the Summer! how pleasing the Autumn! and how venerable the Winter!—But there is no thinking of these things without breaking out into poetry; which is, by-the-by, a plain and undeniable argument of their superior excellence.

For this reason the best, both ancient, and modern, poets have been passionately fond of retirement, and solitude. The wild romantic country was their delight. And they seem never to have been more happy, than when, lost in unfrequented fields, far from the little busy world, they were at leisure, to meditate, and sing the works of Nature.

The book of Job, that noble and ancient poem, which, even, strikes so forcibly through a mangling translation, is crowned with a description of the grand works of Nature; and that, too, from the mouth of their Almighty Author.

It was this devotion to the works of Nature that, in his Georgics, inspired the rural Virgil to write so inimitably; and who can forbear joining with him in this declaration of his, which has been the rapture of ages?

> Me vero primum dulces ante omnia Musae,
> Quarum sacra fero ingenti perculsus amore,
> Accipiant: caelique vias et sidera monstrent,
> Defectus solis varios, lunaeque labores:
> Unde tremor terris: qua vi maria alta tumescant
> Obicibus ruptis, rursusque in seipsa residant:
> Quid tantum oceano properent se tingere soles
> Hyberni: vel quae tardis mora noctibus obstet.
> Sin, has ne possim naturae accedere partes,
> Frigidus obstiterit circum praecordia sanguis;
> Rura mihi et rigui placeant in vallibus amnes,
> Flumina amem silvasque inglorius.[2]

[2] *Georgics* II, 475–86.

Which may be Englished thus:—

> Me may the Muses, my supreme delight!
> Whose priest I am, smit with immense desire,
> Snatch to their care; the starry tracts disclose,
> The sun's distress, the labours of the moon:
> Whence the earth quakes: and by what force the deeps
> Heave at the rocks, then on themselves reflow:
> Why winter-suns to plunge in ocean speed:
> And what retards the lazy summer-night.
> But, lest I should these mystic-truths attain,
> If the cold current freezes round my heart,
> The country me, the brooky vales may please
> Mid woods and streams unknown.

[The rest of the "Preface" consists of compliments to Aaron Hill, David Malloch (David Mallet), and an anonymous "Mira," all of whom had written prefatory poems in praise of *Winter*.]

EDWARD YOUNG
[1683–1765]

———

Young's father was rector of Upham and later Dean of
Salisbury and chaplain to William and Mary. Most of Young's
early good fortune seems attributable to the merit of his
father. After graduation from Oxford he attempted to make
his way in London, not without some success, but without
the success he thought he deserved. In 1725–1728 he
published a series of satires, Love of Fame, The Universal
Passion, generally somewhat undervalued by comparison
with Pope's satires, which they may have influenced. It was
George II's first parliamentary speech which prompted
Young to produce "Ocean: An Ode" with its prefatory
essay on lyric poetry. Sir Leslie Stephen calls the essay
"commonplace," and it is so in that it reflects the neoclassic
view of the proper form and function of the lyric; it is not
commonplace to remember that such theories were a part of
the critical equipment of authors writing in the first quarter
of the eighteenth century. In 1730 Young was presented
the rectory of Welwyn in Hertfordshire, where, beginning
in 1742, he wrote the incredibly popular Night Thoughts
which established his international reputation.

 The decision to omit Young's major critical work,
Conjectures on Original Composition (1759), was not taken
lightly. That essay is, however, for the most part an enormous
expansion of the sentences in "On Lyric Poetry" beginning,
"Above all, in this, as in every work of genius, somewhat
of an original spirit should be, at least, attempted." In
retrospect, Johnson's comment on the Conjectures seems
sound. Boswell records that "[Johnson] was surprized to find

Young receive as novelties, what he thought very common maxims." (Journal of a Tour to the Hebrides, *Thursday, 30th September.*) *Johnson was very likely more familiar with the common maxims of 1759 than modern commentators who have overpraised the* Conjectures *as a document heralding a literary revolution.*

The text printed here is adapted from that of Alexander Chalmers, 1810. "*On Lyric Poetry*" *is also collected by Elledge. This essay seems not to have been the subject of scholarly investigation, but the following essays are informative on Young's criticism:*

Kelly, Richard M.: "*Imitation of Nature: Edward Young's Attack upon Alexander Pope,*" Xavier University Studies, IV (1964), 168–76.
McKillop, Alan D.: "*Richardson, Young, and the* Conjectures," MP, XXII (1925), 391–404.

ON LYRIC POETRY
[1728]

How imperfect soever my own composition may be, yet am
I willing to speak a word or two of the nature of lyric poetry
to show that I have, at least, some idea of perfection in that
kind of poem in which I am engaged, and that I do not think
myself poet enough entirely to rely on inspiration for success
in it.

To our having, or not having, this idea of perfection in
the poem we undertake is chiefly owing the merit or demerit
of our performances, as also the modesty or vanity of our
opinions concerning them. And in speaking of it I shall show
how it unavoidably comes to pass that *bad* poets, that is,
poets in general, are esteemed, and really *are*, the most vain,

the most irritable, and most ridiculous set of men upon earth.
But poetry in its own nature is certainly

—Non hos quæsitum munus in usus.

He that has an idea of perfection in the work he undertakes *may* fail in it; he that has not, *must:* and yet he will be
vain. For every little degree of beauty, how short or improper
soever, will be looked on fondly by him because it is all pure
gains, and more than he promised to himself, and because he
has no test, or standard in his judgment, with which to chastise
his opinion of it.

Now this idea of perfection is, in poetry, more refined
than in other kinds of writing; and because more refined,
therefore more difficult; and because more difficult, therefore
more rarely attained; and the non-attainment of it is, as I have
said, the source of our vanity. Hence the poetic clan are more
obnoxious to vanity than others. And from vanity consequently
flows that great sensibility of disrespect, that quick resentment, that tinder of the mind that kindles at every spark, and
justly marks them out for the *genus irritabile* among mankind.
And from this combustible temper, this serious anger for no
very serious things, things looked on by most as foreign to the
important points of life, as consequentially flows that inheritance of ridicule which devolves on them, from generation to
generation. As soon as they become authors, they become like
Ben Jonson's angry boy, and learn the art of quarrel.

> Concordes amimæ—dum nocte premuntur;
> Heu! quantum inter se bellum, si lumina vitæ
> Attigerint, quantas acies stragemque ciebunt!
> Qui Juvencs! quantas ostentant, aspice, vires.
> Ne, pueri! ne tanta animis assuescite bella.
> Tuque prior, tu parce, genus qui ducis Olympo,
> Sidereo flagrans clypeo, et cœlestibus armis,
> Projice tela manu, sanguis meus!
> Nec te ullæ facies, non terruit ispe Typhœus

---

[1] *Æneid* IV, 647: "A gift besought for no such end!"

Arduus, arma tenens; non te Messapus et Ufens,
Contemptorque Deûm Mezentius.   VIRG.[2]

But to return. He that has this idea of perfection in the work he undertakes, however successful he is, will yet be modest, because to rise up to that idea which he proposed for his model is almost, if not absolutely, impossible.

These two observations account for what may seem as strange, as it is infallibly true; I mean, they show us why good writers have the lowest, and bad writers the highest, opinion of their own performances. They who have only a *partial* idea of this perfection, as their portion of ignorance or knowledge of it is greater or less, have proportionable degrees of modesty or conceit.

Nor, though natural good understanding makes a tolerably just judgment in things of this nature, will the reader judge the worse for forming to himself a notion of what he ought to expect from the piece he has in hand before he begins his perusal of it.

The Ode, as it is the eldest kind of poetry, so it is more spiritous, and more remote from prose than any other in sense, sound, expression, and conduct. Its thoughts should be uncommon, sublime, and moral; its numbers full, easy, and most harmonious; its expression pure, strong, delicate, yet unaffected; and of a *curious felicity* beyond other poems; its conduct should be rapturous, somewhat abrupt, and immethodical to a vulgar eye. That apparent order, and connexion, which gives form and life to *some* compositions, takes away the very soul of *this*. Fire, elevation, and select thought,

---

[2] Elledge has identified this as "a cento of lines from the Aeneid," and gives the following translation: "Souls harmonious now while they are wrapped in night, alas, if they but reach the light of life, what mutual war and carnage shall they arouse. What youths! Behold what strengths they show. O my sons, make not a home within your hearts for such warfare; and do thou first forbear, thou who drawest thy race from heaven ablaze with the starry shield and celestial arms, cast from thy hand, thou blood of mine! No shape daunted thee, no, not Typhoeus' self, towering aloft in arms, nor you, Messapus and Ufens, and Mezentius, scorner of the gods. [Elledge, I, 559.]

are indispensable; an humble, tame, and vulgar ode is the most pitiful errour a pen can commit.

> Musa dedit Fidibus divos, puerosque deorum.[3]

And as its subjects are sublime, its writer's genius should be so too, otherwise it becomes the meanest thing in writing, viz. an involuntary burlesque.

It is the genuine character and true merit of the ode a little to startle some apprehensions. Men of cold complexions are very apt to mistake a want of vigour in their imaginations for a delicacy of taste in their judgments, and, like persons of a tender sight, they look on bright objects in their natural lustre as too glaring; what is most delightful to a stronger eye is painful to them. Thus Pindar, who has as much logic at the bottom as Aristotle or Euclid, to some critics has appeared as mad, and must appear so to all who enjoy no portion of his own divine spirit. Dwarf-understandings, measuring others by their own standard, are apt to think they see a monster when they see a man.

And indeed it seems to be the amends which Nature makes to those whom she has not blessed with an elevation of mind, to indulge them in the comfortable mistake that all is wrong which falls not within the narrow limits of their own comprehensions and relish.

Judgment, indeed, that masculine power of the mind, in ode, as in all compositions, should bear the supreme sway; and a beautiful imagination, as its mistress, should be subdued to its dominion. Hence, and hence only, can proceed the fairest offspring of the human mind.

But then in ode there is this difference from other kinds of poetry, that there the imagination, like a very beautiful mistress, is indulged in the appearance of domineering, though the judgment, like an artful lover, in reality carries its point; and the less it is suspected of it, it shows the more masterly conduct and deserves the greater commendation.

It holds true in this province of writing, as in war, "The

---

[3] Horace, *Ars Poetica*, 83: "To the Lyre the Muse granted tales of Gods and children of gods."

more danger, the more honour." It must be very enterprising;
it must, in Shakespeare's style, have hair-breadth 'scapes, and
often tread the very brink of errour: nor can it ever deserve
the applause of the *real* judge, unless it renders itself obnoxious to the misapprehensions of the contrary.

Such is Casimire's[4] strain among the moderns, whose
lively wit, and happy fire, is an honour to them. And Buchanan[5] might justly be much admired if any thing more than
the sweetness of his numbers and the purity of his diction
were his own: his original, from which I have taken my motto,
through all the disadvantages of a northern prose translation,
is still admirable; and, Cowley says, as preferable in beauty
to Buchanan, as Judæa is to Scotland.

Pindar, Anacreon, Sappho, and Horace, are the great
masters of lyric poetry among Heathen writers. Pindar's Muse,
like Sacharissa, is a stately, imperious, and accomplished
beauty, equally disdaining the use of art and the fear of any
rival, so intoxicating that it was the highest commendation
that could be given an antient that he was not afraid to taste
of her charms:

Pindarici fontis qui non expalluit haustus,[6]

a danger which Horace declares he durst not run.

Anacreon's Muse is like Amoret, most sweet, natural, and
delicate; all over flowers, graces, and charms; inspiring complacency, not awe; and she seems to have good-nature enough
to *admit* a rival, which she cannot *find*.

Sappho's Muse, like Lady ——, is passionately tender, and
glowing; like oil set on fire, she is soft and warm, in excess.
Sappho has left us a few fragments only; Time has swallowed
the rest; but that little which remains, like the remaining jewel

---

[4] Maciej Kazimierz Sarbiewski (1595–?1640). Polish Jesuit poet, "the
Polish Horace." His Odes were translated into English in 1646 by G. Hils.
[5] George Buchanan (1506–1582). Scottish humanist, for a time tutor to
James I (as James VI of Scotland), defender of absolutism, and author
of Latin verse frequently cited as the most accomplished written in Great
Britain.
[6] Horace, *Epistle* I, iii, 10: "Who quailed not at draughts of the Pindaric
spring."

of Cleopatra after the other was dissolved at her banquet, may be esteemed (as was that jewel) a sufficient ornament for the goddess of beauty herself.

Horace's Muse (like one I shall not presume to name) is correct, solid, and moral; she joins all the sweetness and majesty, all the sense and the fire of the former in the justest proportions and degrees, superadding a felicity of dress entirely her own. She moreover is distinguishable by this particularity, that she abounds in hidden graces and secret charms which none but the discerning can discover; nor are any capable of doing full justice, in their opinion, to her excellencies without giving the world, at the same time, an incontestable proof of refinement in their own understandings.

But, after all, to the honour of our own country I must add that I think Mr. Dryden's Ode on St. Cecilia's Day inferior to no composition of this kind. Its chief beauty consists in adapting the numbers most happily to the variety of the occasion. Those by which he has chosen to express Majesty, (viz.)

> Assumes the God,
> Affects to nod,
> And seems to shake the spheres,

are chosen in the following ode because the subject of it is great.

For the more harmony likewise, I chose the frequent return of rhyme, which laid me under great difficulties. But difficulties overcome give grace and pleasure. Nor can I account for the pleasure of rhyme in general (of which the moderns are too fond) but from this truth.

But then the writer must take care that the difficulty *is* overcome. That is, he must make rhyme consistent with as perfect sense and expression as could be expected if he was free from that shackle. Otherwise, it gives neither grace to the work, nor pleasure to the reader, nor, consequently, reputation to the poet.

To sum the whole: Ode should be peculiar, but not strained; moral, but not flat; natural, but not obvious; delicate, but not affected; noble, but not ambitious; full, but not obscure; fiery, but not mad; thick, but not loaded in its numbers, which should be most harmonious, without the least sacrifice of expression or of sense. Above all, in this, as in every work of genius, somewhat of an original spirit should be, at least, attempted; otherwise the poet, whose character disclaims mediocrity, makes a secondary praise his ultimate ambition, which has something of a contradiction in it. Originals only have true life, and differ as much from the best imitations as men from the most animated pictures of them. Nor is what I say at all inconsistent with a due deference for the great standards of antiquity; nay, that very deference is an argument for it, for doubtless their example is on my side in this matter. And we should rather imitate their example in the general motives and fundamental methods of their working, than in their works themselves. This is a distinction, I think, not hitherto made, and a distinction of consequence. For the first may make us their equals; the second must pronounce us their inferiors even in our utmost success. But the first of these prizes is not so readily taken by the moderns, as valuables too massy for easy carriage are not so liable to the thief.

The antients had a particular regard to the choice of their subjects, which were generally national and great. My subject is, in its own nature, noble, most proper for an Englishman, never more proper than on this occasion, and (what is strange) hitherto unsung.

If I stand not absolutely condemned by my own rules; if I have hit the spirit of ode in general; if I cannot think with Mr. Cowley that "Music alone, sometimes, makes an excellent ode,"

Versus inopes rerum, nugæque canoræ,[7]

if there is any thought, enthusiasm, and picture, which are as the body, soul, and robe of Poetry; in a word, if in any degree I have provided rather food for men, than air for wits; I hope smaller faults will meet indulgence for the sake of the design, which is the glory of my country and my king.

And indeed, this may be said, in general, that great sub-

---

[7] Horace, *Ars Poetica,* 322: "Verses void of thought and sonorous trifles."

jects are above being nice; that dignity and spirit ever suffer
from scrupulous exactness; and that the minuter cares ef-
feminate a composition. Great masters of poetry, painting, and
statuary, in their nobler works, have even affected the contrary: and justly; for a truly-masculine air partakes more
of the negligent than of the neat both in writings, and in life—

Grandis oratio haberet majestatis suæ pondus.[8]

PETRON.

A poem, like a criminal under too severe correction, may
lose all its spirit and expire. We know it was Faberrimus, that
was such an artist at a hair or a nail. And we know the cause
was

Quia ponere totum
Nescius.[9]   HOR.

To close: If a piece of this nature wants an apology, I
must own that those who have strength of mind sufficient
profitably to devote the whole of their time to the *severer*
studies, I despair of imitating, I can only envy and admire.
The mind is relieved and strengthened by variety, and he that
sometimes is sporting with his pen is only taking the most
effectual means of giving a general importance to it. This truth
is clear from the knowledge of human nature and of history,
from which I could cite very celebrated instances did I not
fear that, by citing them, I should condemn myself, who am so
little qualified to follow their example in its full extent.

[8] *Satyr.* iv: "The grand style of oratory would have its full force and
splendour."
[9] *Ars Poetica,* 34: "Because he cannot represent a whole figure."

MARK AKENSIDE
[1721–1770]

Son of a dissenting butcher of Newcastle-on-Tyne, Akenside very early showed literary promise. At sixteen he sent to the Gentleman's Magazine a poem in Spenserian stanzas, "The Virtuoso," which anticipated the better known pieces in that measure by Shenstone and Thomson, and at seventeen, in 1738, he is said to have begun working on The Pleasures of Imagination. In 1739 he was sent by the dissenting congregation of Newcastle to Edinburgh to study for the ministry, but while there he became attracted to medicine, and after repaying the Newcastle congregation devoted himself to a medical career, in which he was later enormously successful.

The Pleasures of Imagination, his masterwork, was published in 1744 by Dodsley, who had taken Pope's advice that "this is no every day writer." The poem was highly commended at the time, and Akenside never equalled this achievement, though he published more poetry, mostly rather stilted odes, and a considerable quantity of prose—the latter as editor of Dodsley's Museum.

A. O. Aldridge, in "Akenside and Imagination" [Studies in Philology XLII (1945), 769–92], has opposed the usual contention that Akenside's theory of imagination anticipates romantic theory, and suggests that we are to think of it "in connection with established moral and esthetic traditions of the eighteenth century . . . Akenside's concept of imagination is an amalgamation of nearly all the characteristics attributed to it in esthetic speculation up to the year 1744." This is surely true, and readers of this

*anthology will recognize, at least, echoes of Shaftesbury. But
the following selection from the end of the third book may
none the less be of interest to students of the early nineteenth
century as demonstrating, if such demonstration still be
needed, that certain aspects of romantic theory were entering
into common literary thought before the death of Pope.*

There were at least sixteen separate editions of The
Pleasures of Imagination *during the eighteenth century,
plus at least eight editions of Akenside's collected poems.
The poetical works in one form or another were published
regularly until the latter nineteenth century. Akenside
made considerable revisions in his major poem (see Jeffrey
Hart, below). The text used here is that of Mrs. Barbauld's
edition of 1796, and, for the part selected, represents
essentially the 1744 version.*

S. H. Monk *comments on the poem in* The Sublime. *See also:*

Aldridge, A. O.: "The Eclecticism of Mark Akenside's 'The
    Pleasures of Imagination,' " Journal of the History of
    Ideas, V (1944), 292–314.
Hart, Jeffrey: "Akenside's Revision of The Pleasures of
    Imagination," PMLA, LXXIV (1959), 67–74.
Houpt, Charles T.: Mark Akenside: a biographical and
    critical study, Philadelphia, 1944.
Thorpe, Clarence D.: "Addison and Hutcheson on the
    Imagination," ELH, II (1935), 215–234.
Williams, Iolo A.: Seven XVIIIth Century Bibliographies,
    London, 1924.

FROM THE PLEASURES
OF IMAGINATION
[1744]

BOOK III

    For when the different images of things   312
By chance combin'd, have struck the attentive soul
With deeper impulse, or, connected long,
Have drawn her frequent eye; howe'er distinct
The external scenes, yet oft the ideas gain
From that conjunction an eternal tie,
And sympathy unbroken. Let the mind
Recall one partner of the various league,
Immediate, lo! the firm confederates rise,   320
And each his former station straight resumes:
One movement governs the consenting throng,

And all at once with rosy pleasure shine,
Or all are sadden'd with the glooms of care. . . .
Such is the secret union, when we feel   337
A song, a flower, a name, at once restore
Those long-connected scenes where first they mov'd
The attention: backward through her mazy walks
Guiding the wanton fancy to her scope,
To temples, courts, or fields; with all the band
Of painted forms, of passions and designs
Attendant: whence, if pleasing in itself,
The prospect from that sweet accession gains
Redoubled influence o'er the listening mind.

    By these mysterious ties the busy power
Of memory her ideal train preserves
Entire; or when they would elude her watch,   350
Reclaims their fleeting footsteps from the waste
Of dark oblivion; thus collecting all
The various forms of being to present,
Before the curious aim of mimic art,
Their largest choice: like spring's unfolded blooms
Exhaling sweetness, that the skilful bee
May taste at will, from their selected spoils
To work her dulcet food. For not the expanse
Of living takes in summer's noontide calm,
Reflects the bordering shade, and sun-bright heavens   360
With fairer semblance; not the sculptur'd gold
More faithful keeps the graver's lively trace,
Than he whose birth the sister powers of art
Propitious view'd, and from his genial star
Shed influence to the seeds of fancy kind;
Than his attemper'd bosom must preserve
The seal of nature. There alone unchang'd,
Her form remains. The balmy walks of May
There breathe perennial sweets; the trembling chord
Resounds for ever in the abstracted ear,   370
Melodious: and the virgin's radiant eye,
Superior to disease, to grief, and time,
Shines with unbating lustre. Thus at length

Endow'd with all that nature can bestow,
The child of fancy oft in silence bends
O'er these mixt treasures of his pregnant breast,
With conscious pride. From them he oft resolves
To frame he knows not what excelling things;
And win he knows not what sublime reward
Of praise and wonder. By degrees, the mind   380
Feels her young nerves dilate: the plastic powers
Labour for action: blind emotions heave
His bosom; and with loveliest frenzy caught,
From earth to heaven he rolls his daring eye,
From heaven to earth. Anon ten thousand shapes,
Like spectres trooping to the wizard's call,
Flit swift before him. From the womb of earth,
From ocean's bed they come: the eternal heavens
Disclose their splendors, and the dark abyss
Pours out her births unknown. With fixed gaze   390
He marks the rising phantoms. Now compares
Their different forms; now blends them, now divides,
Enlarges and extenuates by turns;
Opposes, ranges in fantastic bands,
And infinitely varies. Hither now,
Now thither fluctuates his inconstant aim,
With endless choice perplex'd. At length his plan
Begins to open. Lucid order dawns;
And as from Chaos old the jarring seeds
Of nature at the voice divine repair'd   400
Each to its place, till rosy earth unveil'd
Her fragrant bosom, and the joyful sun
Sprung up the blue serene; by swift degrees
Thus disentangled, his entire design
Emerges. Colours mingle, features join,
And lines converge: the fainter parts retire;
The fairer eminent in light advance;
And every image on its neighbour smiles
Awhile he stands, and with a father's joy
Contemplates. Then with Promethéan art,   410
Into its proper vehicle he breathes
The fair conception; which, embodied thus,

And permanent, becomes to eyes or ears
An object ascertain'd: while thus inform'd,
The various organs of his mimic skill,
The consonance of sounds, the featur'd rock,
The shadowy picture and impassion'd verse,
Beyond their proper powers attract the soul
By that expressive semblance, while in sight
Of nature's great original we scan   420
The lively child of art; while line by line,
And feature after feature we refer
To that sublime exemplar whence it stole
Those animating charms. Thus beauty's palm
Betwixt them wavering hangs: applauding love
Doubts where to chuse; and mortal man aspires
To tempt creative praise. . . .

    Such various bliss the well-tun'd heart enjoys,   437
Favour'd of heaven! while, plung'd in sordid cares,
The unfeeling vulgar mocks the boon divine:
And harsh austerity, from whose rebuke   440
Young love and smiling wonder shrink away
Abash'd and chill of heart, with sager frowns
Condemns the fair enchantment. On my strain,
Perhaps even now, some cold, fastidious judge
Casts a disdainful eye; and calls my toil,
And calls the love and beauty which I sing,
The dream of folly. Thou, grave censor! say,
Is beauty then a dream, because the glooms
Of dulness hang too heavy on the sense,
To let her shine upon thee? So the man   450
Whose eye ne'er open'd on the light of heaven,
Might smile with scorn while raptur'd vision tells
Of the gay-colour'd radiance flushing bright
O'er all creation. From the wise be far
Such gross unhallow'd pride; nor needs my song
Descend so low; but rather now unfold,
If human thought could reach, or worlds unfold,
By what mysterious fabric of the mind,
The deep-felt joys and harmony of sound

Result from airy motion; and from shape   460
The lovely phantoms of sublime and fair.
By what fine ties hath God connected things
When present in the mind, which in themselves
Have no connection? Sure the rising sun
O'er the cœrulean convex of the sea,
With equal brightness, and with equal warmth
Might roll his fiery orb; nor yet the soul
Thus feel her frame expanded, and her powers
Exulting in the splendor she beholds;
Like a young conqueror moving through the pomp   470
Of some triumphal day. When join'd at eve,
Soft-murmuring streams and gales of gentlest breath
Melodious Philomela's wakeful strain
Attemper, could not man's discerning ear
Through all its tones the sympathy pursue;
Nor yet this breath divine of nameless joy
Steal through his veins and fan the awaken'd heart,
Mild as the breeze, yet rapturous as the song.

      But were not nature still endow'd at large
With all which life requires, though unadorn'd   480
With such enchantment? Wherefore then her form
So exquisitely fair? her breath perfum'd
With such ætherial sweetness? whence her voice
Inform'd at will to raise or to depress
The impassion'd soul? and whence the robes of light
Which thus invest her with more lovely pomp
Than fancy can describe? Whence but from thee,
O source divine of ever-flowing love,
And thy unmeasur'd goodness? Not content
With every food of life to nourish man,   490
By kind illusions of the wondering sense
Thou mak'st all nature beauty to his eye,
Or music to his ear: well-pleas'd he scans
The goodly prospect; and with inward smiles
Treads the gay verdure of the painted plain;
Beholds the azure canopy of heaven,
And living lamps that over-arch his head

With more than regal splendor; bends his ears
To the full choir of water, air, and earth;
Nor heeds the pleasing error of his thought,   500
Nor doubts the painted green or azure arch,
Nor questions more the music's mingling sounds
Than space, or motion, or eternal time;
So sweet he feels their influence to attract
The fixed soul; to brighten the dull glooms
Of care, and make the destin'd road of life
Delightful to his feet. So fables tell,
The adventurous hero, bound on hard exploits,
Beholds with glad surprise, by secret spells
Of some kind sage, the patron of his toils,   510
A visionary paradise disclos'd
Amid the dubious wild; with streams, and shades,
And airy songs, the enchanted landscape smiles,
Cheers his long labours and renews his frame.

     What then is taste, but these internal powers
Active, and strong, and feelingly alive
To each fine impulse? a discerning sense
Of decent and sublime, with quick disgust
From things deform'd, or disarrang'd, or gross
In species? This, nor gems, nor stores of gold,   520
Nor purple state, nor culture can bestow;
But God alone, when first his active hand
Imprints the secret bias of the soul.
He, mighty parent! wise and just in all,
Free as the vital breeze or light of heaven,
Reveals the charms of nature. Ask the swain
Who journeys homeward from a summer-day's
Long labour, why, forgetful of his toils
And due repose, he loiters to behold
The sunshine gleaming as through amber clouds,   530
O'er all the western sky; full soon, I ween,
His rude expression and untutor'd airs,
Beyond the power of language, will unfold
The form of beauty smiling at his heart,
How lovely! how commanding! But though heaven

In every breast hath sown these early seeds
Of love and admiration, yet in vain,
Without fair culture's kind parental aid,
Without enlivening suns, and genial showers,
And shelter from the blast, in vain we hope   540
The tender plant should rear its blooming head,
Or yield the harvest promis'd in its spring.
Nor yet will every soil with equal stores
Repay the tiller's labour; or attend
His will, obsequious, whether to produce
The olive or the laurel. Different minds
Incline to different objects: one pursues
The vast alone, the wonderful, the wild;
Another sighs for harmony, and grace,
And gentlest beauty. Hence when lightning fires   550
The arch of heaven, and thunders rock the ground,
When furious whirlwinds rend the howling air,
And ocean, groaning from his lowest bed,
Heaves his tempestuous billows to the sky;
Amid the mighty uproar, while below
The nations tremble, Shakespeare looks abroad
From some high cliff, superior, and enjoys
The elemental war. But Waller longs,
All on the margin of some flowery stream
To spread his careless limbs amid the cool   560
Of plantane shades, and to the listening deer
The tale of slighted vows and love's disdain
Resound soft-warbling, all the live-long day:
Consenting Zephyr sighs; the weeping rill
Joins in his plaint, melodious; mute the groves;
And hill and dale with all their echoes mourn.
Such and so various are the tastes of men.

      Oh! blest of heaven, whom not the languid songs
Of luxury, the syren! not the bribes
Of sordid wealth, nor all the gaudy spoils   570
Of pageant honour can seduce to leave
Those ever-blooming sweets, which from the store
Of nature fair imagination culls

To charm the enliven'd soul! What though not all
Of mortal offspring can attain the heights
Of envied life; though only few possess
Patrician treasures or imperial state;
Yet nature's care, to all her children just,
With richer treasures and an ampler state
Endows at large whatever happy man   580
Will deign to use them. His the city's pomp,
The rural honours his. Whate'er adorns
The princely dome, the column and the arch
The breathing marbles and the sculptur'd gold,
Beyond the proud possessor's narrow claim,
His tuneful breast enjoys. For him, the spring
Distils her dews, and from the silken gem
Its lucid leaves unfolds: for him, the hand
Of autumn tinges every fertile branch
With blooming gold and blushes like the morn.   590
Each passing hour sheds tribute from her wings;
And still new beauties meet his lonely walk,
And loves unfelt attract him. Not a breeze
Flies o'er the meadow, not a cloud imbibes
The setting sun's effulgence, not a strain
From all the tenants of the warbling shade
Ascends, but whence his bosom can partake
Fresh pleasure, unreprov'd. Nor thence partakes
Fresh pleasure only: for the attentive mind,
By this harmonious action on her powers   600
Becomes herself harmonious: wont so oft
In outward things to meditate the charm
Of sacred order, soon she seeks at home
To find a kindred order, to exert
Within herself this elegance of love,
This fair inspir'd delight: her temper'd powers
Refine at length, and every passion wears
A chaster, milder, more attractive mien.
But if to ampler prospects, if to gaze
On nature's form, where, negligent of all   610
These lesser graces, she assumes the port
Of that eternal majesty that weigh'd

The world's foundations, if to these the mind
Exalts her daring eye; then mightier far
Will be the change, and nobler. Would the forms
Of servile custom cramp her generous powers?
Would sordid policies, the barbarous growth
Of ignorance and rapine, bow her down
To tame pursuits, to indolence and fear?
Lo! she appeals to nature, to the winds   620
And rolling waves, the sun's unwearied course,
The elements and seasons: all declare
For what the eternal Maker has ordain'd
The powers of man: we feel within ourselves
His energy divine: he tells the heart,
He meant, he made us to behold and love
What he beholds and loves, the general orb
Of life and being; to be great like him,
Beneficent and active. Thus the men
Whom nature's works can charm, with God himself   630
Hold converse; grow familiar, day by day,
With his conceptions, act upon his plan;
And form to his, the relish of their souls.

JOHN BROWN
[1715–1766]

Born the son of a Northumberland curate, Brown received
a Cambridge B.A. with distinction from St. John's College
in 1735. He took orders, his career in the Church being
furthered by the ubiquitous William Warburton, who had
observed a compliment to himself in Brown's "An Essay
on Satire, Occasion'd by the Death of Mr. Pope" (1745),
and who also, in respect to Brown's disapproval of Shaftesbury,
found that piece to his liking. Brown was perhaps too careful
not to let the friendship lapse.

In 1751 Brown published Essays on the Characteristicks,
which Leslie Stephen describes as "a remarkably clear
statement of the utilitarian theory." J. S. Mill praised the
book highly in his essay upon Bentham. Brown's most
popular and influential work, however, was An Estimate of
the Manners and Principles of the Times (1757), in which
he expresses forcibly the common complaints against
effeminancy and luxury, and suggests that these weaknesses
result from an excess of Progress. After the publication of
this book Brown was distinguished as "Estimate Brown."
He also worte A Dissertation on the Rise, Union, and
Power, the Progressions, Separations, and Corruptions of
Poetry and Music (1763), in which he takes the primitivistic
view that these arts arose together out of savage rites.

The selection reprinted here does not very accurately
represent the point of view of the Essays on the
Characteristicks as a whole, and should not be read in that
light. It is interesting, however, as a late example of genre
criticism, and as illustrating what happened to that mode

when it was associated with later ideas of imagination and passion. The selection is adapted from the fifth edition, 1764.

There has been no significant comment on Brown's literary criticism. Hermann M. Flasdieck has written (*in German*) John Brown (1715–1766) und seine Dissertation on Poetry and Music, *Halle, 1924.*

ESSAYS ON THE CHARACTERISTICKS

[1751]

From "Essay on Ridicule"

Perhaps there is no species in writing (except only that of mere narration) but what will fall under the denomination of *Poetry, Eloquence, or Argument.* The first lays hold of the imagination; the second, through the imagination, seizes the passions; the last addresseth itself to the Reason of mankind. The immediate, essential end therefore of Poetry is to *please*, of Eloquence to *persuade*, of Argument to *instruct*. To this end, the poet dwells on such images as are *beautiful;* the orator selects every circumstance that is *affecting;* the philosopher only admits what is *true.* But as all these, in their several kinds of writing, address themselves to Man, who is compounded of imagination, passion, and reason; so they seldom confine themselves to their respective provinces, but lay hold of each other's art, the more effectually to gain admission and success to their own. Yet still the Masters in these various kinds of composition know how to keep their several boundaries distinct, not to make unwarrantable inroads into each other's provinces, nor remove those lines which Nature hath prescribed, but so to limit their excursions that the intelligent may always know what is designed: a *Poem,* an *Oration,* or an *Argument.*

Thus the judicious Poet, though his immediate and universal aim is beautiful imitation, yet, in order to become more pleasing, endeavours often to be interesting, always to be rational. His application being made to Man, should he let loose Imagination to its random-flights, he must shock the reason of every penetrating observer. Hence appears the necessity of cultivating that maxim in poetical composition, which the two best of French critics, Boileau and Bouhours have so much insisted on, "that all poetical Beauty must be founded in Truth." Because in the unlimited excursions of Fancy, though one faculty should approve, yet another is disgusted: though Imagination acquiesce in false beauty, Reason will reject it with disdain. Thus, although the primary and essential end of poetry is to please by imitation, yet as it is addressed to Man, *instruction* makes a necessary though an adventitious part of its character. *

From this view of things we may, in passing, further see the nature, limits, and comparative excellence of the various Kinds of poetry. The descriptive holds entirely of the Imagination, and may be termed *pure poetry* or Imitation; yet, with regard to the secondary end of instruction, it seems to merit only the lowest place, because it is then perfect

---

* Hence the debate mentioned by Strabo (l.i.) between Eratosthenes and some of the Ancients may easily be decided. The first insisting that *pleasure,* the other that *instruction* was the only end of poetry. They were both wrong: as it appears that these two ends must always be united in some degree. However, Eratosthenes was nearer the truth, as he alleged the essential end. 'Tis no bad description, given by Mr. Dryden and others, of the end of poetry, that it is "to instruct, by pleasing," though upon the whole it throws more weight on the circumstance of instruction than the thing will bear. Perhaps it had better been said that it is "to please, consistently with instruction."

when it satisfies the imagination; and while it offends not reason or the affections nothing further with regard to these faculties is expected from it. The *tragic, comic, satiric,* and the *elegy,* as they chiefly regard the Passions and the heart of man, so they draw much of their force from the sources of eloquence. On the other hand, the *didactic,* as it makes its chief application to Reason, though it retains so much of the graces of imagination as to merit the name of poetry, is principally of the *logical* species. The *epic,* by its great extent, includes all these Kinds by turns, and is therefore the noblest, both in its primary and secondary intention. Much indeed hath been occasionally asserted by several writers concerning the superior dignity of the tragic species*: But this hath been more in the way of affirmation than proof. Their opinion seems to have been founded on a mistaken interpretation of Aristotle, whose supposed authority on this subject hath generally passed unquestioned. But whoever shall thoroughly examine the sentiments of the *grand Master* will find he only meant to assert that the *mode of imitation* in tragedy is more forcible, and therefore superior to that of the epic Kind, because in the last the action is only told, in the former it is visibly represented. This is the truth. But if we consider not the mode of imitation but the subjects imitated; if we consider the comparative greatness of the action which these two Kinds of poetry can comprehend, and the moral ends of instruction no less than the variety and beauty of description, which constitutes the very essence of poetry, we shall find the epic greatly superior on account of the extent and importance of those actions, and the variety of characters which it is capable of involving. Thus, for instance, such an action as the death of Oepidus or Cato may be more perfectly imitated (because visibly represented) in tragedy than in the epos: But a much greater and more extensive action, such as the establishment of an empire, with all its subordinate episodes, religious, political, and moral, cannot be comprehended or

---

* Thus the excellent Mr. Addison: "A perfect Tragedy is the noblest Production of human Nature." Spectator, No. 39.

exhibited in tragedy, while yet they may be perfectly described in the *Epopée*.

So much concerning poetry will be found to have relation to our subject. But as the question concerning ridicule will turn chiefly to the proper subordination of eloquence, it will be necessary to consider this Kind of composition in a more particular manner.

Eloquence, then, is no other than a species of poetry applied to the particular end of persuasion. For persuasion can only be effected by rowzing the passions of the soul; and these, we have seen, are only to be moved by a force impressed on the imagination, assuming the appearance of Truth, which is the essential nature of poetical composition. Thus the Lord Verulam: "In all persuasions that are wrought by eloquence, and other impression of like nature which paint and disguise the true appearance of things, the chief recommendation unto reason is from the imagination."[1] And the judicious Strabo, consistently with this theory, tells us that in fact "the oratorial elocution was but an imitation of the poetical: This appeared first, and was approved. They who imitated it took off the measures, but still preserved all the other parts of poetry in their writings. Such were Cadmus the Milesian, Pherecydes, and Hecataeus. Their followers then took something more from what was left, and at length elocution descended into the prose which is now among us."[2]

Thus, as the passions must have an apparent object of good or evil offered by the imagination in order to excite them, so eloquence must offer apparent evidence ere it can be received and acquiesced in, for the mind cannot embrace known falsehood. So that every opinion which eloquence instills, though it be the pure result of certain fictitious images impressed on the fancy, is always regarded as the result of rational conviction, and received by the mind as truth.

Hence we may perceive the just foundation of the well-known maxim in rhetorical composition, *Artis est celare artem* [3]

---

[1] *De Aug. Scient. I. ii.* (Brown's citation).
[2] Strabo, Book I (Brown's citation).
[3] Proverbial: *Ars est celare artem* (art consists in concealing art).

In every other art, where the end is pleasure, instruction, or admiration, the greater art the master displays, the more effectually he gains his purpose; but where the end is persuasion, the discovery of his art must defeat its force and design. For ere he can persuade he must seem to apply to his hearer's reason, while in fact he is working on his imagination and affections. Now this, once known, must defeat his purpose, because nothing can persuade but what has the appearance of truth.

Hence too we may see where the true medium lies between the too frequent use and delicate avoidance of poetical images in eloquence. Metaphors, similies, bold figures, and glowing expressions are proper so far as they point the imagination to the main subject on which the passion is to be excited; when they begin to amuse they grow absurd. And here, by the way, lies the essential difference between the epic and tragic composition. For the epic, tending chiefly to admiration and instruction, allows a full display of art; but the tragic, being of the persuasive kind, must only regard and touch upon poetical images in this single view, as they tend to rowze the passions of the soul. Macrobius* hath collected many elegant examples of this poetic elocution from the *Eneid*. He hath ranged them in classes, and pointed out the fountains whence the great poet drew his pathos: and sure it may with truth be affirmed, that "the Master-strokes of that divine work are rather of the Tragic than the Epic species."

These remarks will enable us to discover the impropriety of an opinion commonly held † "that the reason why eloquence had such power, and wrought such wonders in Athens and Rome, was because it had become the general taste and study of the times; that consequently these cities were more sensible to its charms, and therefore more warmly affected by it." Now, though with regard to pure poetry or strict argument, where either pleasure or truth are the purposed ends, this reasoning might hold, yet, when applied to eloquence,

---

* Saturnal, 1, iv. passim.
† See Mr. Hume's Essay on Eloquence.

it seems to be without foundation. For where ignorance is predominant, there any application to the fancy or the passions is most likely to wear the appearance of reason, and therefore the most likely to persuade. As men improve in knowledge, such application must proportionably lose its force, and true reasoning prevail. Hence it should seem that they who make the constituent principles of eloquence familiar to their imagination, must of all others be best enabled to separate *Truth* from its *Appearances,* and distinguish between *Argument* and *Colouring.* An artful oration will indeed afford great pleasure to one who hath applied himself to the study of rhetoric, yet not so as that he shall be persuaded by it. On the contrary, his pleasure consists in a reflex act of the understanding, and arises from the very circumstance which prevents persuasion, a *Discovery of the Master's Art.*

The true reason, therefore, why eloquence gained such mighty power in these famed Republics was "because the orators addressed themselves to the people as their judges." Here the art triumphed: for it had not reason to instruct, but imagination and passion to controul.

SAMUEL JOHNSON
[1709–1784]

Johnson's most carefully considered critical statement is
undoubtedly the "Preface" to his edition of Shakespeare,
whose plays all through the eighteenth century provided,
for obvious reasons, the greatest challenge to critics. This
"Preface" is easily accessible, and is therefore omitted
from this anthology, though not without regret; for no place
else does Johnson so ably display those qualities—erudition
corrected by clearsightedness, intellect tempered by wisdom,
the standards of literature adjusted to the standards of the
perceiving reader—which while he was alive and ever since
have assured him recognition as the greatest critic of the
eighteenth century, and one of the major critics in
English. That piece is also a rhetorical tour de force, a fact
insufficiently acknowledged by those who will carp at
Johnson's carpings without recognizing their function in
giving unimportant points to an opponent (for Johnson
seldom wrote without thinking of an opponent to be tossed
and gored), while reserving the ground on which he was
to stand. The retreat is strategic; most of the terrain
abandoned would not even in this day of Shakespeare idolatry
be very strongly defended; the victory is superb and decisive.
That battle over the unities has never had to be fought
again; though Johnson was not the first to fight it, he was
the last.

    Johnson has often been regarded as the last great
neoclassic critic, indeed as the last bulwark of an outmoded
creed, stubbornly and insensitively upholding critical positions
untenable by their very nature and inapplicable to any

*literature at any time, but particularly to any literature
produced since 1800. A partial reading of Johnson can
indeed support this view, but only if one ignores much of
his criticism. That criticism, it is true, he wrote without the
benefit of having read Coleridge; but it is also true that
Coleridge may have derived no little benefit from having
perused Johnson, for a close reading of the "Preface" to
Shakespeare demonstrates that in that essay most of the
neoclassic critical ikons are smashed beyond repair: the
ikon of the five act structure, of Horatian decorum, of the
single plot (though not of the unity of action, of course),
of the unities of place and time, of absolute and a priori
standards of criticism. Johnson was by no means the first
to wield the hammer, but his blows were decisive, coming
as they did from his conviction that literature, to use his
own phrase (and a neoclassic phrase, but hardly used in the
neoclassic sense), "mirrors life." The emphasis is on life—
"This reasoning," he says in refuting the idea that the
mixture of comic and serious scenes is indecorous, "is so
specious [that is, plausible] that it is received as true even
by those who in daily experience feel it to be false." "In
every real, and therefore in every imitative action, the
intervals may be more or fewer . . ." "His story requires
Romans or kings, but he thinks only on men."*

*There remain two other aspects of Johnson's
neoclassicism, his didacticism and his use of the term
"general nature." "Nothing can please many and please
long but just representations of general nature." The term
is certainly neoclassic, as is Johnson's use of it, a use which,
however, does not necessarily render it intolerably remote.
For why do we, today, still acclaim Shakespeare? Why,
indeed, Aeschylus and Sophocles if it be not for the
representations of "general nature," that is, because their
plays are "universal," because in Aeschylus, Sophocles, and
Shakespeare our minds do "repose on the stability of truth"?*

*As to the didacticism, that to be sure is neoclassic; it is
also Platonic, mediaeval, Victorian, and sometimes modern.
The idea that literature ought to be instructive, that it
ought to instruct while delighting, no matter how much it
might have repelled Poe and may still repel the modern
romantics, is hardly one peculiar to neoclassicism. We may
find this view limiting Johnson's ability to focus on some*

*aspects of literature which attract us, but though it is a
limitation more prevalent in his criticism and in his age
than in ours, it is peculiar to none.*

*Johnson's critical standards are not, then, simply
neoclassic standards; but this is not to say that they are our
standards, or those of Wordsworth or Coleridge. They are,
however, nearer our standards than are those of Dryden,
Dennis, or Pope, and they move nearer because what Johnson
ultimately asks of literature is nearer to what we ask: that
it represent real life and real emotions, that it engage us as
men rather than engaging our attention to literary constructs
in themselves. This is implied in the "Notes" to Shakespeare,
where Johnson occasionally responded with an intensity
he did not allow himself in formal pronouncements.*

*Having said this much, we must turn to the selections
presented here, which may at first reading seem not only odd
but somewhat perverse. Of the papers from* The Rambler,
*the first is on a topic upon which Johnson was as well
prepared as any critic of his age to pronounce, and a subject
about which modern students of the eighteenth century are
peculiarly uninformed. Johnson's analysis of Milton's
versification repays the closest attention, not only as
demonstrating the exactness of Johnson's own standards and
the nicety of his apprehension, but as illuminating for us
conceptions about verse (perhaps near to Milton's own) now
as remote as the Dead Sea Scrolls, though still vital for the
mid-eighteenth century. The last sentence of the essay is
worth attention: Johnson much more frequently than not
pays Milton the highest compliments in his power.*

*Ramblers 93 and 156 exemplify the good sense, the
manliness, the independence of the critic, tempered by his
awareness of "the treachery of the human heart," "the
resistless vicissitudes of the heart." No. 156 adumbrates
much of what Johnson was to say more memorably in the
"Preface" to Shakespeare. If this be neoclassic criticism—and
there is no reason to deny it that appellation—one can
hardly ask for better.*

*Rambler 168 again concerns a subject remote from
modern critics and poets, but one still much alive for Johnson
and his age. We will all immediately disagree with
Johnson's point, because on the issue of diction, as of
metre, Johnson is exactly in the neoclassic center, and*

his view is one to be remembered when reading the poetry of the age. We may note that almost alone in matters of language does an attitude really difficult for us to accept manifest itself in Johnson's criticism.

To the admirable and famous Chapter X of Rasselas we must bring the skepticism of that book as a whole. The chapter is indeed an exposition of the creed of the ideal renaissance poet, who is acquainted with all stations of life, learned in all arts, and who does not paint the streaks of the tulip. The fact, however, that Imlac found all this difficult of accomplishment does not force us to believe that the creed is Johnson's own, as the opening paragraph of Chapter XI may show. Rasselas is such a dense tissue of ironies that we must beware of pointing to any one statement with the conviction that "here is what Johnson believed"; to say this of Imlac's remarks at a point in the story where he has been recounting a succession of failures is doubly dangerous. Johnson just as likely intends us to understand that this particular poetic creed is outworn beyond recovery: no human being by these exertions can be a poet. The poetic creed expressed may, then, represent an ideal goal to which the critic looks back not without regret, but hardly for Johnson a practical goal, no matter how desirable, and the remarks on the general and particular—the famous tulip passage—become, like the rest of the book, shaded with double meanings.

The Lives of the English poets is possibly the work which has done most to keep alive Johnson's reputation as an author. The biographies are good reading, and the criticism astute. The critical selections anthologized here have an obvious unity in that each deals with a poet who wrote most memorably in blank verse; they also show that Johnson was capable of somewhat wider sympathies than he is frequently credited with.

The text reproduced here is from the 1825 Oxford edition of Johnson's Works. This remains the standard edition until the Yale edition, in progress, is completed. Johnson's criticism has been and continues to be a challenge to scholarship. For supplementation or correction of the views stated above, the student is referred to the bibliography by James L. Clifford, Johnsonian Studies 1887–1950 (Minneapolis, 1951) and its continuation to 1960 by James L.

Clifford and Donald J. Greene in Johnsonian Studies *(ed.*
Magdi Wahba, Cairo, 1962). Jean H. Hagstrum's Samuel
Johnson's Literary Criticism (Minneapolis, 1952; revised
edition, including "Studies of Johnson's Literary Criticism
since 1952," Chicago, 1967) will not soon be superseded.
Chapters on Johnson are found in all general treatments
of English criticism or of eighteenth-century criticism.
Atkins' view is conventionally complimentary, while that
of René Wellek in A History of Modern Criticism,
1750–1950, vol. I (New Haven, 1955) suffers from
inconsistencies. Emerson R. Marks' chapter in The Poetics
of Reason *(New York, 1968) is sensible and readable. See also:*

Hardy, John: "The 'Poet of Nature' and Self-Knowledge:
    One Aspect of Johnson's Moral Reading of Shakespeare,"
    University of Toronto Quarterly, XXXVI (1967),
    141–160.
Kallich, Martin: "Samuel Johnson's Principles of Criticism
    and Imlac's 'Dissertation upon Poetry,'" Journal of
    Aesthetics and Art Criticism, XXV (1966), 71–82.
Misenheimer, James B., Jr.: "Dr. Johnson's Concept of
    Literary Fiction," Modern Language Review, LXII
    (1967), 598–605.
Sachs, Arieh: "Generality and Particularity in Johnson's
    Thought," SEL, V (1965), 491–511.
————: Passionate Intelligence: Imagination and Reason in
    the Work of Samuel Johnson, Baltimore, 1967.
Sigworth, Oliver F.: "Johnson's Lycidas: The End of
    Renaissance Criticism," Eighteenth Century Studies, I
    (1967), 159–168.

FROM THE RAMBLER
[1751]

In tenui labor. VIRG. Geor. iv. 6.
What toil in slender things!

It is very difficult to write on the minuter parts of literature without failing either to please or instruct. Too much nicety of detail disgusts the greatest part of readers, and to throw a multitude of particulars under general heads, and lay down rules of extensive comprehension, is to common understandings of little use. They who undertake these subjects are, therefore, always in danger, as one or other inconvenience arises to their imagination, of frighting us with rugged science, or amusing us with empty sound.

In criticising the work of Milton, there is, indeed, opportunity to intersperse passages that can hardly fail to relieve the languors of attention; and since, in examining the variety and choice of the pauses with which he has diversified his numbers, it will be necessary to exhibit the lines in which they are to be found, perhaps the remarks may be well compensated by the examples, and the irksomeness of grammatical disquisitions somewhat alleviated.

Milton formed his scheme of versification by the poets of Greece and Rome, whom he proposed to himself for his models, so far as the difference of his language from theirs would permit the imitation. There are, indeed, many inconveniencies inseparable from our heroick measure compared with that of Homer and Virgil; inconveniencies, which it is no reproach to Milton not to have overcome, because they are in their own nature insuperable; but against which he has struggled with so much art and diligence, that he may at least be said to have deserved success.

The hexameter of the ancients may be considered as consisting of fifteen syllables, so melodiously disposed, that, as every one knows who has examined the poetical authors, very pleasing and sonorous lyrick measures are formed from the fragments of the heroick. It is, indeed, scarce possible to break them in such a manner, but that *invenias etiam disjecta membra poetæ,*[1] some harmony will still remain, and the due proportions of sound will always be discovered. This measure, therefore, allowed great variety of pauses, and great liberties of connecting one verse with another, because wherever the line was interrupted, either part singly was musical. But the ancients seem to have confined this privilege to hexameters; for in their other measures, though longer than the English heroick, those who wrote after the refinements of versification, venture so seldom to change their pauses, that every variation may be supposed rather a compliance with necessity than the choice of judgment.

Milton was constrained within the narrow limits of a measure not very harmonious in the utmost perfection; the single parts, therefore, into which it was to be sometimes broken by pauses, were in danger of losing the very form

---

[1] Horace, *Satires,* I, iv, 62: "The poet remains, despite his scattered members."

of verse. This has, perhaps, notwithstanding all his care, sometimes happened.

As harmony is the end of poetical measures, no part of a verse ought to be so separated from the rest as not to remain still more harmonious than prose, or to show, by the disposition of the tones, that it is part of a verse. This rule in the old hexameter might be easily observed, but in English will very frequently be in danger of violation; for the order and regularity of accents cannot well be perceived in a succession of fewer than three syllables, which will confine the English poet to only five pauses; it being supposed, that when he connects one line with another, he should never make a full pause at less distance than that of three syllables from the beginning or end of a verse.

That this rule should be universally and indispensably established, perhaps cannot be granted; something may be allowed to variety, and something to the adaptation of the numbers to the subject; but it will be found generally necessary, and the ear will seldom fail to suffer by its neglect.

Thus when a single syllable is cut off from the rest, it must either be united to the line with which the sense connects it, or be sounded alone. If it be united to the other line, it corrupts its harmony; if disjoined, it must stand alone, and with regard to musick be superfluous; for there is no harmony in a single sound, because it has no proportion to another:

> ———Hypocrites austerely talk,
> Defaming as impure what God declares
> *Pure;* and commands to some, leaves free to all.

When two syllables likewise are abscinded from the rest, they evidently want some associate sounds to make them harmonious:

> ———Eyes———
> ———more wakeful than to drowse,
> Charm'd with Arcadian pipe, the pastoral reed
> Of *Hermes,* or his opiate rod. *Meanwhile*
> To re-salute the world with sacred light
> *Leucothea* wak'd.

> He ended, and the sun gave signal high
> To the bright minister that watch'd: *he blew*
> His trumpet.
>
> First in the east his glorious lamp was seen,
> Regent of day; and all th' horizon round
> Invested with bright rays, jocund to run
> His longitude through heav'n's high road; *the gray*
> Dawn, and the Pleiades, before him danc'd,
> Shedding sweet influence.

The same defect is perceived in the following line, where the pause is at the second syllable from the beginning:

> ————————————————The race
> Of that wild rout that tore the Thracian hard
> In *Rhodope,* where woods and rocks had ears
> To rapture, till the savage clamour drown'd
> Both harp and voice; nor could the muse defend
> *Her son.* So fail not thou, who thee implores.

When the pause falls upon the third syllable or the seventh, the harmony is better preserved; but as the third and seventh are weak syllables, the period leaves the ear unsatisfied, and in expectation of the remaining part of the verse:

> ——He, with his horrid crew,
> Lay vanquish'd, rolling in the fiery gulph,
> Confounded though immor*tal.* But his doom
> Reserv'd him to more wrath; for now the thought
> Both of lost happiness and lasting pain
> Torments *him.*
>
> God,—with frequent intercourse,
> Thither will send his winged messengers
> On errands of supernal grace. So sung
> The glorious train ascend*ing.*

It may be, I think, established as a rule, that a pause which concludes a period should be made for the most part upon a strong syllable, as the fourth and sixth; but those pauses which only suspend the sense may be placed upon the weaker. Thus the rest in the third line of the first passage

satisfies the ear better than in the fourth, and the close of
the second quotation better than of the third:

> ————————————The evil soon
> Drawn back, redounded (as a flood) on those
> From whom it *sprung;* impossible to mix
> With *Blessedness.*

> ————————What we by day
> Lop overgrown, or prune, or prop, or bind,
> One night or two with wanton growth derides,
> Tending to *wild.*

> The paths and bow'rs doubt not but our joint hands
> Will keep from wilderness with ease as wide
> As we need walk, till younger hands ere long
> Assist *us.*

The rest in the fifth place has the same inconvenience as
in the seventh and third, that the syllable is weak:

> Beast now with beast 'gan war, and fowl with fowl,
> And fish with fish, to graze the herb all leaving,
> Devour'd each *other:* nor stood much in awe
> Of man, but fled *him,* or with countenance grim,
> Glar'd on him pas*sing.*

The noblest and most majestick pauses which our versification admits, are upon the fourth and sixth syllables, which
are both strongly sounded in a pure and regular verse, and
at either of which the line is so divided, that both members
participate of harmony:

> But now at last the sacred influence
> Of light *appears,* and from the walls of heav'n
> Shoots far into the bosom of dim night
> A glimmering *dawn:* here nature first begins
> Her farthest verge, and chaos to retire.

But far above all others, if I can give any credit to my
own ear, is the rest upon the sixth syllable, which, taking
in a complete compass of sound, such as is sufficient to
constitute one of our lyrick measures, makes a full and solemn
close. Some passages which conclude at this stop, I could

never read without some strong emotions of delight or admiration:

> Before the hills appear'd, or fountain flow'd,
> Thou with the eternal wisdom didst converse,
> Wisdom thy sister, and with her didst play
> In presence of the almighty Father, pleas'd
> With thy celestial *song*.
>
> Or other worlds they seem'd, or happy isles,
> Like those Hesperian gardens fam'd of old,
> Fortunate fields, and groves, and flow'ry vales,
> Thrice happy isles! But who dwelt happy there,
> He staid not to in*quire*.
>
> —————————————————————He blew
> His trumpet, heard in Oreb since, perhaps,
> When God descended; and, perhaps, once more
> To sound at general *doom*.

If the poetry of Milton be examined, with regard to the pauses and flow of his verses into each other, it will appear that he has performed all that our language would admit; and the comparison of his numbers with those who have cultivated the same manner of writing, will show that he excelled as much in the lower as the higher parts of his art, and that his skill in harmony was not less than his invention or his learning.

NO. 93 TUESDAY, FEBRUARY 5, 1751

> ——*Experiar quid concedatur in illos,*
> *Quorum flaminia tegitur cinis, atque Latina.*   Juv. Sat. i. 170.

> More safely truth to urge her claim presumes,
> On names now found alone on books and tombs.

There are few books on which more time is spent by young students, than on treatises which deliver the characters of authors; nor any which oftener deceive the expectation of the reader, or fill his mind with more opinions which the progress of his studies and the increase of his knowledge oblige him to resign.

Baillet[2] has introduced his collection of the decisions of
the learned, by an enumeration of the prejudices which mislead the critick, and raise the passions in rebellion against the
judgment. His catalogue, though large, is imperfect; and who
can hope to complete it? The beauties of writing have been
observed to be often such as cannot in the present state of
human knowledge be evinced by evidence, or drawn out into
demonstrations; they are, therefore, wholly subject to the imagination, and do not force their effects upon a mind preoccupied by unfavourable sentiments, nor overcome the counteraction of a false principle or of stubborn partiality.

To convince any man against his will is hard, but to
please him against his will is justly pronounced by Dryden
to be above the reach of human abilities. Interest and passion
will hold out long against the closest siege of diagrams and
syllogisms, but they are absolutely impregnable to imagery
and sentiment; and will for ever bid defiance to the most
powerful strains of Virgil or Homer, though they may give
way in time to the batteries of Euclid or Archimedes.

In trusting, therefore, to the sentence of a critick, we are
in danger not only from that vanity which exalts writers too
often to the dignity of teaching what they are yet to learn,
from that negligence which sometimes steals upon the most
vigilant caution, and that fallibility to which the condition of
nature has subjected every human understanding; but from a
thousand extrinsick and accidental causes, from every thing
which can excite kindness or malevolence, veneration or contempt.

Many of those who have determined with great boldness
upon the various degrees of literary merit, may be justly
suspected of having passed sentence, as Seneca remarks of
Claudius,

> *Una tantum parte audita,*
> *Sæpe et nulla,*[3]

without much knowledge of the cause before them; for it

---

[2] Adrien Baillet (1649–1760), *Jugements des savants sur les principaux
ouvrages des auteurs* (1685–1686).
[3] *Ludus de morte Claudii* xii.

will not easily be imagined of Langbaine, Borrichius, or Rapin,[4] that they had very accurately perused all the books which they praise or censure; or that, even if nature and learning had qualified them for judges, they could read for ever with the attention necessary to just criticism. Such performances, however, are not wholly without their use; for they are commonly just echoes to the voice of fame, and transmit the general suffrage of mankind when they have no particular motives to suppress it.

Criticks, like the rest of mankind, are very frequently misled by interest. The bigotry with which editors regard the authors whom they illustrate or correct, has been generally remarked. Dryden was known to have written most of his critical dissertations only to recommend the work upon which he then happened to be employed: and Addison is suspected to have denied the expediency of poetical justice, because his own Cato was condemned to perish in a good cause.[5]

There are prejudices which authors, not otherwise weak or corrupt, have indulged without scruple; and, perhaps, some of them are so complicated with our natural affections, that they cannot easily be disentangled from the heart. Scarce any can hear with impartiality a comparison between the writers of his own and another country; and though it cannot, I think, be charged equally on all nations, that they are blinded with this literary patriotism, yet there are none that do not look upon their authors with the fondness of affinity, and esteem them as well for the place of their birth, as for their knowledge or their wit. There is, therefore, seldom much respect due to comparative criticism, when the competitors are of different countries, unless the judge is of a nation equally indifferent to both. The Italians could not for a long time believe, that there was any learning beyond the mountains; and the French seem generally persuaded, that there are no wits or reasoners equal to their own. I can scarcely conceive

---

[4] Gerard Langbaine (1656–1692), *An account of the English Dramatic Poets* (1691); Oluf Borch (1626–1690), *Dissertationes academicae de poetis* (1683); René Rapin (1621–1687), *Réflexions sur la poétique d'Aristote et sur les ouvrages des poëtes anciens et modernes* (1674).

[5] See *Spectator* 40.

that if Scaliger had not considered himself as allied to Virgil, by being born in the same country, he would have found his works so much superiour to those of Homer, or have thought the controversy worthy of so much zeal, vehemence, and acrimony.

There is, indeed, one prejudice, and only one, by which it may be doubted whether it is any dishonour to be sometimes misguided. Criticism has so often given occasion to the envious and ill-natured of gratifying their malignity, that some have thought it necessary to recommend the virtue of candour without restriction, and to preclude all future liberty of censure. Writers possessed with this opinion are continually enforcing civility and decency, recommending to cricks the proper diffidence of themselves, and inculcating the veneration due to celebrated names.

I am not of opinion that these professed enemies of arrogance and severity have much more benevolence or modesty than the rest of mankind; or that they feel in their own hearts, any other intention than to distinguish themselves by their softness and delicacy. Some are modest because they are timorous, and some are lavish of praise because they hope to be repaid.

There is, indeed, some tenderness due to living writers, when they attack none of those truths which are of importance to the happiness of mankind, and have committed no other offence than that of betraying their own ignorance, or dulness. I should think it cruelty to crush an insect which had provoked me only by buzzing in my ear; and would not willingly interrupt the dream of harmless stupidity, or destroy the jest which makes its author laugh. Yet I am far from thinking this tenderness universally necessary; for he that writes may be considered as a kind of general challenger, whom every one has a right to attack; since he quits the common rank of life, steps forward beyond the lists, and offers his merit to the publick judgment. To commence author is to claim praise, and no man can justly aspire to honour, but at the hazard of disgrace.

But whatever be decided concerning contemporaries, whom he that knows the treachery of the human heart, and considers how often we gratify our own pride or envy under the appearance of contending for elegance and propriety, will find himself not much inclined to disturb; there can surely be no exemptions pleaded to secure them from criticism, who can no longer suffer by reproach, and of whom nothing now remains but their writings and their names. Upon these authors the critick is undoubtedly at full liberty to exercise the strictest severity, since he endangers only his own fame, and, like Æneas, when he drew his sword in the infernal regions, encounters phantoms which cannot be wounded. He may, indeed, pay some regard to established reputation; but he can by that show of reverence consult only his own security, for all other motives are now at an end.

The faults of a writer of acknowledged excellence are more dangerous, because the influence of his example is more extensive; and the interest of learning requires that they should be discovered and stigmatized, before they have the sanction of antiquity conferred upon them, and become precedents of indisputable authority.

It has, indeed, been advanced by Addison, as one of the characteristicks of a true critick, that he points out beauties rather than faults. But it is rather natural to a man of learning and genius to apply himself chiefly to the study of writers who have more beauties than faults to be displayed: for the duty of criticism is neither to depreciate, nor dignify by partial representations, but to hold out the light of reason, whatever it may discover; and to promulgate the determinations of truth, whatever she shall dictate.

NO. 156 SATURDAY, SEPTEMBER 14, 1751

Nunquam aliud Natura, aliud Sapientia dicit.   Juv. Sat. xiv. 321.

For Wisdom ever echoes Nature's voice.

Every government, say the politicians, is perpetually degenerating towards corruption, from which it must be rescued at certain periods by the resuscitation of its first principles, and the re-establishment of its original constitution. Every

animal body, according to the methodick physicians, is, by
the predominance of some exuberant quality, continually declining towards disease and death, which must be obviated by
a seasonable reduction of the peccant humour to the just
equipoise which health requires.

In the same manner the studies of mankind, all at least
which, not being subject to rigorous demonstration, admit
the influence of fancy and caprice, are perpetually tending
to errour and confusion. Of the great principles of truth
which the first speculatists discovered, the simplicity is embarrassed by ambitious additions, or the evidence obscured
by inaccurate argumentation; and as they descend from one
succession of writers to another, like light transmitted from
room to room, they lose their strength and splendour, and
fade at last in total evanescence.

The systems of learning therefore must be sometimes
reviewed, complications analyzed into principles, and knowledge disentangled from opinion. It is not always possible,
without a close inspection, to separate the genuine shoots
of consequential reasoning, which grow out of some radical
postulate, from the branches which art has ingrafted on it.
The accidental prescriptions of authority, when time has
procured them veneration, are often confounded with the
laws of nature, and those rules are supposed coëval with
reason, of which the first rise cannot be discovered.

Criticism has sometimes permitted fancy to dictate the
laws by which fancy ought to be restrained, and fallacy to
perplex the principles by which fallacy is to be detected;
her superintendence of others has betrayed her to negligence
of herself; and, like the ancient Scythians, by extending her
conquests over distant regions, she has left her throne vacant
to her slaves.

Among the laws of which the desire of extending authority, or ardour of promoting knowledge, has prompted the
prescription, all which writers have received, had not the same
original right to our regard. Some are to be considered as
fundamental and indispensable, others only as useful and convenient; some as dictated by reason and necessity, others as
enacted by despotick antiquity; some as invincibly supported

by their conformity to the order of nature and operations of
the intellect; others as formed by accident, or instituted by
example, and therefore always liable to dispute and alteration.

That many rules have been advanced without consulting
nature or reason, we cannot but suspect, when we find it
peremptorily decreed by the ancient masters, that *only three
speaking personages should appear at once upon the stage;*
a law, which, as the variety and intricacy of modern plays
has made it impossible to be observed, we now violate without
scruple, and, as experience proves, without inconvenience.

The original of this precept was merely accidental.
Tragedy was a monody, or solitary song in honour of Bacchus,
improved afterwards into a dialogue by the addition of another speaker; but the ancients, remembering that the tragedy
was at first pronounced only by one, durst not for some time
venture beyond two; at last, when custom and impunity had
made them daring, they extended their liberty to the admission of three, but restrained themselves by a critical edict
from further exorbitance.

By what accident the number of acts was limited to five,
I know not that any author has informed us; but certainly
it is not determined by any necessity arising either from
the nature of action, or propriety of exhibition. An act is
only the representation of such a part of the business of the
plays as proceeds in an unbroken tenour, or without any intermediate pause. Nothing is more evident than that of every
real, and by consequence of every dramatick action, the intervals may be more or fewer than five; and indeed the rule
is upon the English stage every day broken in effect, without
any other mischief than that which arises from an absurd
endeavour to observe it in appearance. Whenever the scene is
shifted the act ceases, since some time is necessarily supposed
to elapse while the personages of the drama change their
place.

With no greater right to our obedience have the criticks
confined the dramatick action to a certain number of hours.
Probability requires that the time of action should approach
somewhat nearly to that of exhibition, and those plays will
always be thought most happily conducted which crowd the

greatest variety into the least space. But since it will frequently happen that some delusion must be admitted, I know
not where the limits of imagination can be fixed. It is rarely
observed that minds, not prepossessed by mechanical criticism, feel any offence from the extension of the intervals between the acts; nor can I conceive it absurd or impossible,
that he who can multiply three hours into twelve or twenty-
four, might imagine with equal ease a greater number.

I know not whether he that professes to regard no other
laws than those of nature, will not be inclined to receive
tragi-comedy to his protection, whom, however generally condemned, her own laurels have hitherto shaded from the
fulminations of criticism. For what is there in the mingled
drama which impartial reason can condemn? The connexion
of important with trivial incidents, since it is not only common but perpetual in the world, may surely be allowed upon
the stage, which pretends only to be the mirror of life. The
impropriety of suppressing passions before we have raised
them to the intended agitation, and of diverting the expectation from an event which we keep suspended only to raise
it, may be speciously urged. But will not experience shew this
objection to be rather subtle than just? Is it not certain that
the tragick and comick affections have been moved alternately
with equal force, and that no plays have oftener filled the eye
with tears, and the breast with palpitation, than those which
are variegated with interludes of mirth?

I do not however think it safe to judge of works of genius
merely by the event. The resistless vicissitudes of the heart,
this alternate prevalence of merriment and solemnity, may
sometimes be more properly ascribed to the vigour of the
writer than the justness of the design: and, instead of vindicating tragi-comedy by the success of Shakspeare, we ought, perhaps, to pay new honours to that transcendent and unbounded
genius that could preside over the passions in sport; who, to
actuate the affections, needed not the slow gradation of common means, but could fill the heart with instantaneous jollity
or sorrow, and vary our disposition as he changed his scenes.
Perhaps the effects even of Shakspeare's poetry might have
been yet greater, had he not counteracted himself; and we

might have been more interested in the distresses of his heroes, had we not been so frequently diverted by the jokes of his buffoons.

There are other rules more fixed and obligatory. It is necessary that of every play the chief action should be single; for since a play represents some transaction, through its regular maturation to its final event, two actions equally important must evidently constitute two plays.

As the design of tragedy is to instruct by moving the passions, it must always have a hero, a personage apparently and incontestably superior to the rest, upon whom the attention may be fixed, and the anxiety suspended. For though, of two persons opposing each other with equal abilities and equal virtue, the auditor will inevitably, in time, choose his favourite, yet as that choice must be without any cogency of conviction, the hopes or fears which it raises will be faint and languid. Of two heroes acting in confederacy against a common enemy, the virtues or dangers will give little emotion, because each claims our concern with the same right, and the heart lies at rest between equal motives.

It ought to be the first endeavour of a writer to distinguish nature from custom; or that which is established because it is right, from that which is right only because it is established; that he may neither violate essential principles by a desire of novelty, nor debar himself from the attainment of beauties within his view, by a needless fear of breaking rules which no literary dictator had authority to enact.

NO. 168 SATURDAY, OCTOBER 26, 1751

——————————*Decipit*
Frons prima multos: rara mens intelligit,
Quod interiore condidit cura angulo.

PHÆDRUS, Lib. iv. Fab. i. 5.

The tinsel glitter, and the specious mien,
Delude the most; few pry behind the scene.

It has been observed by Boileau, that "a mean or common thought expressed in pompous diction, generally pleases more than a new or noble sentiment delivered in low and vulgar language; because the number is greater of those whom custom has enabled to judge of words, than whom study has qualified to examine things."

This solution might satisfy, if such only were offended with meanness of expression as are unable to distinguish propriety of thought, and to separate propositions or images from the vehicles by which they are conveyed to the understanding. But this kind of disgust is by no means confined to the ignorant or superficial; it operates uniformly and universally upon readers of all classes; every man, however profound or abstracted, perceives himself irresistibly alienated by low terms; they who profess the most zealous adherence to truth are forced to admit that she owes part of her charms to her ornaments; and loses much of her power over the soul, when she appears disgraced by a dress uncouth or ill-adjusted.

We are all offended by low terms, but are not disgusted alike by the same compositions, because we do not all agree to censure the same terms as low. No word is naturally or intrinsically meaner than another; our opinion therefore of words, as of other things arbitrarily and capriciously established, depends wholly upon accident and custom. The cottager thinks those apartments splendid and spacious, which an inhabitant of palaces will despise for their inelegance; and to him who has passed most of his hours with the delicate and polite, many expressions will seem sordid, which another, equally acute, may hear without offence; but a mean term never fails to displease him to whom it appears mean, as poverty is certainly and invariably despised, though he who is poor in the eyes of some, may, by others, be envied for his wealth.

Words become low by the occasions to which they are applied, or the general character of them who use them; and the disgust which they produce, arises from the revival of those images with which they are commonly united. Thus if, in the most solemn discourse, a phrase happens to occur which has been successfully employed in some ludicrous narrative, the gravest auditor finds it difficult to refrain from laughter, when they who are not prepossessed by the same

accidental association, are utterly unable to guess the reason
of his merriment. Words which convey ideas of dignity in one
age, are banished from elegant writing or conversation in another, because they are in time debased by vulgar mouths,
and can be no longer heard without the involuntary recollec-
tion of unpleasing images.

When Macbeth is confirming himself in the horrid purpose of stabbing his king, he breaks out amidst his emotions
into a wish natural to a murderer:

> ——Come, thick night!
> And pall thee in the dunnest smoke of hell,
> That my keen knife see not the wound it makes;
> Nor heav'n peep through the blanket of the dark,
> To cry, Hold! hold!——

In this passage is exerted all the force of poetry; that force
which calls new powers into being, which embodies sentiment, and animates matter: yet, perhaps, scarce any man now
peruses it without some disturbance of his attention from the
counteraction of the words to the ideas. What can be more
dreadful than to implore the presence of night, invested, not
in common obscurity, but in the smoke of hell? Yet the efficacy
of this invocation is destroyed by the insertion of an epithet
now seldom heard but in the stable, and *dun* night may come
or go without any other notice than contempt.

If we start into raptures when some hero of the Iliad tells
us that δόρυ μαίνεται, his lance rages with eagerness to destroy;
if we are alarmed at the terrour of the soldiers commanded
by Cæsar to hew down the sacred grove, who dreaded, says
Lucan, lest the axe aimed at the oak should fly back upon the
striker:

> ——*Si robora sacra ferirent,*
> *In sua credebant redituras membra secures;*
> None dares with impious steel the grove to rend,
> Lest on himself the destin'd stroke descend;

we cannot surely but sympathise with the horrours of a
wretch about to murder his master, his friend, his benefactor,
who suspects that the weapon will refuse its office, and start
back from the breast which he is preparing to violate. Yet

this sentiment is weakened by the name of an instrument used by butchers and cooks in the meanest employments: we do not immediately conceive that any crime of importance is to be committed with a *knife;* or who does not, at last, from the long habit of connecting a knife with sordid offices, feel aversion rather than terrour?

Macbeth proceeds to wish, in the madness of guilt, that the inspection of heaven may be intercepted, and that he may, in the involutions of infernal darkness, escape the eye of Providence. This is the utmost extravagance of determined wickedness; yet this is so debased by two unfortunate words, that while I endeavour to impress on my reader the energy of the sentiment, I can scarce check my risibility, when the expression forces itself upon my mind; for who, without some relaxation of his gravity, can hear of the avengers of guilt *peeping through a blanket?*

These imperfections of diction are less obvious to the reader, as he is less acquainted with common usages; they are therefore wholly imperceptible to a foreigner, who learns our language from books, and will strike a solitary academick less forcibly than a modish lady.

Among the numerous requisites that must concur to complete an author, few are of more importance than an early entrance into the living world. The seeds of knowledge may be planted in solitude, but must be cultivated in publick. Argumentation may be taught in colleges, and theories formed in retirement; but the artifice of embellishment, and the powers of attraction, can be gained only by general converse.

An acquaintance with prevailing customs and fashionable elegance is necessary likewise for other purposes. The injury that grand imagery suffers from unsuitable language, personal merit may fear from rudeness and indelicacy. When the success of Æneas depended on the favour of the queen upon whose coasts he was driven, his celestial protectress thought him not sufficiently secured against rejection by his piety or bravery, but decorated him for the interview with preternatural beauty. Whoever desires, for his writings or himself, what none can reasonably contemn, the favour of mankind, must add grace to strength, and make his thoughts

agreeable as well as useful. Many complain of neglect who
never tried to attract regard. It cannot be expected that the
patrons of science or virtue should be solicitous to discover
excellencies, which they who possess them shade and disguise.
Few have abilities so much needed by the rest of the world
as to be caressed on their own terms; and he that will not
condescend to recommend himself by external embellishments, must submit to the fate of just sentiment meanly expressed, and be ridiculed and forgotten before he is understood.

FROM RASSELAS, PRINCE OF ABISSINIA
[1759]

CHAPTER X

Imlac's History Continued
A Dissertation upon Poetry

"Wherever I went, I found that poetry was considered as the highest learning, and regarded with a veneration, somewhat approaching to that which man would pay to the angelick nature. And yet it fills me with wonder, that, in almost all countries, the most ancient poets are considered as the best: whether it be that every other kind of knowledge is an acquisition gradually attained, and poetry is a gift conferred at once; or that the first poetry of every nation surprised them as a novelty, and retained the credit by consent, which it received by accident at first: or whether, as the province of poetry is to describe nature and passion, which are always the same, the first writers took possession of the most striking objects for description, and the most probable occurrences for fiction, and left nothing to those that followed them, but transcription of the same events, and new combinations of the same images. Whatever be the reason, it is commonly observed, that the early writers are in possession of nature, and their followers of art: that the first excel in strength and invention, and the latter in elegance and refinement.

"I was desirous to add my name to this illustrious fraternity. I read all the poets of Persia and Arabia, and was able to repeat, by memory, the volumes that are suspended in the mosque of Mecca. But I soon found, that no man was ever great by imitation. My desire of excellence impelled me to transfer my attention to nature and to life. Nature was to be my subject, and men to be my auditors: I could never describe what I had not seen; I could not hope to move those with delight or terrour, whose interest and opinions I did not understand.

"Being now resolved to be a poet, I saw every thing with a new purpose; my sphere of attention was suddenly magnified: no kind of knowledge was to be overlooked. I ranged mountains and deserts for images and resemblances, and pictured upon my mind every tree of the forest and flower of the valley. I observed, with equal care, the crags of the rock and the pinnacles of the palace. Sometimes I wandered along the mazes of the rivulet, and sometimes watched the changes of the summer clouds. To a poet, nothing can be useless. Whatever is beautiful, and whatever is dreadful, must be familiar to his imagination: he must be conversant with all that is awfully vast, or elegantly little. The plants of the garden, the animals of the wood, the minerals of the earth, and meteors of the sky, must all concur to store his mind with inexhaustible variety; for every idea is useful for the enforcement or decoration of moral religious truth; and he, who knows most, will have most power of diversifying his scenes, and of gratifying his reader with remote allusions and unexpected instruction.

"All the appearances of nature I was, therefore, careful to study, and every country, which I have surveyed, has contributed something to my poetical powers."

"In so wide a survey," said the prince, "you must surely have left much unobserved. I have lived till now, within the circuit of these mountains, and yet cannot walk abroad without the sight of something, which I had never beheld before, or never heeded."

"The business of a poet," said Imlac, "is to examine, not the individual, but the species; to remark general properties and large appearances: he does not number the streaks of the tulip, or describe the different shades in the verdure of the forest. He is to exhibit, in his portraits of nature, such prominent and striking features, as recall the original to every mind; and must neglect the minuter discriminations, which one may have remarked, and another have neglected, for those characteristics which are alike obvious to vigilance and carelessness.

"But the knowledge of nature is only half the task of a poet; he must be acquainted, likewise, with all the modes of life. IIis character requires, that he estimate the happiness and misery of every condition; observe the power of all the passions in all their combinations, and trace the changes of the human mind, as they are modified by various institutions, and accidental influences of climate or custom, from the sprightliness of infancy to the despondence of decrepitude. He must divest himself of the prejudices of his age or country; he must consider right and wrong in their abstracted and invariable state; he must disregard present laws and opinions, and rise to general and transcendental truths, which will always be the same; he must, therefore, content himself with the slow progress of his name; contemn the applause of his own time, and commit his claims to the justice of posterity. He must write, as the interpreter of nature, and the legislator of mankind, and consider himself, as presiding over the thoughts and manners of future generations; as a being superiour to time and place.

"His labour is not yet at an end: he must know many languages and many sciences; and, that his style may be worthy of his thoughts, must, by incessant practice, familiarize to himself every delicacy of speech and grace of harmony."

CHAPTER XI

Imlac's Narrative Continued
A Hint on Pilgrimage

Imlac now felt the enthusiastick fit, and was proceeding to aggrandize his own profession, when the prince cried out: "Enough! thou hast convinced me, that no human being can ever be a poet. Proceed with thy narration."

"To be a poet," said Imlac, "is, indeed, very difficult." "So difficult," returned the prince, "that I will, at present, hear no more of his labours. Tell me whither you went, when you had seen Persia." . . .

FROM LIVES OF THE ENGLISH POETS
[1781]

THOMSON

As a writer he is entitled to one praise of the highest kind:
his mode of thinking, and of expressing his thoughts, is
original. His blank verse is no more the blank verse of Milton,
or of any other poet, than the rhymes of Prior are the rhymes
of Cowley. His numbers, his pauses, his diction, are of his
own growth, without transcription, without imitation. He
thinks in a peculiar train, and he thinks always as a man of
genius; he looks round on nature and on life with the eye
which nature bestows only on a poet; the eye that distinguishes, in every thing presented to its view, whatever
there is on which imagination can delight to be detained,
and with a mind that at once comprehends the vast, and attends to the minute. The reader of the *Seasons* wonders that

he never saw before what Thomson shows him, and that he never yet has felt what Thomson impresses.

His is one of the works in which blank verse seems properly used. Thomson's wide expansion of general views, and his enumeration of circumstantial varieties, would have been obstructed and embarrassed by the frequent intersection of the sense, which are the necessary effects of rhyme.

His descriptions of extended scenes and general effects bring before us the whole magnificence of nature, whether pleasing or dreadful. The gaiety of spring, the splendour of summer, the tranquillity of autumn, and the horrour of winter, take, in their turns, possession of the mind. The poet leads us through the appearances of things as they are successively varied by the vicissitudes of the year, and imparts to us so much of his own enthusiasm, that our thoughts expand with his imagery, and kindle with his sentiments. Nor is the naturalist without his part in the entertainment; for he is assisted to recollect and to combine, to arrange his discoveries, and to amplify the sphere of his contemplation.

The great defect of the Seasons is want of method; but for this I know not that there was any remedy. Of many appearances subsisting all at once, no rule can be given why one should be mentioned before another; yet the memory wants the help of order, and the curiosity is not excited by suspense or expectation.

His diction is in the highest degree florid and luxuriant, such as may be said to be to his images and thoughts, "both their lustre and their shade:" such as invest them with splendour, through which, perhaps, they are not always easily discerned. It is too exuberant, and sometimes may be charged with filling the ear more than the mind.

These poems, with which I was acquainted at their first appearance, I have since found altered and enlarged by subsequent revisals, as the author supposed his judgment to grow more exact, and as books or conversation extended his knowledge and opened his prospects. They are, I think, improved in general; yet I know not whether they have not lost part of what Temple calls their "race;" a word which, applied to wines, in its primitive sense, means the flavour of the soil.

Liberty, when it first appeared, I tried to read, and soon desisted. I have never tried again, and, therefore, will not hazard either praise or censure.

The highest praise which he has received ought not to be suppressed; it is said by lord Lyttelton, in the prologue to his posthumous play, that his works contained

No line which, dying, he could wish to blot.

YOUNG

Of Young's poems it is difficult to give any general character; for he has no uniformity of manner: one of his pieces has no great resemblance to another. He began to write early, and continued long; and at different times had different modes of poetical excellence in view. His numbers are sometimes smooth, and sometimes rugged; his style is sometimes con-catenated, and sometimes abrupt; sometimes diffusive, and sometimes concise. His plan seems to have started in his mind at the present moment; and his thoughts appear the effect of chance, sometimes adverse, and sometimes lucky, with very little operation of judgment.

He was not one of those writers whom experience improves, and who, observing their own faults, become gradually correct. His poem on the Last Day, his first great performance, has an equability and propriety, which he afterwards either never endeavoured or never attained. Many paragraphs are noble, and few are mean, yet the whole is languid: the plan is too much extended, and a succession of images divides and weakens the general conception; but the great reason why the reader is disappointed is, that the thought of the Last Day makes every man more than poetical, by spreading over his mind a general obscurity of sacred horrour, that oppresses distinction, and disdains expression.

His story of Jane Grey was never popular. It is written with elegance enough; but Jane is too heroick to be pitied.

The *Universal Passion* is, indeed, a very great performance. It is said to be a series of epigrams; but, if it be, it is what the author intended; his endeavour was at the production of striking distichs and pointed sentences; and his distichs have the weight of solid sentiment, and his points the sharpness of resistless truth.

His characters are often selected with discernment, and drawn with nicety; his illustrations are often happy, and his reflections often just. His species of satire is between those of Horace and Juvenal; and he has the gaiety of Horace without his laxity of numbers, and the morality of Juvenal, with greater variation of images. He plays, indeed, only on the surface of life; he never penetrates the recesses of the mind, and, therefore, the whole power of his poetry is exhausted by a single perusal; his conceits please only when they surprise.

To translate he never condescended, unless his Paraphrase on Job may be considered as a version; in which he has not, I think, been unsuccessful; he, indeed, favoured himself, by choosing those parts which most easily admit the ornaments of English poetry.

He had least success in his lyrick attempts, in which he seems to have been under some malignant influence: he is always labouring to be great, and at last is only turgid.

In his *Night Thoughts* he has exhibited a very wide display of original poetry, variegated with deep reflections and striking allusions, a wilderness of thought, in which the fertility of fancy scatters flowers of every hue and of every odour. This is one of the few poems in which blank verse could not be changed for rhyme but with disadvantage. The wild diffusion of the sentiments, and the digressive sallies of imagination, would have been compressed and restrained by confinement to rhyme. The excellence of this work is not exactness, but copiousness; particular lines are not to be regarded; the power is in the whole; and in the whole there is a magnificence like that ascribed to Chinese plantations, the magnificence of vast extent and endless diversity.

His last poem was *Resignation;* in which he made, as he was accustomed, an experiment of a new mode of writing, and succeeded better than in his "Ocean" or his "Merchant." It was very falsely represented as a proof of decaying faculties. There is Young in every stanza, such as he often was in his highest vigour.

His tragedies, not making part of the collection, I had forgotten, till Mr. Steevens recalled them to my thoughts by remarking, that he seemed to have one favourite catastrophe, as his three plays all concluded with lavish suicide; a method by which, as Dryden remarked, a poet easily rids his scene of persons whom he wants not to keep alive. In *Busiris* there are the greatest ebullitions of imagination: but the pride of Busiris is such as no other man can have, and the whole is too remote from known life to raise either grief, terrour, or indignation. *The Revenge* approaches much nearer to human practices and manners, and, therefore, keeps possession of the stage: the first design seems suggested by Othello; but the reflections, the incidents, and the diction, are original. The moral observations are so introduced, and so expressed, as to have all the novelty that can be required. Of the *Brothers* I may be allowed to say nothing, since nothing was ever said of it by the publick.

It must be allowed of Young's poetry, that it abounds in thought, but without much accuracy or selection. When he lays hold of an illustration, he pursues it beyond expectation, sometimes happily, as in his parallel of Quicksilver with Pleasure, which I have heard repeated with approbation by a lady, of whose praise he would have been justly proud, and which is very ingenious, very subtile, and almost exact: but sometimes he is less lucky, as when, in his *Night Thoughts*, having it dropped into his mind, that the orbs floating in space might be called the *cluster* of creation, he thinks of a cluster of grapes, and says, that they all hang on the great vine, drinking the "nectareous juice of immortal life."

His conceits are sometimes yet less valuable. In the *Last Day* he hopes to illustrate the reassembly of the atoms that compose the human body at the "trump of doom" by the collection of bees into a swarm at the tinkling of a pan.

The prophet says of Tyre, that "her merchants are princes." Young says of Tyre, in his Merchant,

         Her merchants princes, and each *deck a throne*.

Let burlesque try to go beyond him.

He has the trick of joining the turgid and familiar: to buy the alliance of Britain, "Climes were paid down." Antithesis is his favourite: "They for kindness hate;" and, "because she's right, she's ever in the wrong."

His versification is his own: neither his blank nor his rhyming lines have any resemblance to those of former writers; he picks up no hemistichs, he copies no favourite expressions; he seems to have laid up no stores of thought or diction, but to owe all to the fortuitous suggestions of the present moment. Yet I have reason to believe that, when once he had formed a new design, he then laboured it with very patient industry; and that he composed with great labour and frequent revisions.

His verses are formed by no certain model; he is no more like himself in his different productions than he is like others. He seems never to have studied prosody, nor to have had any direction but from his own ear. But, with all his defects, he was a man of genius and a poet.

AKENSIDE

Akenside is to be considered as a didactick and lyrick poet. His great work is the *Pleasures of Imagination*; a performance which, published as it was, at the age of twenty-three, raised expectations that were not very amply satisfied. It has undoubtedly a just claim to very particular notice, as an example of great felicity of genius, and uncommon amplitude of acquisitions, of a young mind stored with images, and much exercised in combining and comparing them.

With the philosophical or religious tenets of the author, I have nothing to do; my business is with his poetry. The subject is well chosen, as it includes all images that can strike or please, and thus comprises every species of poetical delight. The only difficulty is in the choice of examples and illustrations; and it is not easy, in such exuberance of matter, to find the middle point between penury and satiety. The parts seem artificially disposed, with sufficient coherence, so as that they cannot change their places without injury to the general design.

His images are displayed with such luxuriance of expression, that they are hidden, like Butler's Moon, by a "veil of light;" they are forms fantastically lost under superfluity of dress. "Pars minima est ipsa puella sui." [6] The words are multiplied till the sense is hardly perceived; attention deserts the mind, and settles in the ear. The reader wanders through the gay diffusion, sometimes amazed, and sometimes delighted; but, after many turnings in the flowery labyrinth, comes out as he went in. He remarked little, and laid hold on nothing.

To his versification, justice requires that praise should not be denied. In the general fabrication of his lines he is, perhaps, superiour to any other writer of blank verse: his flow is smooth, and his pauses are musical; but the concatenation of his verses is commonly too long continued, and the full close does not recur with sufficient frequency. The sense is carried on through a long intertexture of complicated clauses, and, as nothing is distinguished, nothing is remembered.

The exemption which blank verse affords from the necessity of closing the sense with the couplet, betrays luxuriant and active minds into such self-indulgence, that they pile image upon image, ornament upon ornament, and are not easily persuaded to close the sense at all. Blank verse will, therefore, I fear, be too often found in description exuberant, in argument loquacious, and in narration tiresome.

His diction is certainly poetical as it is not prosaick, and elegant as it is not vulgar. He is to be commended as having fewer artifices of disgust than most of his brethren of the blank song. He rarely either recalls old phrases, or twists his

---

[6] Ovid, *Remedia Amoris*, 344: *Auferimur cultu; gemmis auroque teguntur Omnia; pars minima est ipsa puella sui.*

"We are won by dress; all is concealed by gems and gold; a woman is the least part of herself."

metre into harsh inversions. The sense, however, of his words is strained, when "he views the Ganges from Alpine heights;" that is, from mountains like the Alps: and the pedant surely intrudes, (but when was blank verse without pedantry?) when he tells how "planets *absolve* the stated round of time."

It is generally known to the readers of poetry that he intended to revise and augment this work, but died before he had completed his design. The reformed work as he left it, and the additions which he had made, are very properly retained in the late collection. He seems to have somewhat contracted his diffusion; but I know not whether he has gained in closeness what he has lost in splendour. In the additional book, the Tale of Solon is too long.

One great defect of his poem is very properly censured by Mr. Walker,[7] unless it may be said, in his defence, that what he has omitted was not properly in his plan. "His picture of man is grand and beautiful, but unfinished. The immortality of the soul, which is the natural consequence of the appetites and powers she is invested with, is scarcely once hinted throughout the poem. This deficiency is amply supplied by the masterly pencil of Dr. Young; who, like a good philosopher, has invincibly proved the immortality of man, from the grandeur of his conceptions, and the meanness and misery of his state; for this reason, a few passages are selected from the Night Thoughts, which, with those from Akenside, seem to form a complete view of the powers, situation, and end of man." Exercises for Improvement in Elocution, p. 66.

His other poems are now to be considered; but a short consideration will despatch them. It is not easy to guess why he addicted himself so diligently to lyric poetry, having neither the ease and airiness of the lighter, nor the vehemence and elevation of the grander ode. When he lays his ill-fated hand upon his harp, his former powers seem to desert him; he has no longer his luxuriance of expression, nor variety of images. His thoughts are cold, and his words inelegant. Yet

[7] John Walker (1732–1807), actor, elocutionist, and lexicographer who quit the stage in 1768 to become a lecturer on elecution. Compiled a dictionary of rhymes, 1775, and a pronouncing dictionary, 1791.

such was his love of lyricks, that, having written, with great vigour and poignancy, his "Epistle to Curio," he transformed it afterwards into an ode disgraceful only to its author.

Of his odes nothing favourable can be said; the sentiments commonly want force, nature, or novelty; the diction is sometimes harsh and uncouth, the stanzas ill-constructed and unpleasant, and the rhymes dissonant, or unskilfully disposed, too distant from each other, or arranged with too little regard to established use, and, therefore, perplexing to the ear, which, in a short composition, has not time to grow familiar with an innovation.

To examine such compositions singly cannot be required; they have, doubtless, brighter and darker parts; but, when they are once found to be generally dull, all further labour may be spared: for to what use can the work be criticised that will not be read?

JOSEPH WARTON
[1722–1800]

Joseph, brother of Thomas the Younger, was the son of Thomas Warton, vicar of Basingstoke and Professor of Poetry at Oxford. From grammar school at Basingstoke Joseph went to Winchester, where he was a friend of William Collins, and where, after he was appointed usher (or second master) in 1755, he was to spend most of the rest of his life. After leaving Winchester as a student, he went to Oriel College, Oxford, and graduated B.A. in 1743–4, taking Orders immediately. In 1744 he published his first acknowledged poems, including "The Enthusiast, or the Lover of Nature," by which he is chiefly remembered as a poet.

It is commonly said that his critique of Pope, as well as his poetry, anticipates romanticism; however, even in his poetry he seldom got far from the neoclassic norms which are ultimately those he is applying to Pope. Warton criticizes Pope, in essence, because he did not attempt the highest genres—epic, tragedy, and the great ode—not because he was less than supreme in what he did attempt. It is amusing to speculate whether Pope himself would seriously have disagreed with Warton's estimate: it is, after all, no small compliment to be placed "next to Milton and just above Dryden"!

In 1797 Warton published an edition of Pope in which he attempted to dispel the impression, by then grown common, that he unduly disparaged Pope's poetry, meanwhile using as notes many of the remarks in the Essay. Yet despite Warton's insistence to the last on the importance of the Renaissance genres, his emphasis on the

*imagination as a critical standard, while hardly surprising
in view of Addison and Akenside, can be regarded as at
least symptomatic of a change of emphasis in English
criticism. The "imagination," however, is not a simple
concept, nor is it quite our concept of the word.*

The first volume of the Essay on the Genius and
Writings of Pope *(1756) was reviewed, generally favorably,
by Samuel Johnson in* The Literary Magazine, *and the second
volume, which did not appear until 1782 (perhaps because
of Joseph's timidity, since sheets had been printed years
before), was noticed in the* Monthly Review *for April of
that year. The* Essay *remains Joseph's chief claim to notice
as a critic, but he also wrote a number of essays for the*
Adventurer, *and retranslated, with a by no means
despicable critical preface, the minor poetry of Virgil.*

*The text of the "Dedication" to Edward Young
reprinted here is taken from the 1756 edition. The remarks
on Thomson and the conclusion are from the edition of
1806. See also:*

*Allison, James: "Joseph Warton's reply to Dr. Johnson's
    Lives,"* JEGP, LI *(1952), 186–91.*

*Griffith, Philip M.: "Joseph Warton's Criticism of
    Shakespeare,"* Tulane Studies in English, XIV *(1965),
    17–56.*

*Leedy, Paul F.: "Genre Criticism and the Significance of
    Warton's Essays on Pope,"* JEGP, XLV *(1946), 140–
    146. [See also the review of this essay by W. J. Bate
    in* PQ, XXVI *(1947), 143–4.]*

MacClintock, William D.: Joseph Warton's Essay on Pope;
    a history of the five editions, Chapel Hill, *1933.*

*Pittock, Joan: "Joseph Warton and his Second Volume of
    the* Essay on Pope," RES, XVIII *(1966), 264–73.*

*Schick, George Baldwin: "Joseph Warton's Conception of
    the Qualities of a True Poet,"* Boston University Studies
    in English, III *(1957), 77–87.*

Trowbridge, Hoyt: "Joseph Warton on the Imagination,"
    MP, XXXV *(1937), 73–87.*

ESSAY ON THE GENIUS AND WRITINGS OF POPE

[1756]

DEDICATION

TO THE REVEREND

DR. YOUNG,

RECTOR OF WELWYN

IN HERTFORDSHIRE

Dear Sir:

Permit me to break into your retirement, the residence of virtue and literature, and to trouble you with a few reflections on the merits and real character of an admired author, and on other collateral subjects, that will naturally arise. No love of singularity, no affectation of paradoxical opinions, gave rise to the following work. I revere the memory of Pope, I respect and honour his abilities; but I do not think him at the head of his profession. In other words, in that species of poetry wherein Pope excelled, he is superior to all mankind, and I only say that this species of poetry is not the most excellent one of the art. We do not, it should seem, sufficiently attend to the difference there is, betwixt a man of wit, a man of sense, and a true poet. Donne and Swift were undoubtedly men of wit and men of sense, but what traces have they left of Pure Poetry?

Fontenelle and La Motte[1] are entitled to the former character; but what can they urge to gain the latter? Which of these characters is the most valuable and useful, is entirely out of the question; all I plead for is to have their several provinces kept distinct from each other, and to impress on the reader that a clear head and acute understanding are not sufficient, alone, to make a poet; that the most solid observations on human life, expressed with the utmost elegance and brevity, are *morality,* and not *poetry;* that the *Epistles* of Boileau in rhyme, are no more poetical, than the *Characters* of Bruyere in prose; and that it is a creative and glowing imagination, "acer spiritus ac vis," [2] and that alone, that can stamp a writer with this exalted and very uncommon character, which so few possess, and of which so few can properly judge.

For one person who can adequately relish and enjoy a work of imagination, twenty are to be found who can taste and judge of observations on familiar life, and the manners of the age. The satires of Ariosto are more read than the *Orlando Furioso,* or even Dante. Are there so many cordial admirers of Spenser and Milton as of *Hudibras* if we strike out of the number of these supposed admirers those who appear such out of fashion, and not of feeling? Swift's rhapsody on poetry is far more popular than Akenside's noble ode to Lord Huntingdon. The Epistles on the characters of men and women, and your sprightly satires, my good friend, are more frequently perused, and quoted than "L'Allegro" and "Il Penseroso" of Milton. Had you written only these satires, you would indeed have gained the title of a man of wit and a man of sense; but, I am confident, would not insist on being denominated a *Poet* merely on their account.

Non satis est puris versum perscribere verbis.[3]

It is amazing this matter should ever have been mistaken, when Horace has taken particular and repeated pains to settle and adjust

---

[1] Bernard le Bovier de Fontenelle (1659–1757). A literary critic, popularizer of science, and precursor of the encyclopedists, he took the side of the moderns in the *Digression sur les Anciens et les Modernes* (1688). Antoine Houdar de La Motte (1672–1731), known also as Lamotte-Houdar. French poet and literary critic who in 1713–14 translated the *Iliad* into verse with a prefatory *Discours sur Homère,* which in discrediting Mme. Dacier's prose translation led to a brief resumption of the ancients-modern controversy.

[2] Horace, *Serm.* I, iv, 46. "The fire and force of inspiration."

[3] *Ibid.,* line 54. "It is not enough to write out a line of simple words."

the opinion in question. He has more than once disclaimed all right and title to the name of *Poet* on the score of his ethic and satiric pieces.

> ———*Neque enim concludere versum*
> *Dixeris esse satis*———[4]

are lines often repeated, but whose meaning is not extended and weighed as it ought to be. Nothing can be more judicious than the method he prescribes of trying whether any composition be essentially poetical or not, which is to drop entirely the measures and numbers, and transpose and invert the order of the words: and in this unadorned manner to peruse the passage. If there be really in it a true poetical spirit, all your inversions and transpositions will not disguise and extinguish it; but it will retain its lustre like a diamond unset and thrown back into the rubbish of the mine. Let us make a little experiment on the following well-known lines:

> "Yes, you despise the man that is confined to books, who rails at human kind from his study; tho' what he learns he speaks, and may perhaps advance some general maxims, or may be right by chance. The coxcomb bird, so grave and so talkative, that cries whore, knave, and cuckold from his cage, tho' he rightly call many a passenger, you hold him no philosopher. And yet, such is the fate of all extremes, men may be read too much as well as books. We grow more partial, for the sake of the observer, to observations which we ourselves make; less so to written wisdom, because another's. Maxims are drawn from notions, and those from guess." [5]

What shall we say of this passage?—Why, that it is most excellent sense, but just as poetical as the "Qui fit Mæcenas" of the author who recommends this method of trial. Take any ten lines of the *Iliad, Paradise Lost,* or even of the *Georgics* of Virgil, and see whether by any process of critical chemistry you can lower and reduce them to the tameness of prose. You will find that they will appear like Ulysses in his disguise of rags, still a hero, though lodged in the cottage of the herdsman Eumæus.

The Sublime and the Pathetic are the two chief nerves of all genuine poesy. What is there very sublime or very pathetic in

---

[4] *Ibid.,* line 40. "For you would not call it enough to round off a verse."
[5] The passage quoted reduces to prose Pope's *Moral Essay* I ("Epistle to Cobham"), 1–14.

Pope? In his works there is indeed, *"nihil inane, nihil arcessitum;—puro tamen fonti quam magno flumini propior,"* [6] as the excellent Quintilian remarks of Lysias. And because I am perhaps ashamed or afraid to speak out in plain English, I will adopt the following passage of Voltaire, which, in my opinion, as exactly characterizes Pope as it does his model Boileau, for whom it was originally designed. *"Incapable peutêtre du sublime qui élève l'âme, et du sentiment qui l'attendrit, mais fait pour éclairer ceux à qui la nature accorda l'un et l'autre, laborieux, sévère, précis, pur, harmonieux, il devint, enfin, le poète de la raison."* [7]

Our English poets may, I think, be disposed in four different classes and degrees. In the first class I would place, first, our only three sublime and pathetic poets: *Spenser, Shakespeare, Milton;* and then, at proper intervals, *Otway* and *Lee*. In the second class should be placed such as possessed the true poetical genius in a more moderate degree, but had noble talents for moral and ethical poesy. At the head of these are *Dryden, Donne, Denham, Cowley, Congreve*. In the third class may be placed men of wit, of elegant taste, and some fancy in describing familiar life. Here may be numbered, *Prior, Waller, Parnell, Swift, Fenton*. In the fourth class the mere versifiers, however smooth and mellifluous some of them may be thought, should be ranked. Such as *Pitt, Sandys, Fairfax, Broome, Buckingham, Lansdown*. In which of these classes *Pope* deserves to be placed, the following work is intended to determine.

[Following is the conclusion as it appeared in Warton's final revision, published in 1806.]

Our English poets may, I think, be disposed in four different classes and degrees. In the first class I would place our only three sublime and pathetic poets: *Spenser, Shakespeare, Milton*. In the second class should be ranked such as possessed the true poetical genius in a more moderate degree, but who had noble talents for moral, ethical, and panegyrical poesy. At the head of these are *Dryden, Prior, Addison, Cowley, Waller, Garth, Fenton, Gay, Denham, Parnell*. In the third class may be placed men of wit, of elegant taste, and lively fancy in describing familiar life, though not the

---

[6] Quintilian, *Inst.* X, i, 78. "Nothing irrelevant or far-fetched; nevertheless I would compare him to a clear spring rather than a mighty river."

[7] *Discours à sa réception à l'Académie française* . . . "Incapable, perhaps, of the sublimity which exalts the soul, and of the sentiment which softens it, but capable of illuminating those to whom nature has vouchsafed both the one and the other, laborious, correct, precise, pure, harmonious, he becomes, finally, the poet of reason."

higher scenes of poetry. Here may be numbered *Butler, Swift, Rochester, Donne, Dorset, Oldham*. In the fourth class, the mere versifiers, however smooth and mellifluous some of them may be thought, should be disposed. Such as *Pitt, Sandys, Fairfax, Broome, Buckingham, Lansdown*. This enumeration is not intended as a complete catalogue of writers, and in their proper order, but only to mark out briefly the different species of our celebrated authors. In which of these classes *Pope* deserves to be placed the following work is intended to determine.

FROM SECTION II

Of 'Windsor Forest' and Lyric Pieces

It would be unpardonable to conclude these remarks on descriptive poesy, without taking notice of the *Seasons* of Thomson, who had peculiar and powerful talents for this species of composition. Let the reader, therefore, pardon a digression, if such it be, on his merits and character.

Thomson was blessed with a strong and copious fancy; he hath enriched poetry with a variety of new and original images, which he painted from nature itself, and from his own actual observations: his descriptions have, therefore, a distinctness and truth, which are utterly wanting to those of poets who have only copied from each other, and have never looked abroad on the objects themselves. Thomson was accustomed to wander away into the country for days, and for weeks, attentive to "each rural sight, each rural sound;" while many a poet, who has dwelt for years in the Strand, has attempted to describe fields and rivers, and generally succeeded accordingly. Hence that nauseous repetition of the same circumstances; hence that disgusting impropriety of introducing what may be called a set of hereditary images, without proper regard to the age, or climate, or occasion in which they were formerly used. Though the diction of the *Seasons* is sometimes harsh and inharmonious, and sometimes turgid and obscure, and though, in many instances, the numbers are not sufficiently diversified by different pauses, yet is this poem, on the whole, from the

numberless strokes of nature in which it abounds, one of the
most captivating and amusing in our language; and which, as
its beauties are not of a transitory kind, as depending on particular customs and manners, will ever be perused with delight.
The scenes of Thomson are frequently as wild and romantic as
those of Salvator Rosa, varied with precipices and torrents,
and "castled cliffs," and deep valleys, with piny mountains,
and the gloomiest caverns. Innumerable are the little circumstances in his descriptions, totally unobserved by all his predecessors. What poet hath ever taken notice of the leaf, that,
towards the end of autumn,

> Incessant rustles from the mournful grove,
> Oft startling such as, studious, walk below,
> And slowly circles through the waving air?
>
> [*Autumn*, 990] [8]

Or who, in speaking of a summer evening, hath ever mentioned

> The quail that clamours for his running mate?
>
> [*Summer*, 1657]

Or the following natural image at the same time of the year?

> Wide o'er the thistly lawn, as swells the breeze,
> A whitening shower of vegetable down
> Amusive floats. — — —
>
> [*Summer*, 1658]

In what other poet do we find the silence and expectation that
precedes an April shower insisted on, as in ver. 165 of *Spring*?
Or where,

> The stealing shower is scarce to patter heard,
> By such as wander through the forest walks,
> Beneath th' umbrageous multitude of leaves.
>
> [*Spring*, 177]

How full, particular, and picturesque, is this assemblage of circumstances that attend a very keen frost in a night of winter!

---

[8] The line numbers are keyed to Thomson's *Poetical Works*, ed. J. Logie
Robertson (*Oxford Standard Authors*, 1908–1965), but the quotations
have not been corrected in accordance with that edition.

Loud rings the frozen earth, and hard reflects
A double noise; while at his evening watch
The village dog deters the nightly thief;
The heifer lows; the distant water-fall
Swells in the breeze; and with the hasty tread
Of traveller, the hollow-sounding plain
Shakes from afar.

[*Winter*, 732]

In no one subject are common writers more confused and unmeaning than in their descriptions of rivers, which are generally said only to wind and to murmur, while their qualities
and courses are seldom accurately marked. Examine the exactness of the ensuing description, and consider what a perfect
idea it communicates to the mind.

Around th' adjoining brook, that purls along
The vocal grove, now fretting o'er a rock,
Now scarcely moving through a reedy pool,
Now starting to a sudden stream, and now
Gently diffus'd into a limpid plain;
A various groupe the herds and flocks compose,
Rural confusion.

[*Summer*, 482]

A group worthy the pencil of Giacomo da Bassano, and so
minutely delineated that he might have worked from this
sketch:

— — — On the grassy bank
Some ruminating lie; while others stand
Half in the flood, and often bending sip
The circling surface. — — —

He adds, that the ox, in the middle of them,

— — — — From his sides
The troublous insects lashes, to his sides
Returning still.

[*Summer*, 486]

A natural circumstance, that, to the best of my remembrance,
hath escaped even the natural Theocritus. Nor do I recollect
that any poet hath been struck with the murmurs of the numberless insects that swarm abroad at the noon of a summer's

day: as attendants of the evening, indeed, they have been
mentioned;

> Resounds the living surface of the ground:
> Nor undelightful is the ceaseless hum
> To him who muses through the woods at noon;
> Or drowsy shepherd, as he lies reclin'd
> With half-shut eyes.
>
> [*Summer*, 281]

But the novelty and nature we admire in the descriptions of
Thomson, are by no means his only excellencies; he is equally
to be praised for impressing on our minds the effects, which
the scene delineated would have on the present spectator or
hearer. Thus having spoken of the roaring of the savages in a
wilderness of Africa, he introduces a captive, who, though just
escaped from prison and slavery under the tyrant of Morocco,
is so terrified and astonished at the dreadful uproar, that

> The wretch half wishes for his bonds again.
>
> [*Summer*, 936]

Thus also having described a caravan lost and overwhelmed
in one of those whirlwinds that so frequently agitate and lift
up the whole sands of the desert, he finishes his picture by
adding, that,

> — — — In Cairo's crouded streets,
> Th' impatient merchant, wondering waits in vain,
> And Mecca saddens at the long delay.
>
> [*Summer*, 977]

And thus, lastly, in describing the pestilence that destroyed the
British troops at the siege of Carthagena, he has used a circumstance inimitably lively, picturesque, and striking to the
imagination; for he says that the admiral not only heard the
groans of the sick that echoed from ship to ship, but that he
also pensively stood and listened at midnight to the dashing of
the waters, occasioned by throwing the dead bodies into the
sea:

> Heard, nightly, plung'd into the sullen waves,
> The frequent corse. — — — —
>
> [*Summer*, 1048]

A minute and particular enumeration of circumstances judiciously selected, is what chiefly discriminates poetry from history, and renders the former, for that reason, a more close and
faithful representation of nature than the latter. And if our
poets would accustom themselves to contemplate fully every
object, before they attempted to describe it, they would not
fail of giving their readers more new and more complete
images than they generally do.

These observations on Thomson, which, however, would
not have been so large, if there had been already any considerable criticism on his character, might be still augmented by an
examination and development of the beauties in the loves of
the birds, in *Spring*, verse 580; a view of the torrid zone in
Summer, verse 630; the rise of fountains and rivers in *Autumn*,
verse 781; a man perishing in the snows, in *Winter*, verse 277;
the wolves descending from the Alps, and a view of winter
within the polar circle, verse 389; which are all of them highly-
finished originals, excepting a few of those blemishes intimated
above. *Winter* is, in my apprehension, the most valuable of
these four poems; the scenes of it, like those of "Il Penseroso"
of Milton, being of that awful, solemn, and pensive kind, on
which a great genius best delights to dwell.

Pope, it seems, was of opinion, that descriptive poetry is a
composition as absurd as a feast made up of sauces: and I
know many other persons that think meanly of it. I will not
presume to say it is equal, either in dignity or utility, to those
compositions that lay open the internal constitution of man,
and that *imitate* characters, manners, and sentiments. I may,
however, remind such contemners of it that, in a sister-art,
landscape-painting claims the very next rank to history-paint-
ing, being ever preferred to single portraits, to pieces of still-
life, to droll-figures, to fruit and flower-pieces; that Titian
thought it no diminution of his genius to spend much of his
time in works of the former species; and that, if their principles
lead them to condemn Thomson, they must also condemn the
Georgics of Virgil and the greatest part of the noblest descriptive poem extant, I mean that of Lucretius.

FROM SECTION XIV AND LAST

Thus have I endeavoured to give a critical account, with freedom, but it is hoped with impartiality, of each of Pope's works; by which review it will appear, that the largest portion of them is of the didactic, moral, and satyric kind, and consequently not of the most poetic species of poetry; whence it is manifest that good sense and judgment were his characteristical excellencies, rather than fancy and invention: not that the author of the *Rape of the Lock* and *Eloisa* can be thought to want imagination; but because his imagination was not his predominant talent, because he indulged it not, and because he gave not so many proofs of this talent as of the other. This turn of mind led him to admire French models; he studied Boileau attentively; formed himself upon him as Milton formed himself upon the Grecian and Italian sons of fancy. He stuck to describing modern manners; but those manners, because they are familiar, uniform, artificial, and polished, are, in their very nature, unfit for any lofty effort of the Muse. He gradually became one of the most correct, even, and exact poets that ever wrote, polishing his pieces with a care and assiduity that no business or avocation ever interrupted: so that if he does not frequently ravish and transport his reader, yet he does not disgust him with unexpected inequalities and absurd improprieties. Whatever poetical enthusiasm he actually possessed he withheld and stifled. The perusal of him affects not our minds with such strong emotions as we feel from Homer and Milton, so that no man of a true poetical spirit *is master of himself while he reads them.* Hence he is a writer fit for universal perusal, adapted to all ages and stations—for the old and for the young, the man of business and the scholar. He who would think the *Faery Queen, Palamon and Arcite,* the *Tempest,* or *Comus* childish and romantic might relish Pope. Surely it is no narrow and niggardly encomium, to say he is the great Poet of Reason, the first of ethical authors in verse. And this species

of writing is, after all, the surest road to an extensive reputation. It lies more level to the general capacities of men than
the higher flights of more genuine poetry. We all remember
when even a Churchill was more in vogue than a Gray. He
that treats of fashionable follies and the topics of the day, that
describes present persons and recent events, finds many readers whose understandings and whose passions he gratifies. The
name of Chesterfield on one hand, and of Walpole on the
other, failed not to make a poem bought up and talked of. And
it cannot be doubted that the *Odes* of Horace which celebrated, and the *Satires* which ridiculed, well-known and real
characters at Rome, were more eagerly read, and more frequently cited, than the *Æneid* and the *Georgics* of Virgil.

Where then, according to the question proposed at the
beginning of this Essay, shall we with justice be authorized to
place our admired Pope? Not, assuredly, in the same rank with
Spenser, Shakespeare, and Milton, however justly we may applaud the *Eloisa* and *Rape of the Lock*; but, considering the
correctness, elegance, and utility of his works, the weight of
sentiment, and the knowledge of man they contain, we may
venture to assign him a place next to Milton, and just above
Dryden. Yet, to bring our minds steadily to make this decision,
we must forget for a moment the divine *Music Ode* of Dryden;
and may, perhaps, then be compelled to confess, that though
Dryden be the greater genius, yet Pope is the better artist.

The preference here given to Pope above other modern
English poets, it must be remembered, is founded on the excellencies of his works *in general* and *taken all together;* for there
are parts and passages in other modern authors, in Young and
in Thomson, for instance, equal to any of Pope; and he has
written nothing in a strain so truly sublime as *The Bard* of
Gray.

DAVID HUME
[1711–1776]

As a philosopher, both critical and constructive, Hume ranks
among the major figures; fortunately an attempt to
represent the subtlety and point of his thought in two
brief essays is not necessary. What can be represented is
a clarity and urbanity of style now virtually extinct among
writers on subjects the least abstruse, and a mastery of the
essay form—a form now outmoded for serious discussions
by the scholarly article. Despite the deceptive surface, Hume's
discussion of art is serious and subtle, and his is one of the few
treatments of the subject one could wish longer.

In his most important remarks on aesthetics, Of the
Standard of Taste (1757), Hume raises the central problem
of aesthetic evaluation, which he likens to perceptual
judgments in that ultimately a consensus must be brought
to bear to determine truth: our own predispositions may
lead us to an extreme of approval or disapproval, just as a
diseased vision may make a ripe apple appear gray or brown;
but the general view of men with appropriate training
and normal sensibility will enable us to arrive at a true
standard, just as all healthy eyes see the apple as red.
Hume as a philosopher is empirical and deterministic,
positions which seem not to accord well with an exalted
view of art; his view of taste, then, may appear from some
abstracted standard unsatisfactorily shallow. Those
philosophical positions also, however, may lead naturally
to an unbridled and "deep" subjectivity, as the history of
the Western mind for the last two hundred years can
demonstrate. The lucidity of Hume's discussion can conceal

the potential depths, just as a fishpond may look *as deep
as the ocean, and the waters of a mountain lake as shallow
as a fishpond—which is one of Hume's points exactly.*

*Ernest C. Mossner has written a splendid biography of
Hume (Austin, 1954), and has also contributed an essay,
"Hume's 'Of Criticism,' " to* Studies in Criticism and
Aesthetics 1660–1800. *(ed Anderson and Shea, Minneapolis,
1967), among many other contributions.* See also:

Brunet, Olivier: Philosophie et esthétique chez David Hume,
    Paris, 1965.

Brunius, Teddy: David Hume on Criticism, *Stockholm,
    1952* [see review by Elder Olson, *PQ, XXXII (1953),
    272–73*].

Cohen, Ralph: *"David Hume's Experimental Method and
    the Theory of Taste," ELH, XXV (1958), 270–87.

————: "The Transformation of Passion: A Study of Hume's
    Theories of Tragedy," PQ, XLI (1962), 450–64.*

Kallich, Martin: *"The Associationist Criticism of Francis
    Hutcheson and David Hume," SP, XLIII (1946),
    644–67.*

ESSAYS
[1741]

ESSAY I

Of the Delicacy of Taste and Passion

Some people are subject to a certain *delicacy* of *passion*, which makes them extremely sensible to all the accidents of life, and gives them a lively joy upon every prosperous event, as well as a piercing grief when they meet with misfortunes and adversity. Favours and good offices easily engage their friendship, while the smallest injury provokes their resentment. Any honour or mark of distinction elevates them above measure; but they are as sensibly touched with contempt. People of this character have, no doubt, more lively enjoyments, as well as more pungent sorrows, than men of cool and sedate tempers: But, I believe, when every thing is balanced, there is no one who would not rather be of the latter character, were he entirely master of his own disposition. Good or ill fortune is very little at our disposal: And when a person that has this sensibility of temper meets with any misfortune, his sorrow or resentment takes entire possession of him, and deprives him of all relish in the common occurrences of life, the right enjoyment of which forms the chief part of our happiness. Great pleasures are much less frequent than great pains, so that a sensible temper must meet with fewer trials in the former way than in the latter. Not to mention, that men of such lively passions are apt to be transported beyond all bounds of prudence and discretion, and to take false steps in the conduct of life which are often irretrievable.

There is a *delicacy of taste* observable in some men, which very much resembles this *delicacy* of *passion,* and produces the same sensibility to beauty and deformity of every kind as that does to prosperity and adversity, obligations, and injuries. When you present a poem or a picture to a man possessed of this talent, the delicacy of his feeling makes him be sensibly touched with every part of it; nor are the masterly strokes perceived with more exquisite relish and satisfaction, than the negligences or absurdities with disgust and uneasiness. A polite and judicious conversation affords him the highest entertainment; rudeness or impertinence is as great a punishment to him. In short, delicacy of taste has the same effect as delicacy of passion: It enlarges the sphere both of our happiness and misery, and makes us sensible to pains as well as pleasures, which escape the rest of mankind.

I believe, however, every one will agree with me, that, notwithstanding this resemblance, delicacy of taste is as much to be desired and cultivated as delicacy of passion is to be lamented, and to be remedied, if possible. The good or ill accidents of life are very little at our disposal; but we are pretty much masters what books we shall read, what diversions we shall partake of, and what company we shall keep. Philosophers have endeavoured to render happiness entirely independent of every thing external. That degree of perfection is impossible to be *attained:* But every wise man will endeavour to place his happiness on such objects chiefly as depend upon himself: and *that* is not to be *attained* so much by any other means as by this delicacy of sentiment. When a man is possessed of that talent, he is more happy by what pleases his taste than by what gratifies his appetites, and receives more enjoyment from a poem or a piece of reasoning than the most expensive luxury can afford.*

Whatever connexion there may be originally between these two species of delicacy, I am persuaded, that nothing is so proper to cure us of this delicacy of passion, as the cultivating of that higher and more refined taste, which enables us to judge of the characters of men, of compositions of genius, and of the productions of the nobler arts. A greater or less relish for those obvious beauties which strike the senses, depends entirely upon the greater or less sensibility of the temper: But with regard to the sciences and liberal arts, a fine taste is, in some measure, the same with strong sense, or at least depends so much upon it that they are inseparable. In order to judge aright of a composition of genius, there are so many views to be taken in, so many circumstances to be compared, and such a knowledge of human nature requisite, that no man who is not possessed of the soundest judgment will ever make a tolerable critic in such performances. And this is a new reason for cultivating a relish in the liberal arts. Our judgment will strengthen by this exercise: We shall form juster notions of life: Many things, which please or afflict others, will appear to us too frivolous to engage our attention: And we shall lose by degrees that sensibility and delicacy of passion, which is so incommodious.

But perhaps I have gone too far in saying that a cultivated taste for the polite arts extinguishes the passions, and renders us indifferent to those objects which are so fondly pursued by the rest of mankind. On farther reflection, I find that it rather improves our sensibility for all the tender and

* [How far delicacy of taste, and that of passion, are connected together in the original frame of the mind, it is hard to determine. To me there appears a very considerable connexion between them. For we may observe that women, who have more delicate passions than men, have also a more delicate taste of the ornaments of life, of dress, equipage, and the ordinary decencies of behaviour. Any excellency in these hits their taste much sooner than ours; and when you please their taste, you soon engage their affections.—Omitted in later editions.]

agreeable passions, at the same time that it renders the mind
incapable of the rougher and more boisterous emotions.

Ingenuas didicisse fideliter artes,
Emollit mores, nec sinit esse feros.[1]

For this, I think there may be assigned two very natural
reasons. In the *first* place, nothing is so improving to the
temper as the study of the beauties, either of poetry, eloquence, music, or painting. They give a certain elegance of
sentiment to which the rest of mankind are strangers. The
emotions which they excite are soft and tender. They draw
off the mind from the hurry of business and interest; cherish
reflection; dispose to tranquillity; and produce an agreeable
melancholy, which, of all dispositions of the mind, is the best
suited to love and friendship.

In the *second* place, a delicacy of taste is favourable to
love and friendship, by confining our choice to few people,
and making us indifferent to the company and conversation
of the greater part of men. You will seldom find that mere
men of the world, whatever strong sense they may be endowed with, are very nice in distinguishing characters, or in
marking those insensible differences and gradations which
make one man preferable to another. Any one that has competent sense is sufficient for their entertainment: They talk to
him of their pleasure and affairs with the same frankness
that they would to another; and finding many who are fit
to supply his place, they never feel any vacancy or want in
his absence. But to make use of the allusion of a celebrated
French° author, the judgment may be compared to a clock
or watch, where the most ordinary machine is sufficient to
tell the hours, but the most elaborate alone can point out
the minutes and seconds, and distinguish the smallest differences of time. One that has well digested his knowledge
both of books and men, has little enjoyment but in the company of a few select companions. He feels too sensibly how
much all the rest of mankind fall short of the notions which

---

[1] Ovid, *Epistolae ex Ponto* II. 9. 48: "A faithful study of the liberal arts
humanizes a character and permits it not to be cruel."
° *Mons.* FONTENELLE, *Pluralité des Mondes.* Soir. 6.

he has entertained. And, his affections being thus confined within a narrow circle, no wonder he carries them further than if they were more general and undistinguished. The gaiety and frolic of a bottle companion improves with him into a solid friendship: And the ardours of a youthful appetite become an elegant passion.

ESSAY XX

Of Simplicity and Refinement in Writing

Fine writing, according to Mr. Addison, consists of sentiments which are natural without being obvious. There cannot be a juster and more concise definition of fine writing.

Sentiments which are merely natural affect not the mind with any pleasure, and seem not worthy of our attention. The pleasantries of a waterman, the observations of a peasant, the ribaldry of a porter or hackney coachman, all of these are natural, and disagreeable. What an insipid comedy should we make of the chit-chat of the tea-table, copied faithfully and at full length? Nothing can please persons of taste but nature drawn with all her graces and ornaments, *la belle nature;* or if we copy low life, the strokes must be strong and remarkable, and must convey a lively image to the mind. The absurd naivety* of *Sancho Pancho* is represented in such inimitable colours by Cervantes, that it entertains as much as the picture of the most magnanimous hero or softest lover.

The case is the same with orators, philosophers, critics, or any author who speaks in his own person, without introducing other speakers or actors. If his language be not elegant, his observations uncommon, his sense strong and masculine, he will in vain boast his nature and simplicity. He may be correct, but he never will be agreeable. It is the unhappiness

---

* [Naivety, a word which I have borrow'd from the *French,* and which is wanted in our language.]

of such authors, that they are never blamed or censured. The good fortune of a book, and that of a man, are not the same. The secret deceiving path of life, which Horace talks of, *fallentis semita vitæ*,[2] may be the happiest lot of the one, but is the greatest misfortune which the other can possibly fall into.

On the other hand, productions which are merely surprising, without being natural, can never give any lasting entertainment to the mind. To draw chimeras is not, properly speaking, to copy or imitate. The justness of the representation is lost, and the mind is displeased to find a picture which bears no resemblance to any original. Nor are such excessive refinements more agreeable in the epistolary or philosophic style than in the epic or tragic. Too much ornament is a fault in every kind of production. Uncommon expressions, strong flashes of wit, pointed similes, and epigrammatic turns, especially when they recur too frequently, are a disfigurement, rather than any embellishment of discourse. As the eye, in surveying a Gothic building, is distracted by the multiplicity of ornaments, and loses the whole by its minute attention to the parts; so the mind, in perusing a work overstocked with wit, is fatigued and disgusted with the constant endeavour to shine and surprize. This is the case where a writer overabounds in wit, even though that wit, in itself, should be just and agreeable. But it commonly happens to such writers that they seek for their favourite ornaments even where the subject does not afford them, and by that means have twenty insipid conceits for one thought which is really beautiful.

There is no subject in critical learning more copious than this of the just mixture of simplicty and refinement in writing; and therefore, not to wander in too large a field, I shall confine myself to a few general observations on that head.

First, I observe, *That though excesses of both kinds are to be avoided, and though a proper medium ought to be studied in all productions; yet this medium lies not in a point, but admits of a considerable latitude.* Consider the wide distance,

---

[2] *Epistles* I, viii, 103: "Path of the deceitful life."

in this respect, between Mr. Pope and Lucretius. These seem to lie in the two greatest extremes of refinement and simplicity in which a poet can indulge himself, without being guilty of any blameable excess. All this interval may be filled with poets who may differ from each other, but may be equally admirable, each in his peculiar stile and manner. Corneille and Congreve, who carry their wit and refinement somewhat farther than Mr. Pope (if poets of so different a kind can be compared together), and Sophocles and Terence, who are more simple than Lucretius, seem to have gone out of that medium in which the most perfect productions are found, and to be guilty of some excess in those opposite characters. Of all the great poets, Virgil and Racine, in my opinion, lie nearest the center, and are the farthest removed from both the extremities.

My *second* observation on this head is, *That it is very difficult, if not impossible, to explain by words, where the just medium lies between the excesses of simplicity and refinement, or to give any rule by which we can know precisely the bounds between the fault and the beauty.* A critic may not only discourse very judiciously on this head without instructing his readers, but even without understanding the matter perfectly himself. There is not a finer piece of criticism than *the dissertation on pastorals* by Fontenelle, in which, by a number of reflections and philosophical reasonings, he endeavours to fix the just medium which is suitable to that species of writing. But let any one read the pastorals of that author, and he will be convinced that this judicious critic, notwithstanding his fine reasonings, had a false taste, and fixed the point of perfection much nearer the extreme of refinement than pastoral poetry will admit of. The sentiments of his shepherds are better suited to the toilettes of Paris than to the forests of Arcadia. But this it is impossible to discover from his critical reasonings. He blames all excessive painting and ornament as much as Virgil could have done, had that great poet writ a dissertation on this species of poetry. However different the tastes of men, their general discourse on these subjects is commonly the same. No criticism can be instructive which descends not to particulars, and is not full of examples and illustrations. It is allowed on all hands that beauty, as well as virtue, always lies in a medium; but where this medium is placed is the great question, and can never be sufficiently explained by general reasonings.

I shall deliver it as a *third* observation in this subject, *That we ought to be more on our guard against the excess of refinement than that of simplicity; and that because the former excess is both less* beauty, *and more* dangerous *than the latter.*

It is a certain rule, that wit and passion are entirely incompatible. When the affections are moved, there is no place for the imagination. The mind of man being naturally limited, it is impossible that all its faculties can operate at once: And the more any one predominates, the less room is there for the others to exert their vigour. For this reason, a greater degree of simplicity is required in all compositions where men, and actions, and passions are painted, than in such as consist of reflections and observations. And as the former species of writing is the more engaging and beautiful, one may safely, upon this account, give the preference to the extreme of simplicity above that of refinement.

We may also observe, that those compositions, which we read the oftenest, and which every man of taste has got by heart, have the recommendation of simplicity, and have nothing surprising in the thought, when divested of that elegance of expression and harmony of numbers with which it is cloathed. If the merit of the composition lie in a point of wit, it may strike at first; but the mind anticipates the thought in the second perusal, and is not longer affected by it. When I read an epigram of Martial, the first line recalls the whole, and I have no pleasure in repeating to myself what I know already. But each line, each word in Catullus, has its merit; and I am never tired with the perusal of him. It is sufficient to run over Cowley once: But Parnel, after the fiftieth reading, is as fresh as at the first. Besides, it is with books as with women, where a certain plainness of manner and of dress is more engaging than that glare of paint and airs and apparel, which may dazzle the eye, but reaches not the affections. Terence is a modest and bashful beauty, to whom we grant everything because he assumes nothing, and whose purity and nature make a durable, though not a violent impression on us.

But refinement, as it is the less *beautiful,* so is it the more *dangerous* extreme, and what we are the aptest to fall into. Simplicity passes for dulness when it is not accompanied with great elegance and propriety. On the contrary, there is something surprizing in a blaze of wit and conceit. Ordinary readers are mightily struck with it, and falsely imagine it to be the most difficult, as well as most excellent way of writing. Seneca abounds with agreeable faults, says Quintilian, *abundat dulcibus vitiis;*[3] and for that reason is the more dangerous, and the more apt to pervert the taste of the young and inconsiderate.

I shall add, that the excess of refinement is now more to be guarded against than ever, because it is the extreme which men are the most apt to fall into after learning has made some progress, and after eminent writers have appeared in every species of composition. The endeavour to please by novelty leads men wide of simplicity and nature, and fills their writings with affectation and conceit. It was thus the Asiatic eloquence degenerated so much from the Attic: It was thus the age of Claudius and Nero became so much inferior to that of Augustus in taste and genius: And perhaps there are, at present, some symptoms of a like degeneracy of taste, in France as well as in England.

[3] *Institutio Oratio* X, 129.

EDMUND BURKE
[1729–1797]

———————

Burke as statesman, orator, and political writer cannot concern us, though it was for his political writing that he produced that prose which at its best remains in majesty of utterance second only to Johnson's (and some would deny that precedence) in the latter eighteenth century. Burke had tentatively begun A Philosophical Enquiry into the Origin of Our Ideas on the Sublime and the Beautiful when he was nineteen, and published it when only twenty-eight, as yet unsettled and unestablished. He always after took a discriminating interest in literary and artistic matters, but, although he was a member of the famous Club and highly regarded by Johnson, he made no further contributions to pure literature or criticism, except for an "Essay on Taste" prefixed to the second edition (1759) of the Enquiry. From 1759 to 1788, however, he conducted Dodsley's Annual Register, and it is very likely that the book reviews and comments on literature scattered through that publication are to be attributed mostly to him.

Professor Boulton, in the long and excellent introduction to his edition of the Enquiry (see below), asserts that Burke "was the first writer on aesthetics in English to take up an uncompromising sensationist viewpoint." He further remarks, "Burke, of course, followed in a great tradition in holding his sensationist philosophy: the dependence of the mind, for its ideas, on the senses was fundamental to the work of Locke, Berkeley, and Hume. Addison used this principle as the starting-point for an analysis of aesthetic

*experience. To him sight is the principal source of material
for the imagination:*

> We cannot indeed have a single Image in the Fancy
> that did not make its first Entrance through the Sight;
> but we have the Power of retaining, altering and com-
> pounding those Images, which we have once received,
> into all the Varieties of Picture and Vision that are most
> agreeable to the Imagination.
>
> [*Spectator* No. 411]

*From this premise it was argued that aesthetic values are
appreciated through the senses. Thus the senses became
accepted as the faculties involved in the enjoyment of beauty;
beauty was thought to depend on physical properties in
objects—properties, therefore, apprehended through
sensation." (p. xxxvi) The writer thus dependent on his
sensations for aesthetic judgment cannot, of course, make
the judgment until he examines his sensations. Subjectivity
is thus enforced. The philosophical and psychological basis
for the dominant romantic and the popular twentieth-century
aesthetic thought is discoverable in Locke (and perhaps
in Descartes with his "I think, therefore I am"), but
Burke gives it its most important eighteenth-century
statement, one immensely influential. How much, for an
example, nineteenth-century taste in architecture may look
back to Part II, Section XV I leave the curious reader to
determine.*

*The text below is derived from the second edition, 1759.
The admirable edition of the* Enquiry, *with splendid
introduction and notes, by J. T. Boulton, 1958, must be
consulted. My annotations, in particular, are much indebted
to Professor Boulton's labors. See also:*

Harris, Eileen: "Burke and Chambers on the Sublime and
    Beautiful," Essays in the History of Architecture
    Presented to Rudolph Wittkower (ed. Douglas Fraser,
    Howard Hibbard, and Milton J. Levine), London,
    1967, pp. 207–13.
Morpurgo Tagliabue, Guido: "La nozione del gusto nel
    XVIII seculo: E. Burke," Acme (1962), 97–120.

Price, Martin: *"The Sublime Poem: Pictures and Powers,"*
    Yale Review, LVIII (1968), 194–213.
Stanlis, Peter J.: *"Burke and the Sensibility of Rousseau,"*
    Thought, XXXVI (1961), 246–76.
Wector, Dixon: *"Burke's Theory of Words, Images, and
    Emotion,"* PMLA, LV (1940), 167–81.

FROM A PHILOSOPHICAL ENQUIRY
INTO THE ORIGIN OF OUR IDEAS
OF THE SUBLIME AND BEAUTIFUL
[1754]

PART I

SECTION VI

Of the Passions Which Belong to Self-Preservation

Most of the ideas which are capable of making a powerful
impression on the mind, whether simply of pain or pleasure, or
of the modifications of those, may be reduced very nearly to
these two heads, *self-preservation,* and *society;* to the ends of
one or the other of which all our passions are calculated to
answer. The passions which concern self-preservation, turn
mostly on *pain* or *danger.* The ideas of *pain, sickness,* and
death, fill the mind with strong emotions of horror; but *life* and
health, though they put us in a capacity of being affected with
pleasure, make no such impression by the simple enjoyment.
The passions therefore which are conversant about the preservation of the individual turn chiefly on *pain* and *danger,* and
they are the most powerful of all the passions.

SECTION VII

Of the Sublime

Whatever is fitted in any sort to excite the ideas of pain and danger, that is to say, whatever is in any sort terrible, or is conversant about terrible objects, or operates in a manner analogous to terror, is a source of the *sublime;* that is, it is productive of the strongest emotion which the mind is capable of feeling. I say the strongest emotion, because I am satisfied the ideas of pain are much more powerful than those which enter on the part of pleasure. Without all doubt, the torments which we may be made to suffer are much greater in their effect on the body and mind, than any pleasures which the most learned voluptuary could suggest, or than the liveliest imagination, and the most sound and exquisitely sensible body, could enjoy. Nay, I am in great doubt whether any man could be found, who would earn a life of the most perfect satisfaction at the price of ending it in the torments, which justice inflicted in a few hours on the late unfortunate regicide in France.[1] But as pain is stronger in its operation than pleasure, so death is in general a much more affecting idea than pain; because there are very few pains, however exquisite, which are not preferred to death: nay, what generally makes pain itself, if I may say so, more painful, is, that it is considered as an emissary of this king of terrors. When danger or pain press too nearly, they are incapable of giving any delight, and are simply terrible; but at certain distances, and with certain modifications, they may be, and they are, delightful, as we every day experience. The cause of this I shall endeavor to investigate hereafter.

---

[1] Burke refers to Robert Francis Damiens, who, after attempting the life of Louis XV, was put to death in 1757 after incredible tortures. The incident was much discussed in England, and may have inspired Johnson's famous reference to "a malefactor who ceases to feel the cords that bind him when the pincers are tearing his flesh." (Review of *Soame Jenyns' Free Inquiry* . . . , 1757) This remark was added to the 1759 edition.

SECTION VIII

Of the Passions Which Belong to Society

The other head under which I class our passions, is that of
society, which may be divided into two sorts. 1. The society of
the *sexes,* which answers the purpose of propagation; and next,
that more *general society,* which we have with men and with
other animals, and which we may in some sort be said to have
even with the inanimate world. The passions belonging to the
preservation of the individual turn wholly on pain and danger:
those which belong to *generation* have their origin in gratifica-
tions and *pleasures;* the pleasure most directly belonging to this
purpose is of a lively character, rapturous and violent, and
confessedly the highest pleasure of sense; yet the absence of
this so great an enjoyment scarce amounts to an uneasiness;
and, except at particular times, I do not think it affects at all.
When men describe in what manner they are affected by pain
and danger, they do not dwell on the pleasure of health and the
comfort of security, and then lament the *loss* of these satisfac-
tions: the whole turns upon the actual pains and horrors which
they endure. But if you listen to the complaints of a forsaken
lover, you observe that he insists largely on the pleasures which
he enjoyed, or hoped to enjoy, and on the perfection of the
object of his desires; it is the *loss* which is always uppermost
in his mind.[2] The violent effects produced by love, which has
sometimes been even wrought up to madness, is no objection
to the rule which we seek to establish. When men have suffered
their imaginations to be long affected with any idea, it so
wholly engrosses them as to shut out by degrees almost every
other, and to break down every partition of the mind which
would confine it. Any idea is sufficient for the purpose, as is

[2] Boulton points out that Burke had been intimately acquainted with a
"forsaken lover" whose "loss" resulted in suicide. (A. P. I. Samuels,
The Early Life . . . of Burke, Cambridge, 1923, pp. 50–52.)

evident from the infinite variety of causes, which give rise to madness: but this at most can only prove, that the passion of love is capable of producing very extraordinary effects, not that its extraordinary emotions have any connection with positive pain.

SECTION IX

The Final Cause of the Difference Between the Passions Belonging to Self-Preservation, and Those Which Regard the Society of the Sexes

The final cause of the difference in character between the passions which regard self-preservation, and those which are directed to the multiplication of the species, will illustrate the foregoing remarks yet further; and it is, I imagine, worthy of observation even upon its own account. As the performance of our duties of every kind depends upon life, and the performing them with vigor and efficacy depends upon health, we are very strongly affected with whatever threatens the destruction of either: but as we were not made to acquiesce in life and health, the simple enjoyment of them is not attended with any real pleasure, lest, satisfied with that, we should give ourselves over to indolence and inaction. On the other hand, the generation of mankind is a great purpose, and it is requisite that men should be animated to the pursuit of it by some great incentive. It is therefore attended with a very high pleasure; but as it is by no means designed to be our constant business, it is not fit that the absence of this pleasure should be attended with any considerable pain. The difference between men and brutes, in this point, seems to be remarkable. Men are at all times pretty equally disposed to the pleasures of love, because they are to be guided by reason in the time and manner of indulging them. Had any great pain arisen from the want of this satisfaction, reason, I am afraid, would find great difficulties in the performance of its office. But brutes that obey laws, in the execution of which their own reason has but little share, have their stated seasons; at such times it is not improbable that the sensation from the want is very troublesome, because the end must be then answered, or be missed in many, perhaps forever; as the inclination returns only with its season.

SECTION X

Of Beauty

The passion which belongs to generation, merely as such, is lust only. This is evident in brutes, whose passions are more unmixed, and which pursue their purposes more directly than ours. The only distinction they observe with regard to their mates, is that of sex. It is true, that they stick severally to their own species in preference to all others. But this preference, I imagine, does not arise from any sense of beauty which they find in their species, as Mr. Addison supposes,[3] but from a law of some other kind, to which they are subject; and this we may fairly conclude, from their apparent want of choice amongst those objects to which the barriers of their species have confined them. But man, who is a creature adapted to a greater variety and intricacy of relation, connects with the general passion the idea of some *social* qualities, which direct and heighten the appetite which he has in common with all other animals; and as he is not designed like them to live at large, it is fit that he should have some thing to create a preference, and fix his choice; and this in general should be some sensible quality; as no other can so quickly, so powerfully, or so surely produce its effect. The object therefore of this mixed passion, which we call love, is the *beauty* of the *sex*. Men are carried to the sex in general, as it is the sex, and by the common law of

---

[3] *Spectator* No. 413.

nature; but they are attached to particulars by personal *beauty*. I call beauty a social quality; for where women and men, and not only they, but when other animals give us a sense of joy and pleasure in beholding them (and there are many that do so), they inspire us with sentiments of tenderness and affection towards their persons; we like to have them near us, and we enter willingly into a kind of relation with them, unless we should have strong reasons to the contrary. But to what end, in many cases, this was designed, I am unable to discover; for I see no greater reason for a connection between man and several animals who are attired in so engaging a manner, than between him and some others who entirely want this attraction, or possess it in a far weaker degree. But it is probable that Providence did not make even this distinction, but with a view to some great end; though we cannot perceive distinctly what it is, as his wisdom is not our wisdom, nor our ways his ways.

PART II

SECTION I

Of the Passion Caused by the Sublime

The passion caused by the great and sublime in *nature*, when those causes operate most powerfully, is astonishment: and astonishment is that state of the soul in which all its motions are suspended, with some degree of horror. In this case the mind is so entirely filled with its object, that it cannot entertain any other, nor by consequence reason on that object which employs it. Hence arises the great power of the sublime, that, far from being produced by them, it anticipates our reasonings, and hurries us on by an irresistible force. Astonishment, as I have said, is the effect of the sublime in its highest degree; the inferior effects are admiration, reverence, and respect.

SECTION II

Terror

No passion so effectually robs the mind of all its powers of acting and reasoning as *fear*. For fear being an apprehension of
pain or death, it operates in a manner that resembles actual
pain. Whatever therefore is terrible, with regard to sight, is
sublime too, whether this cause of terror be endued with greatness of dimensions or not; for it is impossible to look on anything as trifling, or contemptible, that may be dangerous. There
are many animals, who, though far from being large, are yet
capable of raising ideas of the sublime, because they are considered as objects of terror. As serpents and poisonous animals
of almost all kinds. And to things of great dimensions, if we
annex an adventitious idea of terror, they become without comparison greater. A level plain of a vast extent on land, is certainly no mean idea; the prospect of such a plain may be as
extensive as a prospect of the ocean; but can it ever fill the
mind with anything so great as the ocean itself? This is owing
to several causes; but it is owing to none more than this, that
the ocean is an object of no small terror. Indeed terror is in all
cases whatsoever, either more openly or latently, the ruling
principle of the sublime. Several languages bear a strong testi-
mony to the affinity of these ideas. They frequently use the
same word to signify indifferently the modes of astonishment
or admiration and those of terror. Θάμβος is in Greek either
fear or wonder; δεινός is terrible or respectable; αἰδέω, to reverence or to fear. *Vereor* in Latin is what αἰδέω is in Greek. The
Romans used the verb *stupeo*, a term which strongly marks the
state of an astonished mind, to express the effect either of simple fear, or of astonishment; the word *attonitus* (thunder-
struck) is equally expressive of the alliance of these ideas; and
do not the French *étonnement*, and the English *astonishment*
and *amazement*, point out as clearly the kindred emotions

which attend fear and wonder? They who have a more general knowledge of languages, could produce, I make no doubt, many other and equally striking examples.

SECTION III

Obscurity

To make anything very terrible, obscurity seems in general to be necessary. When we know the full extent of any danger, when we can accustom our eyes to it, a great deal of the apprehension vanishes. Every one will be sensible of this, who considers how greatly night adds to our dread, in all cases of danger, and how much the notions of ghosts and goblins, of which none can form clear ideas, affect minds which give credit to the popular tales concerning such sorts of beings. Those despotic governments which are founded on the passions of men, and principally upon the passion of fear, keep their chief as much as may be from the public eye. The policy has been the same in many cases of religion. Almost all the heathen temples were dark. Even in the barbarous temples of the Americans at this day, they keep their idol in a dark part of the hut, which is consecrated to his worship. For this purpose too the Druids performed all their ceremonies in the bosom of the darkest woods, and in the shade of the oldest and most spreading oaks. No person seems better to have understood the secret of heightening, or of setting terrible things, if I may use the expression, in their strongest light, by the force of a judicious obscurity than Milton. His description of death in the second book is admirably studied; it is astonishing with what a gloomy pomp, with what a significant and expressive uncertainty of strokes and coloring, he has finished the portrait of the king of terrors:

> "The other shape,
> If shape it might be called that shape had none
> Distinguishable, in member, joint, or limb;

> Or substance might be called that shadow seemed;
> For each seemed either; black he stood as night;
> Fierce as ten furies; terrible as hell;
> And shook a deadly dart. What seemed his head
> The likeness of a kingly crown had on." [4]

In this description all is dark, uncertain, confused, terrible, and sublime to the last degree.

SECTION IV

Of the Difference Between Clearness and Obscurity with Regard to the Passions

---

It is one thing to make an idea clear, and another to make it *affecting* to the imagination. If I make a drawing of a palace, or a temple, or a landscape, I present a very clear idea of those objects; but then (allowing for the effect of imitation which is something) my picture can at most affect only as the palace, temple, or landscape, would have affected in the reality. On the other hand, the most lively and spirited verbal description I can give raises a very obscure and imperfect *idea* of such objects; but then it is in my power to raise a stronger *emotion* by the description than I could do by the best painting. This experience constantly evinces. The proper manner of conveying the *affections* of the mind from one to another is by words; there is a great insufficiency in all other methods of communication; and so far is a clearness of imagery from being absolutely necessary to an influence upon the passions, that they may be considerably operated upon, without presenting any image at all, by certain sounds adapted to that purpose; of which we have a sufficient proof in the acknowledged and powerful effects of instrumental music. In reality, a great clearness helps but little towards affecting the passions, as it is in some sort an enemy to all enthusiasms whatsoever.

[4] *Paradise Lost*, II, 666–73, slightly misquoted.

SECTION [IV]

The Same Subject Continued

There are two verses in Horace's Art of Poetry that seem to contradict this opinion; for which reason I shall take a little more pains in clearing it up. The verses are,

> Segnius irritant animos demissa per aures,
> Quam quæ sunt oculis subjecta fidelibus.[5]

On this the Abbé du Bos founds a criticism, wherein he gives painting the preference to poetry in the article of moving the passions; principally on account of the greater *clearness* of the ideas it represents. I believe this excellent judge was led into this mistake (if it be a mistake) by his system; to which he found it more conformable than I imagine it will be found to experience. I know several who admire and love painting, and yet who regard the objects of their admiration in that art with coolness enough in comparison of that warmth with which they are animated by affecting pieces of poetry or rhetoric. Among the common sort of people, I never could perceive that painting had much influence on their passions. It is true that the best sorts of painting, as well as the best sorts of poetry, are not much understood in that sphere. But it is most certain that their passions are very strongly roused by a fanatic preacher, or by the ballads of Chevy Chase, or the Children in the Wood, and by other little popular poems and tales that are current in that rank of life. I do not know of any paintings, bad or good, that produce the same effect. So that poetry, with all its obscurity, has a more general, as well as a more powerful dominion over the passions, than the other art. And I think there are reasons in nature, why the obscure idea, when prop-

---

[5] *Ars Poetica* 180–81: "Less vividly is the mind stirred by what finds entrance through the ears than by what is brought before the trusty eyes." Horace: *per aurem.*

erly conveyed, should be more affecting than the clear. It is our
ignorance of things that causes all our admiration, and chiefly
excites our passions. Knowledge and acquaintance make the
most striking causes affect but little. It is thus with the vulgar;
and all men are as the vulgar in what they do not understand.
The ideas of eternity, and infinity, are among the most affecting
we have: and yet perhaps there is nothing of which we really
understand so little, as of infinity and eternity. We do not anywhere meet a more sublime description than this justly-cele-
brated one of Milton, wherein he gives the portrait of Satan
with a dignity so suitable to the subject:

> He above the rest
> In shape and gesture proudly eminent
> Stood like a tower; his form had yet not lost
> All her original brightness, nor appeared
> Less than archangel ruined, and th' excess
> Of glory obscured: as when the sun new risen
> Looks through the horizontal misty air
> Shorn of his beams; or from behind the moon
> In dim eclipse disastrous twilight sheds
> On half the nations; and with fear of change
> Perplexes monarchs.[6]

Here is a very noble picture; and in what does this poetical
picture consist? In images of a tower, an archangel, the sun
rising through mists, or in an eclipse, the ruin of monarchs and
the revolutions of kingdoms. The mind is hurried out of itself,
by a crowd of great and confused images; which affect because
they are crowded and confused. For separate them, and you
lose much of the greatness; and join them, and you infallibly
lose the clearness. The images raised by poetry are always of
this obscure kind; though in general the effects of poetry are by
no means to be attributed to the images it raises; which point
we shall examine more at large hereafter. But painting, when
we have allowed for the pleasure of imitation, can only affect
simply by the images it presents; and even in painting, a judicious obscurity in some things contributes to the effect of the
picture; because the images in painting are exactly similar to

[6] *Paradise Lost*, I, 589–99.

those in nature; and in nature, dark, confused, uncertain
images have a greater power on the fancy to form the grander
passions, than those have which are more clear and determinate. But where and when this observation may be applied
to practice, and how far it shall be extended, will be better
deduced from the nature of the subject, and from the occasion,
than from any rules that can be given.

I am sensible that this idea has met with opposition, and is
likely still to be rejected by several. But let it be considered
that hardly anything can strike the mind with its greatness,
which does not make some sort of approach towards infinity;
which nothing can do whilst we are able to perceive its bounds;
but to see an object distinctly, and to perceive its bounds, is
one and the same thing. A clear idea is therefore another name
for a little idea. There is a passage in the book of Job amazingly
sublime, and this sublimity is principally due to the terrible
uncertainty of the thing described: *In thoughts from the visions of the night, when deep sleep falleth upon men, fear came
upon me and trembling, which made all my bones to shake.
Then a spirit passed before my face. The hair of my flesh stood
up. It stood still,* but I could not discern the form thereof; *an
image was before mine eyes; there was silence; and I heard a
voice,—Shall mortal man be more just than God?* [7] We are first
prepared with the utmost solemnity for the vision; we are first
terrified, before we are let even into the obscure cause of our
emotion: but when this grand cause of terror makes its appearance, what is it? Is it not wrapt up in the shades of its own incomprehensible darkness, more awful, more striking, more terrible, than the liveliest description, than the clearest painting,
could possibly represent it? When painters have attempted to
give us clear representations of these very fanciful and terrible
ideas, they have, I think, almost always failed; insomuch that I
have been at a loss, in all the pictures I have seen of hell, to
determine whether the painter did not intend something ludicrous. Several painters have handled a subject of this kind,
with a view of assembling as many horrid phantoms as their
imagination could suggest; but all the designs I have chanced

[7] *Job* 4:13–17.

to meet of the temptations of St. Anthony were rather a sort of odd, wild grotesques, than any thing capable of producing a serious passion. In all these subjects poetry is very happy. Its apparitions, its chimeras, its harpies, its allegorical figures, are grand and affecting; and though Virgil's Fame and Homer's Discord are obscure, they are magnificent figures. These figures in painting would be clear enough, but I fear they might become ridiculous.

SECTION V

Power

Besides those things which *directly* suggest the idea of danger, and those which produce a similar effect from a mechanical cause, I know of nothing sublime, which is not some modification of power. And this branch rises, as naturally as the other two branches, from terror, the common stock of everything that is sublime. The idea of power, at first view, seems of the class of those indifferent ones, which may equally belong to pain or to pleasure. But in reality, the affection arising from the idea of vast power is extremely remote from that neutral character. For first, we must remember that the idea of pain, in its highest degree, is much stronger than the highest degree of pleasure; and that it preserves the same superiority through all the subordinate gradations. From hence it is, that where the chances for equal degrees of suffering or enjoyment are in any sort equal, the idea of the suffering must always be prevalent. And indeed the ideas of pain, and, above all, of death, are so very affecting, that whilst we remain in the presence of whatever is supposed to have the power of inflicting either, it is impossible to be perfectly free from terror. Again, we know by experience, that, for the enjoyment of pleasure, no great efforts of power are at all necessary; nay, we know that such efforts would go a great way towards destroying our satisfaction: for pleasure must be stolen, and not forced upon us; pleasure follows the will; and therefore we are generally affected with it by many things of a force greatly inferior to our own. But pain is always inflicted by a power in some way superior, because we never submit to pain willingly. So that strength, violence, pain, and terror, are ideas that rush in upon the mind together. Look at a man, or any other animal of prodigious strength, and what is your idea before reflection? Is it that this strength will be subservient to you, to your ease, to your pleasure, to your interest in any sense? No; the emotion you feel is, lest this enormous strength should be employed to the purposes of rapine and destruction. That power derives all its sublimity from the terror with which it is generally accompanied, will appear evidently from its effect in the very few cases, in which it may be possible to strip a considerable degree of strength of its ability to hurt. When you do this, you spoil it of everything sublime, and it immediately becomes contemptible. An ox is a creature of vast strength; but he is an innocent creature, extremely serviceable, and not at all dangerous; for which reason the idea of an ox is by no means grand. A bull is strong too; but his strength is of another kind; often very destructive, seldom (at least amongst us) of any use in our business; the idea of a bull is therefore great, and it has frequently a place in sublime descriptions, and elevating comparisons. Let us look at another strong animal, in the two distinct lights in which we may consider him. The horse in the light of an useful beast, fit for the plough, the road, the draft; in every social useful light, the horse has nothing sublime; but is it thus that we are affected with him, *whose neck is clothed with thunder, the glory of whose nostrils is terrible, who swalloweth the ground with fierceness and rage, neither believeth that it is the sound of the trumpet?* [8] In this description, the useful character of the horse entirely disappears, and the terrible and sublime blaze out together. We have continually about us animals of a strength that is considerable, but not pernicious. Amongst these we never look for the sublime; it comes upon us in the gloomy forest, and in the howling wilderness, in the form of the lion, the tiger, the panther, or rhinoceros. Whenever

[8] *Job* 39: semi-verses from 19, 20, 24.

strength is only useful, and employed for our benefit or our pleasure, then it is never sublime; for nothing can act agreeably to us, that does not act in conformity to our will; but to act agreeably to our will, it must be subject to us, and therefore can never be the cause of a grand and commanding conception. The description of the wild ass, in Job, is worked up into no small sublimity, merely by insisting on his freedom, and his setting mankind at defiance; otherwise the description of such an animal could have had nothing noble in it. *Who hath loosed* (says he) *the bands of the wild ass? whose house I have made the wilderness and the barren land his dwellings. He scorneth the multitude of the city, neither regardeth he the voice of the driver. The range of the mountains is his pasture.*[9] The magnificent description of the unicorn and of leviathan, in the same book, is full of the same heightening circumstances: *Will the unicorn be willing to serve thee? canst thou bind the unicorn with his band in the furrow? wilt thou trust him because his strength is great?—Canst thou draw out leviathan with an hook? will he make a covenant with thee? wilt thou take him for a servant forever? shall not one be cast down even at the sight of him?* [10] In short, wheresoever we find strength, and in what light soever we look upon power, we shall all along abserve the sublime the concomitant of terror, and contempt the attendant on a strength that is subservient and innoxious. The race of dogs, in many of their kinds, have generally a competent degree of strength and swiftness; and they exert these and other valuable qualities which they possess, greatly to our convenience and pleasure. Dogs are indeed the most social, affectionate, and amiable animals of the whole brute creation; but love approaches much nearer to contempt than is commonly imagined; and accordingly, though we caress dogs, we borrow from them an appellation of the most despicable kind, when we employ terms of reproach; and this appellation is the common mark of the last vileness and contempt in every language. Wolves have not more strength than several species of dogs; but, on

[9] *Job* 39:5–8, slightly misquoted.
[10] *Job* 39: semi-verses from 9–11; 41:1, 4, 9 in pastiche.

account of their unmanageable fierceness, the idea of a wolf is not despicable; it is not excluded from grand descriptions and similitudes. Thus we are affected by strength, which is *natural* power. The power which arises from institution in kings and commanders, has the same connection with terror. Sovereigns are frequently addressed with the title of *dread majesty*. And it may be observed, that young persons, little acquainted with the world, and who have not been used to approach men in power, are commonly struck with an awe which takes away the free use of their faculties. *When I prepared my seat in the street,* (says Job,) *the young men saw me, and hid themselves.*[11] Indeed so natural is this timidity with regard to power, and so strongly does it inhere in our constitution, that very few are able to conquer it, but by mixing much in the business of the great world, or by using no small violence to their natural dispositions. I know some people are of opinion, that no awe, no degree of terror, accompanies the idea of power; and have hazarded to affirm, that we can contemplate the idea of God himself without any such emotion. I purposely avoided, when I first considered this subject, to introduce the idea of that great and tremendous Being, as an example in an argument so light as this; though it frequently occurred to me, not as an objection to, but as a strong confirmation of, my notions in this matter. I hope, in what I am going to say, I shall avoid presumption, where it is almost impossible for any mortal to speak with strict propriety. I say then, that whilst we consider the Godhead merely as he is an object of the understanding, which forms a complex idea of power, wisdom, justice, goodness, all stretched to a degree far exceeding the bounds of our comprehension, whilst we consider the divinity in this refined and abstracted light, the imagination and passions are little or nothing affected. But because we are bound, by the condition of our nature, to ascend to these pure and intellectual ideas, through the medium of sensible images, and to judge of these divine qualities by their evident acts and exertions, it becomes extremely hard to disentangle our idea of the cause from the effect by which

[11] *Job* 39:7–8.

we are led to know it. Thus, when we contemplate the Deity, his attributes and their operation, coming united on the mind, form a sort of sensible image, and as such are capable of affecting the imagination. Now, though in a just idea of the Deity, perhaps none of his attributes are predominant, yet, to our imagination, his power is by far the most striking. Some reflection, some comparing, is necessary to satisfy us of his wisdom, his justice, and his goodness. To be struck with his power, it is only necessary that we should open our eyes. But whilst we contemplate so vast an object, under the arm, as it were, of almighty power, and invested upon every side with omnipresence, we shrink into the minuteness of our own nature, and are, in a manner, annihilated before him. And though a consideration of his other attributes may relieve, in some measure, our apprehensions; yet no conviction of the justice with which it is exercised, nor the mercy with which it is tempered, can wholly remove the terror that naturally arises from a force which nothing can withstand. If we rejoice, we rejoice with trembling; and even whilst we are receiving benefits, we cannot but shudder at a power which can confer benefits of such mighty importance. When the prophet David contemplated the wonders of wisdom and power which are displayed in the economy of man, he seems to be struck with a sort of divine horror, and cries out, *fearfully and wonderfully am I made!* [12] An heathen poet has a sentiment of a similar nature; Horace looks upon it as the last effort of philosophical fortitude, to behold without terror and amazement, this immense and glorious fabric of the universe:

> Hunc solem, et stellas, et decedentia certis
> Tempora momentis sunt qui formidine nulla
> Imbuti spectent. [13]

Lucretius is a poet not to be suspected of giving way to superstitious terrors; yet, when he supposes the whole mechanism of nature laid open by the master of his philosophy, his transport

[12] Psalms 139:14, "I will praise thee; for I am fearfully and wonderfully made . . ."
[13] *Epistles*, I, vi, 3–5: "You sun, the stars and seasons that pass in fixed courses—some can gaze upon these with no strain of fear."

on this magnificent view, which he has represented in the
colors of such bold and lively poetry, is overcast with a shade
of secret dread and horror:

> His ibi me rebus quædam divina voluptas
> Percipit, atque horror; quod sic natura, tua vi
> Tam manifesta patens, ex omni parte retecta est.[14]

But the Scripture alone can supply ideas answerable to the
majesty of this subject. In the Scripture, wherever God is represented as appearing or speaking, everything terrible in nature
is called up to heighten the awe and solemnity of the Divine
presence. The Psalms, and the prophetical books, are crowded
with instances of this kind. *The earth shook,* (says the Psalm-
ist,) *the heavens also dropped at the presence of the Lord.*[15]
And what is remarkable, the painting preserves the same character, not only when he is supposed descending to take vengeance upon the wicked, but even when he exerts the like
plenitude of power in acts of beneficence to mankind. *Tremble,
thou earth! at the presence of the Lord; at the presence of the
God of Jacob; which turned the rock into standing water, the
flint into a fountain of waters!* [16] It were endless to enumerate
all the passages, both in the sacred and profane writers, which
establish the general sentiment of mankind, concerning the
inseparable union of a sacred and reverential awe, with our
ideas of the divinity. Hence the common maxim, *Primus in
orbe deos fecit timor.*[17] This maxim may be, as I believe it is,
false with regard to the origin of religion. The maker of the
maxim saw how inseparable these ideas were, without considering that the notion of some great power must be always
precedent to our dread of it. But this dread must necessarily
follow the idea of such a power, when it is once excited in the
mind. It is on this principle that true religion has, and must

[14] *De Rerum Natura,* III, 38–40 (slightly misquoted): "O, here in these
affairs some new divine delight and trembling awe takes hold through
me, and thus by power of thine, Nature, so plain and manifest at last,
hath been on every side laid bare." (W. E. Leonard translation.)
[15] *Psalms* 68:8.
[16] *Psalms* 114:7–8.
[17] Statius, *Thebiad* III, 661: "Fear first made Gods in the world."

have, so large a mixture of salutary fear; and that false religions have generally nothing else but fear to support them. Before the Christian religion had, as it were, humanized the idea of the Divinity, and brought it somewhat nearer to us, there was very little said of the love of God. The followers of Plato have something of it, and only something; the other writers of pagan antiquity, whether poets or philosophers, nothing at all. And they who consider with what infinite attention, by what a disregard of every perishable object, through what long habits of piety and contemplation it is that any man is able to attain an entire love and devotion to the Deity, will easily perceive that it is not the first, the most natural, and the most striking effect which proceeds from that idea. Thus we have traced power through its several gradations unto the highest of all, where our imagination is finally lost; and we find terror, quite throughout the progress, its inseparable companion, and growing along with it, as far as we can possibly trace them. Now, as power is undoubtedly a capital source of the sublime, this will point out evidently from whence its energy is derived, and to what class of ideas we ought to unite it.

SECTION VI

Privation

All *general* privations are great, because they are all terrible; *vacuity, darkness, solitude,* and *silence.* With what a fire of imagination, yet with what severity of judgment, has Virgil amassed all these circumstances, where he knows that all the images of a tremendous dignity ought to be united at the mouth of hell! Where, before he unlocks the secrets of the great deep, he seems to be seized with a religious horror, and to retire astonished at the boldness of his own design:

> Dii, quibus imperium est animarum, umbræque *silentes!*
> Et Chaos, et Phlegethon! loca *nocte silentia* late!
> Sit mihi fas audita loqui! sit numine vestro

Pandere res alta terra et *caligine* mersas!
Ibant *obscuri, sola* sub *nocte,* per *umbram,*
Perque domos Ditis *vacuas,* et *inania* regna.[18]

"Ye subterraneous gods! whose awful sway
The gliding ghosts, and *silent* shades obey:
O Chaos hoar! and Phlegethon profound!
Whose solemn empire stretches wide around;
Give me, ye great, tremendous powers, to tell
Of scenes and wonders in the depth of hell;
Give me your mighty secrets to display
From those *black* realms of darkness to the day."

PITT.[19]

"*Obscure* they went through dreary *shades* that led
Along the *waste* dominions of the *dead.*"

DRYDEN.[20]

SECTION VII

Vastness

Greatness of dimension is a powerful cause of the sublime.
This is too evident, and the observation too common, to need
any illustration; it is not so common to consider in what ways
greatness of dimension, vastness of extent or quantity, has
the most striking effect. For, certainly, there are ways and
modes wherein the same quantity of extension shall produce
greater effects than it is found to do in others. Extension is
either in length, height, or depth. Of these the length strikes
least; a hundred yards of even ground will never work such
an effect as a tower a hundred yards high, or a rock or mountain of that altitude. I am apt to imagine, likewise, that height
is less grand than depth; and that we are more struck at looking down from a precipice, than looking up at an object of

[18] *Æneid,* VI, 264–69.
[19] *Æneid,* VI, 371–78 (1740).
[20] *Æneid,* VI, 378–79.

equal height; but of that I am not very positive. A perpen-
dicular has more force in forming the sublime, than an inclined
plane, and the effects of a rugged and broken surface seem
stronger than where it is smooth and polished. It would carry
us out of our way to enter in this place into the cause of these
appearances, but certain it is they afford a large and fruitful
field of speculation. However, it may not be amiss to add to
these remarks upon magnitude, that as the great extreme of
dimension is sublime, so the last extreme of littleness is in some
measure sublime likewise; when we attend to the infinite
divisibility of matter, when we pursue animal life into these
excessively small, and yet organized beings, that escape the
nicest inquisition of the sense; when we push our discoveries
yet downward, and consider those creatures so many degrees
yet smaller, and the still diminishing scale of existence, in
tracing which the imagination is lost as well as the sense; we
become amazed and confounded at the wonders of minuteness;
nor can we distinguish in its effect this extreme of littleness
from the vast itself. For division must be infinite as well as
addition; because the idea of a perfect unity can no more be
arrived at, than that of a complete whole, to which nothing
may be added.

SECTION VIII

Infinity

Another source of the sublime is *infinity;* if it does not rather
belong to the last. Infinity has a tendency to fill the mind with
that sort of delightful horror, which is the most genuine effect,
and truest test of the sublime. There are scarce any things
which can become the objects of our senses, that are really
and in their own nature infinite. But the eye not being able to
perceive the bounds of many things, they seem to be infinite,
and they produce the same effects as if they were really so.
We are deceived in the like manner, if the parts of some large

object are so continued to any indefinite number, that the imagination meets no check which may hinder its extending them at pleasure.

Whenever we repeat any idea frequently, the mind, by a sort of mechanism, repeats it long after the first cause has ceased to operate. After whirling about when we sit down, the objects about us still seem to whirl. After a long succession of noises, as the fall of waters, or the beating of forge-hammers, the hammers beat and the waters roar in the imagination long after the first sounds have ceased to affect it; and they die away at last by gradations which are scarcely perceptible. If you hold up a straight pole, with your eye to one end, it will seem extended to a length almost incredible. Place a number of uniform and equi-distant marks on this pole, they will cause the same deception, and seem multiplied without end. The senses, strongly affected in some one manner, cannot quickly change their tenor, or adapt themselves to other things; but they continue in their old channel until the strength of the first mover decays. This is the reason of an appearance very frequent in madmen; that they remain whole days and nights, sometimes whole years, in the constant repetition of some remark, some complaint, or song; which having struck powerfully on their disordered imagination in the beginning of their frenzy, every repetition reinforces it with new strength, and the hurry of their spirits, unrestrained by the curb of reason, continues it to the end of their lives.

SECTION XIV

Light

Having considered extension, so far as it is capable of raising ideas of greatness; *color* comes next under consideration. All colors depend on *light*. Light therefore ought previously to be examined; and with it its opposite, darkness. With regard to light, to make it a cause capable of producing the sublime, it must be attended with some circumstances, besides its bare faculty of showing other objects. Mere light is too common a thing to make a strong impression on the mind, and without a strong impression nothing can be sublime. But such a light as that of the sun, immediately exerted on the eye, as it overpowers the sense, is a very great idea. Light of an inferior strength to this, if it moves with great celerity, has the same power; for lightning is certainly productive of grandeur, which it owes chiefly to the extreme velocity of its motion. A quick transition from light to darkness, or from darkness to light, has yet a greater effect. But darkness is more productive of sublime ideas than light. Our great poet was convinced of this; and indeed so full was he of this idea, so entirely possessed with the power of a well-managed darkness, that in describing the appearance of the Deity, amidst that profusion of magnificent images, which the grandeur of his subject provokes him to pour out upon every side, he is far from forgetting the obscurity which surrounds the most incomprehensible of all beings, but

> "With majesty of *darkness* round
> Circles his throne." [21]

And what is no less remarkable, our author had the secret of preserving this idea, even when he seemed to depart the farthest from it, when he describes the light and glory which flows from the Divine presence; a light which by its very excess is converted into a species of darkness:—

> "*Dark* with excessive *light* thy skirts appear." [22]

Here is an idea not only poetical in a high degree, but strictly and philosophically just. Extreme light, by overcoming the organs of sight, obliterates all objects, so as in its effect exactly to resemble darkness. After looking for some time at the sun, two black spots, the impression which it leaves, seem to dance before our eyes. Thus are two ideas as opposite as can be imagined reconciled in the extremes of both; and both, in spite of their opposite nature, brought to concur in producing

---

[21] *Paradise Lost*, II, 266–67: "*Covers* his throne."
[22] *Paradise Lost*, III, 380: "Dark with excessive *bright* thy skirts appear."

the sublime. And this is not the only instance wherein the opposite extremes operate equally in favor of the sublime, which in all things abhors mediocrity.

SECTION XV

Light in Building

As the management of light is a matter of importance in architecture, it is worth inquiring, how far this remark is applicable to building. I think, then, that all edifices calculated to produce an idea of the sublime, ought rather to be dark and gloomy, and this for two reasons; the first is, that darkness itself on other occasions is known by experience to have a greater effect on the passions than light. The second is, that to make an object very striking, we should make it as different as possible from the objects with which we have been immediately conversant; when therefore you enter a building, you cannot pass into a greater light than you had in the open air; to go into one some few degrees less luminous, can make only a trifling change; but to make the transition thoroughly striking, you ought to pass from the greatest light, to as much darkness as is consistent with the uses of architecture. At night the contrary rule will hold, but for the very same reason; and the more highly a room is then illuminated, the grander will the passion be.

SECTION XVI

Color Considered as Productive of the Sublime

Among colors, such as are soft or cheerful (except perhaps a strong red, which is cheerful) are unfit to produce grand images. An immense mountain covered with a shining green turf, is nothing, in this respect, to one dark and gloomy; the cloudy sky is more grand than the blue; and night more sublime and solemn than day. Therefore in historical painting, a gay or gaudy drapery can never have a happy effect: and in buildings, when the highest degree of the sublime is intended, the materials and ornaments ought neither to be white, nor green, nor yellow, nor blue, nor of a pale red, nor violet, nor spotted, but of sad and fuscous colors, as black, or brown, or deep purple, and the like. Much of gilding, mosaics, painting, or statues, contribute but little to the sublime. This rule need not be put in practice, except where an uniform degree of the most striking sublimity is to be produced, and that in every particular; for it ought to be observed, that this melancholy kind of greatness, though it be certainly the highest, ought not to be studied in all sorts of edifices, where yet grandeur must be studied; in such cases the sublimity must be drawn from the other sources; with a strict caution however against anything light and riant; as nothing so effectually deadens the whole taste of the sublime.

PART III

SECTION I

Of Beauty

It is my design to consider beauty as distinguished from the sublime; and, in the course of the inquiry, to examine how far it is consistent with it. But previous to this, we must take a short review of the opinions already entertained of this quality; which I think are hardly to be reduced to any fixed principles; because men are used to talk of beauty in a figurative manner, that is to say, in a manner extremely uncertain, and indeterminate. By beauty, I mean that quality, or those qualities in bodies, by which they cause love, or some passion similar to it.

I confine this definition to the merely sensible qualities of things, for the sake of preserving the utmost simplicity in a subject, which must always distract us whenever we take in those various causes of sympathy which attach us to any persons or things from secondary considerations, and not from the direct force which they have merely on being viewed. I likewise distinguish love, (by which I mean that satisfaction which arises to the mind upon contemplating anything beautiful, of whatsoever nature it may be,) from desire or lust; which is an energy of the mind, that hurries us on to the possession of certain objects, that do not affect us as they are beautiful, but by means altogether different. We shall have a strong desire for a woman of no remarkable beauty; whilst the greatest beauty in men, or in other animals, though it causes love, yet excites nothing at all of desire. Which shows that beauty, and the passion caused by beauty, which I call love, is different from desire, though desire may sometimes operate along with it; but it is to this latter that we must attribute those violent and tempestuous passions, and the consequent emotions of the body which attend what is called love in some of its ordinary acceptations, and not to the effects of beauty merely as it is such.

SECTION XII

The Real Cause of Beauty

Having endeavored to show what beauty is not, it remains that we should examine, at least with equal attention, in what it really consists. Beauty is a thing much too affecting not to depend upon some positive qualities. And since it is no creature of our reason, since it strikes us without any reference to use, and even where no use at all can be discerned, since the order and method of nature is generally very different from our measures and proportions, we must conclude that beauty is, for the greater part, some quality in bodies acting mechanically upon the human mind by the intervention of the senses. We ought, therefore, to consider attentively in what manner those sensible qualities are disposed, in such things as by experience we find beautiful, or which excite in us the passion of love, or some correspondent affection.

SECTION XVIII

Recapitulation

On the whole, the qualities of beauty, as they are merely sensible qualities, are the following: First, to be comparatively small. Secondly, to be smooth. Thirdly, to have a variety in the direction of the parts; but, fourthly, to have those parts not angular, but melted, as it were, into each other. Fifthly, to be of a delicate frame, without any remarkable appearance of strength. Sixthly, to have its colors clear and bright, but not very strong and glaring. Seventhly, or if it should have any glaring color, to have it diversified with others. These are, I believe, the properties on which beauty depends; properties that operate by nature, and are less liable to be altered by caprice, or confounded by a diversity of tastes, than any other.

SECTION XXVII

The Sublime and Beautiful Compared

On closing this general view of beauty, it naturally occurs that we should compare it with the sublime; and in this comparison there appears a remarkable contrast. For sublime objects are vast in their dimensions, beautiful ones comparatively small; beauty should be smooth and polished; the great, rugged and negligent: beauty should shun the right line, yet deviate from it insensibly; the great in many cases loves the right line; and when it deviates, it often makes a strong deviation: beauty should not be obscure; the great ought to be dark and gloomy: beauty should be light and delicate; the great ought to be solid, and even massive. They are indeed ideas of a very different nature, one being founded on pain, the other on pleasure; and, however they may vary afterwards from the direct nature of their causes, yet these causes keep up an eternal distinction between them, a distinction never to be forgotten by any whose business it is to affect the passions. In the infinite variety of natural combinations, we must expect to find the qualities of things the most remote imaginable from each other united in the same object. We must expect also to find combinations of the same kind in the works of art. But when we consider the power of an object upon our passions, we must know that when anything is intended to affect the mind by the force of some predominant property, the affection produced is like to be the more uniform and perfect, if all the other properties or qualities of the object be of the same nature, and tending to the same design as the principal.

> "If black and white blend, soften, and unite
> A thousand ways, are there no black and white?" [23]

If the qualities of the sublime and beautiful are sometimes found united, does this prove that they are the same; does it prove that they are any way allied; does it prove even that they are not opposite and contradictory? Black and white may soften, may blend; but they are not therefore the same. Nor, when they are so softened and blended with each other, or with different colors, is the power of black as black, or of white as white, so strong as when each stands uniform and distinguished.

---

[23] Pope, *Essay on Man*, II, 213–14: "If white and black blend, soften, and unite / A thousand ways, is there no black or white?"

PART IV

SECTION I

Of the Efficient Cause of the Sublime and Beautiful

When I say, I intend to inquire into the efficient cause of sublimity and beauty, I would not be understood to say, that I can come to the ultimate cause. I do not pretend that I shall ever be able to explain why certain affections of the body produce such a distinct emotion of mind, and no other; or why the body is at all affected by the mind, or the mind by the body. A little thought will show this to be impossible. But I conceive, if we can discover what affections of the mind produce certain emotions of the body; and what distinct feelings and qualities of body shall produce certain determinate passions in the mind, and no others, I fancy a great deal will be done; something not unuseful towards a distinct knowledge of our passions, so far at least as we have them at present under our consideration. This is all, I believe, we can do. If we could advance a step farther, difficulties would still remain, as we should be still equally distant from the first cause. When Newton first discovered the property of attraction, and settled its laws, he found it served very well to explain several of the most remarkable phenomena in nature; but yet, with reference to the general system of things, he could consider attraction but as an effect, whose cause at that time he did not attempt to trace. But when he afterwards began to account for it by a subtle elastic ether, this great man (if in so great a man it be not impious to discover anything like a blemish) seemed to have quitted his usual cautious manner of philosophizing; since, perhaps, allowing all that has been advanced on this subject to be sufficiently proved, I think it leaves us with as many difficulties as it found us. That great chain of causes, which, linking one to another, even to the throne of God himself, can never be unravelled by any industry of ours. When we go but one step beyond the immediate sensible qualities of things, we go out of our depth. All we do after is but a faint struggle, that shows we are in an element which does not belong to us. So that when I speak of cause, and efficient cause, I only mean certain affections of the mind, that cause certain changes in the body; or certain powers and properties in bodies, that work a change in the mind. As, if I were to explain the motion of a body falling to the ground, I would say it was caused by gravity; and I would endeavor to show after what manner this power operated, without attempting to show why it operated in this manner: or, if I were to explain the effects of bodies striking one another by the common laws of percussion, I should not endeavor to explain how motion itself is communicated.

PART V

SECTION V

Examples That Words May Affect without Raising Images

I find it very hard to persuade several that their passions are affected by words from whence they have no ideas; and yet harder to convince them that in the ordinary course of conversation we are sufficiently understood without raising any images of the things concerning which we speak. It seems to be an odd subject of dispute with any man, whether he has ideas in his mind or not. Of this, at first view, every man, in his own forum, ought to judge without appeal. But, strange as it may appear, we are often at a loss to know what ideas we have of things, or whether we have any ideas at all upon some subjects. It even requires a good deal of attention to be thoroughly satisfied on this head. Since I wrote these papers, I found two very striking instances of the possibility there is, that a man may hear words without having any idea of the things which they represent, and yet afterwards be capable of returning them to others, combined in a new way, and with great propriety, energy, and instruction. The first instance is that of Mr. Blacklock, a poet blind from his birth.[24] Few men blessed with the most perfect sight can describe visual objects with more spirit and justness than this blind man; which cannot possibly be attributed to his having a clearer conception of the things he describes than is common to other persons. Mr. Spence, in an elegant preface which he has written to the works of this poet, reasons very ingeniously, and, I imagine, for the most part, very rightly, upon the cause of this extraordinary phenomenon; but I cannot altogether agree with him, that some improprieties in language and thought, which occur in these poems, have arisen from the blind poet's imperfect conception of visual objects, since such improprieties, and much greater, may be found in writers even of a higher class than Mr. Blacklock, and who, notwithstanding, possessed the faculty of seeing in its full perfection. Here is a poet doubtless as much affected by his own descriptions as any that reads them can be; and yet he is affected with this strong enthusiasm by things of which he neither has, nor can possibly have, any idea further than that of a bare sound: and why may not those who read his works be affected in the same manner that he was; with as little of any real ideas of the things described? The second instance is of Mr. Saunderson, professor of mathematics in the University of Cambridge.[25] This learned man had acquired great knowledge in natural philosophy, in astronomy, and whatever sciences depend upon mathematical skill. What was the most extraordinary and the most to my purpose, he

[24] Thomas Blacklock (1721–91), a Scottish poet blind from the age of six months, published his *Poems* 1746, which brought him to the attention of Hume, who recommended them to Joseph Spence. Spence published his *Account of the Life, Character and Poems of Mr. Blacklock* as a preface to the second edition of the *Poems* in 1756. Spence comments on some "improprieties" e.g. the use of "Blaze" as "a Characteristic of Beauty"; the "Application of the Epithet of Rayless to Silence." These criticisms appeared in the original 1754 edition of Spence's *Account*, but were omitted in 1756. (v. Boulton's note, pp. 168–69).

[25] Dr. Nicolas Saunderson (1682–1739), Professor of Mathematics at Cambridge from 1711.

gave excellent lectures upon light and colors; and this man
taught others the theory of those ideas which they had, and
which he himself undoubtedly had not. But it is probable that
the words red, blue, green, answered to him as well as the
ideas of the colors themselves; for the ideas of greater or lesser
degrees of refrangibility being applied to these words, and
the blind man being instructed in what other respects they
were found to agree or to disagree, it was as easy for him to
reason upon the words as if he had been fully master of the
ideas. Indeed it must be owned he could make no new discoveries in the way of experiment. He did nothing but what
we do every day in common discourse. When I wrote this last
sentence, and used the words *every day* and *common discourse,*
I had no images in my mind of any succession of time; nor of
men in conference with each other; nor do I imagine that the
reader will have any such ideas on reading it. Neither when I
spoke of red, or blue, and green, as well as refrangibility, had
I these several colors, or the rays of light passing into a different
medium, and there diverted from their course, painted before
me in the way of images. I know very well that the mind
possesses a faculty of raising such images at pleasure; but then
an act of the will is necessary to this; and in ordinary conversation or reading it is very rarely that any image at all is excited in the mind. If I say, "I shall go to Italy next summer,"
I am well understood. Yet I believe nobody has by this painted
in his imagination the exact figure of the speaker passing by
land or by water, or both; sometimes on horseback, sometimes
in a carriage: with all the particulars of the journey. Still less
has he any idea of Italy, the country to which I proposed to go;
or of the greenness of the fields, the ripening of the fruits, and
the warmth of the air, with the change to this from a different
season, which are the ideas for which the word *summer* is
substituted; but least of all has he any image from the word
next; for this word stands for the idea of many summers, with
the exclusion of all but one: and surely the man who says
next summer has no images of such a succession, and such an
exclusion. In short, it is not only of those ideas which are
commonly called abstract, and of which no image at all can
be formed, but even of particular, real beings, that we con-

verse without having any idea of them excited in the imagination; as will certainly appear on a diligent examination of our own minds. Indeed, so little does poetry depend for its effect on the power of raising sensible images, that I am convinced it would lose a very considerable part of its energy, if this were the necessary result of all description. Because that union of affecting words, which is the most powerful of all poetical instruments, would frequently lose its force along with its propriety and consistency, if the sensible images were always excited. There is not, perhaps, in the whole Æneid a more grand and labored passage than the description of Vulcan's cavern in Etna, and the works that are there carried on. Virgil dwells particularly on the formation of the thunder which he describes unfinished under the hammers of the Cyclops. But what are the principles of this extraordinary composition?

> Tres imbris torti radios, tres nubis aquosæ
> Addiderant; rutili tres ignis, et alitis austri:
> Fulgores nunc terrificos, sonitumque, metumque
> Miscebant operi, flammisque sequacibus iras.[26]

This seems to me admirably sublime: yet if we attend coolly to the kind of sensible images which a combination of ideas of this sort must form, the chimeras of madmen cannot appear more wild and absurd than such a picture. *"Three rays of twisted showers, three of watery clouds, three of fire, and three of the winged south wind; then mixed they in the work terrific lightnings, and sound, and fear, and anger, with pursuing flames."* This strange composition is formed into a gross body; it is hammered by the Cyclops, it is in part polished, and partly continues rough. The truth is, if poetry gives us a noble assemblage of words corresponding to many noble ideas, which are connected by circumstances of time or place, or related to each other as cause and effect, or associated in any natural way, they may be moulded together in any form, and perfectly answer their end. The picturesque connection is not demanded; because no real picture is formed; nor is the effect of the description at all the less upon this account. What is

[26] *Æneid*, VIII, 429–32. The passage is translated below.

said of Helen by Priam and the old men of his council, is generally thought to give us the highest possible idea of that fatal beauty.

> Οὐ νέμεσις, Τρῶας καὶ ἐϋκνήμιδας Ἀχαιοὺς
> Τοιῇδ᾽ ἀμφὶ γυναικὶ πολὺν χρόνον ἄλγεα πάσχειν·
> Αἰνῶς ἀθανάτῃσι θεῇς εἰς ὦπα ἔοικεν·

> "They cried, No wonder such celestial charms
> For nine long years have set the world in arms;
> What winning graces! what majestic mien!
> She moves a goddess, and she looks a queen."
>
>   POPE.[27]

Here is not one word said of the particulars of her beauty; nothing which can in the least help us to any precise idea of her person; but yet we are much more touched by this manner of mentioning her, than by those long and labored descriptions of Helen, whether handed down by tradition, or formed by fancy, which are to be met with in some authors. I am sure it affects me much more than the minute description which Spenser has given of Belphebe;[28] though I own that there are parts, in that description, as there are in all the descriptions of that excellent writer, extremely fine and poetical. The terrible picture which Lucretius has drawn of religion in order to display the magnanimity of his philosophical hero in opposing her, is thought to be designed with great boldness and spirit:—

> Humana ante oculos fœdè cum vita jaceret,
> In terris, oppressa gravi sub religione,
> Quæ caput e cœli regionibus ostendebat
> Horribili super aspectu mortalibus instans;
> Primus Graius homo mortales tollere contra
> Est oculos ausus.[29]

---

[27] *Iliad* 205–208. Pope is translating *Iliad* 156–58, above.

[28] *Faerie Queene* II, iii, 21–31.

[29] *De Rerum Natura* I, 62–67 (slightly misquoted): "Whilst human kind throughout the lands lay miserably crushed before all eyes beneath Religion—who would show her head along the region skies, glowering on mortals with her hideous face—a Greek it was who first opposing dared raise mortal eyes that terror to withstand." (W. E. Leonard translation.)

What idea do you derive from so excellent a picture? none at all, most certainly: neither has the poet said a single word which might in the least serve to mark a single limb or feature of the phantom, which he intended to represent in all the horrors imagination can conceive. In reality, poetry and rhetoric do not succeed in exact description so well as painting does; their business is, to affect rather by sympathy than imitation; to display rather the effect of things on the mind of the speaker, or of others, than to present a clear idea of the things themselves. This is their most extensive province, and that in which they succeed the best.

SECTION VI

Poetry Not Strictly an Imitative Art

Hence we may observe that poetry, taken in its most general sense, cannot with strict propriety be called an art of imitation. It is indeed an imitation so far as it describes the manners and passions of men which their words can express; where *animi motus effert interprete lingua.*[30] There it is strictly imitation; and all merely *dramatic* poetry is of this sort. But *descriptive* poetry operates chiefly by *substitution;* by the means of sounds, which by custom have the effect of realities. Nothing is an imitation further than as it resembles some other thing; and words undoubtedly have no sort of resemblance to the ideas for which they stand.

[30] Horace, *Ars Poetica,* 111: *effert animi motus interprete lingua,* "with the tongue for interpreter she proclaims the motions of the soul."

SECTION VII

How Words Influence the Passions

Now, as words affect, not by any original power, but by representation, it might be supposed, that their influence over the
passions should be but light; yet it is quite otherwise; for we
find by experience, that eloquence and poetry are as capable,
nay indeed much more capable, of making deep and lively
impressions than any other arts, and even than nature itself
in very many cases. And this arises chiefly from these three
causes. First, that we take an extraordinary part in the passions
of others, and that we are easily affected and brought into
sympathy by any tokens which are shown of them; and there
are no tokens which can express all the circumstances of most
passions so fully as words; so that if a person speaks upon any
subject, he can not only convey the subject to you, but likewise
the manner in which he is himself affected by it. Certain it is,
that the influence of most things on our passions is not so
much from the things themselves, as from our opinions concerning them; and these again depend very much on the opinions of other men, conveyable for the most part by words only.
Secondly, there are many things of a very affecting nature,
which can seldom occur in the reality, but the words that
represent them often do; and thus they have an opportunity
of making a deep impression and taking root in the mind,
whilst the idea of the reality was transient; and to some perhaps never really occurred in any shape, to whom it is notwithstanding very affecting, as war, death, famine, &c. Besides
many ideas have never been at all presented to the senses of
any men but by words, as God, angels, devils, heaven, and hell,
all of which have however a great influence over the passions.
Thirdly, by words we have it in our power to make such
combinations as we cannot possibly do otherwise. By this
power of combining we are able, by the addition of well-chosen

circumstances, to give a new life and force to the simple object. In painting we may represent any fine figure we please; but we never can give it those enlivening touches which it may receive from words. To represent an angel in a picture, you can only draw a beautiful young man winged: but what painting can furnish out anything so grand as the addition of one word, "the angel of the *Lord*"? It is true, I have here no clear idea; but these words affect the mind more than the sensible image did; which is all I contend for. A picture of Priam dragged to the altar's foot, and there murdered, if it were well executed, would undoubtedly be very moving; but there are very aggravating circumstances, which it could never represent:

> Sanguine fœdantem *quos ipse sacraverat* ignes.[31]

As a further instance, let us consider those lines of Milton, where he describes the travels of the fallen angels through their dismal habitation:

> "O'er many a dark and dreary vale
> They passed, and many a region dolorous;
> O'er many a frozen, many a fiery Alp;
> Rocks, caves, lakes, fens, bogs, dens, and shades of death,
> A universe of death." [32]

Here is displayed the force of union in

> "Rocks, caves, lakes, dens, bogs, fens, and shades"

which yet would lose the greatest part of their effect, if they were not the

> "Rocks, caves, lakes, dens, bogs, fens, and shades—of *Death*."

This idea or this affection caused by a word, which nothing but a word could annex to the others, raises a very great degree of the sublime, and this sublime is raised yet higher by what follows, a "*universe of death.*" Here are again two ideas not presentable but by language, and an union of them great

---

[31] *Æneid* II, 502: "polluting with his blood the fires he himself had hallowed."
[32] *Paradise Lost*, II, 618–22.

and amazing beyond conception; if they may properly be called ideas which present no distinct image to the mind; but still it will be difficult to conceive how words can move the passions which belong to real objects, without representing these objects clearly. This is difficult to us, because we do not sufficiently distinguish, in our observations upon language, between a clear expression and a strong expression. These are frequently confounded with each other, though they are in reality extremely different. The former regards the understanding, the latter belongs to the passions. The one describes a thing as it is, the latter describes it as it is felt. Now, as there is a moving tone of voice, an impassioned countenance, an agitated gesture, which affect independently of the things about which they are exerted, so there are words, and certain dispositions of words, which being peculiarly devoted to passionate subjects, and always used by those who are under the influence of any passion, touch and move us more than those which far more clearly and distinctly express the subject-matter. We yield to sympathy what we refuse to description. The truth is, all verbal description, merely as naked description, though never so exact, conveys so poor and insufficient an idea of the thing described, that it could scarcely have the smallest effect, if the speaker did not call in to his aid those modes of speech that mark a strong and lively feeling in himself. Then, by the contagion of our passions, we catch a fire already kindled in another, which probably might never have been struck out by the object described. Words, by strongly conveying the passions by those means which we have already mentioned, fully compensate for their weakness in other respects. It may be observed, that very polished languages, and such as are praised for their superior clearness and perspicuity, are generally deficient in strength. The French language has that perfection and that defect. Whereas the Oriental tongues, and in general the languages of most unpolished people, have a great force and energy of expression, and this is but natural. Uncultivated people are but ordinary observers of things, and not critical in distinguishing them; but, for that reason they admire more, and are more affected with what they see, and therefore express themselves in a warmer and more passionate manner.

If the affection be well conveyed, it will work its effect without any clear idea, often without any idea at all of the thing which has originally given rise to it.

It might be expected, from the fertility of the subject, that I should consider poetry, as it regards the sublime and beautiful, more at large; but it must be observed, that in this light it has been often and well handled already. It was not my design to enter into the criticism of the sublime and beautiful in any art, but to attempt to lay down such principles as may tend to ascertain, to distinguish, and to form a sort of standard for them; which purposes I thought might be best effected by an inquiry into the properties of such things in nature, as raise love and astonishment in us; and by showing in what manner they operated to produce these passions. Words were only so far to be considered as to show upon what principle they were capable of being the representatives of these natural things, and by what powers they were able to affect us often as strongly as the things they represent, and sometimes much more strongly.

THOMAS WARTON
[1728–1790]

_Thomas Warton was the younger brother of Joseph. His
education was directed by his father until he was sixteen,
when he went to Trinity College, Oxford, receiving the
B.A. in 1747, the year in which he published his famous
juvenile poem "The Pleasures of Melancholy," a boyish
pastiche of passages from Spenser and Milton evidencing that
interest in older English poetry which was later to
constitute his chief claim to regard. He took orders, becoming
a tutor in the college, and received his M.A. in 1750.
Receiving a fellowship the next year, he spent the rest of
his life at Oxford. After publishing the_ Observations on the
Fairie Queene _of Spenser in 1754 he was awarded the
Professorship of Poetry, which he retained until 1767. His
lectures, of course, were delivered in Latin, but he was not
otherwise a typical Oxford don, preferring beer-drinking
in taverns to claret in the common room. Fanny Burney's
younger sister described him as "the greatest clod I ever saw,
and so vulgar a figure with his clunch wig that I took him
for a shoemaker at first." George III appointed him Poet
Laureate in 1785._

Thomas's major work was his History of English Poetry,
from the Close of the Eleventh Century to the
Commencement of the Eighteenth Century, _which in
three large volumes published between 1775 and 1781 he
only managed to bring up to the reign of Elizabeth I. This
work is not a critical history, but it is a history, and marks
an important turning of attitudes from a priori critical
approaches toward historical relativism. His method had_

been adumbrated in his Observations on The Fairie Queene, *though we must note the debt he owed (and acknowledged) to Theobald in the application of historical materials to literary criticism.*

The second edition of the Observations, *"corrected and enlarged," 1762, represents some considerable revisions, and it is this edition which is the basis for the present text.* See also:

Havens, Raymond D.: "Thomas Warton and the
  Eighteenth-century Dilemma," SP, XXV (1928), 36–50.
Kinghorn, A.M.: "Warton's History and Early English
  Poetry," Essays and Studies, XLIV (1962), 197–204.
Miller, Frances Schouler: "The Historic Sense of Thomas
  Warton, Junior," ELH, V (1938), 71–92.
Smith, David Nichol: Warton's History of English Poetry
  (The Warton Lecture), London, 1929.
Wellek, René: The Rise of English Literary History,
  Chapel Hill, 1941.

OBSERVATIONS ON THE FAIRY QUEEN OF SPENSER
[1754]

SECTION I

Of the plan and conduct of the Fairy Queen

When the works of Homer and of Aristotle began to be restored and studied in Italy, when the genuine and uncor-
rupted sources of ancient poetry and ancient criticism were
opened and every species of literature at last emerged from
the depths of Gothic ignorance and barbarity, it might have
been expected that, instead of the romantic manner of poetical
composition introduced and established by the Provencial
bards, a new and more legitimate taste of writing would have
succeeded. With these advantages it was reasonable to conclude that unnatural events, the machinations of imaginary
beings, and adventures entertaining only as they were improbable, would have given place to justness of thought and
design, and to that decorum which nature dictated, and which

the example and the precept of antiquity had authorized. But it was a long time before such a change was effected. We find Ariosto, many years after the revival of letters, rejecting truth for magic, and preferring the ridiculous and incoherent excursions of Boyardo[1] to the propriety and uniformity of the Grecian and Roman models. Nor did the restoration of ancient learning produce any effectual or immediate improvement in the state of criticism. Beni, one of the most celebrated critics of the sixteenth century, was still so infatuated with a fondness for the old Provencial vein, that he ventured to write a regular dissertation* in which he compares Ariosto with Homer.

. . .

Such was the prevailing taste when Spenser projected the Fairy Queen: a poem which, according to the practice of Ariosto, was to consist of allegories, enchantments, and romantic expeditions, conducted by knights, giants, magicians, and fictitious beings. It may be urged that Spenser made an unfortunate choice, and discovered but little judgment in adopting Ariosto for his example rather than Tasso, who had so evidently exceeded his rival, at least in conduct and decorum. But our author naturally followed the poem which was most celebrated and popular. For although the French critics universally gave the preference to Tasso, yet in Italy the partisans on the side of Ariosto were by far the most powerful, and consequently in England: for Italy, in the age of queen Elizabeth, gave laws to our island in all matters of taste, as France has done ever since. At the same time it may be supposed that, of the two, Ariosto was Spenser's favourite, and that he was naturally biassed to prefer that plan which would admit the most extensive range for his unlimited imagination. What was Spenser's particular plan, in

[1] Boyardo: Matteo Maria Boiardo (1434–1494). The sixty-nine cantos of his uncompleted historical epic *Orlando Innamorato*, in which he treated Carolingian epic matter in the style of the Arthurian romances, served as a point of departure for Ariosto's *Orlando Furioso*.

* *Comparazione di T. Tasso con Omero e Virgilio, insieme con la difesa dell' Ariosto paragonato ad Omero*, etc.

consequence of this choice, and how it was conducted, I now proceed to examine.

The poet supposes* that the Faerie Queene, according to an established annual custom, held a magnificent feast which continued twelve days, on each of which, respectively, twelve several complaints are presented before her. Accordingly, in order to redress the injuries which were the occasion of these several complaints, she dispatches, with proper commissions, twelve different Knights, each of which, in the particular adventure allotted to him, proves an example of some particular virtue, as of holiness, temperance, justice, chastity; and has one complete book assigned to him, of which he is the hero. But besides these twelve knights, severally exemplifying twelve moral virtues, the poet has constituted one principal knight or general hero, viz. Prince Arthur. This personage represents magnificence, a virtue which is supposed to be the perfection of all the rest. He moreover assists in every book, and the end of his actions is to discover, and win, *Gloriana*, or Glory. In a word, in this character the poet professes to portray *The Image of a brave knight perfected in the twelve private moral virtues.*

It is evident that our author in establishing one hero who, seeking and attaining one grand end, which is *Gloriana*, should exemplify one grand character, or a brave Knight perfected in the twelve private moral virtues, copied the cast and construction of the ancient Epic. But sensible as he was of the importance and expediency of the unity of the hero and of his design, he does not, in the meantime, seem convinced of the necessity of that unity of action, by the means of which such a design should be properly accomplished. At least, he has not followed the method practiced by Homer and Virgil in conducting their respective heroes to the proposed end.

It may be asked with great propriety, how does Arthur execute the grand, simple, and ultimate design intended by the poet? It may be answered, with some degree of plausibility, that by lending his respective assistance to each of the

* See Spenser's Letter to Sir W. Raleigh, etc.

twelve knights who patronize the twelve virtues, in his allotted defence of each *Arthur* approaches still nearer and nearer to Glory, till at last he gains a complete possession. But surely to assist is not a sufficient service. This secondary merit is inadequate to the reward. The poet ought to have made this "brave knight" the leading adventurer. *Arthur* should have been the principal agent in vindicating the cause of holiness, temperance, and the rest. If our hero had thus, in his own person, exerted himself in the protection of the twelve virtues, he might have been deservedly styled the perfect Pattern of all, and consequently would have succeeded in the task assigned, the attainment of Glory. At present he is only a subordinate or accessory character. The difficulties and obstacles which we expect him to surmount in order to accomplish his final achievement are removed by others. It is not he who subdues the dragon in the first book, or quells the magician Busirane in the third. These are the victories of St. George and of Britomart. On the whole, the twelve knights do too much for *Arthur* to do anything, or at least, so much as may be reasonably required from the promised plan of the poet. While we are attending to the design of the hero of the book, we forget that of the hero of the poem. Dryden remarks, "We must do Spenser that justice to observe, that magnanimity (magnificence) which is the true character of Prince Arthur, shines throughout the whole poem; and succours the rest when they are in distress.* If the magnanimity of Arthur did, in reality, thus shine in every part of the poem with a superior and steady lustre, our author would fairly stand acquitted. At present it bursts forth but seldom, in obscure and interrupted flashes. "To succour the rest when they are in distress," is, as I have hinted, a circumstance of too little importance in the character of this universal champion. It is a service to be performed in the cause of the hero of the epic poem by some dependent or inferior chief, the business of a Gyas or a Cloanthus [2]

On the whole, we may observe that Spenser's adventures,

---

* Dedication to the Translation of Juvenal.

[2] Minor characters in the *Æneid*, I, 222.

separately taken as the subject of each single book, have not
always a mutual dependence upon each other, and consequently do not properly contribute to constitute one legitimate
poem. Hughes, not considering this, has advanced a remark
in commendation of Spenser's critical conduct, which is indeed one of the most blameable parts of it. "If we consider
the first book as an entire work of itself, we shall find it to
be no irregular contrivance. There is one principal action,
which is completed in the twelfth canto, and the several
incidents are proper, as they tend either to obstruct or promote it." *

As the heroic poem is required to be one *whole*, compounded of many various parts, relative and dependent, it is
expedient that not one of those parts should be so regularly
contrived, and so completely finished, as to become a *whole*
of itself. For the mind, being once satisfied in arriving at the
consummation of an orderly series of events, acquiesces in
that satisfaction. Our attention and curiosity are in the midst
diverted from pursuing, with due vigour, the final and general
catastrophe. But while each part is left incomplete, if separated from the rest, the mind still eager to gratify its expectations is irresistibly and imperceptibly drawn from part to
part, 'till it receives a full and ultimate satisfaction from the
accomplishment of one great event, which all those parts,
following and illustrating each other, contributed to produce.

Our author was probably aware that by constituting
twelve several adventures for twelve several heroes the want
of a general connection would often appear. On this account,
as I presume, he sometimes resumes and finishes in some
distant book a tale formerly begun and left imperfect. But
as numberless interruptions necessarily intervene, this proceeding often occasions infinite perplexity to the reader. And
it seems to be for the same reason that after one of the
twelve knights has achieved the adventure of his proper book,
the poet introduces him, in the next book, acting perhaps in

---

* Remarks on the Fairy Queen. Hughes's Edit. of Spenser, vol. 1. [1715;
republished 1750.]

an inferior sphere, and degraded to some less dangerous exploit. But this conduct is highly inartificial: for it destroys that repose which the mind feels after having accompanied a hero, through manifold struggles and various distresses, to success and victory. Besides, when we perceive him entering upon any less illustrious attempt, our former admiration is in some measure diminished. Having seen him complete some memorable conquest, we become interested in his honour, and are jealous concerning his future reputation. To attempt, and even to achieve, some petty posterior enterprise, is to derogate from his dignity, and to sully the transcendent lustre of his former victories.

Spenser perhaps would have embarrassed himself and the reader less had he made every book one entire detached poem of twelve cantos, without any reference to the rest. Thus he would have written twelve different books, in each of which he might have completed the pattern of a particular virtue in twelve knights respectively: at present he has remarkably failed in endeavouring to represent all the virtues exemplified in one. The poet might either have established *twelve Knights* without an *Arthur*, or an *Arthur* without twelve *Knights*. Upon supposition that Spenser was resolved to characterise the twelve moral virtues, the former plan perhaps would have been best: the latter is defective as it necessarily wants simplicity. It is an action consisting of twelve actions, all equally great and unconnected between themselves, and not compounded of one uninterrupted and coherent chain of incidents tending to the accomplishment of one design.

I have before remarked that Spenser intended to express the character of a hero perfected in the twelve moral virtues by representing him as assisting in the service of all, till at last he becomes possessed of all. This plan, however injudicious, he certainly was obliged to observe. But in the third book, which is styled the Legend of Chastity, Prince Arthur does not so much as lend his assistance in the vindication of that virtue. He appears indeed, but not as an agent, or even an auxiliary, in the adventure of the book.

Yet it must be confessed, that there is something artificial

in the poet's manner of varying from historical precision.
This conduct is rationally illustrated by himself.* According
to this plan, the reader would have been agreeably surprised
in the last book, when he came to discover that the series
of adventures, which he had just seen completed, were undertaken at the command of the *Fairy Queen;* and that the
knights had severally set forward to the execution of them
from her annual birth-day festival. But Spenser, in most of
the books, has injudiciously forestalled the first of these particulars which certainly should have been concealed 'till the
last book, not only that a needless repetition of the same
thing might be prevented, but that an opportunity might
be secured of striking the reader's mind with a circumstance
new and unexpected.

But notwithstanding [that] the plan and conduct of
Spenser, in the poem before us, is highly exceptionable, yet
we may venture to pronounce that the scholar has more merit
than his master in this respect; and that the *Fairy Queen* is
not so confused and irregular as the Orlando Furioso. There
is indeed no general unity which prevails in the former: but,
if we consider every book or adventure as a separate poem,
we shall meet with so many distinct, however imperfect,
unities, by which an attentive reader is less bewildered, than
in the maze of indigestion and incoherence of which the
latter totally consists, where we seek in vain either for partial
or universal integrity.

　　　　　———Cum nec pes nec caput uni
　　　　　Reddatur Formae.†———

Ariosto has his admirers, and most deservedly. Yet every
classical, every reasonable critic must acknowledge that the
poet's conception in celebarting the *madness,* or, in other
words, describing the irrational acts of a hero, implies extravagance and absurdity. Orlando does not make his appearance till the eighth book, where he is placed in a situation

---

* Letter to Sir W. Raleigh.
† Hor. Art. Poet. v. 8. ["So that neither head nor foot can be assigned to
a single shape."]

not perfectly heroic. He is discovered to us in bed, desiring
to sleep. His ultimate design is to find Angelica, but his
pursuit of her is broken off in the thirtieth book, after which
there are sixteen books, in none of which Angelica has the
least share. Other heroes are likewise engaged in the same
pursuit. After reading the first stanza, we are inclined to
think that the subject of the poem is the expedition of the
Moors into France, under the emperor Agramante, to fight
against Charlemagne; but this business is the most insignifi-
cant and inconsiderable part of it. Many of the heroes perform
exploits equal, if not superior, to those of Orlando, particularly Ruggiero, who closes the poem with a grand and important achievement, the conquest and death of Rodomont.
But this event is not the completion of a story carried on,
principally and perpetually, through the work.

This spirited Italian passes from one incident to another,
and from region to region with such incredible expedition and
rapidity, that one would think he was mounted upon his
winged steed Ippogrifo. Within the compass of ten stanzas
he is in England and the Hesperides, in the earth and the
moon. He begins the history of a knight in Europe, and suddenly breaks it off to resume the unfinished catastrophe of
another in Asia. The reader's imagination is distracted, and
his attention harrassed, amidst the multiplicity of tales, in the
relation of which the poet is at the same instant equally engaged. To remedy this inconvenience the compassionate ex-
positors have affixed, in some of the editions, marginal hints
informing the bewildered reader in what book and stanza
the poet intends to recommence an interrupted episode. This
expedient reminds us of the awkward artifice practised by the
first painters. However, it has proved the means of giving
Ariosto's admirers a clear comprehension of his stories, which
otherwise they could not have obtained without much difficulty. This poet is seldom read a second time in order, that
is, by passing from the first canto to the second, and from
the second to the rest in succession: by thus persuing, without any regard to the proper course of the books and stanzas,
the different tales, which though all somewhere finished, yet
are at present so mutually complicated that the incidents of

one are perpetually clashing with those of another. The judicious Abbé du Bos observes happily enough, that "Homer is a geometrician in comparison of Ariosto." His miscellaneous contents cannot be better expressed than by the two first verses of his exordium.

> *Le Donni, i Cavallier, l'Arme, gli Amori,*
> *Le Cortegie, le' audaci Imprese, io canto.*[3]

But it is absurd to think of judging either Ariosto or Spenser by precepts which they did not attend to. We who live in the days of writing by rule are apt to try every composition by those laws which we have been taught to think the sole criterion of excellence. Critical taste is universally diffused, and we require the same order and design which every modern performance is expected to have in poems where they never were regarded or intended. Spenser, and the same may be said of Ariosto, did not live in an age of planning. His poetry is the careless exuberance of a warm imagination and a strong sensibility. It was his business to engage the fancy, and to interest the attention by bold and striking images in the formation and the disposition of which little labour or art was applied. The various and the marvellous were the chief sources of delight. Hence we find our author ransacking alike the regions of reality and romance, of truth and fiction, to find the proper decorations and furniture for his fairy structure. Born in such an age, Spenser wrote rapidly from his own feelings, which at the same time were naturally noble. Exactness in his poem would have been like the cornice which a painter introduced in the grotto of Calypso. Spenser's beauties are like the flowers in Paradise.

> ————————Which not nice Art
> In beds and curious knots, but Nature boon
> Pour'd forth profuse, on hill, and dale, and plain;
> Both were the morning sun first warmly smote

---

[3] Of loves and ladies, knights and arms, I sing,
  Of courtesies, and many a daring feat. (tr. Wm. Stewart Rose)

> The open field, or where the unpierc'd shade
> Imbrown'd the noon-tide bowers.°————

If the *Fairy Queen* be destitute of that arrangement and œconomy which epic severity requires, yet we scarcely regret the loss of these while their place is so amply supplied by something which more powerfully attracts us: something which engages the affections, the feelings of the heart, rather than the cold approbation of the head. If there be any poem whose graces please because they are situated beyond the reach of art, and where the force and faculties of creative imagination delight because they are unassisted and unrestrained by those of deliberate judgment, it is this. In reading Spenser if the critic is not satisfied, yet the reader is transported.

.   .   .

POSTSCRIPT

At the close of this work I shall beg leave to subjoin an apology for the manner in which it has been conducted and executed.

I presume it will be objected that these remarks would have appeared with greater propriety connected with Spenser's text, and arranged according to their respective references; at least it may be urged that such a plan would have prevented much unnecessary transcription. But I was dissuaded from this method by two reasons. The first is, that these Observations, thus reduced to general heads, form a series of distinct essays on Spenser, and exhibit a course of systematical criticism on the *Faerie Queene*. But my principal argument was that a formal edition of this poem with notes would have been at once impertinent and superfluous; as two publications of Spenser,[4] under that form, are at present expected

---

° Parad. Lost, b. iv. v. 241.
[4] Two publications of Spenser: Thomas Birch's edition had appeared in 1751. Ralph Church (1758) and John Upton (1759) published editions, the latter with glossary and notes marking an advance on Hughes's edition of 1715.

from the hands of two learned and ingenious critics. Besides,
it was never my design to give so complete and perpetual a
comment on every part of our author, as such an attempt
seemed to require. But while some passages are entirely
overlooked, or but superficially touched, others will be found
to have been discussed more at large, and investigated with
greater research and accuracy than such an attempt would
have permitted.

As to more particular objections, too many, I am sensible,
must occur; one of which will probably be that I have been
more diligent in remarking the faults than the beauties of
Spenser. That I have been deficient in encomiums on particular passages did not proceed from a want of perceiving or
acknowledging beauties, but from a persuasion that nothing
is more absurd or useless than the panegyrical comments of
those who criticise from the imagination rather than from
the judgment, who exert their admiration instead of their
reason, and discover more of enthusiasm than discernment.
And this will most commonly be the case of those critics who
profess to point out beauties, because, as [beauties] approve
themselves to the reader's apprehension by their own force,
no reason can often be given why they please. The same
cannot always be said of faults, which I have frequently displayed without reserve or palliation.

It was my chief aim to give a clear and comprehensive
estimate of the characteristical merits and manner of this
admired, but neglected, poet. For this purpose I have considered the customs and genius of his age; I have searched
his cotemporary writers; and examined the books on which
the peculiarities of his style, taste, and composition, are confessedly founded.

I fear I shall be censured for quoting too many pieces
of this sort. But experience has frequently and fatally proved
that the commentator whose critical enquiries are employed
on Spenser, Jonson, and the rest of our elder poets, will in
vain give specimens of his classical erudition, unless, at the
same time, he brings to his work a mind intimately acquainted
with those books which, though now forgotten, were yet in
common use and high repute about the time in which his

authors respectively wrote, and which they consequently must have read. While these are unknown, many allusions and many imitations will either remain obscure, or lose half their beauty and propriety: "as the figures vanish when the canvas is decayed."

Pope laughs at Theobald for giving us, in his edition of Shakespeare, a sample of

All such *reading* as was never read.

But these strange and ridiculous books which Theobald quoted were unluckily the very books which Shakespeare himself had studied, the knowledge of which enabled that useful editor to explain so many difficult allusions and obsolete customs in his poet, which otherwise could never have been understood. For want of this sort of literature, Pope tells us that the "Dreadful Sagittary" in *Troilus and Cressida* signifies Teucer, so celebrated for his skill in archery. Had he deigned to consult an old history called the *Destruction of Troy*, a book which was the delight of Shakespeare and of his age, he would have found that this formidable archer was no other than an imaginary beast which the Grecian army brought against Troy. If Shakespeare is worth reading he is worth explaining, and the researches used for so valuable and elegant a purpose merit the thanks of genius and candour, not the satire of prejudice and ignorance. That labour, which so essentially contributes to the service of true taste, deserves a more honourable repository than The Temple of Dulness. In the same strain of false satire, Pope observes with an air of ridicule than Caxton speaks of the Æneid "as a *history*, as a book *hardly known*." * But the satirist perhaps would have expressed himself with not much more precision or propriety concerning the Æneid had he been Caxton's cotemporary. Certainly, had he wrote English poetry in so unenlightened a period, the world would have lost his refined diction and harmonious versification, the fortunate effects of better times. Caxton, rude and uncouth as he is, co-operated in the noblest cause: he was a very considerable instrument in the grand

* Dunciad, 149. Note.

work of introducing literature into his country. In an illiterate
and unpolished age he multiplied books, and consequently
readers. The books he printed, besides the grossest barbarisms
of style and composition, are chiefly written on subjects of
little importance and utility, almost all, except the works of
Gower and Chaucer, translations from the French: yet, such
as they were, we enjoy their happy consequences at this day.
Science, the progressive state of which succeeding generations
have improved and completed, dates her original from these
artless and imperfect efforts.

Mechanical critics will perhaps be disgusted at the liberties I have taken in introducing so many anecdotes of ancient
chivalry. But my subject required frequent proofs of this
sort. Nor could I be persuaded that such enquiries were, in
other respects, either useless or ridiculous, as they tended at
least to illustrate an institution of no frivolous or indifferent
nature. Chivalry is commonly looked upon as a barbarous
sport, or extravagant amusement, of the dark ages. It had however no small influence on the manners, policies, and consti-
tutions of ancient times, and served many public and important purposes. It was the school of fortitude, honour, and
affability. Its exercises, like the Grecian games, habituated the
youth to fatigue and enterprise, and inspired the noblest sentiments of heroism. It taught gallantry and civility to a savage
and ignorant people, and humanised the native ferocity of
the northern nations. It conduced to refine the manners of
the combatants by exciting an emulation in the devices and
accoutrements, the splendour and parade, of their tilts and
tournaments: while its magnificent festivals, thronged with
noble dames and courteous knights, produced the first efforts
of wit and fancy.

I am still further to hope that, together with other specimens of obsolete literature in general, hinted at before, the
many references I have made, in particular to Romances, the
necessary appendage of ancient Chivalry, will also plead their
pardon. For however monstrous and unnatural these compositions may appear to this age of reason and refinement, they
merit more attention than the world is willing to bestow.
They preserve many curious historical facts, and throw con-

siderable light on the nature of the feudal system. They are
the pictures of ancient usages and customs, and represent the
manners, genius, and character of our ancestors. Above all,
such are their Terrible Graces of magic and enchantment, so
magnificently marvellous are their fictions and fablings, that
they contribute, in a wonderful degree, to rouse and in-
vigorate all the powers of imagination: to store the fancy
with those sublime and alarming images which true poetry
best delights to display.

Lastly, in analysing the plan and conduct of this poem, I
have so far tried it by epic rules as to demonstrate the inconveniencies and incongruities which the poet might have
avoided had he been more studious of design and uniformity.
It is true that his romantic materials claim great liberties, but
no materials exclude order and perspicuity. I have endeavoured
to account for these defects, partly from the peculiar bent
of the poet's genius, which at the same time produced infinite
beauties, and partly from the predominant taste of the times
in which he wrote.

Let me add, that if I have treated some of the Italian
poets, on certain occasions, with too little respect, I did not
mean to depreciate their various incidental excellencies. I
only suggested that those excellencies, like some of Spenser's,
would have appeared to greater advantage had they been
more judiciously disposed. I have blamed, indeed, the vicious
excess of their fictions; yet I have found no fault, in general,
with their use of magical machinery; notwithstanding, I have
so far conformed to the reigning maxims of modern criticism
as, in the mean time, to recommend classical propriety.

I cannot take my final leave of the reader without the
satisfaction of acknowledging that this work has proved a
most agreeable task, and I hope this consideration will at
least plead my pardon for its length, whatever censure or
indulgence the rest of its faults may deserve. The business of
criticism is commonly laborious and dry; yet it has here more
frequently amused than fatigued my attention in its excursions
upon an author who makes such perpetual and powerful appeals to the fancy. Much of the pleasure that Spenser experi-
enced in composing the *Fairy Queen* must, in some measure,

be shared by his commentator; and the critic, on this occasion, may speak in the words, and with the rapture, of the poet.

> The wayes through which my weary steppes I guyde
> In this *delightful land of Faerie*,
> Are so exceeding spacious and wyde,
> And sprinkled with such sweet varietie
> Of all that pleasant is to ear or eye,
> That I nigh ravisht with rare thoughts delight,
> My *tedious travel* do forgett thereby:
> And when I gin to feele decay of might,
> It strength to me supplies, and cheares my dulled spright.
>
> 6. I. I.

RICHARD HURD
[1720–1808]

An edition of Horace's Ars Poetica in 1749, in the preface
to which Hurd complimented William Warburton, won
him the attention of that powerful divine, who saw to his
advancement in the church. Hurd engaged in philosophical
dispute with Hume as a result of editing Warburton's
"Remarks" on Hume's Natural History of Religion, and in
1751 he contributed a "Dissertation on Poetical Imitation"
to an edition of Horace's "Epistle to Augustus." In 1759 he
published the Dialogues Moral and Political, followed in
1762 by the Letters on Chivalry and Romance, which served
as a sequel to the dialogue "On the Age of Elizabeth." The
Letters attracted considerable attention, going through
six editions by 1788. As not infrequently occurred in the
case of clerics offering Warburton his proper meed of flattery,
Hurd's advancement in the church was rapid, and in 1775
he became Bishop of Lichfield and Coventry; in 1781 he
was translated to the richer See of Worcester.

Hoyt Trowbridge, in "Bishop Hurd: a reinterpretation"
[PMLA, LVIII (1943), 450–65], remarks, "For [Hurd's]
way of reasoning in criticism, the closest parallel is to be
found not in Wordsworth or Coleridge but in Hurd's
philosophical contemporaries—in Hume, Kames, Reynolds,
and Burke. If the conclusions Hurd reaches are not those
of the early neoclassicists, they are at least representative
of the systematic and rational neoclassicism of the 1750s
and 60s." The kind of historical criticism Hurd uses was
not new, nor, strictly speaking, is Hurd's approach to the
idea of organic form, which Aristotle had at least hinted

*at; but then one would not expect such a confirmed
Warburtonian (as he called himself) to be adventuresome.
It is the very evidence that Hurd's position was not a daring
one which adds to its interest.*

The selection from the Dialogues *is adapted from the
edition of 1771; that of the* Letters *is modernized from
Edith Morley's edition of 1911.* See also:

The Correspondence of Richard Hurd and William Mason
    and Letters of Richard Hurd to Thomas Gray
    (*Introduction and notes by Ernest Harold Pearce.*
    Edited by Leonard Whibley), Cambridge, 1932.
Smith, Audley L.: "*Richard Hurd's* Letters on Chivalry
    and Romance," ELH, VI (1939), 58–81.

DIALOGUES MORAL
AND POLITICAL
[1759]

FROM ON THE AGE OF ELIZABETH [1]

And, now the poets have fallen in my way, let me further
observe that the manifest superiority of this class of writers
in Elizabeth's reign, and that of her successor, over all others
who have succeeded to them is, among other reasons, to be
ascribed to the taste which then prevailed for these moral
representations [masques]. This taught them to animate and
impersonate every thing. Rude minds, you will say, naturally
give in to this practice. Without doubt. But art and genius do
not disdain to cultivate and improve it. Hence it is that we
find in the phraseology and mode of thinking of that time,

[1] This dialogue takes place among the ruins of Kenilworth Castle between Addison and Arbuthnot.

and of that time only, the essence of the truest and sublimest poetry.

Without doubt, Mr. Addison said, the poetry of that time is of a better taste than could well have been expected from its barbarism in other instances. But such prodigies as Shakespear and Spenser would do great things in any age, and under every disadvantage.

Most certainly they would, returned Dr. Arbuthnot, but not the things that you admire so much in these immortal writers. And, if you will excuse the intermixture of a little philosophy in these ramblings, I will attempt to account for it.

There is, I think, in the revolutions of taste and language, a certain point which is more favourable to the purposes of poetry than any other. It may be difficult to fix this point with exactness. But we shall hardly mistake in supposing it lies somewhere between the rude essays of uncorrected fancy, on the one hand, and the refinements of reason and science on the other.

And such appears to have been the condition of our language in the age of Elizabeth. It was pure, strong, and perspicuous, without affectation. At the same time, the high figurative manner, which fits a language so peculiarly for the uses of the poet, had not yet been controlled by the prosaic genius of philosophy and logic. Indeed this character had been struck so deeply into the English tongue that it was not to be removed by any ordinary improvements in either: the reason of which might be the delight which was taken by the English very early in their old Mysteries and Moralities, and the continuance of the same spirit in succeeding times by means of their Masques and Triumphs. And something like this, I observe, attended the progress of the Greek and Roman poetry, which was the truest poetry, on the clown's maxim in Shakespear, because it was *the most feigning*. It had its rise, you know, like ours, from religion: and pagan religion, of all others, was the properest to introduce and encourage a spirit of allegory and moral fiction. Hence we easily account for the allegoric cast of their old dramas, which have a great resemblance to our ancient moralities. *Necessity* is brought in as a person of the drama in one of Aeschylus's plays, and

Death in one of Euripides, to say nothing of many shadowy persons in the comedies of Aristophanes. The truth is, the pagan religion *deified* every thing, and delivered these deities into the hand of their painters, sculptors, and poets. In like manner, Christian superstition, or, if you will, modern barbarism, impersonated every thing; and these persons, in proper form, subsisted for some time on the stage, and almost to our days in the masques. Hence the picturesque style of our old poetry, which looks so fanciful in Spenser, and which Shakespear's genius hath carried to the utmost sublimity.

I will not deny, said Mr. Addison, but there may be something in this deduction of the causes by which you account for the strength and grandeur of the English poetry, unpolished as it still was in the hands of Elizabeth's great poets. But for the masques themselves—

You forget, I believe, *one*, interrupted Dr. Arbuthnot, which does your favourite poet, Milton, almost as much honour as his *Paradise Lost*.—But I have no mind to engage in a further vindication of these fancies. I only conclude that the taste of the age, the state of letters, the genius of the English tongue was such as gave a manliness to their compositions of all sorts, and even an elegance to those of the lighter forms, which we might do well to emulate, and not deride, in this era of politeness.

But I am aware, as you say, I have been transported too far. My design was only to hint to you, in opposition to your invective against the memory of the old times awakened in us by the sight of this castle, that what you object to is capable of a much fairer interpretation. You have a proof of it in two or three instances in their festivals, their exercises, and their poetical fictions: or, to express myself in the classical forms, you have seen by this view of their convivial, gymnastic, and musical character, that the times of Elizabeth may pass for golden, notwithstanding what a fondness for this age of baser metal may incline us to represent it.

LETTERS ON CHIVALRY AND ROMANCE

[1762]

LETTER VIII

I spoke of "criticizing Spenser's poem, under the idea, not of a classical but Gothic composition."

It is certain much light might be thrown on that singular work, were an able critic to consider it in this view. For instance, he might go some way towards explaining, perhaps justifying, the general plan and *conduct* of the *Faery Queen*, which, to classical readers has appeared indefensible.

I have taken the fancy, with your leave, to try my hand on this curious subject.

When an architect examines a Gothic structure by Grecian rules, he finds nothing but deformity. But the Gothic architecture has its own rules,[2] by which when it comes to be examined, it is

---

[2] The reference here may be to Batty Langley (1696–1751), architec-

seen to have its merit, as well as the Grecian. The question is not which of the two is conducted in the simplest or truest taste, but, whether there be not sense and design in both, when scrutinized by the laws on which each is projected.

The same observation holds of the two sorts of poetry. Judge of the *Faery Queen* by the classic models, and you are shocked with its disorder: consider it with an eye to its Gothic original, and you find it regular. The unity and simplicity of the former are more complete, but the latter has that sort of unity and simplicity which results from its nature.

The *Faery Queen* then, as a Gothic poem, derives its method, as well as the other characters of its composition, from the established modes and ideas of chivalry.

It was usual, in the days of knight-errantry, at the holding of any great feast, for knights to appear before the prince, who presided at it, and claim the privilege of being sent on any adventure to which the solemnity might give occasion. For it was supposed that, when such a *throng of knights and barons bold* as Milton speaks of were got together, the distressed would flock in from all quarters, as to a place where they knew they might find and claim redress for all their grievances.

This was the real practice, in the days of pure and ancient chivalry. And an image of this practice was afterwards kept up in the castles of the great on any extraordinary festival or solemnity, of which, if you want an instance, I refer you to the description of a feast made at Lisle in 1453, in the court of Philip the Good, Duke of Burgundy, for a crusade against the Turks, as you may find it given at large in the memoirs of *Matthieu de Conci, Olivier de la Marche,* and *Monstrelet.*

That feast was held for twelve days, and each day was distinguished by the claim and allowance of some adventure.

Now laying down this practice as a foundation for the poet's design, you will see how properly the *Faery Queen* is conducted.

—"I devise," says the poet himself in his Letter to Sir W. Raleigh, "that the *Faery Queen* kept her annual feaste xii days: upon which xii several days, the occasions of the xii several adventures hapened; which being undertaken by xii several knights, are in these xii books severally handled."

----

tural writer and builder, who in *Ancient Architecture, Restored and Improved* (1741–1747) attempted to remodel Gothic architecture by the invention of five "orders."

Here you have the poet delivering his own method, and the reason of it. It arose out of the order of his subject. And would you desire a better reason for his choice?

"Yes," you will say, "a poet's method is not that of his subject." I grant you, as to the order of time in which the recital is made, for here, as Spenser observes (and his own practice agrees to the rule) lies the main difference between the *poet historical,* and the *historiographer*: The reason of which is drawn from the nature of epic composition itself, and holds equally, let the subject be what it will, and whatever the system of manners be on which it is conducted. Gothic or Classic makes no difference in this respect.

But the case is not the same with regard to the general plan of a work, or what may be called the order of distribution, which is and must be governed by the subject matter itself. It was as requisite for the *Faery Queen* to consist of the adventures of twelve knights, as for the Odyssey to be confined to the adventures of one hero: Justice had otherwise not been done to his subject.

So that if you will say any thing against the poet's method, you must say that he should not have chosen this subject. But this objection arises from your classic ideas of unity, which have no place here and are in every view foreign to the purpose, if the poet has found means to give his work, though consisting of many parts, the advantage of unity. For in some reasonable sense or other, it is agreed, every work of art must be *one,* the very idea of a work requiring it.

If you ask then, what is this unity of Spenser's poem, I say it consists in the relation of its several adventures to one common original, the appointment of the Faery Queen, and to one common end, the completion of the Faery Queen's injunctions. The knights issued forth on their adventures on the breaking up of this annual feast; and the next annual feast, we are to suppose, is to bring them together again from the achievement of their several charges.

This, it is true, is not the classic unity, which consists in the representation of one entire action; but it is an unity of another sort, an unity resulting from the respect which a number of related actions have to one common purpose. In other words, it is an unity of *design,* and not of action.

This Gothic method of design in poetry may be, in some sort, illustrated by what is called the Gothic method of design in gardening. A wood or grove cut out into many separate avenues or glades was amongst the most favourite of the works of art which our fathers attempted in this species of cultivation. These walks were distinct from each other, had each their several destination, and terminated on their own proper objects. Yet the whole was brought together and considered under one view by the relation which these various openings had, not to each other, but to their common and concurrent center. You and I are, perhaps, agreed that this sort of gardening is not of so true a taste as that which *Kent and Nature*[3] have brought us acquainted with, where the supreme art of the designer consists in disposing his ground and objects into an entire landscape, and grouping them, if I may use the term, in so easy a manner that the careless observer, though he be taken with the symmetry of the whole, discovers no art in the combination:

> In lieto aspetto il bel giardin s'aperse,
> Acque stagnanti, mobili cristalli,
> Fior vari, e varie piante, herbe diverse,
> Apriche Collinette, ombrose valli,
> Selve, e spelunche in UNA VISTA offerse:
> E quel, che'l bello, e'l caro accresce à l'opre,
> L'Arte, che tutto fà, nulla si scopre.[4]
>   *Tasso. C xvi. S. ix.*

This, I say, may be the truest taste in gardening, because the simplest. Yet there is a manifest regard to unity in the other method, which has had its admirers, as it may have again, and is certainly not without its design and beauty.

But to return to our poet. Thus far he drew from Gothic ideas, and these ideas, I think, would lead him no farther. But, as Spenser knew what belonged to classic composition, he was tempted to tie his subject still closer together by one expedient of his own, and by another taken from his classic models.

His own was to interrupt the proper story of each book by dis-

---

[3] William Kent (1684–1748), primarily remembered as a designer and architectural protegé of the Earl of Burlington, can also with some justification be called, as Walpole called him, "the father of modern gardening" in the natural style.

[4] When they had passed all those troubled ways,
      The garden sweet spread forth her green to show,
   The moving crystal from the fountains plays,
      Fair trees, high plants, strange herbs, and flow'rets new,
   Sun shiny hills, dales hid from Phœbus' rays,
      Groves, arbors, mossy caves, at once they view;
   And that which beauty most, most wonder brought,
   Nowhere appear'd the art which all this wrought.
                                                    [tr. Fairfax]

persing it into several, involving by this means, and as it were inter-
twisting the several actions together, in order to give something like
the appearance of one action to his twelve adventures. And for this
conduct, as absurd as it seems, he had some great examples in the
Italian poets, though I believe they were led into it by different
motives.

The other expedient which he borrowed from the classics, was
by adopting one superior character, which should be seen throughout. Prince Arthur, who had a separate adventure of his own, was to
have his part in each of the others; and thus several actions were
to be embodied by the interest which one principal hero had in
them all. It is even observable that Spenser gives this adventure of
Prince Arthur in quest of Gloriana as the proper subject of his poem,
and upon this idea the late learned editor of the *Faery Queen* has
attempted, but I think without success, to defend the unity and
simplicity of its fable. The truth was, the violence of classic prejudices forced the poet to affect this appearance of unity, though
in contradiction to his Gothic system. And, as far as we can judge of
the tenour of the whole work from the finished half of it, the adventure of Prince Arthur, whatever the author pretended and his
critic too easily believed, was but an after thought and at least with
regard to the historical fable, which we are now considering, was
only one of the expedients by which he would conceal the disorder
of his Gothic plan.

And if this was his design, I will venture to say that both his
expedients were injudicious. Their purpose was to ally two things in
nature incompatible, the Gothic and the classic unity, the effect of
which misalliance was to discover and expose the nakedness of the
Gothic.

I am of opinion then, considering the *Faery Queen* as an epic
or narrative poem constructed on Gothic ideas, that the poet had
done well to affect no other unity than that of design, by which
his subject was connected. But his poem is not simply narrative; it
is throughout *allegorical:* he calls it *a perpetual allegory or dark
conceit:* and this character, for reasons I may have occasion to
observe hereafter, was even predominant in the *Faery Queen*. His
narration is subservient to his moral, and but serves to colour it.
This he tells us himself at setting out.

Fierce wars and faithful loves shall moralize my song,

that is, shall serve for a vehicle, or instrument to convey the moral.

Now under this idea, the unity of the *Faery Queen* is more
apparent. His twelve knights are to exemplify as many virtues, out

of which one illustrious character is to be composed. And in this view the part of Prince Arthur in each book becomes essential, and yet not principal, exactly as the poet has contrived it. They who rest in the literal story, that is, who criticize it on the footing of a narrative poem, have constantly objected to this management. They say it necessarily breaks the unity of design. Prince Arthur, they affirm, should either have had no part in the other adventures, or he should have had the chief part. He should either have done nothing, or more. And the objection is unanswerable; at least I know of nothing that can be said to remove it but what I have supposed above might be the purpose of the poet, and which I myself have rejected as insufficient.

But how faulty soever this conduct be in the literal story, it is perfectly right in the moral, and that for an obvious reason, though his critics seem not to have been aware of it. His chief hero was not to have the twelve virtues in the degree in which the knights had, each of them, their own (such a character would be a monster), but he was to have so much of each as was requisite to form his superior character. Each virtue, in its perfection, is exemplified in its own knight: they are all, in a due degree, concentered in Prince Arthur.

This was the poet's moral: and what way of expressing this moral in the *history* but by making Prince Arthur appear in each adventure, and in a manner subordinate to its proper hero? Thus, though inferior to each in his own specific virtue, he is superior to all by uniting the whole circle of their virtues in himself. And thus he arrives, at length, at the possession of that bright form of Glory, whose ravishing beauty, as seen in a dream or vision, had led him out into these miraculous adventures in the land of *Faery*.

The conclusion is that, as an allegorical poem, the method of the *Faery Queen* is governed by the justness of the moral; as a narrative poem it is conducted on the ideas and usages of chivalry. In either view, if taken by itself, the plan is defensible. But from the union of the two designs there arises a perplexity and confusion which is the proper, and only considerable, defect of this extraordinary poem.

LETTER XII

The wonders of chivalry were still in the memory of men, were still existing, in some measure, in real life, when Chaucer undertook to expose the barbarous relaters of them.

This ridicule, we may suppose, hastened the fall both of chivalry and romance. At least from that time the spirit of both declined very fast, and at length fell in such discredit that when now Spenser arose, and with a genius singularly fitted to immortalize the land of faery, he met with every difficulty and disadvantage to obstruct his design.

The age would no longer bear the naked letter of these amusing stories, and the poet was so sensible of the misfortune that we find him apologizing for it on a hundred occasions. But apologies, in such circumstances, rarely do any good. Perhaps they only served to betray the weakness of the poet's cause, and to confirm the prejudices of his reader. However, he did more than this. He gave an air of mystery to his subject, and pretended that his stories of knights and giants were but the cover to abundance of profound wisdom.

In short, to keep off the eyes of the profane from prying too nearly into his subject, he threw about it the mist of allegory: he moralized his song, and the virtues and vices lay hid under his warriors and enchanters—a contrivance which he had learned indeed from his Italian masters, for Tasso had condescended to allegorize his own work, and the commentators of Ariosto had even converted the extravagances of the *Orlando Furioso* into moral lessons.

And this, it must be owned, was a sober attempt in comparison of some projects that were made about the same time to serve the cause of the old, and now expiring, romances. For it is to be observed, that the idolizers of these romances did by them what the votaries of Homer had done by him. As the times improved and would less bear his strange tales, they *moralized* what they could, and turned the rest into mysteries of natural science. And as this last contrivance was principally designed to cover the monstrous stories of the pagan gods, so it served the lovers of romance to palliate the no less monstrous stories of magic and enchantments. . . .

But to return to Spenser, who, as we have seen, had no better way to take in his distress than to hide his faery fancies under the mystic cover of moral allegory. The only favourable circumstance that attended him (and this no doubt encouraged, if it did not produce, his untimely project) was that he was somewhat befriended in these fictions, even when interpreted according to the letter, by the romantic spirit of his age, much countenanced, and for a time brought into fresh credit, by the romantic Elizabeth. Her inclination for the fancies of chivalry is well known, and obsequious wits and courtiers would not be wanting to feed and flatter it. In short, tilts

and tournaments were in vogue: the *Arcadia,* and the *Faery Queen*
were written.

With these helps the new spirit of chivalry made a shift to
support itself for a time, when reason was but dawning, as we may
say, and just about to gain the ascendant over the portentous spectres of the imagination. Its growing splendour, in the end, put them
all to flight, and allowed them no quarter even amongst the poets.
So that Milton, as fond as we have seen he was of the Gothic fictions, durst only admit them on the bye, and in the way of simile
and illustration only.

And this, no doubt, was the main reason of his relinquishing his
long-projected design of Prince Arthur, at last, for that of the
Paradise Lost, where, instead of giants and magicians, he had angels
and devils to supply him with the marvellous with greater probability. Yet, though he dropped the tales, he still kept to the allegories
of Spenser. And even this liberty was thought too much, as appears
from the censure passed on his Sin and Death by the severer critics.

Thus at length the magic of the old romances was perfectly
dissolved. They began with reflecting an image indeed of the feudal
manners, but an image magnified and distorted by unskilful design-
ers. Common sense being offended with these perversions of truth
and nature (still accounted the more monstrous, as the ancient
manners they pretended to copy after were now disused, and of
most men forgotten), the next step was to have recourse to *allegories.* Under this disguise they walked the world a while, the excellence of the moral and the ingenuity of the contrivance making
some amends, and being accepted as a sort of apology for the
absurdity of the literal story.

Under this form the tales of faery kept their ground, and even
made their fortune at court, where they became, for two or three
reigns, the ordinary entertainment of our princes. But reason, in the
end (assisted, however, by party and religious prejudices), drove
them off the scene, and would endure these lying wonders neither in
their own proper shape nor as masked in figures.

Henceforth, the taste of wit and poetry took a new turn, and
Fancy, that had wantoned it so long in the world of fiction, was now
constrained, against her will, to ally herself with strict truth if she
would gain admittance into reasonable company.

What we have gotten by this revolution, you will say, is a great
deal of good sense. What we have lost is a world of fine fabling, the
illusion of which is so grateful to the *charmed spirit* that, in spite
of philosophy and fashion, *Faery* Spenser still ranks highest among

the poets; I mean with all those who are either come of that house,
or have any kindness for it.

Earth-born critics, my friend, may blaspheme,

"But all the GODS are ravish'd with delight
Of his celestial Song, and music's wondrous might."

HENRY HOME, LORD KAMES
[1696–1782]

Henry Home was the son of a Scottish country gentleman.
Badly educated at home by a tutor, he did not repair the
defects of his education until he conceived a desire to
become an advocate. In 1724 he was called to the bar, and
to the bench in 1752, when he assumed the title Lord Kames
after the place of his birth. Kames wrote on a wide variety
of subjects: on British antiquities, on legal and historical
subjects, and upon logic, education, and agriculture.
He wrote an Essay on the Principles of Morality and Natural
Religion upon which Jonathan Edwards commented.

    Walter J. Hipple remarks that "The Elements of
Criticism of Henry Home, Lord Kames, remains today one
of the most elaborate and systematic treatises on aesthetics
and criticism of any age or nation; and it ranks, alongside
Archibald Alison's Essays on Taste, as the major effort of
philosophical criticism in eighteenth-century Britain."
Readers of Boswell, however, will remember that at his
first meeting with Johnson, the year after the Elements
was published, Ursa Major pronounced, "Sir, this book is a
pretty essay, and deserves to be held in some estimation,
though much of it is chimerical." And a few years later
Johnson had occasion slightly to elaborate: "The Scotchman
has taken the right method in his Elements of Criticism.
I do not mean that he has taught us any thing; but he has told
us old things in a new way." The chimerical qualities of
the essay certainly did not immediately appear, for it was
reprinted as an authoritative treatise until the mid-nineteenth
century and after, and was published in New York with

"translations of ancient and foreign illustrations" as late as
1871; but in retrospect the "new way" seems to have
been lost among the "old things"—the Essay, finally, is yet
another effort at an empirical aesthetics.

The somewhat repellant concluding chapter reprinted
here (from which the essentials of Kames's system can be
deduced) is probably the most thoroughgoing of many
eighteenth-century efforts to establish a universal taste on
immutable principles. We cannot help observing, however,
that this taste is ultimately to be established upon the
perceptions of a man not unlike what Henry Home, Lord
Kames conceived himself to be, a man not unlike what
almost any gentleman of the time would have conceived
himself to be. There may very well be worse standards, but
the problem is not often considered relevant in the
twentieth century.

Hipple *in* The Beautiful, the Sublime, and the
Picturesque . . . *devotes a chapter to Kames, and Elledge*
anthologizes Kames's remarks on fiction. Atkins gives a
generally sympathetic account of his Shakespeare criticism,
and devotes some attention to other aspects of his work
(English Literary Criticism, 17th and 18th Centuries).
See also:

Horn, Audras: "Kames and the Anthropological
    Approach to Criticism," PQ, XLIV (1964), 211–33.
McKenzie, Gordon: "Lord Kames and the Mechanist
    Tradition," Essays and Studies by Members of the
    Department of English, University of California
    (*University of California Publications in English*, XIV,
    1943), *pp*. 93–121.
Randall, Helen Whitcomb: The Critical Theory of Lord
    Kames (*Smith College Studies in Modern Languages*),
    Northampton, Mass., 1944.

FROM ELEMENTS OF CRITICISM

[1762]

CHAPTER XXV

Standard of Taste

"That there is no disputing about taste," meaning taste in its figurative as well as proper sense, is a saying so generally received as to have become a proverb. One thing even at first view is evident, that if the proverb holds true with respect to taste in its proper meaning, it must hold equally true with respect to our other external senses: if the pleasures of the palate disdain a comparative trial, and reject all criticism, the pleasures of touch, of smell, of sound, and even of sight, must be equally privileged. At that rate, a man is not within the reach of censure, even where he prefers the Saracen's head upon a sign-post before the best tablature of Raphael, or a rude Gothic tower before the finest Grecian building: or where he prefers the smell of a rotten carcass before that of

the most odoriferous flower, or discords before the most exquisite harmony.

But we cannot stop here. If the pleasures of external sense
be exempted from criticism, why not every one of our pleasures, from whatever source derived? if taste in its proper sense
cannot be disputed, there is little room for disputing it in its
figurative sense. The proverb accordingly comprehends both;
and in that large sense may be resolved into the following general proposition. That with respect to the perceptions of sense,
by which some objects appear agreeable, some disagreeable,
there is not such a thing as a *good* or a *bad*, a *right* or a *wrong;*
that every man's taste is to himself an ultimate standard
without appeal; and consequently that there is no ground of
censure against any one, if such a one there be, who prefers
Blackmore before Homer, selfishness before benevolence, or
cowardice before magnanimity.

The proverb in the foregoing examples is indeed carried
very far: it seems difficult, however, to sap its foundation,
or with success to attack it from any quarter: for is not every
man equally a judge of what ought to be agreeable or disagreeable to himself? doth it not seem whimsical, and perhaps
absurd, to assert that a man *ought not* to be pleased when
he is, or that he *ought* to be pleased when he is not?

This reasoning may perplex, but will never afford conviction:
everyone of taste will reject it as false, however unqualified
to detect the fallacy. At the same time, though no man of
taste will assent to the proverb as holding true in every
case, no man will affirm that it holds true in no case: objects
there are, undoubtedly, that we may like or dislike indifferently, without any imputation upon our taste. Were a
philosopher to make a scale for human pleasures, he would
not think of making divisions without end; but would rank
together many pleasures arising perhaps from different objects,
either as equally conducing to happiness, or differing so imperceptibly as to make a separation unnecessary. Nature hath
taken this course, at least it appears so to the generality of
mankind. There may be subdivisions without end; but we are
only sensible of the grosser divisions, comprehending each of
them various pleasures equally affecting; to these the proverb

is applicable in the strictest sense; for with respect to pleasures of the same rank, what ground can there be for preferring one before another? if a preference in fact be given by any individual, it cannot proceed from taste, but from custom, imitation, or some peculiarity of mind.

Nature in her scale of pleasures, has been sparing of divisions: she hath wisely and benevolently filled every division with many pleasures, in order that individuals may be contented with their own lot, without envying that of others. Many hands must be employed to procure us the conveniences of life; and it is necessary that the different branches of business, whether more or less agreeable, be filled with hands: a taste too refined would obstruct that plan; for it would crowd some employments, leaving others no less useful, totally neglected. In our present condition, lucky it is that the plurality are not delicate in their choice, but fall in readily with the occupations, pleasures, food and company, that fortune throws in their way; and if at first there be any displeasing circumstance, custom soon makes it easy.

The proverb will hold true as to the particulars now explained; but when applied in general to every subject of taste, the difficulties to be encountered are insuperable. We need only to mention the difficulty that arises from human nature itself; do we not talk of a good and a bad taste? of a right and a wrong taste? and upon that supposition, do we not, with great confidence, censure writers, painters, architects, and every one who deals in the fine arts? Are such criticisms absurd, and void of common sense? have the foregoing expressions, familiar in all languages and among all people, no sort of meaning? This can hardly be; for what is universal, must have a foundation in nature. If we can reach that foundation, the standard of taste will no longer be a secret.

We have a sense or conviction of a common nature, not only in our own species, but in every species of animals: and our conviction is verified by experience; for there appears a remarkable uniformity among creatures of the same kind, and a deformity no less remarkable among creatures of different kinds. This common nature is conceived to be a model or standard for each individual that belongs to the kind. Hence it is a wonder to find an individual deviating from the common nature of the species, whether in its internal or external construction: a child born with aversion to its mother's milk, is a wonder, no less than if born without a mouth, or with more than one. This conviction of a common nature in every species paves the way finely for distributing things into *genera* and *species,* to which we are extremely prone, not only with regard to animals and vegetables, where nature has led the way, but also with regard to many other things, where there is no ground for such distribution, but fancy merely.

With respect to the common nature of man in particular, we have a conviction that it is invariable not less than universal; that it will be the same hereafter as at present, and as it was in time past; the same among all nations and in all corners of the earth. Nor are we deceived; because, giving allowance for the difference of culture and gradual refinement of manners, the fact corresponds to our conviction.

We are so constituted, as to conceive this common nature, to be not only invariable, but also *perfect* or *right;* and consequently that individuals *ought* to be made conformable to it. Every remarkable deviation from the standard makes accordingly an impression upon us of imperfection, irregularity, or disorder: it is disagreeable, raises in us a painful emotion; monstrous births, exciting the curiosity of a philosopher, fail not at the same time to excite a sort of horror.

This conviction of a common nature or standard and of its perfection, accounts clearly for that remarkable conception we have of a right and a wrong sense or taste in morals. It accounts not less clearly for the conception we have of a right and a wrong sense or taste in the fine arts. A man who, avoiding objects generally agreeable, delights in objects generally disagreeable, is condemned as a monster: we disapprove his taste as bad or wrong, because we have a clear conception that he deviates from the common standard. If man were so framed as not to have any notion of a common standard, the proverb mentioned in the beginning would hold universally, not only in the fine arts, but in morals: upon that supposition, the taste of every man, with respect to both, would to himself be an ultimate standard. But as the conviction of a common standard is universal and a branch of our nature, we intuitively conceive a taste to be right or good, if conformable to the common standard, and wrong or bad if disconformable.

No particular in human nature is more universal, than the uneasiness a man feels when in matters of importance his opinions are rejected by others: why should difference in opinion create uneasiness, more than difference in stature, in countenance, or in dress? The conviction of a common standard explains the mystery: every man, generally speaking, taking it for granted that his opinions agree with the common sense of mankind, is therefore disgusted with those who think differently, not as differing from him, but as differing from the common standard: hence in all disputes, we find the parties, each of them equally appealing constantly to the common sense of mankind as the ultimate rule or standard. With respect to points arbitrary or indifferent, which are not supposed to be regulated by any standard, individuals are permitted to think for themselves with impunity: the same liberty is not indulged with respect to points that are reckoned of moment: for what reason, other than that the standard by which these are regulated, ought as we judge, to produce an uniformity of opinion in all men? In a word, to this conviction of a common standard must be wholly attributed the pleasure we take in those who espouse the same principles and opinions with ourselves, as well as the aversion we have at those who differ from us. In matters left indifferent by the standard, we find nothing of the same pleasure or pain: a bookish man, unless swayed by convenience, relisheth not the contemplative man more than the active; his friends and companions are chosen indifferently out of either class: a painter consorts with a poet or musician, as readily as with those of his own art; and one is not the more agreeable to me for loving beef, as I do, nor the less agreeable for preferring mutton.

I have ventured to say, that my disgust is raised not by differing from me, but by differing from what I judge to be the common standard. This point being of importance, ought to be firmly established. Men, it is true, are prone to flatter themselves, by taking it for granted that their opinions and their taste are in all respects conformable to the common standard; but there may be exceptions, and experience shews there are some: there are instances without number of persons who [are] addicted to the grosser amusements of gaming, eating, drinking, without having any relish for more elegant pleasures such, for example, as are afforded by the fine arts; yet these very persons, talking the same language with the rest of mankind, pronounce in favour of the more elegant pleasures, and they invariably approve those who have a more refined taste, being ashamed of their own as low and sensual. It is in vain to think of giving a reason for this singular impartiality, other than the authority of the common standard with respect to the dignity of human nature: and from the instances now given, we discover that the authority of that standard, even upon the most grovelling souls, is so vigorous as to prevail over self-partiality, and to make them despise their own taste compared with the more elevated taste of others.

Uniformity of taste and sentiment resulting from our conviction of a common standard, leads to two important final causes; the one respecting our duty, the other our pastime. Barely to mention the first shall be sufficient, because it does not properly belong to the present undertaking. Unhappy it would be for us did not uniformity prevail in morals: that our actions should uniformly be directed to what is good and against what is ill, is the greatest blessing in society; and in order to uniformity of action, uniformity of opinion and sentiment is indispensable.

With respect to pastime in general, and the fine arts in particular, the final cause of uniformity is illustrious. Uniformity of taste gives opportunity for sumptuous and elegant buildings, for fine gardens, and extensive embellishments, which please universally; and the reason is that without uniformity of taste, there could not be any suitable reward, either of profit or honour, to encourage men of genius to labour in such works, and to advance them toward perfection. The same uniformity of taste is equally necessary to perfect the art of music, sculpture, and painting, and to support the expense they require after they are brought to perfection. Nature is in every particular consistent with herself: we are framed by Nature to have a high relish for the fine arts, which are a great source of happiness, and friendly in a high degree to virtue: we are, at the same time, framed with uniformity of taste, to furnish proper objects for that high relish; and if uniformity did not prevail, the fine arts could never have made any figure.

And this suggests another final cause no less illustrious. The separation of men into different classes, by birth, office, or occupation, however necessary, tends to relax the connexion that ought be among members of the same state; which bad effect is in some measure prevented by the access all ranks of people have to public spectacles, and to amusements that are best enjoyed in company. Such meetings, where every one partakes of the same pleasures in common, are no slight support to the social affections.

Thus, upon a conviction common to the species is erected a standard of taste, which without hesitation is applied to the taste of every individual.—That standard, ascertaining what actions are right, what wrong, what proper, what improper, hath enabled moralists to establish rules for our conduct, from which no person is permitted to swerve. We have the same standard for ascertaining in all the fine arts what is beautiful or ugly, high or low, proper or improper, proportioned or disproportioned; and here, as in morals, we justly condemn every taste that deviates from what is thus ascertained by the common standard.

That there exists a rule or standard in nature for trying the taste of individuals, in the fine arts as well as in morals, is a discovery; but is not sufficient to complete the task undertaken. A branch still more important remains upon hand: which is, to ascertain what is truly the standard of nature, that we may not lie open to have a false standard imposed on us. But what means shall be employed for bringing to light this natural standard? This is not obvious: for when we have recourse to general opinion and general practice, we are betrayed into endless perplexities. History informs us, that nothing is more variable than taste in the fine arts; judging by numbers, the Gothic taste of architecture must be preferred before that of Greece, and the Chinese taste probably before either. It would be endless to recount the various tastes that have prevailed in different ages with respect to gardening, and still prevail in different countries. Despising the modest colouring of nature, women of fashion in France daub their cheeks with a red powder; nay, an unnatural swelling in the neck, peculiar to the inhabitants of the Alps, is relished by that people. But we ought not to be discouraged by such untoward instances, when we find as great variety in moral opinion; was it not among some nations held lawful for a man to sell his children for slaves, to expose them in their infancy to wild beasts, and to punish them for the crimes of their parents? was any thing more common than to murder an enemy in cold blood? nay more, did not law once authorise the abominable practice of human sacrifices, no less impious than immoral?—Such aberrations from the rules of morality prove only, that men, originally savage and brutal, acquire not rationality nor delicacy of taste till they be long disciplined in society. To ascertain the rules of morality we appeal not to the common sense of savages, but of men in their more perfect state; and we make the same appeal in forming the rules that ought to govern the fine arts: in neither can we safely rely on a local or transitory taste; but on what is the most general and the most lasting among polite nations.

In this very manner, a standard for morals has been ascertained with a good deal of accuracy, and is daily applied by able judges with general satisfaction. The standard of taste in the fine arts is not yet brought to such perfection: and we can account for its slower progress: the sense of right and wrong in actions is vivid and distinct, because its objects are clearly distinguishable from each other; whereas the sense of right and wrong in the fine arts is faint and wavering, because its objects are commonly not so clearly distinguishable from each other, and there appears to me a striking final cause in thus distinguishing the moral sense from the sense of right and wrong in the fine arts. The former, as a rule of conduct, and as a law we ought to obey, must be clear and authoritative. The latter is not entitled to the same privilege, because it contributes to our pleasure and amusement only: were it strong and lively it would usurp upon our duty, and call off the attention from matters of greater moment: were it clear and authoritative, it would banish all difference of taste, leaving no distinction between a refined taste and one that is not so: which would put an end to rivalship, and consequently to all improvement.

But to return to our subject. However languid and cloudy the common sense of mankind may be as to the fine arts, it is nothwithstanding the only standard in these as well as in morals. True it is indeed, that in gathering the common sense of mankind, more circumspection is requisite with respect to the fine arts than with respect to morals: upon the latter, any person may be consulted: but in the former, a wary choice is necessary, for to collect votes indifferently would certainly mislead us. Those who depend for food on bodily labour, are totally void of taste; of such a taste at least as can be of use in the fine arts. This consideration bars the greater part of mankind: and of the remaining part many, by a corrupted taste, are unqualified for voting. The common sense of mankind must then be confined to the few that fall not under these exceptions. But as such selection seems to throw matters again into uncertainty, we must be more explicit upon this branch of our subject.

Nothing tends more than voluptuousness to corrupt the whole internal frame and to vitiate our taste, not only in the fine arts, but even in morals: Voluptuousness never fails in course of time to extinguish all the sympathetic affections, and to bring on a beastly selfishness, which leaves nothing of a man but the shape: about excluding such persons there will be no dispute. Let us next bring under trial, the opulent who delight in expense: the appetite for superiority and respect, inflamed by riches, is vented upon costly furniture, numerous attendants, a princely dwelling, sumptuous feasts, everything superb and gorgeous, to amaze and humble all beholders: simplicity, elegance, propriety, and things natural, sweet, or amiable, are despised or neglected; for these are not appropriated to the rich, nor make a figure in the public eye; in a word, nothing is relished but what serves to gratify pride, by an imaginary exaltation of the possessor above those who surround him. Such sentiments contract the heart and make every principle give way to self-love: benevolence and public spirit, with all their refined emotions, are little felt, and less regarded: and if these be excluded, there can be no place for the faint and delicate emotions of the fine arts.

The exclusion of classes so many and numerous, reduces within a narrow compass those who are qualified to be judges in the fine arts. Many circumstances are necessary to form such a judge: There must be a good natural taste; that is, a taste approaching, at least in some degree, to the delicacy of taste above described: that taste must be improved by education, reflection, and experience:* it must be preserved in vigour by living regularly, by using the goods of fortune with moderation, and by following the dictates of improved nature, which give welcome to every rational pleasure without indulging any excess. This is the tenor of life which of all contributes the most to refinement of taste; and the same tenor of life contributes the most to happiness in general.

* That these particulars are useful, it may be said necessary, for acquiring a discerning tas'e in the fine arts, will appear from the following facts, which show the influence of experience singly. Those who live in the world and in good company, are quick-sighted with respect to every defect or irregularity in behaviour: the very slightest singularity in motion, in speech, or in dress, which to a peasant would be invisible, escapes not their observation. The most minute differences in the human countenance, so minute as to be far beyond the reach of words, are distinctly perceived by the plainest person: while at the same time, the generality have very little discernment in the faces of other animals to which they are less accustomed: Sheep, for example, appear to have all the same face, except to the shepherd, who knows every individual in his flock as he does his relations and neighbours. The very populace in Athens were critics in language, in pronunciation, and even in eloquence, harangue being their daily entertainment. In Rome, at present, the most illiterate shopkeeper is a better judge of statues and of pictures, than persons of refined education in London. These facts afford convincing evidence, that a discerning taste depends still more on experience than on nature. But these facts merit peculiar regard for another reason, that they open to us a sure method of improving our taste in the fine arts; which, with those who have leisure for improvements, ought to be a powerful incitement to cultivate a taste in these arts: an occupation that cannot fail to embellish their manners, and to sweeten society.

If there appear much uncertainty in a standard that requires so painful and intricate a selection, we may possibly be reconciled to it by the following consideration: That with respect to the fine arts, there is less difference of taste than is commonly imagined. Nature hath marked all her works with indelible characters of high or low, plain or elegant, strong or weak: these, if at all perceived, are seldom misapprehended; and the same marks are equally perceptible in works of art. A defective taste is incurable; and it hurts none but the possessor, because it carries no authority to impose upon others. I know not if there be such a thing as a taste naturally bad or wrong; a taste for example, that prefers a grovelling pleasure before one that is high and elegant: grovelling pleasures are never preferred; they are only made welcome by those who know no better. Differences about objects of taste, it is true, are endless; but they generally concern trifles, or possibly matters of equal rank, where preference may be given either way with impunity. If, on any occasion, persons differ where they ought not, a depraved taste will readily be discovered on one or other side, occasioned by imitation, custom, or corrupted manners, such as are described above. And considering that every individual partakes of a common nature, what is there that should occasion any wide difference in taste or sentiment? By the principles that constitute the sensitive part of our nature, a wonderful uniformity is preserved in the emotions and feelings of the different races of men; the same object making upon every person the same impression, the same in kind, if not in degree. There have been, as above observed, aberrations from these principles; but soon or late they prevail, and restore the wanderer to the right track.

I know but of one other means for ascertaining the common sense of mankind, which I mention not in despair, but in great confidence of success. As the taste of every individual ought to be governed by the principles above mentioned, an appeal to these principles must necessarily be decisive of every controversy that can arise upon matters of taste. In general, every doubt with relation to the common sense of man, or standard of taste, may be cleared by the same appeal; and to unfold these principles is the declared purpose of the present undertaking.

ALEXANDER GERARD
[1728–1795]

───────────

An industrious and precocious preacher in the Church of
Scotland and professor in Marischal College and the
University of Aberdeen, Gerard in 1756 won a prize offered
by the Philosophical Society of Edinburgh for the best
essay on "Taste." Gerard's conception of his subject is
somewhat broader than we would consider today; he defined
taste as residing "in the improvement of those principles
which are commonly called the powers of imagination,"
including the senses of novelty, sublimity, beauty, imitation,
harmony, ridicule, and virtue. In giving an important place
to the principle of association, he paved a path which
Archibald Alison was to follow, and which also interested
William Wordsworth.

   Gerard produced An Essay on Genius in 1774. His
most popular work, if one may judge by the number of
editions it went through, seems to have been a sermon
entitled, "Liberty the cloke of maliciousness, both in the
American rebellion, and in the manners of the times," first
printed in Aberdeen in 1778. He produced many other
sermons and theological writings. The "Appendix,
Concerning the question, whether Poetry be properly an
imitative art?" reprinted here appeared first in 1780 in
the third edition of An Essay on Taste, reprinted in facsimile,
Gainesville, Florida, 1963, with an introduction by
W. J. Hipple. See also:

Grene, Marjorie: "Gerard's Essay on Taste," Modern
   Philology, XLI (1943), 45–58.

AN ESSAY ON TASTE

APPENDIX

Concerning the question, whether Poetry be properly an imitative are? and if it be, in what sense it is imitative?

[1780]

Questions merely verbal are frivolous. Yet it is often of importance to ascertain the precise meaning of words, because impropriety in the use of them may occasion confusion of thought and errors in reasoning. This holds true especially of those words which denote the leading ideas on any subject: for these ideas set in a wrong light would necessarily introduce improper modes of expression, and even false conclusions. The rules which are laid down concerning any art must be considerably affected by the idea which is formed of the end of that art, and of the means by which the end may be attained. Whatever idea is formed of the proper nature and end of poetry, it will affect the rules which are laid down for poetry in respect both of their nature, and of the manner of proposing them. It is therefore of importance that that idea be formed with precision.

Aristotle, who was the first that endeavoured to reduce poetry to an art and subject it to rules, calls it an *imitation*, without explaining particularly in what sense it is an imitation: and, on his authority, poetry has ever since been called generally an *imitative art*, without either proof that it is such or explication of how it is such. Some, however, have denied that poetry is imitative, confining this character to painting and sculpture.*

If it be false that poetry is an imitation, it is plain that many of the rules of poetry, by being detached from that idea, may be rendered simpler than they can be when they are proposed with a relation to it. If the idea be just on the whole, but have been left indefinite, an accurate definition of it may prepare the way for rendering the rules of poetry more precise and exact than they would otherwise have been. That poetry, as well as the other fine arts, is imitative has been supposed in the preceding Essay, and some of the general principles there investigated will be affected by the truth or the falsehood of the supposition. I shall therefore briefly attempt a professed examination of it.

To imitate is to produce a resemblance of a thing. Painting and sculpture are in all cases strictly imitative. They produce a proper resemblance of the forms and proportions of visible objects, and exhibit that resemblance to the very same sense which is adapted to the perception of the objects themselves. Even when they go beyond the visible appearances of things, and suggest passions, emotions, and characters, still they suggest these by producing a proper resemblance of the attitudes and features by which the passions or characters show themselves in real life. With respect to some objects, poetry is as properly and strictly imitative: so far as it is dramatic, so far as it introduces persons acting

* [Kames'] Elements of Criticism, chap. 18.

and speaking, and does not merely *describe* how they acted or spoke, it exhibits an exact copy of their conversation and actions.

But whenever poetry ceases to be dramatic, whenever the poet, in his own person, describes or relates, poetry no longer exhibits a resemblance of the things related or described in the same sense as painting does of the things which it represents. Poetry makes use of language, or artificial signs. These bear no resemblance to the things signified by them, and therefore the poem can have no proper resemblance to the subject described in it. It cannot be called an imitation of that subject with any more propriety than an historical narration can be called an imitation of the transaction of which it gives an account.

A poetical description excites an idea of the object described, as conceived by the poet; and, if it be well executed, a very lively idea. But it cannot, for this reason alone, deserve to be denominated an imitation of that object. For, not to insist that the idea is not properly a resemblance of the object, it is sufficient to observe that if every species of composition which excites an idea of the subject were to be called an imitation of it, we might call not only history, but reasoning also, an imitation. But this would, without hesitation, be pronounced by every person to be a gross impropriety.

No doubt, there are many circumstances peculiar to poetical description, and which render the idea excited by it livelier and more affecting than that which is produced by a mere narration of facts, by an exact and minute delineation of a natural object, or by a process of reasoning. This difference might justify our calling the former a livelier imitation than these latter, if both were allowed to be imitations: but it cannot justify our denominating the former an imitation, while we maintain that these latter are not at all imitations.

In consequence of the vivacity of the idea excited by them, poetical descriptions produce effects on the sentiments and passions which cannot be produced by arguments, by historical narrations, or by physiological details. These make an important difference between poetry and other species of composition: but they cannot render that a proper imitation, while these are no imitations. Nothing can establish this precise distinction between them, except it could be proved that poetry produces a resemblance of the things described, and that these other kinds of composition produce no resemblance of their subjects.

Some perhaps, when they called poetry an imitation, and history no imitation, have meant only to say that poetry excites stronger and livelier ideas, sentiments, and emotions, than history; that it in a manner sets the objects before our eyes; that we almost think that we see them. This is very true: but it is improperly expressed; the word *imitation* is used in an indefinite, figurative, and abusive sense: and the use of it in such a sense, when one professes to mark the distinctive nature of poetry, tends to mislead and introduce confusion; especially if he reasons from this figurative sense as if it were the literal.

Poetry is not, nor can be properly imitative, as producing a resemblance of its immediate subject. Its employing language, or instituted signs, renders it absolutely incapable of being in this sense imitative. No combination of significant sounds can form an image or copy, either of sensible or of intellectual objects. An historical narration of any transaction, or a naturalist's description of any visible object, would not, by any man, be called an imitation: but a painting of the same transaction, or of the same object, would be termed an imitation by all men. The only reason of the difference is that in the latter case the artist has produced a resemblance of that transaction or object, in the former no resemblance is produced; and as little could any be produced by poetry.

If poetry, therefore, be, strictly speaking, an imitation, it must be such in some other sense, and for some other reason, than its expressing in words the subject chosen by the poet. What other reason there is for calling poetry an imitation we shall be assisted in conceiving by attending for a little to the nature of painting. On account of its producing a real resemblance of things, painting is in every case an imitation. But it is not in every case an imitation in precisely the same sense. A portrait or a landscape is a copy of the person or the country from which it is taken; and it is an imitation only for this reason, that it exhibits a copy of these individuals. But suppose that a painter, instead of copying an individual object with which he is acquainted, invents a subject; suppose, for instance, that he paints an Hercules from a standard idea in his own mind: in this case, the picture is not an imitation, as being a copy or resemblance of any one individual existing in nature. It is still an imitation, but in a quite different sense: the subject itself is an imitation; it is not a real individual, but a general representation of the make of a strong man. The imitation made by poetry is of this very kind. The poet conceives his subject, and this subject is an imitation; it is not, in all its circumstances, a thing which really exists in nature, or a fact which has really happened; it only resembles things which exist, or which have happened.

All men seem to have an implicit idea that this is the true nature of poetical imitation, though they have not unfolded it distinctly, and though perhaps they have often talked as if their idea had been different. Hence it proceeds that, whenever we speak of poetry as an imitation, we constantly call it an imitation of *Nature*, never an imitation of the poet's particular subject, as we readily would if we considered it as denominated an imitation merely on account of the lively idea of that subject which is excited by it.

It is plainly in the very sense which we have pointed out that Aristotle calls poetry an imitative art. For the distinction which he makes between poetry and history is that history describes things as they *are*, but poetry as they *may be*. The subject of the former is the *real*; the subject of the latter the *probable*, or what resembles the real. And now we can perceive clearly why we call poetry an imitation, history not. History is more than an imitation; it is an accurate detail of real things. But poetry is an imitation, and no more: it is not a description of what has actually been, but a description of something so like to real fact that it might have been, or is probable.

A poet sometimes chuses a real thing for his subject— a particular place, for instance, or a prospect, or a series of events. So far as he adheres strictly to that real thing his description is no more an imitation of that thing than the

geographer's, or naturalist's, or historian's account of it would
be an imitation. But his description may, notwithstanding,
be poetical: it may be embellished and enlivened by images,
etc. not belonging to the real thing, but formed by the poet's
fancy. It is the introduction of these that renders the description poetical; and these are imitations of nature, not actual
appendages of the real thing described. A simple gazette in
verse would be no imitation of the events related, nor would
it be a poem, however harmonious the verse might be; it
would be only a history in metre. Had the Iliad been a mere
detail of certain events of the Trojan war thrown into hexameters it would have been no poem: had it adorned the detail
with a variety of beautiful figures and images it would have
been poetical, but no imitation. Homer only takes his hints
from the real events of the Trojan war; he introduces the
heroes who served in it, but he engages them in whatever
combats he thinks proper; he feigns those circumstances, those
turns of success, and those consequences of the several combats
which produce the best effects on the imagination and the
passions; he brings deities into the field of battle to assist or
to oppose the several combatants, who never appeared there
but who, agreeably to the received mythology of the times,
might have appeared. It is this that renders the Iliad an imitation; and it is this that renders it, in the highest sense, a poem.
The subject of every poem is to a certain degree a fable; and
to the very same degree it is an imitation.

In a word, poetry is called an imitation not because it
produces a lively idea of its immediate subject, but because
this subject itself is an imitation of some part of real nature.
It is not called an imitation to express the exactness with
which it copies real things; for then history would be a more
perfect imitation than poetry. It is called an imitation for
the very contrary reason, to intimate that it is not confined to
the description only of realities, but may take the liberty to
describe all such things as resemble realities, and on account
of that resemblance come within the limits of probability. It
were easy to shew that this very circumstance is the source
from which are derived almost all the rules of poetry, so far
as they differ from those of history and other species of com-

position. Hence it arises, for example, that in descriptions of natural objects the poet is not obliged to take in all their real qualities and appearances, but is allowed to select such as may form a striking picture, and to combine with these such consistent qualities and appearances, not actually belonging to the objects, as are fit for heightening the beauty and force of the picture. Hence it arises that poetical characters represent a whole kind, and are not required to include the peculiar and discriminating circumstances, which never fail to be joined with the generic ones in real individuals. But it is not necessary for our present purpose to point out what influence this view of the nature of poetry has upon its rules; it is sufficient to have ascertained the sense in which poetry is an imitative art.

WILLIAM DUFF
[1732–1815]

_____

Duff was a minister in the Church of Scotland. His life seems
to have been marked only by steady and sedate advancement
in his calling and by the publication in 1767 of the Essay
on Original Genius, followed three years later by Critical
Observations on the Writings of the Most Celebrated
Original Geniuses in Poetry. He also wrote, anonymously,
an Oriental tale, The History of Rhedi, 1773.

In the selection reproduced here, although one surmises
that Duff had read Young's Conjectures, he is very clearly
tying his esthetic notions to the mid-century interest in
primitivism and to the growing interest in mediaeval and
renaissance literature. The Essay may also be in part a
justification of Macpherson's Ossianic poems, the astonishing
popularity of which it certainly helps us to understand.

Duff's Essay seems not to have been republished until
1964, when it was reprinted by Scholars Facsimiles and
Reprints, Gainesville, Florida with an introduction by
John L. Mahoney. The present text is adapted from that
facsimile. See also:

Pearce, Roy H.: "The Eighteenth-Century Scottish
    Primitivists," ELH, XII (1945), 203–20.

FROM AN ESSAY ON ORIGINAL GENIUS; AND ITS VARIOUS MODES OF EXERTION . . . PARTICULARLY IN POETRY

[1767]

A glowing ardor of imagination is indeed (if we may be permitted the expression) the very soul of poetry. It is the principal source of inspiration, and the poet who is possessed of it, like the Delphian priestess, is animated with a kind of divine fury. The intenseness and vigour of his sensations produce the enthusiasm of imagination which, as it were, hurries the mind out of itself, and which is vented in warm and vehement description, exciting in every susceptible breast the same emotions that were felt by the author himself. It is this *enthusiasm* which gives life and strength to poetical representations, renders them striking imitations of nature, and thereby produces that inchanting delight which genuine poetry is calculated to inspire. Without this animating principle all poetical and rhetorical compositions are spiritless and languid, like those bodies that are drained of their vital juices: they are therefore read with indifference or insipidity; the harmony of the numbers, if harmonious, may tickle the ear, but being destitute of nerves, that is of passion and sentiment, they can never affect the heart.

Thus we have pointed out and illustrated the most distinguishing ingredients of *original genius* in poetry; we shall conclude the present section with inquiring into the first and most natural exertions of genius in this divine art.

We may venture then to lay it down as a position highly probable, that the first essays of original genius will be in *allegories, visions,* or the creation of ideal beings of one kind or another. There is no kind of invention in which there is fuller scope afforded to the exercise of imagination than in that of *allegory,* which has this advantage over most other fables, that in it the author is by no means restricted to such an exact probability as is required in those fables that instruct us by a representation of actions which, though not real, must always, however, be such as might have happened. Let it be observed, that we are here speaking of allegory in its utmost latitude. We are not ignorant that there is a species of it which, like the Epic fable, attempts to instruct by the invention of a series of incidents strictly probable. Such are the beautiful and striking allegories contained in different parts of the Sacred Writings. But there is another kind of allegorical fable in which there is very little regard shewn to probability. Its object also is instruction, though it does not endeavour to instruct by real or probable actions; but wrapt in a veil of exaggerated, yet delicate and apposite fiction, is studious at once to delight the imagination and to impress some important maxim upon the mind. Of this kind is the *Fairy Queen* of Spenser. As in this species of allegory we neither expect what is true nor what is like the truth, so we read such fabulous compositions partly for the sake of the morals they contain, but principally for the sake of gratifying that curiosity, so deeply implanted in the human mind, of becoming acquainted with new and marvellous events. We are in this case in a great measure upon our guard against the delusions of fancy, are highly pleased with the narrative, though we do not allow it to impose upon us so far as to obtain our credit. Yet such is the power of ingenious fiction over our minds that we are not only captivated and interested by a relation of surprising incidents, though very improbable, but, during the time of the relation at least, we forget that they are fictitious, and almost fancy them to be real. This deceit, however, lasts no longer than the perusal, in which we are too much agitated to reflect on the probability or improbability of the events related; but when that is over the inchantment vanishes in the cool moment of deliberation, and, being left at leisure to think and reason, we never admit as true what is not strictly probable.

As we are treating of allegorical fables, it may not be amiss to observe, with regard to the kind last mentioned in particular, that the liberties indulged to it, though prodigiously various and extensive, are not however without certain restrictions. Thus, though we do not require probability in the general contexture of the fable, justness of manners must be preserved in this, as well as in the other species of fabulous composition; the incidents must be suitable to the characters to which they are accommodated; those incidents must likewise clearly point out or imply the moral they are intended to illustrate; and they must, in order to captivate the imagination, be new and surprising at the same time that they are to be perfectly consistent with each other. It is evident, however, that these slight restraints prove no real impediment to the natural impulse and excursions of *Genius*, but that they serve rather to point and regulate its course. It is likewise equally evident that this last mentioned species of allegory presents a noble field for the display of a rich and luxuriant imagination, and that to excel in it requires the utmost fertility of invention, since every masterly composition of this kind must be the mere creation of the poet's fancy.

We observed likewise that *original genius* will naturally discover itself in *visions*. This is a species of fiction to succeed in which with applause requires as much poetic inspiration as any other species of composition whatever. That enthusiasm of imagination, which we considered as an essential characteristic of original genius, is indispensibly necessary to the enraptured Bard who would make his readers feel those impetuous transports of passion which occupy and actuate his own mind. He must himself be wrought up to a high pitch of extasy if he expects to throw us into it. Indeed, it is the peculiar felicity of an original author to feel in the most exquisite degree every emotion, and to see every scene he describes. By the vigorous effort of a creative imagination he calls shadowy substances and unreal objects into existence. They are present to his view, and glide, like spectres, in silent, sullen majesty before his astonished and intranced sight. In reading the description of such apparitions we partake of the author's emotion; the blood runs chill in our veins, and our hair stiffens with horror.

It would far exceed the bounds prescribed to this Essay to point out all the particular tracks which an original genius will strike out in the extensive sphere of imagination, as those paths are so various and devious. In the meantime we may observe, that as the hand of Nature hath stamped different minds with a different kind and degree of originality, giving each a particular bent to one certain object or pursuit, original authors will pursue the track marked out by Nature, by faithfully following which they can alone hope for immortality to their writings and reputation. Thus while one writer, obeying the impulse of his genius, displays the exuberance of his fancy in the beautiful and surprising fictions of allegory, another discovers the fertility and extent of his imagination, as well as the justness of his judgment, in the conduct of the epic or dramatic fable, in which he raises our admiration, our terror, or our pity, as occasion may require.

Upon the whole, we need not hesitate to affirm that original genius will probably discover itself either in allegories, visions, or in the creation of ideal figures of one kind or another. The probability that it will do so is derived from that innate tendency to fiction which distinguishes such a genius, and from the natural bias of fiction to run in this particular channel: for the imagination of a poet, whose genius is truly original, finding no objects in the visible creation sufficiently marvellous and new, or which can give full scope to the exercise of its powers, naturally bursts into the ideal world in quest of more surprising and wonderful scenes, which it explores with insatiable curiosity, as well as with exquisite pleasure; and depending in its excursion wholly on its own strength, its success in this province of fiction will be proportionable to the plastic power of which it is possessed. In case, however, the position just advanced should appear problematical to some, we shall confirm it by arguments drawn from experience, which will serve to shew that *original poetic genius* hath in fact exerted its powers in the manner above specified.*

In proof of this assertion, we might adduce the whole system of heathen mythology. What are all the fabulous and allegorical relations of antiquity concerning the nature, generation, powers and offices of the pagan deities, but the inventions of men of genius? Poets and priests were unquestionably the original authors of all the theological systems of the Gentile world. A ray, ultimately derived from divine revelation, did sometimes indeed burst through the cloud of human error, but was soon obscured, if not smothered, by the superstitions of men; and oral tradition, that fallacious guide, was buried under a mass of absurdity and folly. Though the heathen theology must be confessed to be the disgrace and degradation of human reason, yet it must also be acknowledged to be a remarkable proof of the creative power of human imagination; and at the same time that we condemn it as a religious creed, we must admire it as a system of ingenious

* Longinus considers the introducing visions into composition, and the supporting them with propriety, as one of the boldest efforts either of rhetorical or poetic genius. He observes, that they contribute much to the grandeur, to the splendor, and to the efficacy of an oration in particular. . . . He observes [further] that there is a difference betwixt visions adapted to rhetoric, and such as are adapted to poetry; but that they both concur in producing a violent commotion of mind.[1]

[1] Duff is referring to Section XV of *On the Sublime,* where Longinus says, "Images, moreover, contribute greatly . . . to dignity, elevation, and power as a pleader. In this sense some call them mental representations. In a general way the name of *image* or imagination is applied to every idea of the mind, in whatever form it presents itself, which gives birth to speech. But at the present day the word is predominantly used in cases where, carried away by enthusiasm and passion, you think you see what you describe, and you place it before the eyes of your hearers." (Translation by W. Rhys Roberts.)

fiction. The Greek theology was of all other systems the most ingenious. What a strange but fanciful account may we collect from those ancient authors, Homer and Hesiod, of the nature and employment of the numerous deities which Greece acknowledged? We find the celestial divinities, Jupiter and Juno, Minerva and Venus, Mars and Apollo, sometimes quaffing nectar in their golden cups and reposing themselves in indolent tranquility, served by Hebe, and attended by Mercury, the swift-winged messenger of the Gods: at other times we see them mixing among the Trojan and Grecian hosts, taking part in mortal quarrels as partiality or favour dictated, inspiring the army whose cause they embraced with their counsel and aiding it by their power, driving on or stemming the tide of battle and alternately hastening and retarding the decrees of fate. Ceres has the earth for her province, and is the bounteous giver of the golden grain; Neptune sways the ocean with his trident; and Pluto, seated on his throne in gloomy majesty, rules the dominions of the world below. Need we mention, as proofs of wild and exuberant fancy, the pleasures and beauties of Elysium, contrasted with the torments and horrors of dark Tartarus? Need we mention the black Cocytus, the flaming Phlegethon, the punishment of Tantalus, the ever-rolling stone of Sisyphus, the wheel of Ixion, and the fruitless perpetual labours of the Danaids?

.   .   .

From this general and imperfect view of the Greek mythology, it is evident that original genius did in ancient Greece always discover itself in allegorical fiction, or in the creation of ideal figures of one kind or another; in inventing and adding new fables to the received systems of mythology, or in altering and improving those that had been already invented. The immense and multifarious system of the Greek theology was a work of many centuries, and rose gradually to that height in which it now appears. Some additions were daily made to it by the poets and men of lively imagination till that huge pile of superstition was completed which, in its ruins, exhibits so striking a monument of human ingenuity and folly. If, after what has been alleged, any one should question whether the fabulous theology now considered be an effect or indication of *original genius,* we would only desire him to suppose the mythology of Homer annihilated. What a blank would such annihilation make in the divine *Iliad*! Destitute of its celestial machinery, would it not be in a great measure an inanimate mass? It would at least lose much of that variety, dignity and grandeur which we admire in it at present, and much of that pleasing and surprising fiction which gives such exquisite delight to the imagination.

It would be easy to confirm the position we have laid down, that *original genius* always discovers itself in allegories, visions, or the invention of ideal characters, by examples drawn from the Eastern and the Egyptian mythology, which was so full of fable and hieroglyphical emblems; but we shall waive the consideration of these as superfluous after what hath been already urged, and conclude this part of our subject with observing that the Eastern manner of writing is, and hath ever been, characterised by a remarkable boldness of sentiment and expression, by the most rhetorical and poetical figures of speech; and that many of the compositions of the Eastern nations abound with allegories, visions and dreams, of which we have several admirable examples in the sacred writings.

SECTION V

That
Original Poetic
GENIUS
Will in general be displayed in its utmost Vigour
In the Early and Uncultivated
PERIODS OF SOCIETY
Which are peculiarly favorable to it;
And that
It will seldom appear in a very high Degree in
CULTIVATED LIFE,

Having pointed out the exertions of *original genius* in the different arts, and particularly in poetry, we shall now consider the period of society most favourable to the display of originality of genius in the last mentioned art; and this period we affirm to be the earliest and least cultivated.

To assert that this divine art, to an excellence in which the highest efforts of human genius are requisite, should attain its utmost perfection in the infancy of society, when mankind are only emerging from a state of ignorance and barbarity, will appear a paradox to some, though it is an unquestionable truth; and a closer attention will convince us that it is agreeable to reason as well as confirmed by experience.

While arts and sciences are in their first rude and imperfect state, there is great scope afforded for the exertions of Genius. Much is to be observed; much is to be discovered and invented. Imagination, however, in general exerts itself with more success in the arts than in the sciences, in the former of which its success is more rapid than in the latter. Active as this faculty is in its operations, its discoveries in science are for the most part attained by slow and gradual steps. They are the effect of long and severe investigation, and receive their highest improvement in the most civilized state of society. On the other hand the efforts of imagination, in poetry at least, are impetuous, and attain their utmost perfection at once, even in the rudest form of social life. This art does not require long and sedulous application to confer originality and excellence on its productions: its earliest unlaboured essays generally possess both in the highest degree. The reasons why they do so will be assigned immediately. In the meantime we may observe, as a circumstance deserving our attention, that this is by no means the case with the other arts, but is peculiar to poetry alone. Painting, eloquence, music, and architecture attain their highest improvement by the repeated efforts of ingenious artists, as well as the sciences by the reiterated researches and experiments of philosophers, though, as we have already observed, imagination operates with greater rapidity in the improvement of the former than in that of the latter; but still it operates gradually in the improvement of both. There never arose an eminent painter, orator, musician, architect, or philosopher in any age completely self-taught, without being indebted to his predeces-

sors in the art or science he professed. Should it be objected
that the art of painting was revived, and brought to the utmost perfection to which it ever arrived in modern times, in
one single age, that of Leo the Tenth, we answer that the
Italian masters, though they had none of the ancient paintings
to serve them as models, had however some admirable remains both of the Grecian and Roman statuary, which, by
heightening their ideas of excellence in its sister art and
kindling their ambition, contributed greatly to the perfection
of their works. Arts and sciences indeed generally rise and
fall together; but, excepting poetry alone, they rise and fall
by just, though not always by equal degrees: sometimes ad-
vancing with quicker progress to the summit of excellence,
sometimes declining from it by slower steps in proportion
to the different degrees of genius and application with which
they are cultivated, considered in connection with those external causes which promote or obstruct their improvement.
It is very remarkable, however, that in the earliest and most
uncultivated periods of society poetry is by one great effort
of nature, in one age, and by one individual, brought to the
highest perfection to which human genius is capable of ad-
vancing it, not only when the other arts and sciences are in a
languishing state, but when they do not so much as exist.
Thus Homer wrote his *Iliad* and *Odyssey* when there was not
a single picture to be seen in Greece; and Ossian composed
Fingal and *Temora* when none of the arts, whether liberal or
mechanical, were known in his country. This is a curious
phenomenon; let us endeavor to account for it.

The first reason we shall assign of *original poetic genius*
being most remarkably displayed in an early and uncultivated period of society arises from the antiquity of the period itself, and from the appearance of novelty in the objects
which Genius contemplates. A poet or real genius, who lives
in a distant uncultivated age, possesses great and peculiar advantages for original composition by the mere antiquity of the
period in which he lives. He is perhaps the first poet who
hath arisen in this infant state of society, by which means he
enjoys the undivided empire of Imagination without a rival.
The mines of Fancy not having been opened before his

time are left to be digged by him, and the treasures they contain become his own by a right derived from the first discovery. The whole system of nature and the whole region of
fiction yet unexplored by others is subjected to his survey,
from which he culls those rich spoils which adorn his compositions and render them original. It may be said indeed, in
answer to this, and it is true, that the stores of nature are inexhaustible by human imagination, and that her face is ever
various and ever new; but it may be replied that some of her
stores are more readily found than others, being less hid from
the eye of Fancy, and some of her features more easily hit,
because more strongly marked. The first good poet, therefore,
professing those unrifled treasures, and contemplating these
unsullied features, could not fail to present us with a draught
so striking as to deserve the name of a complete *original.*
We may further observe that the objects with which he is
surrounded have an appearance of novelty which, in a more
cultivated period, they in a great measure lose, but which,
in that we are speaking of, excites an attention, curiosity and
surprise highly favourable to the exertion of genius, and
somewhat resembling that which Milton attributes to our
first ancestor:

> Straight toward Heaven my wond'ring eyes I turn'd,
> And gaz'd a while the ample sky.
>
> *Paradise Lost,* Book viii, line 257.

> About me round I saw
> Hill, dale, and shady woods, and funny plains,
> And liquid lapse of murmuring streams.
>
> Line 261.

Such a person looks round him with wonder; every object
is new to him and has the power to affect him with surprise
and pleasure; and as he is not familiarised by previous description to the scenes he contemplates, these strike upon his
mind with their full force; and the imagination, astonished
and enraptured with the survey of the vast, the wild, and
the beautiful in nature, conveyed through the medium of
sense, spontaneously expresses its vivid ideas in bold and
glowing metaphors, in sublime, animated, and picturesque de-

scription. Even a poet of ordinary genius will in such a state of society present us with some original ideas in his composition. For nature, lying open to his view in all its extent and variety, in contemplating this unbounded field so small a part of which hath been yet occupied by others, he can hardly fail to select some distinguishing objects which have escaped the notice of the vulgar, and which described in poetry may stamp upon it a degree of originality.

We may add that the productions of the early ages, when they present to us scenes of nature and a state of life we are little acquainted with, and which are very different from those that now subsist, will to us appear original, though they may not be really such if the true originals are lost of which the works that yet remain are only copies or imitations. Thus the Comedies of Terence are valued because the originals of Menander, which the Roman poet imitated, excepting a few fragments, are lost. Could the works of the latter be recovered, those of the former would lose much of their reputation. Thus far the superiority of poetic genius in those early ages is accidental, and therefore no way meritorious. It is the effect of a particular situation. It is the consequence of antiquity.

The next reason we shall give why original poetic genius appears in its utmost perfection in the first periods of social life is the simplicity and uniformity of manners peculiar to such periods.

Manners have a much greater effect on the exertions of poetic genius than is commonly imagined. The simple manners which prevail among most nations in the infancy of society are peculiarly favourable to such exertions. In this primitive state of nature, when mankind begin to unite in society, the manners, sentiments, and passions are (if we may use the expression) perfectly *original*. They are the dictates of nature, unmixed and undisguised: they are therefore more easily comprehended and described. The poet in describing his own feelings describes also the feelings of others; for in such a state of society these are similar and uniform in all. Their tastes, dispositions, and manners are thrown into the same mould and generally formed upon one and the same model. Artless and tender loves, generous friendships, and warlike exploits compose the history of this uncultivated period, and the poet who relates these, feeling the inspiration of his subject, is himself animated with all the ardor of the *Lover,* the *Friend,* and the *Hero.* Hence, as his sensations are warm and vivid, his sentiments will become passionate or sublime as the occasion may require, his descriptions energetic, his stile bold, elevated, and metaphorical, and the whole, being the effusion of a glowing fancy and an impassioned heart, will be perfectly natural and *original.* Thus far, then, an early and uncultivated state of society, in which the manners, sentiments and passions run in the uniform current above-mentioned (as they do in most infant societies) appears favourable to the display of original poetic genius.

A third cause of this quality's being remarkably exerted in an early period of society is the leisure and tranquillity of uncultivated life, together with the innocent pleasures which generally attend it.

Genius naturally shoots forth in the simplicity and tranquillity of uncultivated life. The undisturbed peace and the innocent rural pleasures of this primeval state are, if we may so express it, congenial to its nature. A poet of true genius delights to contemplate and describe those primitive scenes which recall to our remembrance the fabulous era of the golden age. Happily exempted from that tormenting ambition and those vexatious desires which trouble the current of modern life, he wanders with a serene, contented heart through walks and groves consecrated to the Muses; or, indulging a sublime, pensive, and sweetly-soothing melancholy, strays with a slow and solemn step through the unfrequented desert, along the naked beach, or the bleak and barren heath. In such a situation every theme is a source of inspiration, whether he describes the beauties of nature, which he surveys with transport, or the peaceful innocence of those happy times which are so wonderfully soothing and pleasing to the imagination. His descriptions, therefore, will be perfectly vivid and original, because they are the transcript of his own feelings. Such a situation as that we have above represented is particularly favourable to a pastoral poet, and is very similar to that enjoyed by Theocritus, which no doubt had a happy influence on his compositions, and it is a situation highly propitious to the efforts of every species of poetic genius.

Perhaps we may be thought to refine too much on this point, and it may be questioned whether such tranquillity and innocence as we have above supposed have ever existed in any state of society. To this we may answer, that though the traditionary or even historical accounts of the early ages are not much to be depended on, yet those ancient original poems which we have in our hands give us reason to think that a certain innocence of manners, accompanied with that tranquillity which is its consequence, prevailed among those people whom we are not ashamed to call barbarous in a much higher degree than in more modern and cultivated periods.

The last cause we shall assign why original poetic genius appears in its utmost perfection in the uncultivated ages of society is its exemption from the rules and restraints of criticism, and its want of that knowledge which is acquired from books. When we consider learning and critical knowledge as unfavourable to original poetry we hope we shall not be accused of pleading the cause of ignorance, rusticity, and barbarism any more than, when we speak of the happy influence of the simple, uncultivated periods of society on the productions of the above-mentioned art, we shall be supposed to prefer those rude and artless ages to a highly civilized state of life. The effects of literature and criticism in the improvement of all the sciences and all the arts (excepting poetry alone), and the advantages of a state of civilization in augmenting and refining the pleasures of social life, are too obvious to require to be pointed out. We are at present only concerned to examine the effects of learning and critical knowledge on original poetry, the want of which we affirm to be one of the principal causes of this art being carried to its highest perfection in the first uncultivated periods of human society.

Let us inquire into the effects of these upon the mind of a poet possessed of a high degree of original genius. By an acquaintance with that literature which is derived from books, it will be granted, he may attain the knowledge of a great variety of events, and see human nature in a great variety of forms. By collecting the observations and experience of past ages, by superadding his own, and by reasoning justly from acknowledged principles, he may, no doubt, acquire more accurate and extensive ideas of the works of Nature and Art, and may likewise be thereby qualified to inrich the sciences with new discoveries as well as most of the arts with new inventions and improvements. In his own art only he can never become an original author by such means, nor, strictly speaking, so much as acquire the materials by the use of which he may justly attain this character: for the ideas derived from books, that is, from the ideas of others, can by no process of poetical chymistry confer perfect originality. Those ideas which are the intire creation of the mind, or are the result of the poet's own observations and immediately drawn from nature, are the only original ones in the proper sense. A poet who adopts images, who culls out incidents he has met with in the writings of other authors, and who imitates characters which have been portrayed by other poets, or perhaps by historians, cannot surely with any propriety be considered as an *Original*, though he may at the same time discover considerable powers of imagination in adapting those images and incidents, as well as transforming and molding these characters to the general design of his poem. In order to become a poet perfectly original (cf whom only it must be remembered we are here treating) he must, if he should attempt Epic poetry, invent images, incidents, and characters: tradition may indeed supply him with the groundworks of the poem, as it did Homer, but the superstructure must be altogether his own. In executing such a work, what aid can a truly original poet receive from books? If he borrows aid from the performances of others, he is no longer a complete *Original*. To maintain this character throughout he must rely on his own fund: his own plastic imagination must supply him with every thing.

But such intire originality very rarely happens, especially in a modern age. Many of the most splendid images of poetry have been already exhibited, many of the most striking characters in human life have been delineated, and many of the most beautiful objects of nature, and such as are most obvious, have been described by preceding bards. It will be very difficult, therefore, for their successors to select objects which the eye of Fancy hath never explored, and none but a genius uncommonly original can hope to accomplish it.

There are very different degrees of originality in poetry, and several eminent geniuses in this art, possessing a very considerable share of originality themselves, have, however, been contented to imitate the great Father of Epic Poetry in one circumstance or another, partly perhaps through a consciousness of their being unable to produce any thing of a different kind equal to his compositions, partly through a natural tendency to imitate the excellencies they admired in a model rendered venerable by the concurrent testimonies of all ages in his favour, and partly through the real difficulty of attaining complete originality in the province of the *Epopœa* after him. Thus Virgil copied many of the episodes and images of the Mæonian Bard; Tasso imitated some of this character, as well as adopted a part of his imagery; and even the divine Milton condescended, in a very few instances indeed, to imitate this prince of ancient poets in cases where his own genius, left to its native energy and uninfluenced by an acquaintance with the writings of Homer, would have enabled him to equal the Greek poet. An instance of this kind occurs in the end of the fourth book of *Paradise Lost*, where Milton informs us that Satan, while he was preparing for a dreadful combat with his antagonist, fled away upon observing that one of the scales which were suspended from heaven kicked the beam, thereby presaging to him an unfortunate issue of the encounter. By this cool expedient, which was suggested by that passage of Homer in which Jupiter is supposed to weigh the fates of Hector and Achilles in his golden balance, Milton has prevented the consequences of this horrid fray, sacrificed a real excellence to a frivolous imitation, and very much disappointed the eager expectations of the reader. The poet's own genius, had he been unacquainted with the *Iliad*, would naturally have led him to describe those mighty com-

batants engaged in dreadful fight; but a propensity to the
imitation of so eminent an author repressed the native ardor
of his own imagination. This single instance is sufficient to
shew us the effect of literature on the mind of a poet of
original genius, whose exertions it probably will in some instances suppress but cannot in any instance assist. On the
other hand, a poet living in the more early periods of society,
having few or no preceding bards for his models, is in very
little hazard of being betrayed into imitation, which in a
modern age it is so difficult to avoid; but, giving full scope to
the bent of his genius, he is enabled, if he is possessed of a
high degree of this quality, to produce a work completely original. From this train of reasoning it appears that the literature which is acquired from books, especially from the works
of preceding bards, is unfavourable to originality in poetry,
and that poets who live in the first periods of society, who
are destitute of the means of learning, and consequently are
exempted from the possibility of imitation, enjoy peculiar advantages for original composition.

.   .   .

We observed likewise that an exemption from the rules
and restraints of criticism contributed greatly to the more
remarkable display of original poetic genius in the first ages
of society. Every species of original genius delights to range
at liberty, and especially original poetic genius, which abhors
the fetters of criticism, claims the privilege of the freeborn
sons of Nature, and never relinquishes it without the utmost
regret. This noble talent knows no law, and acknowledges
none in the uncultivated ages of the world, excepting its own
spontaneous impulse, which it obeys without control and
without any dread of the censure of critics. The truth is, criticism was never formed into a system till Aristotle, that penetrating, and (to use an expression by which Voltaire characterises Mr. Locke) "methodical genius" arose, who deduced
his poetics not from his own imagination but from his accurate observations on the works of Homer, Sophocles,
Aeschylus, and Euripides. Let us observe the probable and
natural effects which a strict adherence to the rules of criti-

cism will have on original genius in poetry. One obvious effect of it is that it confines the attention to artificial rules, and ties the mind down to the observance of them, perhaps at the very time that the imagination is upon the stretch and grasping at some idea astonishingly great, which, however, it is obliged, though with the utmost reluctance, to quit, being intimated by the apprehension of incurring censure. By this means, the irregular but noble boldness of Fancy is checked, the divine and impetuous ardor of Genius is, we do not say extinguished, but in a great measure suppressed, and many shining excellencies sacrificed to justness of design and regular uniformity of execution.

The candid reader will observe that the question we have been examining is not whether critical learning be upon the whole really useful to an author of genius so as to render his works more perfect and accurate, but what its particular effect will be upon the productions of a genius truly original. We are far from intending to disregard or censure those rules "for writing well," which have been established by sound judgment and an exact discernment of the various species of composition, an attempt that would be equally weak and vain. On the contrary, we profess a reverence for those laws of writing which good sense and the corresponding voice of ages have pronounced important, and we consider them as what ought never to be violated; though with respect to others of a more trivial nature, however binding they may be upon ordinary authors, we can look upon them in no other light than as the frivolous fetters of original genius, to which it has submitted through fear, always improperly, and sometimes ridiculously, but which it may boldly shake off at pleasure, at least whenever it finds them suppressing its exertion, or whenever it can reach an uncommon excellence by its emancipation.

Upon the whole, from the reasons above assigned, it seems evident, that the *early uncultivated* ages of society are most favourable to the display of original genius in poetry; whence it is natural to expect that in such ages the greatest Originals in this art will always arise. Unhappily for us, this point does not admit of proof from an induction of many particulars, for very few original poems of those nations among whom they might have been expected have descended through the vicissitudes and revolutions of so many ages to our times. Most of the monuments of genius, as well as the works of art, have perished in the general wreck of empire, and we can only conjecture the merit of such as are lost from that of the small number of those which remain. While the works of Homer and Ossian, however, are in our hands, these, without any other examples, will be sufficient to establish the truth of the first part of our assertion, that in the early periods of society original poetic genius will in general be exerted in its utmost vigour. Let us now proceed to shew the truth of the second part of it, which was that this quality will seldom appear in a very high degree in cultivated life, and let us assign the reasons of it.

Shakespeare is the only modern author, (whose times, by the way, compared with the present are not very modern) whom, in point of originality, we can venture to compare with those eminent ancient poets above-mentioned. In sublimity of genius indeed, Milton is inferior to neither of them; but it cannot be pretended that he was so complete an Original as the one or the other, since he was indebted to the sacred writings for several important incidents, and for many sublime sentiments to be met with in *Paradise Lost,* not to mention what was formerly observed, that in a few passages he imitated the great *Father of Poetry.* With respect to Shakespeare therefore, admitting him to be a modern author, he is at any rate but a single exception; though indeed his genius was so strangely irregular and so different from that of every other mortal, *Cui nihil simile aut secundum,*[2] that no argument can be drawn from such an example to invalidate our position, since he would probably have discovered the same great and eccentric genius, which we so much admire at present, in any age or country whatever. External causes, though they have great influence on common minds, would have had very little on such a one as Shakespeare's. Let it be confessed, however,

[2] Horace, *Carmina* I. xii. 18. "Nor does anything flourish like or near to [the Creator]."

in justice to our own age, that if it hath not produced such perfect Originals as those above-mentioned, which perhaps may be partly imputed to the influence of causes peculiar to the present period and state of society, yet it hath produced several elegant, and some exalted geniuses in poetry who are distinguished also by a very considerable degree of originality, and such as is rarely to be met with in a modern age. The names of Young, Gray, Ogilvie, Collins, Akenside, and Mason, as they do honour to the present age, will probably be transmitted with reputation to posterity. But since it must be universally allowed that such intire originality as we have shewn to be competent to an uncultivated period hath never yet appeared in modern times, excepting in the single instance above-mentioned, it may be worth the while to inquire into the causes why it so seldom appears, or can be expected to appear, in cultivated life.

If we have successfully investigated the causes why original poetic genius is most remarkably displayed in the uncultivated state of society, we shall probably discover that the chief causes of its being rarely found in the same degree in more civilized ages are the opposites of the former. Thus the first cause we assigned of this quality's being exerted in a higher degree in the earlier periods of social life was deduced from the antiquity of those periods, and the small progress of cultivation in them. One reason, therefore, why it will so seldom appear in a later period must be the disadvantage of living so long after the field of Fancy hath been preoccupied by the more ancient bards. We have already allowed that a truly original poet will strike out a path for himself, but it must likewise be allowed that to do so after his illustrious predecessors will at least be more difficult. To what hath been above advanced on this head we shall here only add a single observation, that should any modern poet with justice claim an equality of merit with the renowned Ancients in point of originality, he would, considering the disadvantages he must labour under, be intitled to a still superior share of reputation. In the meantime we may reasonably infer that the difference in the period of society above-mentioned will always prove unfavourable to the originality of a modern poet, and may be considered as one cause why this quality rarely appears in a very high degree in polished life.

We considered the *simplicity* and *uniformity* of ancient manners as another cause why original genius is exerted in its utmost vigour in the first periods of society. We may remark, on the other hand, that the diversity, dissipation, and excessive refinements of modern manners will naturally prove unfavourable to its exertion in later and more civilized ages. Where there is a great diversity of manners, it will be difficult to mark and to describe the predominating colours. Where Dissipation prevails, Genius is in danger of being drawn within its vortex; and the false refinements in luxury and pleasure, which are characteristical of later ages, though they are consistent enough with, and even productive of the improvement of all the mechanical, and some of the liberal arts, yet they are unfriendly to the two most sublime of all the liberal arts, original poetry and eloquence. An excess of luxury is indeed almost as unfavourable to the cultivation of genius in these as it is to the cultivation of virtue. It enfeebles the mind, as it corrupts the heart, and gradually suppresses that strenuous exertion of the mental faculties by which consummate excellence is to be attained. Poetic genius in particular cannot flourish either in uninterrupted sunshine or in continual shade. It languishes under the blazing ardor of a summer noon, as its buds are blasted by the damp fogs and chilling breath of a winter sky. Poverty is scarce more unfavourable to the display of true poetic genius than excessive affluence is. The former crushes its early and aspiring efforts at once; the latter more slowly, but no less surely, enervates its powers and dissolves them in luxury and pleasure. It was a sensible observation of a French monarch,* though the conjunction be somewhat fantastical, *Poetæ & equi alendi, non saginandi*.[3] The situation most desirable for a poet is the middle state of life. He ought neither to riot in the fulness of opulence, nor to feel the pinching wants of poverty, but to possess that ease and

---

* Charles the Ninth.
[3] Poets and horses are to be nourished, not fattened.

independence which are necessary to unfold the blossoms of genius to the utmost advantage.

The third cause which we assigned of original poetic genius being most remarkably displayed in the uncultivated state of society was the *leisure* and *tranquillity* naturally resulting from such a state. The cause therefore why it seldom appears in a more advanced period will be just the reverse of the former, namely, the activity and ardor, the hurry and bustle observable in modern ages, occasioned by their eager pursuits and the clashing interests of mankind. As the voice of conscience is often drowned amidst the clamours of tumultuous passion, so the flame of genius is frequently smothered by the busy, bustling cares of an active life. The thorny path of ambition and the painful, patient pursuit of gain, are both unfavourable, though not in an equal degree, to its native ardor. The former occasions a distraction, harassment, and anxiety of thought; the latter an intire depression of the powers of imagination. Genius is misled by the one, perverted by the other. Indeed it scarce ever happens that a high degree of this quality is allied to avarice: it seldom stoops to the drudgery of laborious business for the sake of wealth, of which it is naturally very little solicitous, and with the ardent desire of which it is in a great measure incompatible. Ambition, however, has charms capable of seducing it. Honour and power are objects at which it frequently aspires, and they often prove obstructions to its native exertions in its proper sphere by engaging the mind in pursuits which produce embarrassment and perplexity. True Genius, removed from the din and tumult of business and care, shoots up to the noblest height; it spreads forth all its luxuriance in the peaceful vale of rural tranquillity. Its fate in advanced society, and amidst the croud of mankind, is very different. There it meets with many obstacles to check its progress and to discourage its efforts. Exposed to the assaults of malignity and envy, it falls the victim of unmerited calumny, or, intangled in those vexatious pursuits which interrupt the repose of mankind, its ardor is wasted in the tumultuous career of ambition, and its powers absorbed in the unfathomable gulf of sensual indulgence.

The last cause we took notice of as favourable to original poetry in ancient times, while society was yet in its rudest form, was the *want of literature,* and an *exemption* from the *rules of criticism.* It will follow therefore by just consequence that the acquaintance with literature and critical knowledge, which is so considerably diffused in modern times, must be equally unfavourable to the exertion of original poetic genius in those times.

Having considered the effect of these accomplishments upon the mind of an original poet at great length in the former part of this section, we shall conclude with a remark which will exhibit in one view the substance of what hath been more fully discussed in the preceding pages. It is, that though the progress of Literature, Criticism, and Civilization have contributed to unfold the powers and extend the empire of Reason, have taught men to think more justly as well as to express their sentiments with more precision, have had the happiest influence on the arts and sciences in general (since by communicating the discoveries, inventions, and observations of preceding ages they have facilitated the way to future inventions and discoveries, and have been highly conducive to their improvement), yet the art of original poetry, to an excellence in which the wild exuberance and plastic force of Genius are the only requisites, hath suffered, instead of having gained, from the influence of the above-mentioned causes, and will, for the most part, be displayed in its utmost perfection in the early and uncultivated periods of social life.

JOSEPH PRIESTLEY
[1733–1804]

Joseph Priestley, the son of a nonconforming woollen-cloth
dresser of Yorkshire, was one of the great polymaths of the
eighteenth or any other century. By the time he was twenty
he had learned not only the standard Latin and Greek,
but had added French, German, Italian, Arabic, Syriac,
and Chaldee. After three years at the Daventry Nonconformist
Academy he served a small congregation at Needham
Market, then took a post at the Warrington Academy, where
he composed a course of lectures on the theory of language
and universal grammar, published in 1762. It was at
Warrington that he began the scientific explorations for
which he is best known, and in 1766 his researches in
electricity led to his election to the Royal Society.

A Course of Lectures on Oratory and Criticism was
published while Priestley was in the employment of William
Fitzmaurice-Petty, Earl of Shelburne and afterwards Marquis
of Lansdowne, who had in 1772 engaged him as his "literary
companion," librarian, and supervisor of the education
of his sons. Priestley catalogued Shelburne's books and
manuscripts (now the Lansdowne MSS in the British
Museum), preached, published several theological works,
and pursued his scientific studies. In Experiments and
Observations on Different Kinds of Air, published in three
volumes, 1774–1777, he described the discovery of
"dephlogisted air," or oxygen, although it was the French
chemist Lavoisier, whom Priestley met while accompanying
his patron to Paris in 1774, who realized the true nature
of what Priestley had found. After parting from Shelburne

(*who bestowed on him a pension of £150 a year*), *he moved
to Birmingham, where his writings against the government's
American policy combined with his nonconformism incited
a mob to wreck his house and scientific apparatus. In 1794
he moved to New York, where he spent the rest of his
life completing a six volume* General History of the Christian
Church *and continuing his scientific studies.*

*Of ten and one half folio pages of his writings listed
in the catalogue of the British Museum Library, the vast
majority are works of theology and theological disputation,
in which he was constantly engaged. The precise occasion
for his writing the lectures on oratory and criticism is not
clear, but they may derive from his years at Warrington,
or may have been conceived of as part of his duties as tutor
to Shelburne's sons. The lecture reprinted here is interesting
as showing one of the major minds of the age considering
one of the major aesthetic topics of the age, and applying
to that topic the major psychology of the age—Hartley's
association of ideas. The present text is adapted from the first
edition. See S. H. Monk's discussion in* The Sublime.

A COURSE OF LECTURES
ON ORATORY AND CRITICISM
[1777]

LECTURE XX

OF THE SUBLIME

Great objects please us for the same reason that new objects do,
viz. by the exercise they give to our faculties. The mind, as
was observed before, conforming and adapting itself to the
objects to which its attention is engaged, must, as it were,
enlarge itself, to conceive a great object. This requires a considerable *effort of the imagination,* which is also attended
with a pleasing, though perhaps not a distinct and explicit
consciousness of the strength and extent of our own powers.
    As the ideas of great and little are confessedly relative,
and have no existence but what they derive from a comparison
with other ideas; hence, in all sublime conceptions, there is a
kind of secret retrospect to preceding ideas and states of mind.
The sublime, therefore, of all the species of excellence in

composition, requires the most to be intermixed with ideas of an intermediate nature, as these contribute not a little by their contrast to raise and aggrandize ideas which are of a rank superior to themselves. Whenever any object, how great soever, becomes familiar to the mind, and its relations to other objects is no longer attended to, the sublime vanishes. Milton's battle of the angels, after the prelude to the engagement, would have been read with no greater emotions than are excited by the history of a common battle, had not the poet perpetually reinforced his sublime, as it were, by introducing frequent comparisons of those superior beings and their actions with human combatants and human efforts. It is plainly by means of comparison that Horace gives us so sublime an idea of the unconquerable firmness of Cato:

> Et cuncta terrarum subacta,
>   Preter atrocem animum Catonis.[1]

For the same reason a well-conducted *climax* is extremely favourable to the sublime. In this form of a sentence each subsequent idea is compared with the preceding, so that if the former have been represented as large, the latter, which exceeds it, must appear exceedingly large. The effect of this we see in that sublime passage of Shakespeare, inscribed upon his monument in Westminster Abbey:

> The cloud-capt towers, the gorgeous palaces,
> The solemn temples, the great globe itself,
> And all which it inherit, shall dissolve,
> And, like the baseless fabric of a vision,
> Shall leave no wreck behind.

The intermediate ideas which are introduced to increase

---

[1] Horace, *Carmina*, II, i, 21–24:

> audire magnos iam videor duces
> non indecoro pulvere sordidos,
> et cuncta terrarum subacta
> praeter atrocem animum Catonis

> I have a vision of the great commanders
> Jacketed in grime, their uniform of honor,
> And of a world subdued
> Except for Cato's unforgiving soul. (tr. James Michie)

the sublime by means of comparison with the object whose
grandeur is to be enhanced by them ought to be of a similar
nature, because there is no comparison of things dissimilar.
The difference between them should be nothing more than
that of greater and less: and even in this case it often happens
that the contrast of things between which there is a very great
disparity (as will be explained hereafter) produces the *burlesque,* a sentiment of a quite opposite nature to the sublime.
It is not improbable but that many of Mr. Pope's readers may
affix ludicrous ideas to the following lines, which, in his own
conception, and that of his more philosophical readers, were
very sublime.

> Who sees with equal eye, as God of all,
> A hero perish, or a sparrow fall;
> Atoms, or systems, into ruin hurl'd,
> And now a bubble burst, and now a world.
>
> *Essay on Man,* Ep. 1. [87–90]

Sparrows, atoms, and *bubbles,* do not make the same figure
in the eye of the generality of mankind that they do in that
of a philosopher.

It follows from these principles, that no conception can
be sublime which is not *simple.* If any scene present a crowd
of separate objects, the mind views them in succession, though
in a very quick and rapid one, and exerts no extraordinary
effort to conceive and comprehend any of them. However, an
idea that doth consist of parts may appear sublime if the parts
of which it consists be not attended to, but the aggregate of
them all be perceived as one idea. This is easily illustrated by
the ideas of numbers. Very large numbers, as a *thousand, ten
thousand,* and a *hundred thousand* present great and sublime
ideas upon the first naming of them which continues so long
as we endeavour to survey the whole of them at once without
attempting to resolve them into their component parts; but
the arithmetician, who is used to compose and decompose the
largest numbers, is conscious of no sublime idea, even when
he is performing the operations of addition and multiplication
upon them.

Objects of the first rank in point of magnitude, and which

chiefly constitute the sublime of description, are large rivers, high mountains, and extensive plains; the ocean, the clouds, the heavens, and infinite space; also storms, thunder, lightning, volcanos, and earthquakes, in nature; and palaces, temples, pyramids, cities, etc. in the works of men. See a fine enumeration of those scenes of nature which contribute the most to the sublime in Akenside upon this subject.

> ————————————————Who but rather turns
> To heaven's broad fire his unconstrained view,
> Than to the glimmering of a waxen flame?
> Who that, from Alpine heights, his lab'ring eye
> Shoots round the wide horizon, to survey
> The Nile or Ganges roll his wasteful tide,
> Thro' mountains, plains, thro' empires black with shade,
> And continents of sand, will turn his gaze
> To mark the windings of a scanty rill
> That murmurs at his feet? etc.
>
> *Pleasures of the Imagination,* Lib. I [174-183]

But the account here given of the sublime by no means confines it to the ideas of objects which have sensible and corporeal magnitude. *Sentiments* and *passions* are equally capable of it if they relate to great objects, suppose extensive views of things, require a great effort of the mind to conceive them, and produce great effects. Fortitude, magnanimity, generosity, patriotism, and universal benevolence strike the mind with the idea of the sublime. We are conscious that it requires a great effort to exert them, and in all cases when the mind is conscious of a similar exertion of its faculties it refers its sensations to the same class. If the virtues above mentioned were more common the idea of them would not be so sublime.

Who that considers the sentiments of Diomedes, when he prays to Jupiter to *give him day, and then destroy him;* the answer of Alexander to Parmenio (who had told him that he would accept the offers of Darius, if he were Alexander), *and so would I, if I were Parmenio;* and much more the prayer of our Saviour upon the cross, in behalf of his persecutors, *Father, forgive them, for they know not what they do:* who, I say, that attends to these sentiments, can entertain a doubt that they produce feelings similar to those which we receive from the view of grand elevated objects? Or a person need only to read the following passage from Dr. Akenside to be convinced that there is a true sublime in sentiment:

> Say why was man so eminently raised
> Above the vast creation? Why advanced
> Thro' life and death to dart his piercing eye,
> With thoughts beyond the limits of his frame;
> But that th' Omnipotent might send him forth,
> In sight of mortal and immortal powers,
> As on a boundless theatre, to run
> The great career of justice, to exalt
> His gen'rous aim to all diviner deeds? etc.[2]

There is no surer method of discovering those sensations and ideas which are apprehended to be analogous by mankind in general, than by observing the analogies of words in various languages, for the one will correspond to the other. As mankind, when the bulk of any language was invented, were not in a situation to invent superfluous terms, we may naturally conclude they would content themselves with the same term when there was a great resemblance in the ideas they represented, but in no other case if they could avoid so great an inconvenience. If this clue be allowed to be of any use to us in classing our ideas and sensations, there will remain no doubt but that there are a variety of things, not material, which raise sensations similar to those which are excited by objects which have corporeal magnitude and elevation.

How else came a man of distinguished abilities to be called a *great man?* Why do we say that a benevolent man is of an *open* as well as generous temper? and that a covetous man hath a *narrow* soul? How came the epithets *proud, haughty,* and *lofty,* to be synonymous? and how came the terms *superior taste, advancement in honour, head of the table, high note* in music, *ascending series* in numbers, and *high* and *low, near* or *distant,* with respect to *time,* to prevail so generally, and to become so familiar, that the figure is perfectly evanescent? Moreover, how came robes of state to be made large and full,

[2] *Pleasures* . . . I, 151–59.

and thrones to be lofty, etc.? Whence comes it that largeness of size contributes to make a person look majestic? And how came the Scythian ambassadors to be surprized to find Alexander the Great to be a *little* man?

I might mention a great many more terms borrowed from corporeal magnitude, extension and elevation applied to things which have none of those qualities; but these are sufficient to show that the perception of the sentiments, dispositions, and circumstances to which they are applied are attended with a consciousness of a feeling, similar to that which is excited by the views of objects which have the qualities of corporeal magnitude, extension, and elevation; that is, with the sublime.

The sublime of science consists in general and comprehensive theorems, which, by means of very great and extensive consequences, present the idea of *vastness* to the mind. A person of true taste may perceive many instances of genuine sublime in geometry, and even in algebra; and the sciences of natural philosophy and astronomy exhibit the noblest fields of the sublime that the mind of man was ever introduced to. Theorems may also be sublime by their relating to great objects.

For many things which, considered in themselves and abstracted from every thing that is foreign to them, are incapable of the sublime, inspire that sentiment by their association with others that are capable of it. From this source it is that the ideas of wealth, honour, and power, borrow their sublime. It is the causes, the adjuncts, or the effects of these things that are contemplated when they fill and charm the soul. *Wealth* carries with it the idea of a large estate and abundance of every thing that can contribute to the enjoyment of life. From *honour* we never separate the idea of the strength of body, the capacity of the mind, or the great achievements by which it was procured. With these also we join the number of people among whom a person is renowned, the extent of country through which his name spreads, and the length of time to which it extends. To the idea of *power* we join ideas of the good or evil it may produce and of the multitudes which are subject to its control. In the idea of a *conqueror* we may clearly distinguish the idea of a great extent of country sub-

dued; and in the idea of *nobility* that of a long train of illustrious ancestors. A similar analysis would show us the sublime
of *friendship, patriotism,* and many other abstract ideas.

The grandeur of a palace, besides what it derives from
its exceeding other houses in bulk, is derived from the ideas
of the labour, expence, length of time, and number of persons
necessary to the erection of it; and from ideas of the wealth,
honour, and power of him who inhabits it. Celebrated buildings and cities *in ruins,* along with these ideas, present that of
the length of time that hath elapsed since they flourished, and
the whole sensation is greatly magnified by a comparison of
their former magnificence with their present desolation. The
grandeur and peculiar awfulness with which we are struck
upon the view of a *temple* is, in a great measure, derived from
the ideas we have annexed to it of the power of the Deity to
whom it is sacred, as all that is sublime in the idea of a *senate-
house,* or other public building, arises from the idea of the
use to which it is appropriated.

The *contempt* of power, wealth, and grandeur is more
sublime than the *possession* of them; because, after a view of
those great objects, it presents us with the view of a mind
above them. So that it is not true that "nothing is great the
contempt of which is great."

Though in some cases of this species of transfered sublimity the analysis of a complex idea should present no one
idea which, singly taken, could be called sublime, yet, so long
as those ideas continue separately indistinguishable, the mind
perceives not a number of small objects, but one great one, as
in the case before explained of the sublime of numbers.

As most of our emotions are of a complex nature, we are
in great danger, unless we be extremely attentive, of making
mistakes in the distribution and analysis of them. Hence emotions of *terror* have been often classed with the sublime. But
terror is a mixed sensation composed of the very different
sensations of fear and grandeur, to the latter of which it owes
all its sublimity. For, when we are in a situation in which we
have nothing to fear, the sight of a monstrous beast, of a giant,
or of the sea in a storm, etc. presents little more than the pure
sublime heightened by the secret pleasure we taken in the idea

of our own security. The pure sublime partakes nothing of
fear or of any other painful emotion.

Moreover, the pure sublime, by strongly engaging, tends
to fix the attention and to keep the mind in a kind of awful
stillness, whereas it is of the nature of every species of the
pathetic to throw it into an *agitation*. Hence the sensations we
feel from *darkness* and *profound silence*, resembling the stillness the mind is thrown into when the attention is strongly
fixed by a sublime object, partake of the nature of the sublime,
as we may perceive in the following excellent passage of
Dr. Young.

> Night, sable goddess, from her ebon throne,
> In rayless majesty, now stretches forth
> Her leaden sceptre o'er a slumb'ring world.
> Silence how dead! and darkness how profound!
> Nor eye nor list'ning ear an object finds.
> Creation sleeps. 'Tis as the general pulse
> Of life stood still, and Nature made a pause—
> An awful pause, prophetic of her end.
> And let her prophecy be soon fulfill'd:
> Fate, drop the curtain. I can lose no more.
>
> *Night Thoughts*, I. [18–27]

Hence also deep and slow notes in music bear a nearer
relation to the sublime than shrill and quick sounds.

It may be observed that the account here given of the
Sublime confines it to the *sentiment*. However, as the term
(which hath been used in a more vague sense than almost any
other term in criticism) is frequently applied to *language*, I
shall briefly explain how the sublime is affected by language.

Ideas in themselves sublime may entirely lose that quality
by being expressed in terms which have connexions with trivial
and mean objects, or in metaphors borrowed from such objects. In this case the secondary associations which accompany
those words are transferred upon the object described by them,
and destroy the sublime they would otherwise have. Though,
therefore, in general, the plainest terms are the most favourable
to the sublime, as they exhibit the most just and the strongest
idea of the object, yet every term, however plain and intelligible, that hath ever had the least connexion with mean subjects,
or even which hath been chiefly used by persons of a low

and illiberal class of life, should be carefully avoided. What can be more sublime than the following passage in the Psalms: "He looketh on the earth, and it trembleth. He toucheth the hills, and they smoke"? But it is greatly lowered by some ludicrous images in the following paraphrase:

> The hills forget they're fix'd, and in their fright
> Cast off their weight, and ease themselves for flight.
> The woods, with terror wing'd, outfly the wind,
> And leave the heavy, panting hills behind.

On the other hand, the *mock-heroic* is introduced when words which have generally been annexed to great and important subjects are used to express mean or trivial things. The opposition of ideas so contrary to one another makes a high burlesque.

Sometimes a periphrasis comes seasonably in aid of the sublime by giving the mind an opportunity to dwell upon the idea, and see the whole extent of it. Thus the phrase, *Nine times the space that measures day and night to mortal men,* in Milton, suits the following sublime passage in which it is introduced much better than if he had barely said so many *days.* The former mode of expression, as it were, detains the idea of the *angels rolling in the fiery gulph* longer in the mind, during which time our wonder and astonishment are continually rising higher and higher.

> ———————————Him th' Almighty Power
> Hurl'd headlong flaming from th' ethereal sky,
> With hideous ruin, and combustion, down
> To bottomless perdition, there to dwell
> In adamantine chains and penal fire,
> Who durst defy th' Omnipotent to arms.
> Nine times the space that measures day and night
> To mortal men, he with his horrid crew
> Lay vanquish'd, rolling in the fiery gulph,
> Confounded, though immortal.
> > *Paradise Lost,* Book I. [44–53]

Proper names of great objects are often preferable to general terms, as they realize the ideas and fix the attention to them. Thus, to mention the *Alps,* the *Andes,* or *Teneriffe* presents a greater idea than saying *very high mountains;* and to say, the *Nile*, the *Ganges*, or the *La Plata* is to speak more magnificently than to say great rivers only. Thus, the simple and sublime Ossian affects the imagination of his reader much more strongly by the hill of *Cromla*, the *waves of Inistore*, the reeds of the *lake of Lægo* than he could have done by the use of any more general and abstract terms. This effect would be more sensible if we were acquainted with the objects introduced in this manner.

Next to the *pathetic*, of all the excellencies of good composition the *sublime* promises the most lasting reputation to an author. Compositions which are calculated only to please and to divert are beings of a day. Few of them, even by the favour of a very extraordinary coincidence of circumstances, reach posterity in comparison of those which shake and which elevate our souls. Let us only look into our breasts, and we shall find that we are very differently affected to the writer who pleases the imagination, and to the poet or orator who either raises and enlarges our conceptions, or who thoroughly interests our passions. The former we may admire, but we may also soon forget. Our esteem for the latter rises to reverence, and when the pathetic and the sublime are joined (as they are capable of the most intimate union, and are perhaps never found in a very high degree entirely separate) they produce the strongest and the most lasting attachment.

A genius formed for the sublime is a mind which is naturally disposed to take the most extensive views of things, whose attention is turned to view every thing in the grandest and noblest point of light, whereas other minds are more inclined to attend to what is little and beautiful in the objects they view. And as every thing we are conversant with hath various, and very different properties, every mind hath an opportunity of indulging its own taste by contemplating those forms of things which afford it the most pleasing gratification.

I cannot conclude this article without observing that instances of the true sublime abound no where more than in the Scriptures. Never were grander ideas presented to the human mind than we find in the representations of the Divine Being in Isaiah, particularly chapter XL, in the book of Job, in several places in the Psalms, and in the writings of Moses.

HUGH BLAIR
[1718–1800]

A Scottish Divine (and one of the minor characters in
Boswell's Life of Johnson), Blair proceeded through various
advancements to an appointment to the High Church in
Edinburgh. In 1759 he began to read lectures on composition
in the University, and the next year he was made Professor
of Rhetoric. In 1762 a Regius Professorship of Rhetoric and
Belles Lettres was founded, to which Blair was appointed
at a salary of £70 a year. It was for his duties in this post that
he composed the Lectures on Rhetoric and Belles Lettres,
which he apparently read with virtually no change until
their publication in 1783.

Blair was a member of the distinguished circle of
literati which flourished in Edinburgh during the later
eighteenth century—Hume, Adam Smith, Adam Ferguson
the philosopher, and the historian William Robertson
among others. It was these men who encouraged James
Macpherson to publish the Ossian poems, upon which
Blair wrote an adulatory Dissertation in 1763.

Harold F. Harding says, "As a writer on Rhetoric
[Blair] was neither original, comprehensive, nor profound,"
and Hipple remarks that, "his aesthetic doctrine is less a
system than a conspectus of eighteenth-century opinion."
It is exactly for this reason that Blair is interesting, for his
was one of the most influential books on rhetoric and
composition during the entire nineteenth century, appearing
in many editions and in many forms at least until 1911,
when an abridgement was still used as the text for an
advertised correspondence course. In the United States the

*book was regularly published for a century after its first
appearance in Philadelphia in 1784. The nature of the
interest in Blair may perhaps be partially illustrated by the
appearance in 1810 of* The Beauties of Blair *and in 1819 of*
Sentimental Beauties from the Writings of the Late Dr.
Hugh Blair—*beauties extracted in part from Blair's sermons,
some of which Johnson had praised highly.*

*Blair's view of the Sublime may not mark a great advance
over previous accounts, yet it is worth consideration as
further evidence of the intense mid-century speculation
on the subject, which actually did not progress much beyond
the point to which Blair took it. The present text is adapted
from that of the first edition. This has been reprinted in
facsimile by The Southern Illinois University Press,
Carbondale, 1965, with an introduction by Harold F.
Harding. See also:*

Chapman, R. W.: "Blair on Ossian," RES VII (1931),
      80–83.
Cohen, Herman: "Hugh Blair's Theory of Taste," Quarterly
      Journal of Speech, XLIV (1958), 265–74.
Schmitz, Robert M.: Hugh Blair, New York, 1948.

LECTURES ON RHETORIC AND BELLES LETTRES
[1783]

LECTURE IV

THE SUBLIME IN WRITING

Having treated of Grandeur or Sublimity in external objects, the way seems now to be cleared for treating, with more advantage, of the description of such objects, or of what is called the Sublime in Writing. . . .

Many critical terms have unfortunately been employed in a sense too loose and vague; none more so than that of the Sublime. Every one is acquainted with the character of Caesar's *Commentaries*, and of the style in which they are written— a style remarkably pure, simple, and elegant, but the most remote from the Sublime of any of the classical authors. Yet this author has a German critic, Johannes Gulielmus Bergerus, who wrote no longer ago than the year 1720, pitched upon as the perfect model of the Sublime, and has composed a quarto volume entitled *De naturali pulchritudine Orationis,* the express intention of which is to shew that Caesar's *Commentaries* contain the most complete exemplification of all Longinus's rules relating to Sublime Writing. This I mention as strong proof of the confused ideas which have prevailed concerning this subject. The true sense of Sublime Writing, undoubtedly, is such a description of objects, or exhibition of sentiments, which are in themselves of a Sublime nature, as shall give us strong impressions of them. But there is another very indefinite, and very improper, sense which has been too often put upon it when it is applied to signify any remarkable and distinguishing excellency of composition, whether it raise in us the ideas of grandeur, or those of gentleness, elegance, or any other sort of beauty. In this sense, Caesar's *Commentaries* may, indeed, be termed sublime, and so may many sonnets, pastorals, and love elegies, as well as Homer's *Iliad.* But this evidently confounds the use of words, and marks no one species, or character, of composition whatever.

I am sorry to be obliged to observe that the Sublime is too often used in this last and improper sense by the celebrated critic Longinus, in his treatise on this subject. He sets out, indeed, with describing it in its just and proper meaning, as something that elevates the mind above itself, and fills it with high conceptions and a noble pride. But from this view of it he frequently departs, and substitutes in the place of it whatever, in any strain of composition, pleases highly. Thus, many of the passages which he produces as instances of the Sublime, are merely elegant, without having the most distant relation to proper Sublimity, witness Sappho's famous Ode, on which he descants at considerable length. He points out five sources of the Sublime. The first is boldness or grandeur in the thoughts, the second is the Pathetic; the third, the proper application of figures; the fourth, the use of tropes and beautiful expressions; the fifth, musical structure and arrangement of words. This is the plan of one who was writing a treatise of rhetoric, or of the beauties of writing in general, not of the Sublime in particular. For these five heads, only the two first have any peculiar relation to the Sublime; boldness and grandeur in the thoughts, and, in some instances, the Pathetic, or strong exertions of passion: The other three, tropes, figures, and musical arrangement, have no more relation to the Sublime than to other kinds of good writing; perhaps less to the Sublime than to any other species whatever, because it requires less the assistance of ornament. From this it appears that clear and precise ideas on this head are not to be expected from that writer. I would not, however, be understood as if I meant, by this censure, to represent his treatise as of small value. I know no critic, antient or modern, that discovers a more lively relish of the beauties of fine writing than Longinus; and he has also the merit of being himself an excellent, and in several passages, a truly Sublime writer. But, as his work has been generally considered as a standard on this subject, it was incumbent on me to give my opinion concerning the benefit to be derived from it. It deserves to be consulted not so much for distinct instruction concerning the Sublime, as for excellent general ideas concerning beauty in writing.

I return now to the proper and natural idea of the Sublime in composition. The foundation of it must always be laid in the nature of the object described. Unless it be such an object as, if presented to our eyes, if exhibited to us in reality, would raise ideas of that elevating, that awful, and magnificent kind which we call Sublime, the description, however finely drawn, is not entitled to come under this class. This excludes all objects that are merely beautiful, gay, or elegant. In the next place, the object must not only, in itself, be Sublime, but it must be set before us in a light as is most proper to give us a clear and full impression of it; it must be described with strength, with conciseness, and simplicity. This depends, principally, upon the lively impression which the poet or orator has of the object which he exhibits, and upon his being deeply affected and warmed by the Sublime idea which he would convey. If his own feeling be languid he can never inspire us with any strong emotion. Instances, which are extremely necessary on this subject, will clearly show the importance of all those requisites which I have just now mentioned.

It is, generally speaking, among the most antient authors

that we are to look for the most striking instances of the
Sublime. I am inclined to think that the early ages of the world,
and the rude unimproved state of society, are peculiarly
favourable to the strong emotions of Sublimity. The genius
of men is then much turned to admiration and astonishment.
Meeting with many objects, to them new and strange, their
imagination is kept glowing and their passions are often raised
to the utmost. They think and express themselves boldly and
without restraint. In the progress of society, the genius and
manners of men undergo a change more favourable to accuracy
than to strength or Sublimity.

Of all writings, antient or modern, the Sacred Scriptures
afford us the highest instances of the Sublime. The descriptions
of the Deity, in them, are wonderfully noble; both from the
grandeur of the object, and the manner of representing it. . . .
The noted instance given by Longinus from Moses, "God said,
let there be light; and there was light," is not liable to the
censure which I passed on some of his instances of being
foreign to the subject. It belongs to the true Sublime, and the
Sublimity of it arises from the strong conception it gives of an
exertion of power, producing its effect with the utmost speed
and facility. . . .

            .   .   .

Homer is a poet who, in all ages and by all critics, has
been greatly admired for Sublimity, and he owes much of
his grandeur to that native and unaffected simplicity which
characterises his manner. His descriptions of hosts engaging,
the animation, the fire, and rapidity which he throws into his
battles, present to every reader of the *Iliad* frequent instances
of Sublime Writing. His introduction of the Gods tends often
to heighten, in a high degree, the majesty of his warlike scenes.
Hence Longinus bestows such high and just commendations on
that passage in the XVth book of the *Iliad* where Neptune,
when preparing to issue forth into the engagement, is described
as shaking the mountains with his steps and driving his chariot
along the ocean. Minerva, arming herself for fight in the Vth
book, and Apollo, in the XVth, leading on the Trojans, and
flashing terror with his Ægis on the face of the Greeks, are

similar instances of great Sublimity added to the description of battles by the appearances of those celestial beings. In the XXth book, where all the Gods take part in the engagement according as they severally favour either the Grecians or the Trojans, the poet seems to put forth one of his highest efforts, and the description rises into the most awful magnificence. All nature is represented as in commotion. Jupiter thunders in the heavens; Neptune strikes the earth with his trident; the ships, the city, and the mountain shake; the earth trembles to its centre; Pluto starts from his throne, in dread lest the secrets of the infernal region should be laid open to the view of mortals. . . .

.   .   .

The works of Ossian (as I have elsewhere shewn)[1] abound with examples of the Sublime. The subjects of that author, and the manner in which he writes, are particularly favourable to it. He possesses all the plain and venerable manner of the antient times. He deals in no superfluous or gaudy ornaments, but throws forth his images with a rapid conciseness which enable them to strike the mind with the greatest force. Among poets of more polished times, we are to look for the graces of correct writing, for just proportion of parts, and skillfully conducted narration. In the midst of smiling scenery and pleasureable themes, the gay and the beautiful will appear, undoubtedly, to more advantage. But amidst the rude scenes of nature and of society such as Ossian describes; amidst rocks, and torrents, and whirlwinds, and battles, dwells the Sublime, and naturally associates itself with that grave and solemn spirit which distinguishes the author of Fingal. "As autumn's dark storms pour from two echoing hills, so toward each other approached the heroes. As two dark streams from high rocks meet and mix, and roar on the plain; loud, rough, and dark, in battle, met Lochlin and Inisfail; chief mixed his strokes with chief, and man with man. Steel clanging sounded on steel. Helmets are cleft on high; blood bursts, and smokes around. As the troubled noise of the ocean when roll the waves on

[1] In *Critical Dissertation on the Poems of Ossian,* 1763.

high; as the last peal of the thunder of heaven; such is the noise of battle. The groan of the people spread over the hills. It was like the thunder of night, when the cloud bursts on Cona, and a thousand ghosts shriek at once on the hollow wind." Never were images of more awful Sublimity employed to heighten the terror of battle.

I have produced these instances in order to demonstrate how essential conciseness and simplicity are to Sublime Writing. Simplicity I place in opposition to studied and profuse ornament, and conciseness to superfluous expression. The reason why a defect, either in conciseness or simplicity, is hurtful in a peculiar manner to the Sublime I shall endeavour to explain. The emotion occasioned in the mind by some great or noble object raises it considerably above its ordinary pitch. A sort of enthusiasm is produced, extremely agreeable while it lasts, but from which the mind is tending every moment to fall down into its ordinary situation. Now when an author has brought us, or is attempting to bring us, into this state, if he multiplies words unnecessarily, if he deck the Sublime object which he presents to us round and round with glittering ornaments, nay, if he throws in any one decoration that sinks in the least below the capital image, that moment he alters the key; he relaxes the tension of the mind; the strength of the feeling is emasculated; the Beautiful may remain, but the Sublime is gone.—When Julius Caesar said to the pilot who was afraid to put to sea with him in a storm, "Quid times? Cæsarem vehis," [2] we are struck with the daring magnanimity of one relying with such confidence on his cause and his fortune. These few words convey every thing necessary to give us the impression full. . . .

.   .   .

On account of the great importance of simplicity and conciseness, I conceive rhyme in English verse to be, if not inconsistent with the Sublime, at least very unfavourable to it. The constrained elegance of this kind of verse, and studied

---

[2] Variously quoted: *Caesarem vehis, Caesarisque fortunam; Caesarem portas et fortunam ejus.* Plutarch, *Caesar,* 38: "What do you fear? You carry Caesar and his fortune."

smoothness of the sounds answering regularly to each other at the end of the line, though they be quite consistent with gentle emotions, yet weaken the native force of Sublimity; besides, that the superfluous words which the poet is often obliged to introduce in order to fill up the rhyme tends farther to enfeeble it. Homer's description of the nod of Jupiter, as shaking the heavens, has been admired in all ages as highly Sublime. Literally translated, it runs thus: "He spoke, and bending his sable brows, gave the awful nod; while he shook the celestial locks of his immortal head, all Olympus was shaken." Mr. Pope translates it thus:

> He spoke; and awful bends his sable brows,
> Shakes his ambrosial curls, and gives the nod,
> The stamp of fate, and sanction of a God.
> High Heaven with trembling the dread signal took,
> And all Olympus to its centre shook.[3]

The image is spread out, and attempted to be beautified, but it is, in truth, weakened. The third line—"The stamp of fate, and sanction of a God," is merely expletive and introduced for no other reason but to fill up the rhyme, for it interrupts the description and clogs the image. For the same reason, out of mere compliance with the rhyme, Jupiter is represented as shaking his locks before he gives the nod;—"Shakes his ambrosial curls, and gives the nod," which is trifling and without meaning. Whereas, in the original, the hair of his head shaken is the effect of his nod, and makes a happy picturesque circumstance in the description.

The boldness, freedom, and variety of our blank verse is infinitely more favourable than rhyme to all kinds of Sublime poetry. The fullest proof of this is afforded by Milton, an author whose genius led him eminently to the Sublime. The whole first and second books of *Paradise Lost* are continued instances of it. Take only for an example, the following noted description of Satan, after his fall, appearing at the head of the infernal hosts:

> ————He, above the rest,
> In shape and gesture proudly eminent,

[3] Pope's *Iliad*, I, 683–87.

Stood like a tower: his form had not yet lost
All her original brightness, nor appeared
Less than archangel ruined; and the excess
Of glory obscured: As when the sun, new risen,
Looks through the horizontal misty air,
Shorn of his beams; or, from behind, the moon,
In dim eclipse, disastrous twilight sheds
On half the nations, and with fear of change
Perplexes monarchs. Darken'd so, yet shone
Above them all th' Archangel.————————[4]

Here concur a variety of sources of the Sublime: The principal
object eminently great; a high superior nature, fallen indeed,
but erecting itself against distress; the grandeur of the principal object heightened, by associating it with so noble an
idea as that of the sun suffering an eclipse; this picture shaded
with all those images of change and trouble, of darkness and
terror, which coincide so finely with the Sublime emotion;
and the whole expressed in a style and verification, easy, natural, and simple, but magnificent.

I have spoken of simplicity and conciseness as essential
to Sublime Writing. In my general description of it, I mentioned Strength as another necessary requisite. The Strength
of description arises, in a great measure, from a simple
conciseness; but it supposes also something more, namely,
a proper choice of circumstances in the description, so as
to exhibit the object in its full and most striking point of
view. For every object has several faces, so to speak, by which
it may be presented to us, according to the circumstances with
which we surround it; and it will appear eminently Sublime,
or not, in proportion as all these circumstances are happily
chosen and of a Sublime kind. Here lies the great art of the
writer, and indeed, the great difficulty of Sublime description.
If the description is too general and divested of circumstances,
the object appears in a faint light; it makes a feeble impression,
or no impression at all on the reader. At the same time, if
any trivial or improper circumstances are mingled, the whole
is degraded.

A storm or tempest, for instance, is a Sublime object in

[4] *Paradise Lost,* I, 589–600.

nature. But, to render it Sublime in description, it is not enough either to give us mere general expressions concerning the violence of the tempest, or to describe its common, vulgar effects in overthrowing trees and houses. It must be painted with such circumstances as fill the mind with great and awful ideas. This is very happily done by Virgil, in the following passage:

> Ipse Pater, media nimborum in nocte, corusca
> Fulmina molitur dextra; quo maxima motu
> Terra tremit; fugere feræ, & mortalia corda,
> Per gentes humilis stravit pavor: Ille, flagranti
> Aut Atho, aut Rhodopen, aut alta Ceraunia telo
> Dejicit.*   *Georg.* I [328–333]

Every circumstance in this noble description is the production of an imagination heated and astonished with the grandeur of the object. If there be any defect, it is in the words immediately following those I have quoted: "Ingeminant Austri, et densissimus imber," [5] where the transition is made too hastily, I am afraid, from the preceding Sublime images to a thick shower and the blowing of the south wind; and shews how difficult it frequently is to descend with grace without seeming to fall.

The high importance of the rule which I have been now giving, concerning the proper choice of circumstances when description is meant to be Sublime, seems to me not to have

---

* The Father of the Gods his glory shrouds,
  Involv'd in tempests, and a night of clouds;
  And from the middle darkness flashing out,
  By fits he deals his fiery bolts about.
  Earth feels the motions of her angry God, ⎫
  Her intrails tremble, and her mountains nod, ⎬
  And flying beasts in forests seek abode. ⎭
  Deep horror seizes every human breast;
  Their pride is humbled, and their fears confest;
  While he, from high his rolling thunders throws,
  And fires the mountains with repeated blows;
  The rocks are from their old foundations rent;
  The winds redouble, and the rains augment.
                                            Dryden

[5] *Georgic* I, 333: Dryden: "The winds redouble, and the rains augment."

been sufficiently attended to. It has, however, such a foundation in nature, as renders the least deflexion from it fatal.
When a writer is aiming at the beautiful only, his descriptions
may have improprieties in them and yet be beautiful still.
Some trivial or misjudged circumstances can be overlooked by
the reader; they make only the difference of more or less; the
gay, or pleasing emotion, which he has raised subsists still.
But the case is quite different with the Sublime. There, one
trifling circumstance, one mean idea, is sufficient to destroy the
whole charm. This is owing to the nature of the emotion aimed
at by Sublime description, which admits of no mediocrity and
cannot subsist in a middle state, but must either highly transport us, or, if unsuccessful in the execution, leave us greatly
disgusted and displeased. We attempt to rise along with the
writer; the imagination is awakened and put upon the stretch;
but it requires to be supported; and if, in the midst of its
effort, you desert it unexpectedly, down it comes with a painful shock. When Milton, in his battle of the angels, describes
them as tearing up the mountains and throwing them at one
another, there are, in his description, as Mr. Addison has
observed, no circumstances but what are properly Sublime:

> From their foundations loos'ning to and fro,
> They plucked the seated hills, with all their load,
> Rocks, waters, woods; and by the shaggy tops
> Uplifting, bore them in their hands.————[6]

Whereas Claudian, in a fragment upon the war of the giants,
has contrived to render this idea of their throwing the mountains, which is in itself so grand, burlesque and ridiculous by
this single circumstance, of one of his giants with the mountain Ida upon his shoulders and a river, which flowed from
the mountain, running down along the giant's back as he held
it up in that posture. . . . Such instances shew how much the
Sublime depends upon a just selection of circumstances, and
with how great care every circumstance must be avoided
which, by bordering in the least upon the mean, or even upon
the gay or the trifling, alters the tone of the emotion.

[6] *Paradise Lost,* VI, 643–46.

If it shall now be enquired, What are the proper sources of the Sublime? My answer is, That they are to be looked for everywhere in nature. It is not by hunting after tropes and figures and rhetorical assistances that we can expect to produce it. No: it stands clear, for the most part, of these laboured refinements of art. It must come unsought, if it come at all, and be the natural offspring of a strong imagination. . . . Wherever a great and awful object is presented in nature, or a very magnanimous and exalted affection of the human mind is displayed, thence, if you can catch the impression strongly and exhibit it warm and glowing, you may draw the Sublime. These are its only proper sources. In judging of any striking beauty in composition, whether it is, or is not, to be referred to this class, we must attend to the nature of the emotion which it raises; and only if it be of that elevating, solemn, and awful kind which distinguishes this feeling, we can pronounce it Sublime.

From the account which I have given of the nature of the Sublime, it clearly follows that it is an emotion which can never be long protracted. The mind by no force of genius can be kept for any considerable time so far raised above its common tone, but will, of course, relax into its ordinary situation.

Neither are the abilities of any human writer sufficient to supply a continued run of unmixed Sublime conceptions. The utmost we can expect is that this fire of imagination should sometimes flash upon us like lightning from heaven, and then disappear. In Homer and Milton this effulgence of genius breaks forth more frequently and with greater lustre than in most authors. Shakespeare also rises often into the true Sublime. But no author whatever is Sublime throughout. Some, indeed, there are, who, by a strength and dignity in their conceptions and a current of high ideas that runs through their whole composition, preserve the reader's mind always in a tone nearly allied to the Sublime; for which reason they may, in a limited sense, merit the name of continued Sublime writers; and, in this case, we may justly place Demosthenes and Plato.

As for what is called the Sublime style, it is, for the most part, a very bad one, and has no relation whatever to the real

Sublime. Persons are apt to imagine that magnificent words, accumulated epithets, and a certain swelling kind of expression, by rising above what is usual or vulgar, contributes to, or even forms, the Sublime. Nothing can be more false. In all the instances of Sublime Writing which I have given, nothing of this kind appears. "God said, Let there be light, and there was light." This is striking and Sublime. But put it into what is commonly called the Sublime style: "The Sovereign Arbiter of nature, by the potent energy of a single word, commanded the light to exist," and, as Boileau has well observed, the style indeed is raised, but the thought is fallen. In general, in all good writing, the Sublime lies in the thought, not in the words; and when the thought is truly noble it will, for the most part, clothe itself in a native dignity of language. The Sublime, indeed, rejects mean, low, or trivial expressions; but it is equally an enemy to such as are turgid. The main secret of being Sublime is to say great things in few and plain words. It will be found to hold, without exception, that the most Sublime authors are the simplest in their style; and wherever you find a writer who affects a more than ordinary pomp and parade of words, and is always endeavouring to magnify his subject by epithets, there you may immediately suspect that, feeble in sentiment, he is studying to support himself by mere expression.

The same unfavourable judgment we must pass on all that laboured apparatus with which some writers introduce a passage or description which they intend shall be Sublime, calling on their readers to attend, invoking their Muse, or breaking forth into general, unmeaning exclamations concerning the greatness, terribleness, or majesty of the object which they are to describe. Mr. Addison, in his Campaign, has fallen into an error of this kind, when about to describe the battle of Blenheim.

> But O! my Muse! what numbers wilt thou find
> To sing the furious troops in battle joined?
> Methinks, I hear the drum's tumultous sound,
> The victor's shouts, and dying groans, confound; etc.[7]

---

[7] Addison, *The Campaign* (1705), 273–76.

Introductions of this kind are a forced attempt in a writer to spur up himself, and his reader, when he finds his imagination flagging in vigour. It is like taking artificial spirits in order to supply the want of such as are natural. By this observation, however, I do not mean to pass a general censure on Mr. Addison's *Campaign*, which, in several places, is far from wanting merit; and in particular, the noted comparison of his hero to the angel who rides in the whirlwind and directs the storm is a truly Sublime image.

The faults opposite to the Sublime are chiefly two: the Frigid and the Bombast. The Frigid consists in degrading an object or sentiment which is Sublime in itself, by our mean conception of it, or by our weak, low, and childish description of it. This betrays entire absence, or at least great poverty of genius. Of this there are abundance of examples, and these commented upon with much humour, in the Treatise on the Art of Sinking, in Dean Swift's works, the instances taken chiefly from Sir Richard Blackmore. . . . The Bombast lies in forcing an ordinary or trivial object out of its rank, and endeavouring to raise it into the Sublime; or in attempting to exalt a Sublime object beyond all natural and reasonable bounds. Into this error, which is but too common, writers of genius may sometimes fall by unluckily losing sight of the true point of the Sublime. This is also called fustian, or rant. Shakespeare, a great, but incorrect genius, is not unexceptionable here. Dryden and Lee, in their tragedies, abound with it.

Thus far of the Sublime, of which I have treated fully because it is so capital an excellency in fine writing, and because clear and precise ideas on this head are, as far as I know, not to be met with in critical writers.

SIR JOSHUA REYNOLDS
[1723–1792]

_____

In 1759 Reynolds composed three essays on painting for
Johnson's Idler (nos. 76, 79, and 82), which adumbrate
much of what he was later to say in the remarkable series
of fifteen Discourses which he delivered before the Royal
Academy between 1769 and 1790. Reynolds had been one
of the founders of the Academy in 1768 and, except for a
period of one month, served as its president until his death,
making the biennial awards ceremonies the occasions for
his addresses.

These Discourses represent an articulated but not a
constant or always entirely self-consistent aesthetic theory.
The earlier discourses, through the twelfth, display a certain
unity of doctrine—Reynolds discusses the concepts of
"Nature" and of "imitation" in terms recognizably
Aristotelian and in the best sense of the term "neoclassic."
The Third Discourse is central for this exposition. In the
Seventh Discourse, Reynolds discusses "taste," again in terms
recognizable to a student of earlier eighteenth-century
speculation on the subject: "We may therefore conclude,
that the real substance, as it may be called, of what goes
under the name of taste, is fixed and established in the nature
of things; that there are certain and regular causes by which
the imagination and passions of men are affected; and that
the knowledge of these causes is acquired by a laborious
and diligent investigation of nature."

The Eighth Discourse, with its emphasis upon "the
passions and affections of the mind," marks a turning of
direction, the end of which can be seen in Discourse XIII.

As early as the third of the Idler essays, Reynolds had developed some ideas on the subjective reaction of the perceiver to art, suggesting that we intuitively apprehend what is pleasing to us, for whatever reason of custom, and call it beautiful. By 1786 Reynolds was prepared, in effect, to abandon a priori standards altogether (see the sixth paragraph of the anthologized discourse, beginning, "All theories which attempt to direct or to control the art, upon any principles falsely called rational . . ."), and place his trust in "what is natural for the imagination to be delighted with"—that is, place his trust in art applying itself "like music (and I believe we may add poetry), directly to the imagination, without the intervention of any kind of imitation," the function of art being "to gratify the mind by realizing and embodying what never existed but in the imagination." Mad as Reynolds might no doubt have thought their works, one needs no further aesthetic theory to justify the poetry of Coleridge or the painting of Picasso.

F. W. Hilles has written on The Literary Career of Sir Joshua Reynolds (Cambridge, 1936), and has also edited Reynolds' letters (Cambridge, 1929). The Discourses have been interestingly edited with introduction and notes by Roger Fry (1905), and most recently by Robert R. Work (San Marino, 1959). See also:

Bredvold, Louis I.: "The Tendency Towards Platonism in Neo-Classical Esthetics," ELH, I (1934), 91–119. [Answered by Hoyt Trowbridge, "Platonism and Sir Joshua Reynolds," English Studies, XXI (1939), 1–7.]

Burke, Joseph: Hogarth and Reynolds: a Contrast in English Art Theory, Oxford, 1943.

Goldstein, Harvey D.: "Ut Poesis Pictura: Reynolds on Imitation and Imagination," Eighteenth-Century Studies I (1968), 213–35.

Hipple, Walter J., Jr.: "General and Particular in the Discourses of Sir Joshua Reynolds: a Study in Method," Journal of Aesthetics and Art Criticism, XV (1957), 340–49.

Macklem, Michael: "Reynolds and the Ambiguities of Neo-Classical Criticism," PQ, XXXI (1952), 383–98.

DISCOURSE XIII

DELIVERED TO THE STUDENTS
OF THE ROYAL ACADEMY, ON THE
DISTRIBUTION OF THE PRIZES,
DECEMBER 11, 1786

*Art Not Merely Imitation, but Under the Direction of the
Imagination.—In, What Manner Poetry, Painting, Acting,
Gardening, and Architecture Depart from Nature*

To discover beauties, or to point out faults in the works of
celebrated masters, and to compare the conduct of one artist
with another, is certainly no mean or inconsiderable part of
criticism; but this is still no more than to know the art through
the artist. This test of investigation must have two capital
defects; it must be narrow, and it must be uncertain. To enlarge the boundaries of the art of painting, as well as to fix
its principles, it will be necessary that that art and those
principles should be considered in their correspondence with
the principles of the other arts which, like this, address themselves primarily and principally to the imagination. When
those connected and kindred principles are brought together
to be compared, another comparison will grow out of this;

that is, the comparison of them all with those of human nature, from whence arts derive the materials upon which they are to produce their effects.

When this comparison of art with art, and of all arts with the nature of man, is once made with success, our guiding lines are as well ascertained and established as they can be in matters of this description.

This, as it is the highest style of criticism, is at the same time the soundest; for it refers to the eternal and immutable nature of things.

You are not to imagine that I mean to open to you at large, or to recommend to your research, the whole of this vast field of science. It is certainly much above my faculties to reach it; and though it may not be above yours to comprehend it fully if it were fully and properly brought before you, yet perhaps the most perfect criticism requires habits of speculation and abstraction not very consistent with the employment which ought to occupy, and the habits of mind which ought to prevail in a practical artist. I only point out to you these things, that when you do criticise (as all who work on a plan will criticise more or less), your criticism may be built on the foundation of true principles; and that though you may not always travel a great way, the way that you do travel may be the right road.

I observe, as a fundamental ground, common to all the arts with which we have any concern in this discourse, that they address themselves only to two faculties of the mind,—its imagination and its sensibility.

All theories which attempt to direct or to control the art upon any principles falsely called rational, which we form to ourselves upon a supposition of what ought in reason to be the end or means of art, independent of the known first effect produced by objects on the imagination, must be false and delusive. For though it may appear bold to say it, the imagination is here the residence of truth. If the imagination be affected, the conclusion is fairly drawn; if it be not affected, the reasoning is erroneous, because the end is not obtained,—the effect itself being the test, and the only test, of the truth and efficacy of the means.

There is in the commerce of life, as in art, a sagacity

which is far from being contradictory to right reason, and is superior to any occasional exercise of that faculty which supersedes it; and does not wait for the slow progress of deduction, but goes at once, by what appears a kind of intuition, to the conclusion. A man endowed with this faculty feels and acknowledges the truth, though it is not always in his power, perhaps, to give a reason for it; because he cannot recollect and bring before him all the materials that gave birth to his opinion; for very many and very intricate considerations may unite to form the principle, even of small and minute parts, involved in, or dependent on, a great system of things; though these in process of time are forgotten, the right impression still remains fixed in his mind.

This impression is the result of the accumulated experience of our whole life, and has been collected, we do not always know how or when. But this mass of collective observation, however acquired, ought to prevail over that reason which, however powerfully exerted on any particular occasion, will probably comprehend but a partial view of the subject; and our conduct in life, as well as in the arts, is, or ought to be, generally governed by this habitual reason; it is our happiness that we are enabled to draw on such funds. If we were obliged to enter into a theoretical deliberation on every occasion before we act, life would be at a stand, and art would be impracticable.

It appears to me, therefore, that our first thoughts, that is, the effect which anything produces on our minds on its first appearance, is never to be forgotten; and it demands for that reason, because it is the first, to be laid up with care. If this be not done, the artist may happen to impose on himself by partial reasoning; by a cold consideration of those animated thoughts which proceed, not perhaps from caprice or rashness (as he may afterwards conceit), but from the fulness of his mind, enriched with the copious stores of all the various inventions which he had ever seen, or had ever passed in his mind. These ideas are infused into his design without any conscious effort; but if he be not on his guard he may reconsider and correct them till the whole matter is reduced to a commonplace invention.

This is sometimes the effect of what I mean to caution you against; that is to say, an unfounded distrust of the imagination and feeling in favor of narrow, partial, confined, argumentative theories, and of principles that seem to apply to the design in hand, without considering those general impressions on the fancy in which real principles of *sound reason,* and of much more weight and importance are involved, and, as it were, lie hid under the appearance of a sort of vulgar sentiment.

Reason, without doubt, must ultimately determine everything; at this minute it is required to inform us when that very reason is to give way to feeling.

Though I have often spoken of that mean conception of our art which confines it to mere imitation, I must add that it may be narrowed to such a mere matter of experiment as to exclude from it the application of science, which alone gives dignity and compass to any art. But to find proper foundations for science is neither to narrow nor to vulgarize it; and this is sufficiently exemplified in the success of experimental philosophy. It is the false system of reasoning, grounded on a partial view of things, against which I would most earnestly guard you. And I do it the rather, because those narrow theories, so coincident with the poorest and most miserable practices, and which are adopted to give it countenance, have not had their origin in the poorest minds, but in the mistakes, or possibly in the mistaken interpretations, of great and commanding authorities. We are not, therefore, in this case misled by feeling, but by false speculation.

When such a man as Plato speaks of painting as only an imitative art, and that our pleasure proceeds from observing and acknowledging the truth of the imitation, I think he misleads us by a partial theory. It is in this poor, partial, and, so far, false view of the art, that Cardinal Bembo has chosen to distinguish even Raphael himself, whom our enthusiasm honors with the name of Divine. The same sentiment is adopted by Pope in his epitaph on Sir Godfrey Kneller;* and he turns the panegyric solely on imitation, as it is a sort of deception.

---

* "Kneller, by Heav'n and not a Master taught,
   Whose art was Nature, and whose pictures Thought;

I shall not think my time misemployed if by any means
I may contribute to confirm your opinion of what ought to be
the object of your pursuit; because, though the best critics
must always have exploded this strange idea, yet I know that
there is a disposition towards a perpetual recurrence to it,
on account of its simplicity and superficial plausibility. For
this reason I shall beg leave to lay before you a few thoughts
on this subject; to throw out some hints that may lead your
minds to an opinion (which I take to be the truth) that painting is not only to be considered as an imitation operating by
deception, but that it is, and ought to be, in many points of
view, and strictly speaking, no imitation at all of external
nature. Perhaps it ought to be as far removed from the vulgar
idea of imitation as the refined, civilized state in which we live
is removed from a gross state of nature; and those who have
not cultivated their imaginations, which the majority of mankind certainly have not, may be said, in regard to arts, to
continue in this state of nature. Such men will always prefer
imitation to that excellence which is addressed to another
faculty, that they do not possess; but these are not the persons to whom a painter is to look, any more than a judge of
morals and manners ought to refer controverted points upon
those subjects to the opinions of people taken from the banks
of the Ohio, or from New Holland.

It is the lowest style only of arts, whether of painting,
poetry, or music, that may be said, in the vulgar sense, to be
naturally pleasing. The higher efforts of those arts, we know
by experience, do not affect minds wholly uncultivated. This
refined taste is the consequence of education and habit; we
are born only with a capacity of entertaining this refinement,
as we are born with a disposition to receive and obey all the
rules and regulations of society; and so far it may be said to
be natural to us, and no further.

Now for two ages having snatched from fate
Whate'er was beauteous, or whate'er was great,
Lies crowned with princes' honors, poets' lays,
Due to his merit, and brave thirst of praise.
Living, great Nature feared he might outvie
Her works; and, dying, fears herself may die."

What has been said may show the artist how necessary it is, when he looks about him for the advice and criticism of his friends, to make some distinction of the character, taste, experience, and observation in this art, of those from whom it is received. An ignorant, uneducated man may, like Apelles' critic, be a competent judge of the truth of the representation of a sandal; or, to go somewhat higher, like Molière's old woman, may decide upon what is nature, in regard to comic humor; but a critic in the higher style of art ought to possess the same refined taste which directed the artist in his work.

To illustrate this principle by a comparison with other arts, I shall now produce some instances to show that they, as well as our own art, renounce the narrow idea of nature, and the narrow theories derived from that mistaken principle, and apply to that reason only which informs us, not what imitation is,—a natural representation of a given object,—but what it is natural for the imagination to be delighted with. And perhaps there is no better way of acquiring this knowledge than by this kind of analogy; each art will corroborate and mutually reflect the truth on the other. Such a kind of juxtaposition may likewise have this use, that while the artist is amusing himself in the contemplation of other arts, he may habitually transfer the principles of those arts to that which he professes; which ought to be always present to his mind, and to which everything is to be referred.

So far is art from being derived from, or having any immediate intercourse with, particular nature as its model, that there are many arts that set out with a professed deviation from it.

This is certainly not so exactly true in regard to painting and sculpture. Our elements are laid in gross common nature,—an exact imitation of what is before us; but when we advance to the higher state, we consider this power of imitation, though first in the order of acquisition, as by no means the highest in the scale of perfection.

Poetry addresses itself to the same faculties and the same dispositions as painting, though by different means. The object of both is to accommodate itself to all the natural propensities and inclinations of the mind. The very existence of poetry depends on the license it assumes of deviating from actual nature, in order to gratify natural propensities by other means, which are found by experience full as capable of affording such gratification. It sets out with a language in the highest degree artificial, a construction of measured words, such as never is, nor ever was, used by man. Let this measure be what it may, whether hexameter or any other metre used in Latin or Greek, or rhyme, or blank verse varied with pauses and accents, in modern languages,—they are all equally removed from nature, and equally a violation of common speech. When this artificial mode has been established as the vehicle of sentiment, there is another principle in the human mind to which the work must be referred, which renders it still more artificial, carries it still further from common nature, and deviates only to render it more perfect. That principle is the sense of congruity, coherence, and consistency, which is a real existing principle in man; and it must be gratified. Therefore, having once adopted a style and a measure not found in common discourse, it is required that the sentiments also should be in the same proportion elevated above common nature, from the necessity of there being an agreement of the parts among themselves, that one uniform whole may be produced.

To correspond, therefore, with this general system of deviation from nature, the manner in which poetry is offered to the ear, the tone in which it is recited should be as far removed from the tone of conversation as the words of which that poetry is composed. This naturally suggests the idea of modulating the voice by art, which, I suppose, may be considered as accomplished to the highest degree of excellence in the recitative of the Italian Opera; as we may conjecture it was in the chorus that attended the ancient drama. And though the most violent passions, the highest distress, even death itself, are expressed in singing or recitative, I would not admit as sound criticism the condemnation of such exhibitions on account of their being unnatural.

If it is natural for our senses and our imaginations to be delighted with singing, with instrumental music, with poetry, and with graceful action, taken separately (none of them be-

ing in the vulgar sense natural, even in that separate state),
it is conformable to experience, and therefore agreeable to
reason as connected and referred to experience, that we
should also be delighted with this union of music, poetry,
and graceful action, joined to every circumstance of pomp
and magnificence calculated to strike the senses of the spectator. Shall reason stand in the way, and tell us that we ought
not to like what we know we do like, and prevent us from
feeling the full effect of this complicated exertion of art? This
is what I would understand by poets and painters being allowed to dare everything; for what can be more daring than
accomplishing the purpose and end of art by a complication
of means, none of which have their archetypes in actual
nature?

So far, therefore, is servile imitation from being necessary, that whatever is familiar, or in any way reminds us of
what we see and hear every day, perhaps does not belong to
the higher provinces of art, either in poetry or painting. The
mind is to be transported, as Shakespeare expresses it, *beyond
the ignorant present*, to ages past. Another and a higher order
of beings is supposed; and to those beings everything which
is introduced into the work must correspond. Of this conduct,
under these circumstances, the Roman and Florentine schools
afford sufficient examples. Their style by this means is raised
and elevated above all others; and by the same means the
compass of art itself is enlarged.

We often see grave and great subjects attempted by
artists of another school; who, though excellent in the lower
class of art, proceeding on the principles which regulate that
class, and not recollecting, or not knowing, that they were to
address themselves to another faculty of the mind, have become perfectly ridiculous.

The picture which I have at present in my thoughts is a
sacrifice of Iphigenia, painted by Jan Steen, a painter of whom
I have formerly had occasion to speak with the highest approbation; and even in this picture, the subject of which is
by no means adapted to his genius, there is nature and expression; but it is such expression, and the countenances are so
familiar, and consequently so vulgar, and the whole ac-

companied with such finery of silks and velvets, that one would be almost tempted to doubt whether the artist did not purposely intend to burlesque his subject.

Instances of the same kind we frequently see in poetry. Parts of Hobbes's translation of Homer are remembered and repeated merely for the familiarity and meanness of their phraseology, so ill corresponding with the ideas which ought to have been expressed, and as I conceive, with the style of the original.

We may proceed in the same manner through the comparatively inferior branches of art. There is in works of that class the same distinction of a higher and a lower style; and they take their rank and degree in proportion as the artist departs more or less from common nature, and makes it an object of his attention to strike the imagination of the spectator by ways belonging especially to art,—unobserved and untaught out of the school of its practice.

If our judgments are to be directed by narrow, vulgar, untaught, or rather ill-taught reason, we must prefer a portrait by Denner, or any other high finisher, to those of Titian or Van Dyck; and a landscape of Van der Heyden to those of Titian or Rubens; for they are certainly more exact representations of nature.

If we suppose a view of nature represented with all the truth of the *camera obscura,* and the same scene represented by a great artist, how little and mean will the one appear in comparison with the other,—where no superiority is supposed from the choice of the subject! The scene shall be the same, the difference only will be in the manner in which it is presented to the eye. With what additional superiority, then, will the same artist appear when he has the power of selecting his materials as well as elevating his style. Like Nicholas Poussin, he transports us to the environs of ancient Rome, with all the objects which a literary education makes so precious and interesting to man; or, like Sebastian Bourdon, he leads us to the dark antiquity of the pyramids of Egypt; or, like Claude Lorrain, he conducts us to the tranquillity of Arcadian scenes and fairy-land.

Like the history-painter, a painter of landscapes, in this

style and with this conduct, sends the imagination back into antiquity; and like the poet, he makes the elements sympathize with his subjects,—whether the clouds roll in volumes like those of Titian or Salvator Rosa, or, like those of Claude, are gilded with the setting sun; whether the mountains have sudden and bold projections, or are gently sloped; whether the branches of his trees shoot out abruptly in right angles from their trunks, or follow each other with only a gentle inclination. All these circumstances contribute to the general character of the work, whether it be of the elegant or of the more sublime kind. If we add to this the powerful materials of lightness and darkness, over which the artist has complete dominion, to vary and dispose them as he pleases, to diminish or increase them as will best suit his purpose and correspond to the general idea of his work,—a landscape thus conducted, under the influence of a poetical mind, will have the same superiority over the more ordinary and common views as Milton's "L'Allegro" and "Il Penseroso" have over a cold, prosaic narration or description; and such a picture would make a more forcible impression on the mind than the real scenes, were they presented before us.

If we look abroad to other arts we may observe the same distinction, the same division into two classes; each of them acting under the influence of two different principles, in which the one follows nature, the other varies it, and sometimes departs from it.

The theatre, which is said "to hold the mirror up to nature," comprehends both those ideas. The lower kind of comedy, or farce, like the inferior style of painting, the more naturally it is represented, the better; but the higher appears to me to aim no more at imitation, so far as it belongs to anything like deception, or to expect that the spectators should think that the events there represented are really passing before them, than Raphael in his cartoons, or Poussin in his "Sacraments," expected it to be believed, even for a moment, that what they exhibited were real figures.

For want of this distinction the world is filled with false criticism. Raphael is praised for naturalness and deception, which he certainly has not accomplished, and as certainly never intended; and our late great actor, Garrick, has been as ignorantly praised by his friend Fielding; who doubtless imagined he had hit upon an ingenious device, by introducing in one of his novels (otherwise a work of the highest merit) an ignorant man mistaking Garrick's representation of a scene in "Hamlet" for reality. A very little reflection will convince us that there is not one circumstance in the whole scene that is of the nature of deception. The merit and excellence of Shakespeare, and of Garrick, when they were engaged in such scenes, is of a different and much higher kind. But what adds to the falsity of this intended compliment is that the best stage-representation appears even more unnatural to a person of such a character, who is supposed never to have seen a play before, than it does to those who have had a habit of allowing for those necessary deviations from nature which the art requires.

In theatric representation great allowances must always be made for the place in which the exhibition is represented, —for the surrounding company, the lighted candles, the scenes visibly shifted in your sight, and the language of blank verse, so different from common English, which merely as English must appear surprising in the mouths of Hamlet and all the court and natives of Denmark. These allowances are made, but their being made puts an end to all manner of deception;* and further, we know that the more low, illiterate, and vulgar any person is, the less he will be disposed to make these allowances, and of course to be deceived by any imitation,—the things in which the trespass against nature and common probability is made in favor of the theatre being quite within the sphere of such uninformed men.

Though I have no intention of entering into all the circumstances of unnaturalness in theatrical representations, I

---

* It is false that any representation is mistaken for reality,—that any dramatic fable in its materiality was ever credible, or, for a single moment, was ever credited. . . . The truth is that the spectators are always in their senses, and know, from the first act to the last, that the stage is only a stage, and that the players are only players. They come to hear a certain number of lines recited with just gesture and elegant modulation. —DR. JOHNSON, *Preface to Shakespeare.*

must observe that even the expression of violent passion is not always the most excellent in proportion as it is the most natural; so great terror and such disagreeable sensations may be communicated to the audience that the balance may be destroyed by which pleasure is preserved and holds its predominance in the mind. Violent distortion of action, harsh screamings of the voice, however great the occasions, or however natural on such occasions, are therefore not admissible in the theatric art. Many of these allowed deviations from nature arise from the necessity which there is that everything should be raised and enlarged beyond its natural state; that the full effect may come home to the spectator, which otherwise would be lost in the comparatively extensive space of the theatre. Hence the deliberate and stately step, the studied grace of action, which seems to enlarge the dimensions of the actor, and alone to fill the stage. All this unnaturalness, though right and proper in its place, would appear affected and ridiculous in a private room; *quid enim deformius quam scenam in vitam transferre?* [1]

And here I must observe, and I believe it may be considered as a general rule, that no art can be grafted with success on another art. For though they all profess the same origin, and to proceed from the same stock, yet each has its own peculiar modes both of imitating nature and of deviating from it, each for the accomplishment of its own particular purpose. These deviations, more especially, will not bear transplantation to another soil.

If a painter should endeavor to copy the theatrical pomp and parade of dress and attitude, instead of that simplicity which is not a greater beauty in life than it is in painting, we should condemn such pictures, as painted in the meanest style.

So, also, gardening—as far as gardening is an art, or is entitled to the appellation—is a deviation from nature; for if the true taste consists, as many hold, in banishing every appearance of art, or any traces of the footsteps of man, it would then be no longer a garden. Even though we define it, "nature to advantage dressed,"—and in some sense it is such, and

---

[1] "For what more disgusting than to carry a dramatic scene into life?"

much more beautiful and commodious for the recreation of
man,—it is, however, when so dressed, no longer a subject
for the pencil of a landscape-painter, as all landscape-painters
know, who love to have recourse to nature herself, and to
dress her according to the principles of their own art, which
are far different from those of gardening, even when conducted according to the most approved principles, and such as
a landscape-painter himself would adopt in the disposition
of his own grounds, for his own private satisfaction.

I have brought together as many instances as appear
necessary to make out the several points which I wished to
suggest to your consideration in this discourse,—that your
own thoughts may lead you further in the use that may be
made of the analogy of the arts, and of the restraint which a
full understanding of the diversity of many of their principles
ought to impose on the employment of that analogy.

The great end of all those arts is to make an impression
on the imagination and the feeling. The imitation of nature
frequently does this. Sometimes it fails, and something else
succeeds. I think, therefore, the true test of all the arts is not
solely whether the production is a true copy of nature, but
whether it answers the end of art, which is to produce a
pleasing effect upon the mind.

It remains only to speak a few words of architecture,
which does not come under the denomination of an imitative
art. It applies itself, like music (and, I believe, we may add
poetry), directly to the imagination, without the intervention
of any kind of imitation.

There is in architecture, as in painting, an inferior branch
of art in which the imagination appears to have no concern.
It does not, however, acquire the name of a polite and liberal
art from its usefulness, or administering to our wants or
necessities, but from some higher principle; we are sure that
in the hands of a man of genius it is capable of inspiring sentiment, and of filling the mind with great and sublime ideas.

It may be worth the attention of artists to consider what
materials are in their hands that may contribute to this end,
and whether this art has it not in its power to address itself

to the imagination with effect, by more ways than are generally employed by architects.

To pass over the effect produced by that general symmetry and proportion by which the eye is delighted, as the ear is with music, architecture certainly possesses many principles in common with poetry and painting. Among those which may be reckoned as the first is that of affecting the imagination by means of association of ideas. Thus, for instance, as we have naturally a veneration for antiquity, whatever building brings to our remembrance ancient customs and manners, such as the castles of the barons of ancient chivalry, is sure to give this delight. Hence it is that *towers and battlements** are so often selected by the painter and the poet to make a part of the composition of their ideal landscape; and it is from hence, in a great degree, that in the buildings of Vanbrugh, who was a poet as well as an architect, there is a greater display of imagination than we shall find, perhaps, in any other; and this is the ground of the effect we feel in many of his works, notwithstanding the faults with which many of them are justly charged. For this purpose, Vanbrugh appears to have had recourse to some of the principles of the Gothic architecture; which, though not so ancient as the Grecian, is more so to our imagination, with which the artist is more concerned than with absolute truth.

The barbaric splendor of those Asiatic buildings which are now publishing by a member of this Academy, may possibly, in the same manner, furnish an architect, not with models to copy, but with hints of composition and general effect, which would not otherwise have occurred.

It is, I know, a delicate and hazardous thing (and as such I have already pointed it out) to carry the principles of one art to another, or even to reconcile in one object the various modes of the same art, when they proceed on different principles. The sound rules of the Grecian architecture are

---

* Towers and battlements it sees
  Bosom'd high in tufted trees.

MILTON, L'Allegro

not to be lightly sacrificed. A deviation from them, or even an addition to them, is like a deviation or addition to, or from, the rules of other arts,—fit only for a great master, who is thoroughly conversant in the nature of man, as well as all combinations in his own art.

It may not be amiss for the architect to take advantage *sometimes* of that to which I am sure the painter ought always to have his eyes open,—I mean the use of accidents; to follow when they lead, and to improve them, rather than always to trust to a regular plan. It often happens that additions have been made to houses at various times, for use or pleasure. As such buildings depart from regularity they now and then acquire something of scenery by this accident, which I should think might not unsuccessfully be adopted by an architect in an original plan, if it does not too much interfere with convenience. Variety and intricacy is a beauty and excellence in every other of the arts which address the imagination, and why not in architecture?

The forms and turnings of the streets of London and other old towns are produced by accident, without any original plan or design, but they are not always the less pleasant to the walker or spectator on that account. On the contrary, if the city had been built on the regular plan of Sir Christopher Wren, the effect might have been, as we know it is in some new parts of the town, rather unpleasing; the uniformity might have produced weariness, and a slight degree of disgust.

I can pretend to no skill in the detail of architecture. I judge now of the art merely as a painter. When I speak of Vanbrugh I mean to speak of him in the language of our art. To speak, then, of Vanbrugh in the language of a painter, he had originality of invention, he understood light and shadow, and had great skill in composition. To support his principal object, he produced his second and third groups or masses; he perfectly understood in his art what is the most difficult in ours, the conduct of the background; by which the design and invention is set off to the greatest advantage. What the background is in painting, in architecture is the real ground on which the building is erected; and no architect took greater care than he that his work should not appear crude and hard; that is, it did not abruptly start out of the ground without expectation or preparation.

This is a tribute which a painter owes to an architect who composed like a painter, and was defrauded of the due reward of his merit by the wits of his time, who did not understand the principles of composition in poetry better than he, and who knew little or nothing of what he understood perfectly,—the general ruling principles of architecture and painting. His fate was that of the great Perrault; both were the objects of the petulant sarcasms of factious men of letters, and both have left some of the fairest ornaments which to this day decorate their several countries,—the façade of the Louvre, Blenheim, and Castle Howard.

Upon the whole it seems to me that the object and intention of all the arts is to supply the natural imperfection of things, and often to gratify the mind by realizing and embodying what never existed but in the imagination.

It is allowed on all hands that facts and events, however they may bind the historian, have no dominion over the poet or the painter. With us, history is made to bend and conform to this great idea of art. And why? Because these arts, in their highest province, are not addressed to the gross senses, but to the desires of the mind,—to that spark of divinity which we have within, impatient of being circumscribed and pent up by the world which is about us. Just so much as our art has of this, just so much of dignity, I had almost said of divinity, it exhibits; and those of our artists who possessed this mark of distinction in the highest degree acquired from thence the glorious appellation of Divine.

ARCHIBALD ALISON
[1757–1839]

Alison was educated in Glasgow and took an LL.B. from
Baliol in 1784; he took orders in the Church of England,
and after the publication in 1790 of Essays on the Nature
and Principles of Taste, became a prosperous pluralist.
Finally in 1800 he became the minister of the episcopal
chapel, Cowgate, Edinburgh, where he spent the rest of his
life. His sermons were much admired in his lifetime.

Francis Jeffrey expounded Alison's theories in the
Edinburgh Review for May, 1811: "Alison's main purpose is
to prove that beauty is not a quality of things considered
as existing apart from the mind, but a product of trains
of agreeable ideas, set up in the imagination by objects
associated with, or directly suggestive of, the simple
emotions." Taste, then, as Martin Kallich points out, "is
entirely dependent on the imagination to the exclusion of
judgment and reason." The Essays were influential during
the early nineteenth century, and appeared in the United
States in at least five editions between 1830 and 1856.

Both Samuel H. Monk, in The Sublime, and Walter J.
Hipple, Jr., in The Beautiful, the Sublime, and the
Picturesque . . . discuss Alison at some length. See also:

Kallich, Martin: "The Meaning of Archibald Alison's Essays
on Taste," PQ, XXVII (1948), 314–24.

ESSAYS ON THE NATURE AND PRINCIPLES OF TASTE

[1790]

INTRODUCTION

Taste is, in general, considered as that faculty of the human mind by which we perceive and enjoy whatever is BEAUTIFUL or SUBLIME in the works of Nature or Art.

The perception of these qualities is attended with an emotion of pleasure very distinguishable from every other pleasure of our nature, and which is accordingly distinguished by the name of the EMOTION of TASTE. The distinction of the objects of taste into the sublime and the beautiful has produced a similar division of this emotion, into the EMOTION of SUBLIMITY, and the EMOTION of BEAUTY.

The qualities that produce these emotions are to be found in almost every class of the objects of human knowledge, and the emotions themselves afford one of the most extensive sources of human delight. They occur to us, amid every variety of external scenery, and among many diversities of disposition and affection in the mind of man. The most pleasing arts of human invention are altogether directed to their pursuit: and even the necessary arts are exalted into dignity by the genius that can unite beauty with use. From the earliest period of society to its last stage of improvement, they afford an innocent and elegant amusement to private life, at the same time that they increase the splendour of national character; and in the progress of nations, as well as of individuals, while they attract attention from the pleasures they bestow, they serve to exalt the human mind from corporeal to intellectual pursuits.

These qualities, however, though so important to human happiness, are not the objects of immediate observation; and in the attempt to investigate them various circumstances unite to perplex our research. They are often obscured under the number of qualities with which they are accidentally combined: They result often from peculiar combinations of the qualities of objects, or the relation of certain parts of objects to each other: They are still oftener, perhaps, dependent upon the state of our own minds, and vary in their effects with the dispositions in which they happen to be observed. In all cases, while we feel the emotions they excite, we are ignorant of the causes by which they are produced; and when we seek to discover them, we have no other method of discovery than that varied and patient experiment, by which, amid these complicated circumstances, we may gradually ascertain the peculiar qualities which, by the constitution of our nature, are permanently connected with the emotions we feel.

In the employment of this mode of investigation, there are two great objects of attention and inquiry which seem to include all that is either necessary, or perhaps possible, for us to discover on the subject of taste.

These objects are,

I. To investigate the nature of those qualities that produce the emotions of taste: And,

II. To investigate the nature of that faculty by which these emotions are received.

These investigations, however, are not to be considered only as objects of philosophical curiosity. They have an immediate relation to all the arts that are directed to the production either of the BEAUTIFUL or the SUBLIME; and they afford the only means by which the principles of these various arts can be ascertained. Without a just and accurate conception of the nature of these qualities, the artist must be unable to determine whether the beauty he creates is temporary or permanent, whether adapted to the accidental prejudices of his age, or to the uniform constitution of the human mind; and whatever the science of criticism can afford for the improvement or correction of taste, must altogether depend upon the previous knowledge of the nature and laws of this faculty.

To both these inquiries, however, there is a preliminary investigation which seems absolutely necessary, and without which every conclusion we form must be either imperfect or vague. In the investigation of CAUSES, the first and most important step is the accurate examination of the EFFECT to be explained. In the science of mind, however, as well as in that of body, there are few effects altogether simple, or in which accidental circumstances are not combined with the proper effect. Unless, therefore, by means of repeated experiments, such accidental circumstances are accurately distinguished from the phenomena that permanently characterize the effect, we are under the necessity of including in the cause the causes also of all the accidental circumstances with which the effect is accompanied.

With the emotions of taste, in almost every instance, many other accidental emotions of pleasure are united: the various simple pleasures that arise from other qualities of the object; the pleasure of agreeable sensation, in the case of material objects; and in all, that pleasure which by the constitution of our nature is annexed to the exercise of our faculties. Unless, therefore, we have previously acquired a distinct and accurate conception of that *peculiar* effect which is produced on our minds when the emotions of taste are felt, and can precisely distinguish it from the effects that are produced by these accidental qualities, we must necessarily include in the causes of such emotions those qualities also which are the causes of the accidental pleasures with which this emotion is accompanied. The variety of systems that philosophers have adopted upon this subject, and the various emotions into which they have resolved the emotion of taste, while they afford a sufficient evidence of the numerous accidental pleasures that accompany these emotions, afford also a strong illustration of the necessity of previously ascertaining the nature of this effect before we attempt to investigate its Cause. With regard, therefore, to both these inquiries, the first and most important step is accurately to examine the nature of this emotion itself, and its distinction from every other emotion of pleasure; and our capacity of discovering either the nature of the qualities that produce the emotions of taste, or the nature of the faculty by which they are received, will be exactly proportioned to our accuracy in ascertaining the nature of the emotion itself.

When we look back to the history of these investigations, and to the theories which have been so liberally formed upon the subject, there is one fact that must necessarily strike us, *viz.* That all these theories have uniformly taken for granted the *simplicity* of this emotion; that they have considered it as an emotion too plain, and too commonly felt, to admit of any analysis; that they have as uniformly, therefore, referred it to some *one* principle or law of the human mind; and that they have therefore concluded, that the discovery of that *one* principle was the essential key by which all the pleasures of taste were to be resolved.

While they have assumed this fundamental principle, the various theories of philosophers may, and indeed must, be included in the two following classes of supposition.

I. The first class is that which resolves the emotion of taste directly into an original law of our nature; which supposes a sense, or senses, by which the qualities of Beauty and Sublimity are perceived and felt as their appropriate objects; and concludes, therefore, that the genuine object of the Arts of Taste is to discover, and to imitate, those qualities in every subject which the prescription of Nature has thus made essentially either beautiful or sublime.

To this first class of hypotheses belong almost all the

theories of music, of architecture, and of sculpture; the theory of Mr. Hogarth, of the Abbé Winkelman, and perhaps, in its last result, also the theory of Sir Joshua Reynolds. It is the species of hypothesis which is naturally resorted to by all artists and amateurs—by those, whose habits of thought lead them to attend more to the causes of their emotions than to the nature of the emotions themselves.

II. The second class of hypotheses arises from the opposite view of the subject. It is that which resists the idea of any new or peculiar sense distinct from the common principles of our nature, which supposes some *one* known and acknowledged principle or affection of mind to be the foundation of all the emotions we receive from the objects of taste, and which resolves, therefore, all the various phenomena into some more general law of our intellectual or moral constitution. Of this kind are the hypotheses of M. Diderot, who attributes all our emotions of this kind to the perception of relation; of Mr. Hume, who resolves them into our sense of utility; of the venerable St. Austin, who, with nobler views, a thousand years ago resolved them into the pleasure which belongs to the perception of order and design, &c. It is the species of hypothesis most natural to retired and philosophic minds; to those, whose habits have led them to attend more to the nature of the emotions they felt than to the Causes which produced them.

If the success of these long and varied inquiries has not corresponded to the genius or the industry of the philosophers who have pursued them, a suspicion may arise that there has been something faulty in the principle of their investigation, and that some fundamental assumption has been made which ought first to have been patiently and securely ascertained. It was this suspicion that first led to the following inquiries. It seemed to me that the *simplicity of the emotion of taste* was a principle much too hastily adopted, and that the consequences which followed from it (under both these classes of hypotheses) were very little reconcileable with the most common experience of human feeling; and from the examination of this preliminary question, I was led gradually to conclusions which seemed not only to me, but to others whose opinion I value far more than my own, of an importance not unworthy of being presented to the public. In doing this, I am conscious that I have entered upon a new and untrodden path, and I feel all my own weakness in pursuing it: yet I trust my readers will believe that I should not have pursued it so long, if I were not convinced that it would finally terminate in views not only important to the arts of taste, but important also to the philosophy of the human mind.

The inquiries which follow naturally divide themselves into the following parts, and are to be prosecuted in the following order.

I. I shall begin with an analysis of the effect which is produced upon the mind, when the emotions of Beauty or Sublimity are felt. I shall endeavour to show that this effect is very different from the determination of a *sense;* that it is not in fact a Simple, but a complex emotion; that it involves, in all cases, 1st, the production of some simple emotion, or the exercise of some moral affection, and, 2dly, the consequent excitement of a peculiar exercise of the imagination; that these concomitant effects are distinguishable, and very often distinguished in our experience; and that the *peculiar* pleasure of the Beautiful or the Sublime is only felt when these two effects are conjoined, and the complex emotion produced.

The prosecution of the subject will lead to another inquiry of some difficulty and extent, *viz.* into the origin of the beauty and sublimity of the qualities of matter. To this subordinate inquiry I shall devote a separate essay. I shall endeavour to show that all the phenomena are reducible to the same general principle, and that the qualities of matter are not beautiful or sublime in themselves, but as they are, by various means, the signs or expressions of qualities capable of producing emotion.

II. From this examination of the effect I shall proceed, in the second part, to investigate the *causes* which are productive of it; or, in other words, the sources of the Beautiful and the Sublime in nature and art.

In the course of this investigation I shall endeavour to show, 1st, That there is no single emotion into which these varied effects can be resolved; that on the contrary, every simple emotion, and therefore every object which is capable of producing any simple emotion, *may* be the foundation of the complex emotion of beauty or sublimity. But, *in the second place,* that this complex emotion of beauty or sublimity is never produced, unless, beside the excitement of some simple emotion, the imagination also is excited, and the exercise of the two faculties combined in the general effect. The prosecution of the subject will lead me to the principal object of the inquiry, to show what is that LAW of MIND, according to which, in actual life, this exercise or employment of imagination is excited; and what are the means by which, in the different fine arts, the artist is able to awaken this important exercise of imagination, and to exalt objects of simple and common pleasure into objects of beauty or sublimity.

In this part of the subject, there are two subordinate inquiries which will necessarily demand attention.

1. The qualities of sublimity and beauty are discovered not only in pleasing or agreeable subjects, but frequently also in objects that are in themselves productive of pain, and some of the noblest productions of the fine arts are founded upon subjects of terror and distress. It will form, therefore, an obvious and important inquiry to ascertain by what means this singular effect is produced in real nature, and by what means it may be produced in the compositions of art.

2. There is a distinction in the effects produced upon our minds by objects of taste; and this distinction, both in the emotions and their causes, has been expressed by the terms of SUBLIMITY and BEAUTY. It will form, therefore, a second object of inquiry to ascertain the nature of this distinction, both with regard to these emotions and to the qualities that produce them.

III. From the preceding inquiries I shall proceed, in the last part, to investigate the nature of that faculty by which these emotions are perceived and felt. I shall endeavour to show that it has no resemblance to a sense; that as, whenever it is employed, two distinct and independent powers of mind are employed, it is not to be considered as a separate and peculiar faculty, and that it is finally to be resolved into more general principles of our constitution. These speculations will probably lead to the important inquiry, whether there is any standard by which the perfection or imperfection of our sentiments upon these subjects may be determined; to some explanation of the means by which taste may be corrected or improved; and to some illustration of the purposes which this peculiar constitution of our nature serves in the increase of human happiness, and the exaltation of human character.

I feel it incumbent on me, however, to inform my readers, that I am to employ, in these inquiries, a different kind of evidence from what has usually been employed by writers upon these subjects, and that my illustrations will be derived much less from the compositions of the fine arts than from the appearances of common nature, and the experience of common men. If the fine arts are in reality arts of imitation, their principles are to be sought for in the subject which they imitate; and it is ever to be remembered, "That Music, Architecture, and Painting, as well as Poetry and Oratory, are to deduce their laws and rules from the general Sense and Taste of mankind, and not from the principles of these Arts themselves; in other words, that the Taste is not to conform to the Art, but the Art to the Taste." * In following this mode of illustration, while I am sensible that I render my book less amusing, I trust I may render it more useful. The most effectual method to check the empiricism, either of art or of science, is to multiply, as far as possible, the number of those who can observe and judge; and (whatever may be the conclusions of my readers with regard to my own particular opinions) I shall not have occupied their attention in vain if I can lead them to think and to feel for themselves; to employ the powers which are given them to the ends for which they were given; and, upon subjects where all men are entitled to judge, to disregard alike the abstract refinements of the philosopher who speculates in the closet, and the technical doctrines of the artist who dictates in the school.

* Mr Addison

UVEDALE PRICE
[1747–1829]

―――――
―――――

*Of independent means, Uvedale Price traveled with Charles
James Fox, the eminent statesman and gadfly to George
III, observing the picturesque beauties of Italy and
Switzerland. His interest in gardening began very early,
opposing itself to the system of Lancelot "Capability" Brown
and arguing in favor of a beauty derived from the general
principles of painting, though gardens were not supposed
to reproduce the effects of paintings.* An Essay on the
Picturesque, As Compared with the Sublime and the
Beautiful, and on the Use of Studying Pictures, for the
Purpose of Improving Real Landscape, *1794, is a development
and refinement of positions earlier stated by William
Gilpin (see footnote 1 below), and is an effort to establish
the picturesque as an esthetic category coequal to sublimity
and beauty. The esthetic proposition developed in part
out of literary interests—English poets had been writing
organized "scenes" at least since Denham's "Cooper's
Hill"—and led to literary effects, as one can see from the
explicitly picturesque descriptions in Mrs. Radcliffe's*
Romance of the Forest (1791) *and in certain of
Wordsworth's poems. The volume appeared in editions
enlarged by controversies with the ruling landscape architect
of the time, Humphrey Repton, and with Price's neighbor,
Richard Payne Knight, until it reached its final three-volume
form in 1810.*

Walter J. Hipple, Jr. discusses Price at some length in

The Beautiful, The Sublime, and The Picturesque . . . ,
as does Christopher Hussey in The Picturesque: Studies in a
Point of View, *London, 1927. The present text is taken
from the 1810 edition.*

FROM ESSAYS ON THE PICTURESQUE AS COMPARED WITH THE SUBLIME AND THE BEAUTIFUL

[1794]

CHAPTER III

There are few words, whose meaning has been less accurately determined than that of the word picturesque.

In general, I believe, it is applied to every object, and every kind of scenery, which has been, or might be represented with good effect in painting; just as the word beautiful (when we speak of visible nature) is applied to every object, and every kind of scenery that in any way give pleasure to the eye; and these seem to be the significations of both words, taken in their most extended and popular sense. A more precise and distinct idea of beauty has been given in an essay, the early splendor of which not even the full meridian blaze of its illustrious author has been able to extinguish; but the picturesque, considered as a separate character, has never yet been accurately distinguished from the sublime and the beautiful; though as no one has ever pretended that they are synonymous (for it is sometimes used in contradistinction to them) such a distinction must exist.

Mr. Gilpin,[1] from whose very ingenious and extensive observations on this subject I have received great pleasure and instruction, appears to have adopted this common acceptation, not merely as such, but as giving an exact and determinate idea of the word; for he defines picturesque objects to be those "which please from some quality capable of being illustrated in painting,"* or, as he again defines it in his Letter to Sir Joshua Reynolds "such objects as are proper subjects for painting."† Both these definitions seem to me (what may perhaps appear a contradiction) at once too vague and too confined; for though we are not to expect any definition to be so accurate and comprehensive as both to supply the place and stand the test of investigation, yet if it do not in some degree separate the thing defined from all others, it differs little from any general truth on the same subject. For instance, it is very true that picturesque objects do please from some quality capable of being illustrated in painting; but so also does every object that is represented in painting if it please at all, otherwise it would not have been painted: and hence we ought to conclude, what certainly is

---

[1] Were William Gilpin (1724–1804) not faintly remembered for his "picturesque travels," he might be known as an educational reformer of some interest. At the age of about thirty he became headmaster of a school at Cheam, in Surrey, where, among other innovations, he substituted a system of fines and restrictions instead of corporal punishment, and encouraged the study of the English language, though not to the exclusion of Latin. It was during his summer holidays that he undertook those sketching tours over England which upon their publication provided his slender claims on posterity. These tours occurred between 1769 and 1777, but the first published volume, *Observations on the River Wye and Several Parts of South Wales . . . Relative Chiefly to Picturesque Beauty,* did not appear until 1782. Three other volumes of tours followed, and finally, in 1792, *Three Essays: On Picturesque Beauty; On Picturesque Travel; On Sketching Landscape.* It is to this book that Price refers. See William D. Templeman, *The Life and Work of William Gilpin,* Urbana, 1939.

* Essay on Picturesque Beauty, page 1.

† End of Essay on Picturesque Beauty, page 36.

not meant, that all objects which please in pictures are therefore picturesque; for no distinction or exclusion is made. Were
any other person to define picturesque objects to be those
which please from some striking effect of form, colour, or
light and shadow,—such a definition would indeed give but
a very indistinct idea of the thing defined; but it would be
hardly more vague, and at the same time much less confined
than the others, for it would not have an exclusive reference
to a particular art.

I hope to shew in the course of this work, that the
picturesque has a character not less separate and distinct
than either the sublime or the beautiful, nor less independent
of the art of painting. It has indeed been pointed out and illustrated by that art, and is one of its most striking ornaments; but has not beauty been pointed out and illustrated
by that art also, nay, according to the poet, brought into
existence by it?

> Si Venerem Cous nunquam posuisset Apelles,
> Mersa sub æquoreis illa lateret aquis.[2]

Examine the forms of the early Italian painters, or of
those, who, at a later period, lived where the study of the
antique, then fully operating at Rome on minds highly prepared for its influence, had not yet taught them to separate
what is beautiful from the general mass: you might almost
conclude that beauty did not then exist; yet those painters
were capable of exact imitation, though not of selection. Examine *grandeur* of form in the same manner; look at the dry,
meagre forms of Albert Durer, a man of genius even in Raphael's estimation; of Pietro Perugino, Andrea Mantegna, &c.
and compare them with those of M. Angelo and Raphael:
nature was not more dry and meagre in Germany or Perugia
than at Rome. Compare their landscapes and backgrounds
with those of Titian; nature was not changed, but a mind of
a higher cast, and instructed by the experience of all who had
gone before, rejected minute detail, and pointed out, by

[2] Ovid, *Ars Amatoria*, III, 401-2: "If Coan Apelles had never painted
Venus, she would still be lying hid in the sea's depths."

means of such selections, and such combinations as were congenial to its own sublime conceptions, in what forms, in what colours, and in what effects, grandeur in landscape consisted. Can it then be doubted that grandeur and beauty have been pointed out and illustrated by painting as well as picturesqueness?* Yet, would it be a just definition of sublime or of beautiful objects to say that they were such (and, let the words be taken in their most liberal construction) as *pleased from some quality capable of being illustrated in painting,* or, *that were proper subjects for that art?* The ancients, indeed, not only referred beauty of *form* to painting, but even beauty of *colour;* and the poet who could describe his mistress's complexion by comparing it to the tints of Apelles's pictures, must have thought that beauty of every kind was highly illustrated by the art to which he referred.

The principles of those two leading characters in nature, the sublime and the beautiful, have been fully illustrated and discriminated by a great master; but even when I first read that most original work, I felt that there were numberless objects which give great delight to the eye, and yet differ as widely from the beautiful as from the sublime. The reflections which I have since been led to make have convinced me that these objects form a distinct class, and belong to what may properly be called the picturesque.

That term, as we may judge from its etymology, is applied only to objects of sight; and indeed in so confined a manner as to be supposed merely to have a reference to the art from which it is named. I am well convinced, however, that the name and reference only are limited and uncertain, and that the qualities which make objects picturesque are not only as distinct as those which make them beautiful or sublime, but are equally extended to all our sensations by whatever organs they are received; and that music (though it appears like a solecism) may be as truly picturesque, according to the general principles of picturesqueness, as it may

---

* I have ventured to make use of this word, which I believe does not occur in any writer, from what appeared to me the necessity of having some one word to oppose to beauty and sublimity, in a work where they are so often compared.

be beautiful or sublime, according to those of beauty or sublimity.

But there is one circumstance particularly adverse to this part of my essay; I mean the manifest derivation of the word picturesque. The Italian *pittoresco* is, I imagine, of earlier date than either the English or the French word, the latter of which, *pittoresque,* is clearly taken from it, having no analogy to its own tongue. *Pittoresco* is derived not like picturesque, from the thing painted, but from the painter; and this difference is not wholly immaterial. The English word refers to the performance, and the objects most suited to it: the Italian and French words have a reference to the turn of mind common to painters; who, from the constant habit of examining all the peculiar effects and combinations, as well as the general appearance of nature, are struck with numberless circumstances, even where they are incapable of being represented, to which an unpractised eye pays little or no attention. The English word naturally draws the reader's mind towards pictures; and from that partial and confined view of the subject, what is in truth only an illustration of picturesqueness becomes the foundation of it. The words sublime and beautiful have not the same etymological reference to any one visible art, and therefore are applied to objects of the other senses: sublime indeed, in the language from which it is taken, and in its plain sense, means high, and therefore, perhaps, in strictness, should relate to objects of sight only; yet we no more scruple to call one of Handel's choruses sublime, than Corelli's famous *pastorale* beautiful. But should any person simply, and without any qualifying expressions, call a capricious movement of Scarlatti or Haydn *picturesque,* he would, with great reason, be laughed at, for it is not a term applied to sounds; yet such a movement, from its sudden, unexpected, and abrupt transitions,—from a certain playful wildness of character and appearance of irregularity, is no less analogous to similar scenery in nature than the concerto or the chorus to what is grand or beautiful to the eye.

There is, indeed, a general harmony and correspondence in all our sensations when they arise from similar causes, though they affect us by means of different senses; and these causes, as Mr. Burke has admirably pointed out,* can never be so clearly ascertained when we confine our observations to one sense only.

I must here observe, and I wish the reader to keep it in his mind, that the inquiry is not in what sense certain words are used in the best authors, still less what is their common, and vulgar use, and abuse; but whether there be certain qualities, which uniformly produce the same effects in all visible objects, and, according to the same analogy, in objects of hearing and of all the other senses; and which qualities, though frequently blended and united with others in the same object or set of objects, may be separated from them, and assigned to the class to which they belong.

If it can be shewn that a character composed of these qualities, and distinct from all others, does universally prevail; if it can be traced in the different objects of art and of nature, and appears consistent throughout,—it surely deserves a distinct title; but with respect to the real ground of inquiry, in matters little whether such a character, or the set of objects belonging to it, be called beautiful, sublime, or picturesque, or by any other name, or by no name at all.

Beauty is so much the most enchanting and popular quality, that it is often applied as the highest commendation to whatever gives us pleasure, or raises our admiration, be the cause what it will. Mr. Burke has given several instances of these ill-judged applications, and of the confusion of ideas which result from them; but there is nothing more ill-judged, or more likely to create confusion, if we at all agree with Mr. Burke in his idea of beauty, than the mode which prevails of joining together two words of a different and in some respects of an opposite meaning, and calling the character by the title of Picturesque Beauty.

I must observe, however, that I by no means object to the expression itself; I only object to it as a general term for the *character,* and as comprehending every kind of scenery, and every set of objects which look well in a picture. That is

---

* Sublime and beautiful, page 236. [2nd ed., 1759]

the sense, as far as I have observed, in which it is very commonly used; consequently, an old hovel, an old cart horse, or an old woman, are often, in that sense, full of picturesque *beauty;* and certainly the application of the last term to such objects, must tend to confuse our ideas: but were the expression restrained to those objects only in which the picturesque and the beautiful are mixed together, and so mixed that the result, according to common apprehension, is beautiful; and were it never used when the picturesque (as it no less frequently happens) is mixed solely with what is terrible, ugly, or deformed, I should highly approve of the expression, and wish for more distinctions of the same kind.

In reality, the picturesque not only differs from the beautiful in those qualities which Mr. Burke has so justly ascribed to it, but arises from qualities the most diametrically opposite.

According to Mr. Burke, one of the most essential qualities of beauty is smoothness: now as the perfection of smoothness is absolute equality and uniformity of surface, wherever that prevails there can be but little variety or intricacy; as, for instance, in smooth level banks, on a small, or in open downs, on a large scale. Another essential quality of beauty is gradual variation; that is (to make use of Mr. Burke's expression) where the lines do not vary in a sudden and broken manner, and where there is no sudden protuberance: it requires but little reflection to perceive that the exclusion of all but flowing lines cannot promote variety; and that sudden protuberances, and lines that cross each other in a sudden and broken manner, are among the most fruitful causes of intricacy.

I am therefore persuaded, that the two opposite qualities of roughness,* and of sudden variation, joined to that of irregularity, are the most efficient causes of the picturesque.

This, I think, will appear very clearly, if we take a view

---

* I have followed Mr. Gilpin's example in using roughness as a general term; he observes, however, that, "properly speaking, roughness relates only to the *surface* of bodies; and that when we speak of their *delineation* we use the word ruggedness." In making roughness, in this general sense, a very principal distinction between the beautiful and the picturesque, I believe I am supported by the general opinion of all who have considered the subject, as well as by Mr. Gilpin's authority.

of those objects, both natural and artificial, that are allowed to be picturesque, and compare them with those which are as generally allowed to be beautiful.

A temple or palace of Grecian architecture in its perfect entire state, and with its surface and colour smooth and even, either in painting or reality is beautiful; in ruin it is picturesque. Observe the process by which time, the great author of such changes, converts a beautiful object into a picturesque one. First, by means of weather stains, partial incrustations, mosses, &c. it at the same time takes off from the uniformity of the surface and of the colour; that is, gives a degree of roughness, and variety of tint. Next, the various accidents of weather loosen the stones themselves; they tumble in irregular masses upon what was perhaps smooth turf or pavement, or nicely trimmed walks and shrubberies; now mixed and overgrown with wild plants and creepers that crawl over, and shoot among the fallen ruins. Sedums, wall-flowers, and other vegetables that bear drought, find nourishment in the decayed cement from which the stones have been detached: birds convey their food into the chinks, and yew, elder, and other berried plants project from the sides; while the ivy mantles over other parts, and crowns the top. The even, regular lines of the doors and windows are broken, and through their ivy-fringed openings is displayed in a more broken and picturesque manner, that striking image in Virgil,

> Apparent domus intus, & atria longa patescunt;
> Apparent Priami & veterum penetralia regum.[3]

Gothic architecture is generally considered as more picturesque though less beautiful than Grecian, and upon the same principle that a ruin is more so than a new edifice. The first thing that strikes the eye in approaching any building is the general outline and the effect of the openings: in Grecian buildings, the general lines of the roof are straight; and even when varied and adorned by a dome or a pediment,

---

[3] *Æneid*, II, 483–84: "Open to view is the house within, and the long halls are bared; open to view are the inner chambers of Priam and the kings of old."

the whole has a character of symmetry and regularity. But symmetry, which, in works of art particularly, accords with the beautiful, is in the same degree adverse to the picturesque; and among the various causes of the superior picturesqueness of ruins compared with entire buildings, the destruction of symmetry is by no means the least powerful.

In Gothic buildings, the outline of the summit presents such a variety of forms, of turrents and pinnacles, some open, some fretted and variously enriched, that even where there is an exact correspondence of parts, it is often disguised by an appearance of splendid confusion and irregularity.* In the doors and windows of Gothic churches, the pointed arch has as much variety as any regular figure can well have: the eye too is less strongly conducted, than by the parallel lines in the Grecian style, from the top of one aperture to that of another: and every person must be struck with the extreme richness and intricacy of some of the principal windows of our cathedrals and ruined abbeys. In these last is displayed the triumph of the picturesque; and their charms to a painter's eye are often so great as to rival those which arise from the chaste ornaments and the noble and elegant simplicity of Grecian architecture.

Some people may, perhaps, be unwilling to allow that in ruins of Grecian and Gothic architecture any considerable part of the spectator's pleasure arises from the picturesque circumstances, and may choose to attribute the whole to what may justly claim a great share in that pleasure—the elegance or grandeur of their forms—the veneration of high antiquity—or the solemnity of religious awe; in a word, to the mixture of the two other characters. But were this true, yet there are many buildings highly interesting to all who have united the study of art with that of nature, in which beauty and grandeur are equally out of the question; such as hovels, cottages, mills, insides of old barns, stables, &c. whenever they have any marked and peculiar effect of form, tint, or light and shadow.

---

* There is a line in Dryden's Palamon and Arcite, which might be interpreted according to this idea, though I do not suppose he intended to convey any such meaning;
"And all appeared irregularly great."

In mills particularly, such is the extreme intricacy of the wheels and the wood work; such the singular variety of forms and of lights and shadows, of mosses and weather stains from the constant moisture, of plants springing from the rough joints of the stones; such the assemblage of every thing which most conduces to picturesqueness, that even without the addition of water, an old mill has the greatest charm for a painter.

It is owing to the same causes that a building with scaffolding has often a more picturesque appearance than the building itself when the scaffolding is taken away; that old, mossy, rough-hewn park pales of unequal heights are an ornament to landscape, especially when they are partially concealed by thickets; while a neat post and rail, regularly continued round a field, and seen without any interruption, is one of the most unpicturesque, as being one of the most uniform of all boundaries.

But among all the objects of nature, there is none in which roughness and smoothness more strongly mark the distinction between the two characters, than in water. A calm, clear lake, with the reflections of all that surrounds it, viewed under the influence of a setting sun, at the close of an evening clear and serene as its own surface, is perhaps, of all scenes, the most congenial to our ideas of beauty in its strictest, and in its most general acceptation.

Nay though the scenery around should be the most wild and picturesque (I might almost say the most savage) everything is so softened and melted together by the reflection of such a mirror, that the prevailing idea, even then, might possibly be that of beauty, so long as the water itself was chiefly regarded. On the other hand, all water of which the surface is broken, and the motion abrupt and irregular, as universally accords with our ideas of the picturesque; and whenever the word is mentioned, rapid and stony torrents and waterfalls, and waves dashing against rocks, are among the first objects that present themselves to our imagination. The two characters also approach and balance each other, as roughness or smoothness, as gentle undulation or abruptness prevail.

Among trees, it is not the smooth young beech, nor the
fresh and tender ash, but the rugged old oak, or knotty wych
elm that are picturesque: nor is it necessary they should be
of great bulk; it is sufficient if they are rough, mossy, with a
character of age, and with sudden variations in their forms.
The limbs of huge trees shattered by lightning or tempestuous
winds, are in the highest degree picturesque; but whatever is
caused by those dreaded powers of destruction, must always
have a tincture of the sublime.

If we next take a view of those animals that are called
picturesque, the same qualities will be found to prevail. The
ass is generally thought to be more picturesque than the horse;
and among horses, it is the wild and rough forester, or the
worn out cart-horse to which that title is applied. The sleek
pampered steed, with his high arched crest and flowing mane,
is frequently represented in painting; but his prevailing character, whether there, or in reality, is that of beauty.

In pursuing the same mode of inquiry with respect to
other animals, we find that the Pomeranian, and the rough
water-dog, are more picturesque than the smooth spaniel,
or the greyhound; the shaggy goat than the sheep: and these
last are more so when their fleeces are ragged and worn away
in parts, than when they are of equal thickness, or when
they have lately been shorn. No animal indeed is so constantly
introduced in landscape as the sheep, but that, as I observed
before, does not prove superior picturesqueness; and I imagine,
that besides their innocent character, so suited to pastoral
scenes of which they are the natural inhabitants, it arises from
their being of a tint at once brilliant and mellow, which unites
happily with all objects; and also from their producing when
in groups, however slightly the detail may be expressed,
broader masses of light and shadow than any other animal.
The reverse of this is true with regard to deer: their general
effect in groups, is comparatively meagre and spotty; but
their wild appearance, their lively action, their sudden bounds,
and the intricacy of their branching horns, are circumstances
in the highest degree picturesque.

Wild and savage animals, like scenes of the same description, have generally a marked and picturesque character: and as such scenes are less strongly impressed with that character when all is calm and serene than when the clouds are agitated and variously tossed about, so whatever may be the appearance of any animal in a tranquil state, it becomes more picturesque when suddenly altered by the influence of some violent emotion; and it is curious to observe how all that disturbs inward calm, produces a correspondent roughness without. The bristles of the chafed and foaming boar—the quills on the fretful porcupine—are suddenly raised by sudden emotion; and the angry lion exhibits the same picturesque marks of rage and fierceness . . . It is true that in all animals, where great strength and destructive fierceness are united, there is a mixture of grandeur; but the principles on which a greater or lesser degree of picturesqueness is founded may clearly be distinguished: the lion, for instance, with his shaggy mane, is much more picturesque than the lioness, though she is equally an object of terror.

The effect of smoothness or roughness in producing the beautiful or the picturesque, is again clearly exemplified in birds. Nothing is more truly consonant to our ideas of beauty, than their plumage when smooth and undisturbed, and when the eye glides over it without interruption: nothing, on the other hand, has so picturesque an appearance as their feathers, when ruffled by any accidental circumstance, or by any sudden passion in the animal. When inflamed with anger or with desire, the first symptoms appear in their ruffled plumage: the game cock, when he attacks his rival, raises the feathers of his neck; the purple pheasant his crest; and the peacock, when he feels the return of spring, shews his passion in the same manner,

And every feather shivers with delight.

The picturesque character in birds of prey arises from the angular form of their beak, the rough feathers on their legs, their crooked talons, their action and energy. All these circumstances are in the strongest degree apparent in the eagle; but from his size as well as courage, from the force of his beak and talons, formidable even to man, and likewise from all our earliest associations, the bird of Jove is always very much connected with ideas of grandeur.

Many birds have received from nature the same picturesque appearance which in others happens only accidentally: such are those whose heads and necks are adorned with ruffs, with crests, and with tufts of plumes; not lying smoothly over each other as those of the back, but loosely and irregularly disposed. These are, perhaps, the most striking and attractive of all birds, as having that degree of roughness and irregularity which gives a spirit to smoothness and symmetry; and where in them, or in other objects these last qualities prevail, the result of the whole is justly called beautiful.

In our own species, objects merely picturesque are to be found among the wandering tribes of gypsies and beggars; who in all the qualities which give them that character, bear a close analogy to the wild forester and the worn out carthorse, and again to old mills, hovels, and other inanimate objects of the same kind.—More dignified characters, such as a Belisarius, or a Marius in age and exile, * have the same mixture of picturesqueness and of decayed grandeur as the venerable remains of the magnificence of past ages.

If we ascend to the highest order of created beings, as painted by the grandest of our poets, they, in their state of glory and happiness, raise no ideas but those of beauty and sublimity; the picturesque, as in earthly objects, only shews itself when they are in a state of ruin;† when shadows have obscured their original brightness, and that uniform, though angelic expression of pure love and joy, has been destroyed by a variety of warring passions:

> Darken'd so, yet shone
> Above them all the archangel; but his face
> Deep scars of thunder had entrench'd, and care
> Sat on his faded cheek, but under brows

* The noble picture of Salvator Rosa at Lord Townshend's, which in the print is called Belisarius, has been thought to be a Marius among the ruins of Carthage.

> † Nor appear'd
> Less than archangel *ruin'd,* and the excess
> Of glory obscured.   [*Paradise Lost,* I, 592–94]

Of dauntless courage and considerate pride
Waiting revenge; cruel his eye, but cast
Signs of remorse and passion

[*Paradise Lost*, I, 599–605]

If from nature we turn to that art from which the expression itself is taken, we shall find all the principles of
picturesqueness confirmed. Among painters, Salvator Rosa[4]
is one of the most remarkable for his picturesque effects: in
no other master are seen such abrupt and rugged forms,
such sudden deviations both in his figures and his landscapes;
and the roughness and broken touches of his pencilling admirably accord with the objects they characterise.

Guido,[5] on the other hand, was as eminent for beauty:
in his celestial countenances are the happiest examples of
gradual variation, of lines that melt and flow into each other;
no sudden break, nothing that can disturb that pleasing
languor, which the union of all that constitutes beauty impresses on the soul. The style of his hair is as smooth as its
own character and its effect in accompanying the face will
allow; the flow of his drapery, the sweetness and equality of
his pencilling, and the silvery clearness and purity of his tints,
are all examples of the justness of Mr. Burke's principles of
beauty. But we may learn from the works even of this great
master, how unavoidably an attention to mere beauty and
flow of outline will lead towards sameness and insipidity. If
this has happened to a painter of such high excellence, who
so well knew the value of all that belongs to his art, and
whose touch, when he painted a St. Peter or a St. Jerome,
was as much admired for its spirited and characteristic roughness, as for its equality and smoothness in his angels and
madonnas,—what must be the case with men who have been
tethered all their lives in a clump or a belt?

There is another instance of contrast between two emi-

---

[4] Salvator Rosa (1615–1673), Italian painter whose battle scenes and
landscapes achieved tremendous popularity from the late seventeenth to
the early nineteenth centuries. They were frequently copied, and admired
for their sublime and picturesque qualities.

[5] Guido di Pietro, better known as Fra Angelico (1387–1455), Italian
Dominican friar and painter of religious subjects.

nent painters, Albano[6] and Mola,[7] which I cannot forbear
mentioning, as it confirms the alliance between roughness and
picturesqueness, and between smoothness and beauty; and as
it shews, in the latter case, the consequent danger of sameness. Of all the painters who have left behind them a high
reputation, none perhaps was more uniformly smooth than
Albano, or less often deviated into abruptness of any kind:
none also have greater monotony of character; but, from the
extreme beauty and delicacy of his forms and his tints, and
his exquisite finishing, few pictures are more generally captivating. Mola, the scholar of Albano (and that circumstance
makes it more singular), is as remarkable for many of those
opposite qualities which distinguish S. Rosa, though he has
not the boldness and animation of that original genius. There
is hardly any painter, whose pictures more immediately catch
the eye of a connoisseur than those of Mola, or less attract
the notice of a person unused to painting. Salvator has a
savage grandeur, often in the highest degree sublime; and
sublimity in any shape, will command attention: but Mola's
scenes and figures, are for the most part neither sublime nor
beautiful; they are purely picturesque: his touch is less rough
than Salvator's; his colouring has, in general, more richness
and variety; and his pictures seem to me the most perfect
examples of the higher stile of picturesqueness: infinitely removed from vulgar nature, but having neither the softness
and delicacy of beauty, nor that grandeur of conception which
produces the sublime.

[6] Francesco Albano, or Albani (1578–1660), Italian painter known particularly for pictures of the Holy Family and for frescoes on mythological
subjects.
[7] Pierfrancesco Mola, known also as Mola di Roma (1612–1666). Notable
for the landscape backgrounds in his religious and mythological paintings.

Rinehart Editions